Affirming the Covenant

᪇

A History of Temple B'rith Kodesh
Rochester, New York, 1848–1998

By Peter Eisenstadt

Distributed by
Syracuse University Press

First edition.
99 00 01 02   6 5 4 3 2 1

The paper in this publication meets the minimum requirements of American National Standard for Information Sciences—Permanence of Paper: for Printed Library Materials, ANSI, Z39.48-1984.

ISBN 0-8156-8128-3

Manufactured in the United States of America.

Design and layout by Bash! Studios / Printing by Mercury Print Productions, Inc.

Cover Photo: Temple Dome

"The dome links us to the very beginning of Jewish history. Like the Tabernacle of old, it teaches us to aspire, to build a better world here on earth. It reminds us of the sanctity, the grandeur, the nobility of life. It represents our responsibility to Jewish history to take over the role of the spiritual fountainhead of the future. It symbolizes the greatness, the opportunities, the responsibilities of our period of history, and it is a symbol of the promise of a world of peace and equity for all humanity."

From "The Art and Architecture of Temple B'rith Kodesh, Its Religious Meanings," Rabbi Herbert Bronstein. (Cover photo by Richard Margolis)

Rabbi Philip S. Bernstein

In the last analysis history is made by ordinary people. The history of this congregation is not the history of its rabbis, however useful may have been their role. Nor is it the record of unusual events, like our fire, or a controversy or an interfaith service. It is the history of how ordinary men and women and their children remained loyal to the faith of their fathers. It is the record of people who, week after week, came to worship despite the difficulties of Rochester's winters and the growing diversions of community life. It is the story of children, who, generation after generation, came here to study however reluctant some may have been, and however inadequate may have been their instruction. It is a story of committees and of sisterhoods and of brotherhoods and of women who sewed upstairs and cooked downstairs. It is the record of those who, year after year, sustained a congregation with their resources and with their moral support.

We hail that little band of pioneers, not for being heros or saints but for being typical Jews who were so deeply attached to the faith of their fathers and so profoundly concerned for the welfare of their children that, as their first common act, they established a synagogue and called it by the name, B'rith Kodesh.

—Rabbi Philip S. Bernstein, Rosh Hashanah 1948

Rabbi Laurence A. Kotok

To be a Jew is to have hope. Hope in the future and in the goodness of life. I can only imagine the sense of promise that motivated the founders of Temple B'rith Kodesh. Today, 150 years later, we look back to our beginning and forward to our future with open hearts and minds. We are deeply grateful for the foresight of our founders and those who have led us through the years. We are grateful to those who brought their hopes and dreams to create the vibrant Jewish community we have become. For all who found identity and learning within the walls of our Temple, all who have been touched by the dynamism of our Temple, it is now time to give thanks to God for all that has been accomplished. With our enduring gratitude we thank God for all that has been accomplished, and we look forward to the task before us, praying for vision and guidance to carry on the great tradition of our congregation.

Temple B'rith Kodesh continues to inspire and to lead our community and temple family on the path of Jewish life. We are proud of our many and varied programs and opportunities which provide access to living Jewish expression. We are diverse and welcoming, linking the generations together as a caring community.

Our one hundred and fiftieth year provides us with the special joy of perspective. Over these years Temple B'rith Kodesh has remained true to its founding vision. Times have changed as have we, but leading us forward is our everlasting commitment to God, Torah, and the people of Israel made real and connected through our B'rith Kodesh—our Holy Covenant.

At this time of reflection and thanksgiving, we join together in praising God for continued insight and strength to advance the sacred tasks begun by our ancestors and carried forward—L'dor va dor—from generation to generation. May the coming years find us laboring on behalf of this vision. This is our everlasting commitment as we creatively build the future of our beloved B'rith Kodesh.

We are known as an "Am Sefer," a people of the book. As Jews there are many books we hold special. This book that you hold in your hands tells a part of our people's unfolding story; we need to know where we have come from to know where we are going. It is a magnificent story. I join my voice with yours in thanking all who have made the publication possible.

May the coming years bring us fulfillment and peace. We pray in the words of Psalm 90, "May God bless the work of our hands," and may our efforts be deserving of this blessing.

— Rabbi Laurence A. Kotok, Rosh Hashanah, 1998

UAHC

UNION OF AMERICAN
HEBREW CONGREGATIONS

איחוד ליהדות מתקדמת באמריקה

RABBI ERIC H. YOFFIE, PRESIDENT

Fall 1998/Tishri 5759

Rabbi Laurence Kotok
Temple B'rith Kodesh
2131 Elmwood Avenue
Rochester, NY   14618

Dear Larry:

The commemoration of the 150th Anniversary of Temple B'rith Kodesh is a very special *simcha,* one I look forward to sharing personally with the families of your fine congregation.   I am also pleased to include a special message of *mazal tov* to the wonderful professional staff and members of the congregation, men, women, and youngsters, who make up the B'rith Kodesh family. This is a time for one and all to rejoice!

B'rith Kodesh began serving the North American Jewish community before Reform Judaism reached our shores. It became a charter member of the Union of American Hebrew Congregations when it was founded in 1873 and since that time your fine congregation has been a noble link in our family of congregations. Over the years it has provided great lay and rabbinic leadership to the institutions of Reform Judaism and has created a proud history of service to Judaism and the Jewish people.

May this very special 150th Anniversary mark a new era in the life times of B'rith Kodesh as it flourishes and grows from strength to ever greater strength.

Sincerely,

Eric

Eric H. Yoffie

The sesquicentennial celebration at Temple B'rith Kodesh, fall 1998. L. to r.: Rabbi Eric Yoffie, Temple President Carol Yunker, and Rabbi Laurence Kotok. (Photo by Bruce Kahn)

Introduction

The history of Temple B'rith Kodesh over the past century and a half is in many ways a microcosm of the Reform movement as a whole. The story of the oldest Jewish congregation in Rochester, New York, the remarkable shifts in its understanding of Judaism, the social and economic aspirations of its members, the demographic shifts within its membership, are representative of similar Jewish congregations elsewhere. But if it is a typical history in some ways, in its particularity it is a unique story. *Affirming the Covenant* is a portrait of how the practice of Judaism in the congregation has changed over time and continues to evolve.

All histories are selective and partial. The complete story of Temple B'rith Kodesh, as Rabbi Bernstein suggests, can never be fully told. *Affirming the Covenant* relates the stories of some of the people who have been a part of the history of B'rith Kodesh over the past century and a half. It is a history in which the commonplace and the extraordinary often intersect.

More than most books, this one could not have been written without the assistance and good will of a large number of people. Rabbi Kotok and his staff were unfailingly helpful. Nettie Sheiman, the B'rith Kodesh librarian, became a good friend and raconteur of the temple's history. Sue Klein opened the doors to the riches of the B'rith Kodesh museum. Anne Orwin worked closely with me in many phases of the project. Carol Yunker, the temple president, has a deep and abiding love for and knowledge of the history of B'rith Kodesh, and was an active supporter of this project from the outset. Many people agreed to be interviewed for this book and lent photographs and memorabilia, including Sophy Bernstein, Elizabeth Schwartz, Anita Miller, Harriet Roth, Aaron Braveman, Virginia McConnell, Arthur Herz, and Rabbi Laurence Kotok. I wish to especially thank Rabbi Herbert Bronstein, North Shore Congregation, Glenoe, Ill., who agreed to an interview and granted me access to his personal papers. Dr. Abraham Karp shared with me his unequalled knowledge of the Jewish history of Rochester. Hildegard Herz's superb translation of Simon Tuska's 1854 sermon is a highlight of the book. Walt Nickeson of the Division of Rare Books and Special Collections at the University of Rochester, the archivist of the Philip S. Bernstein Papers, graciously granted me access to the collection before it was fully processed. His detailed knowledge of Bernstein's career has been of inestimable help. Karl Kabelac, of the University of Rochester Library's Division of Rare Books and Special Collections, also provided valuable assistance, as did Amy Barnum, Suzanne Schroeder, and Jean Lombard. At the Rochester Museum and Science Center, Lea Kemp, Ava Petry, and Dan Barbour were extremely helpful.

Many people assisted in various stages of the production and printing of *Affirming the Covenant*. Photographers Richard Margolis, Martin Adwin, and Arthur Lind made important contributions to the volume. Jennifer Alrutz, the volume's photo editor, took painstaking care to ensure that the volume's photographs were of the highest possible quality. David Birnbaum provided valuable assistance in image quality. Ceil Goldman did the copyediting. The superb design and layout was the work of Teri Jankowski of BASH! Studios. Joseph Sloan of Mercury Print Productions shepherded the volume through its print production. Financial assistance for this project was provided by the Lucius N. Littauer Foundation; Barbara and George Morgenstern, in honor of their sons, Jordan and Adrian; the Goldberg Berbeco Foundation, in honor of Nathalie and in loving memory of Emanuel Goldberg; and the American Jewish Archives. Kevin Profitt of the American Jewish Archives was considerate and helpful during my stay in Cincinnati.

Several people are owed a special debt of acknowledgment. Harold Wechsler, Professor of Education at the University of Rochester, welcomed me to Rochester, and gave me access to the 1976 Rochester Jewish Community Oral History Project. Several people read the manuscript, including Aaron Braveman, and my dear friend, Daniel Soyer, Professor of History at Fordham University, a marvelous editor, and one of the leading lights of contemporary scholarship on American Jewish history. George Morgenstern was the chair of the book committee. I don't think either of us really knew what we were getting into when we started this project, but he has been a good friend throughout. My wife, Jane DeLuca, gave me her love and support, as well as her usual toleration of my enthusiasms. I cannot adequately thank Cantor Martha Rock Birnbaum, the project coordinator for *Affirming the Covenant*, for her assistance. Her work on the photographs, and her general commitment to this project and her faith in my efforts, have been a source of joy and inspiration. *Affirming the Covenant* is a far better book for our collaboration. It has been a privilege to work with her and the many others who helped along the way. Let me close with the traditional invocation: for any errors contained herein, I alone am responsible. My father, Joseph Eisenstadt, of blessed memory, died when the volume was in the final stages of production. He would have liked this book.

— *Peter Eisenstadt*
Rochester, New York
February 1, 1999 / 15 Shevat 5759

Contents

This beautiful quilt, depicting scenes from the Bible, was a cherished heirloom of Rabbi Max and Miriam Landsberg. (Courtesy Rochester Museum and Science Center, Rochester, New York, photo by Paul Porell)

Dedication

This book is dedicated to the rabbis who are serving and have served Temple B'rith Kodesh.

From a devoted family, grateful for the blessings they have received: in particular for their close relationships with Rabbi Philip S. Bernstein and Rabbi Judea B. Miller, and grateful for an opportunity to assist with the publication of this sesquicentennial history of their beloved congregation.

Affirming the Covenant

A History of Temple B'rith Kodesh
Rochester, New York, 1848–1998

Chapter I

Beginnings, 1848–1865

Introduction: Two Lifetimes

Gabriel Wile was a founder of Temple B'rith Kodesh—one of the twelve men who met on the day after Yom Kippur in 1848 to organize Rochester's first synagogue. Born in Bavaria in 1820, Wile had come to the United States and Rochester in 1845. A pioneer in Rochester's men's ready-made clothing business, the dominant enterprise among Rochester's German Jews in the nineteenth century, he lived a long and successful life. In 1898, at the ceremony marking the 50th anniversary of the temple, Wile was one of the featured speakers.

"My dear friends," Wile began, "it is a blessed privilege for me to be able to be permitted to address you on this occasion; it is a blessed privilege for me to stand here in the presence of this large congregation and see the fruition, the realization of all of the hopes and anticipations which imbued the hearts and inspired the actions of that little band, which in 1848 organized the congregation 'Berith Kodesh.' "

The original founders were from "a remote land and from widely separated places," Wile remembered. But though their career paths and ambitions were diverse, they were all "imbued with the principles of our holy religion and with deep sense of the obligations thereby imposed. Ours was not, to have the faith that should die with us; ours was not, like the miser who hides his riches, to take the precious heritage which had been entrusted to our care and not permit succeeding generations to profit by it.

Gabriel Wile

Elizabeth Schwartz

We felt that we had a trust to fulfill. *'Veshinantom levonecho'*—and thou shall teach them to thy children."

Wile spoke to a congregation that was in the forefront of "classical" or "radical" Reform Judaism. Its religious service, conducted almost entirely in English, lacked many of the traditional rituals of Judaism. For a Jewish congregation experiencing the freedom of worship possible in the United States, Wile argued, many changes had been necessary. Still, the move to radical Reform had been full of "trials and sufferings." As Wile hinted at in his address, some fourteen years earlier he had threatened to leave the congregation— when its English language ritual was introduced. Nonetheless Gabriel Wile stayed. Many nineteenth-century observers had noted the determination of the members of B'rith Kodesh to hold together, despite occasional ideological disputes. Wile shared this commitment to unity. "As we look back over the long years and the long and devious paths that we have trodden during that time and observe what has been accomplished, we have all come to realize *gam seh l'tovo*—it was all for the best."

The essential truths of Judaism remained the same. Only the outer garb, Wile argued, had changed. "We have endeavored to labor in the vineyard of the Lord and assist, so far as it is in our power, to spread and accomplish the mission of Judaism, until *Bayom hahu yiye adoinoi echod ushemo echod* [On that day shall God be One and his name one]."

In 1904 Gabriel Wile died at the age of 84. He had been a member of B'rith Kodesh almost sixty years. The same year, Elizabeth Schwartz was born in Rochester to parents of Russian Jewish background. About a decade later she first attended the B'rith Kodesh religious school. Like Wile, Elizabeth's parents worked in the garment trade. But they were shop-floor operatives and petty subcontractors, not a grand entrepreneur like Wile. B'rith Kodesh had not always been welcoming to the wave of Eastern European immigrants, especially those who could not afford the expensive membership fees. But in an effort to attract new families, the temple decided in 1906 to permit the children of Russian Jews to attend the religious school without charge. For young Elizabeth, a girl unable to find religious instruction in the orthodox *shules*, B'rith Kodesh soon became a spiritual home.

Elizabeth Schwartz was confirmed at B'rith Kodesh and later became an active member of the congregation, teaching in the religious school and eventually serving as its principal. Over the years, the leadership and direction of the congregation changed. Schwartz's few memories of Max Landsberg, rabbi from 1871 to 1915, an epitome of the spirit of radical Reform, are of an elegant but somewhat distant figure. But she remembers his successor, Rabbi Horace Wolf, as a warm and dynamic leader, who made her feel welcome in the congregation. Wolf died tragically young, in his early forties. Schwartz knew his successor, Rochester native Philip Bernstein, who became rabbi in 1927, from her early girlhood. Bernstein served at B'rith Kodesh for almost half a century, and he was always rooted in his home city. But his career took him far beyond western New York. During World War II Bernstein supervised all the Jewish chaplains in the U.S. military. In the war's immediate aftermath, he served as special advisor on Jewish affairs to the U.S. forces in Germany.

When Bernstein returned to Rochester in 1947, he rejoined the life of the congregation. The postwar baby boom and the growing suburbanization of Rochester's Jewish population led to the construction of a new, larger temple in Brighton, a Rochester suburb, in 1962. Over the years, the congregation changed religiously as well, embracing more of the traditional rituals of Judaism. After Bernstein retired in 1973, Rabbi Judea Miller infused B'rith Kodesh with a new sense of spirituality and social commitment. After Miller's death in 1995, Laurence Kotok became the senior rabbi. Through all of these changes, Elizabeth Schwartz was an active and vital member of B'rith Kodesh. She remains one at the time this is being written, and she has been a participant in the temple sesquicentennial celebrations in 1998, having been associated with the congregation for over seventy years.

One hundred and fifty years seems like an eternity, but it spans less than two lifetimes. Between them, Gabriel Wile and Elizabeth Schwartz have witnessed the entire history of B'rith Kodesh. They form a study in contrasts: one male, one female; a German Jew, a Russian Jew; a businessman, a teacher; a nineteenth century life, a life in the twentieth century. But these two remarkable individuals shared commitment to B'rith Kodesh—through all of its "devious paths," to use Gabriel Wile's phrase—that has been far more important than any differences. Like any religious congregation, B'rith Kodesh is a product and a legacy of the thousands of individuals who have participated in its growth. This volume is a history of the determined people, clergy and laity alike, who have been a part of the story of Temple B'rith Kodesh.

Rochester in 1848

In 1848 Rochester had completed its initial spurt of growth. At first a little hamlet, Rochester, had no more than 800 inhabitants when it was incorporated as a village in 1817. It became a city in 1834, and had over 36,000 inhabitants by mid century.

By 1854, twenty years after its incorporation as a city, Rochester was already a bustling commercial center. (Courtesy Rochester Public Library)

The opening of the Erie Canal in 1825, and the waterpower provided by the Genesee River, propelled Rochester into commercial prominence. Rochester's population was tightly clustered in the downtown area around Four Corners. The present Elmwood Avenue site of the temple would be a long drive into the countryside.

In 1848 Rochester was an excellent place in which to get ahead in life. In its early decades the city's prosperity was largely based on trade generated by the Erie Canal and the fertility of the surrounding countryside. The mills along the rapids and falls of the Genesee River gave Rochester its reputation as the "Flour City," but wheat was by no means the only product of its many small shops and factories. Laborers often came to the city for a few years before pushing on further west. Businessmen generally put down more permanent roots. The city at first had a distinctly "Yankee" character, because its early settlers came mostly from New England. After 1840 the city's population changed dramatically, as immigrants from Ireland and Germany poured into the region. By 1855 almost half the population of Rochester was foreign-born. Among these newcomers were the city's first Jews.

The first Jews probably arrived in Rochester in the mid-1830s. One of the earliest Jews in the area was Joseph Katz, a founding member of B'rith Kodesh. Katz, born in Adelsdorf, Bavaria in 1814, was in Rochester as early as 1834. Meyer Greentree was in Rochester by 1841, and several other early members of B'rith Kodesh were in Rochester by 1845, including Joseph and Gabriel Wile, Asher Beir, and Elias Ettenheimer. From this trickle, the flow of Jews to Rochester soon broadened. By mid century, there were probably around a hundred Jews living in Rochester.

The increase in Rochester's Jewish population was part of the first great wave of Jewish emigration to the United States. Between 1820 and 1880 over 200,000 Jews migrated to the United States from Central Europe. This was the "German" period of American Jewish history. A large number did come from Bavaria, Wurtemberg, and other south-west German states. But many of the

The first recorded activity of the Jewish community of Rochester was the purchase, in April 1848, of a plot at Mt. Hope Cemetery. Meyer Greentree, one of the earliest Jews to settle in Rochester, was in the city by 1843.

immigrants were not raised in the states and kingdoms of Germany proper. A substantial minority was raised in Poznan and Silesia, lands annexed by Prussia from Poland in the late eighteenth century. In these borderlands between central and eastern Europe Jews were still, in the middle of the nineteenth century, as likely to speak Yiddish as German. Still others came from the eastern Hapsburg territories, from the areas of the present-day Czech Republic, Slovakia, and Hungary. A smaller number of Jewish immigrants came from Western Europe, especially from England, Holland, and the Alsace region of France.

Temple B'rith Kodesh in its early decades reflected this ethnic diversity. Through the 1870s over half its members were from Bavaria, but a substantial minority had other origins. The temple's rabbi through the mid 1850s, Mordecai (or Marcus) Tuska, was of Hungarian background, while an English Jew, a Mr. Barnard, served as his assistant and as the primary teacher in the religious school. Tuska's successor, Isaac Mayer, was from the Alsace region of France, and Ferdinand Sarner, Mayer's successor, was born in Poznan, in East Prussia.

Neither was the laity entirely German. An 1855 account describes the congregation, as consisting of "Germans, Englishmen and Poles, who all are acting in harmony." By 1858, however, some of the Eastern European Jews and their sympathizers in B'rith Kodesh organized Adas Jeshrun, a short-lived congregation that followed the Polish *minhag* (rite). The synagogue ceased to exist by 1860, and its leading members returned to B'rith Kodesh. By 1867 there was a new minyan of Polish Jews in the city. Probably between a quarter to a third of the Jews in Rochester before 1880 were either from eastern Prussia, Hapsburg territories, or Western Europe (see Table 1).

The first Jews in Rochester found the city a haven for the free practice of their religion. Perhaps no city in the United States welcomed religious outsiders as much as Rochester did in the 1840s. The city gained a well-deserved reputation for religious enthusiasm, some of it extreme and eccentric. At the center of the "burned-over district," so-called because of the incandescent piety of the faithful, the Rochester area was the birthplace of the urban revival meeting, and of both Mormonism and Spiritualism. The region also harbored a Shaker community and several utopian Socialist settlements.

Rochester also took the social role of religion very seriously. Many residents saw the crusade against slavery as a deep religious commitment. When Frederick Douglass moved to Rochester in 1847, the city was already known as a hotbed of abolitionist sentiment. Rochester was also the first center of the women's rights movement. Rochester feminists were instrumental in organizing, in the same year B'rith Kodesh was founded, the first public meeting in the United States on women's rights in nearby Seneca

Table 1

Birthplaces of Foreign-Born Jews in Rochester By 1880

Western German States

Germany 18
(not further identified)

Bavaria 5

Wurtemburg 2

German 25

Non-German European

England 4

Eastern Prussia 3

Alsace 1

Bohemia 1

Holland 1

Hungary 1

Russian Poland 1

Non-German 12

Total 37

Source: Isaac A. Wile, *History of the Jews of Rochester* (1912)

5

Falls in July 1848. A second, larger women's rights meeting took place several weeks later at the Unitarian Church in Rochester, a congregation that would have a long connection to B'rith Kodesh. Jews in Rochester benefited from the city's tolerance of religious diversity, and would in time significantly contribute to its rich tradition of religiously inspired social reform.

The possibility of business success also brought Jews to Rochester. The *Rochester Democrat* stated in 1855 that Jews "are becoming every year more numerous in this city, as the pursuit of trade attracts them from other sections." The first Jews in Rochester were primarily young, unmarried men, generally of quite limited means. Almost all worked in trade and in small retail businesses, familiar occupations for Central European Jews. Many new immigrants worked as peddlers, a trade that required little initial capital besides a strong back and good legs. A little more than a quarter of the Jews listed in the Rochester City Directory before 1850 give "peddler" as their occupation. Of the nine charter members of B'rith Kodesh whose occupations can be traced, two were peddlers, as was the congregation's first *hazzan* (the reader of the service), Joseph Stieffel.

A peddler's lot was not an easy one. Traveling by canal boat or cart if they were lucky (and by foot if they were not), the peddlers made their rounds to the many small villages and canal towns in the Rochester vicinity. Selling dry goods and jewelry, and doing some tailoring and tinkering as well, the peddlers were on the road six days a week, often carrying a one-hundred-fifty pound pack. On the Sabbath, Jewish peddlers, if observant, stopped where they were for the day, or returned home to Rochester, to start the cycle again on Sunday.

The goal of the peddler was to raise enough money to settle down and open a shop, selling the same sort of goods as before but with more economic and geographic stability. Seven charter members of B'rith Kodesh were small shopkeepers and tailors. In time, many of these men would enter manufacturing and other more lucrative aspects of the garment trade.

Rochester's Jews relied on one another for economic support. Banks seldom granted credit to recent Jewish immigrants, and the more established Jewish settlers frequently extended loans, often in the form of goods, to peddlers recently arrived from Europe. Jewish entrepreneurs commonly pooled their resources and established partnerships. By 1860, Jewish companies dominated Rochester's burgeoning men's ready-made clothing industry.

Of course, Jewish women also came to Rochester, though less is known about them in the first years of Jewish settlement. As with many immigrant populations, men outnumbered women for the first decade or so. The peddler's life was not suited to domestic stability, and many Jewish men in Rochester postponed marriage until they were economically comfortable.

Nevertheless, in 1845 Mr. and Mrs. Jacob Altman became the parents of Bertha Altman, the first Jewish child born in Rochester. In 1849, Berrie Weinstein and Yedda Rothschild became the first couple married at B'rith Kodesh. Some men returned to Europe to find a bride. In 1847 Joseph Katz went to Muehlhausen, Bavaria to marry Jeanette Friedman. The couple then returned to Rochester, where they lived the rest of their days.

Other men married non-Jewish women. In the United States, those who married outside the faith did not have to give up their ties with the Jewish community, as they generally did in Europe. Non-Jewish fiancées or spouses could convert to Judaism without incurring the wrath of either church or state, and many did so. By 1855, the wives of at least three Rochester Jews had converted to the religion of their husbands. Conversion ceremonies—extremely rare in Europe—became an important ritual occasion for Rochester's Jews. The crowd that attended a splendid conversion in 1860 filled the B'rith Kodesh sanctuary. As the writer in the *American Israelite* recounted the event, after the proselyte recited the central declaration of faith, the *Sh'ma*, "her hand lifted up in holy prayer, her eyes fixed with intense reverence upon the sacred arch," everyone in attendance felt "the presence of *Our God* and his true, everlastingly blissful faith."

Life was raw in Rochester in the 1840s and 1850s. It had all the urban problems typical of any big city, as reformers and temperance advocates often noted. Crime was a serious problem, especially near the canal, where many Jewish merchants operated their shops. Fire protection was inadequate. In the spring, the Genesee River regularly overflowed its banks, and flooding was commonplace; the floods of 1855 and 1865 were especially memorable. Public health problems were often severe, and Rochester had serious epidemics of cholera—that scourge of nineteenth-century cities—in 1848 and again in 1852.

Like other residents of the city, Rochester's Jews had a well-developed sense of life's fragility. The infant mortality rate was appallingly high. In the decades before 1880, almost two-thirds of

Table 2

Burials in the B'rith Kodesh plot in Mt. Hope Cemetery, 1848–1880, by decade.

Decade	Children	Adults
1840s	1	2
1850s	49	13
1860s	58	22
1870s	20	10
Total	**128**	47

ROCHESTER. N.Y. The Rev. S. M. Isaacs informs us that he has been called on to prepare a constitution and by-laws for a new congregation about to be organized at the above city.

BUFFALO, N.Y. A congregation is also assembling at this great town of Western New York. There are already twenty-four families, and they have a person officiating as Hazan and Shochet.

SYRACUSE, N.Y. There are at this place fifty families, and have a Synagogue of their own. Their Hazan is the Rev. Mr. Gutman, who also gives instruction in Hebrew.

ALBANY. The choir in the Synagogue is organized upon the plan of Mr. Sulzer, of Vienna, and assists at public worship on the Sabbath, when the stores are generally closed, and the Synagogue is well attended. Dr. Wise's school consists of seventy-six scholars, twenty-four of which belong to the Bible class, and the school fees for ten scholars is paid by the Education Society

By the late 1840s, German Jews were organizing synagogues in all of the major cities in upstate New York. This first attempt to establish a Jewish congregation, as reported in The Occident *in July 1847, in Rochester was unsuccessful, for unknown reasons.*

those buried in the Jewish plots in Mt. Hope Cemetery were children, and in the 1850s alone forty-nine children died in a community that probably did not number more than 150 families (see table 2). Death visited the rich and the poor alike. Sarah Stettheimer, the eight-year-old daughter of one of the city's most prominent Jews, died suddenly in the spring of 1857. A large procession—consisting of 850 people according to newspaper accounts—went to the funeral at Mt. Hope Cemetery. The rabbi of B'rith Kodesh, Isaac Mayer, preached in German to the large crowd, and his eloquence reduced many to tears, including Mayer himself. The *American Israelite* eulogized the little girl as one who "was deemed too frail a flower to be exposed to life's rough storms and trials, and was taken to Himself, by the Lord."

By the time of Sarah Stettheimer's death, Rochester's Jews possessed a full range of religious institutions. But in the mid 1840s they did not. At that time, essential life-cycle rituals were either difficult or impossible to perform. A circuit-riding *mohel* in central and western New York came to Rochester for the occasional circumcision. But there was no *shochet* (ritual slaughterer), no Jewish burial plot, and above all, no synagogue.

The Founding of B'rith Kodesh

Rochester's first Jewish congregation was organized on October 9, 1848, the day after Yom Kippur. Twelve men gathered at the house of Harry Levi, in an upstairs room on the corner of North Clinton and Bowery streets. Some of these men would have long histories of involvement with the congregation. Others soon disappeared from the historical record. What A. Adler, Jacob and Joseph Altman, Jacob Ganz, Joseph Katz, Harry Levi, Samuel Marks, Meyer Rothschild, Abraham Weinberg, Joseph and Gabriel Wile, and Elias Wolf all shared was a commitment to maintaining Judaism in America.

We do not know when the congregation acquired the name B'rith Kodesh; it may have gone without a name for a while. For a short time, it was possibly known as Congregation B'nai B'rith. By 1854 it was known as Congregation Berith Kodesh, the name that appears on the official incorporation papers filed that year. Some, primarily Gentiles, one suspects, called it the Hebrew Congregation of the Holy Covenant. "Beuth Kodash" appears in an advertisement for a new rabbi in early 1859. (This must have been a printer's error of some sort.) "Bris Kaudesch," a more plausible Germanization, appears in a testimonial the following year. At the end of the century, "B'rith Kodesh" slowly replaced "Berith Kodesh" as the preferred spelling; by 1930 the new spelling was official. In its early years B'rith Kodesh was a "shule." The congregation was rarely called a temple before 1871.

Unlike people, religious institutions have complex nativities. Jewish religious activities, both formal and informal, had been ongoing in Rochester for several years prior to 1848. Rochester Jews first hired a shochet in 1846 or 1847. As in many other cities, one of the most important expressions of organized Jewish activity in Rochester was the establishment of a burial society. On April 3, 1848 "Joseph Altman, Joseph Weil, and R. Rotschild, Jews" purchased a plot in Mt. Hope Cemetery for $80. Perhaps they had formed a *khevre kaddisha* (holy society) to perform Jewish funeral rites. The Rochester German Benevolent Society purchased an adjoining lot in December 1849, but no other evidence of their activity survives.

Jews also gathered informally for prayer before 1848, especially on the High Holy Days. Meyer Rothschild, in reminiscences many years after the fact, dated the beginning of the prayer group that became B'rith Kodesh to 1846. According to Rothschild, there were five initial members: the Altman brothers, Samuel Marks, Abraham Weinberg, and Rothschild himself. As the following notice in *The Occident* shows, plans were afoot by July 1847 to start a

Mr. and Mrs. Meyer Rothschild. Meyer Rothschild, a founding member and early president of B'rith Kodesh, was one of three original members who survived to the temple's fiftieth anniversary in 1898.

From 1849 to 1856 the home of Temple B'rith Kodesh was on Front Street. The street is depicted here in the aftermath of the Genesee River flood of 1865. (Courtesy Rochester Museum and Science Center, Rochester, New York)

synagogue. "Rochester, N.Y. The Rev. S. M. Isaacs informs us that he has been called upon to prepare a constitution and by-laws for a congregation about to be organized at the above city." (Isaacs was the traditionally minded rabbi of Congregation B'nai Jeshrun in New York City.) For unknown reasons, the congregation remained unorganized for over a year.

The meetings continued in Harry Levi's quarters for several months after October 1848. Joseph Steifel, the congregation's hazzan, also served as its shochet, receiving an annual salary of $150. By April 1849, when the congregation numbered eighteen members, B'rith Kodesh rented quarters on the third story at No. 2 Front Street, over Stanwix Hall, the home of Rochester's first Odd Fellows' Lodge.

The following decade was perhaps the most complex in the history of B'rith Kodesh. The congregation was organized in the last years before Judaism in the United States divided into ideological camps over questions of ritual observance. There was no Reform movement in the United States in 1850, and no more than one or two Reform congregations. There was no Orthodox movement, and it would be another fifty years before Conservative Judaism came into being. American Judaism consisted of individual congregations, like B'rith Kodesh, each determining its own practices and rituals.

In the congregation, as in American Judaism as a whole, traditional practices declined rapidly. But in their place came not systematic Reform, but a hodgepodge of short-lived innovations and changes. The halting moves toward Reform proved to be a protracted and at times bitterly divisive process. Within ten years the synagogue replaced three rabbis, while various factions with the congregation rose and fell; as Gabriel Wile noted, the founding generation of B'rith Kodesh did not all have similar backgrounds in Jewish learning. Those who joined the congregation included the pious and the casually observant, both scholars and persons of scant Jewish education. If some Rochester Jews felt the lack of organized Jewish life in the city, others did not. As late as 1855, no more than half of the 150 Jewish men in Rochester were members of B'rith Kodesh.

But if it was a time of considerable institutional disorder, it was also a period of great intellectual ferment. It was exciting to be a Jew in America. Rochester Jews found themselves living in a country without an established church, one in which they had civic equality, and enjoyed social acceptance from their Christian neighbors. How should this new circumstance alter their understanding of their ancient faith, which in its beliefs and rituals heightened the sense of Jewish apartness?

Simon Tuska

Mordecai Tuska served as the congregation's first spiritual leader, arriving in Rochester in 1849 to take the position of rabbi, as well as hazzan, schohet, and mohel. (With all those titles to choose from, early Rochester city directories listed his occupation as "priest.") At the time, a rabbi's primary role was to render halachic judgments, while a hazzan led services; one man often performed both functions. Born in Hungary, Tuska was recently arrived in the United States and was living in New York City, when called to Rochester. It is uncertain whether Tuska had actually obtained a proper European *semikhah*, an ordination by a recognized rabbinical authority. In this he resembled many other early American rabbis. Tuska was well regarded by the congregation, which grew rapidly during his tenure. By 1854, when B'rith Kodesh was incorporated, the synagogue had fifty members, who entertained "the most friendly feelings" toward Tuska, who "has ever led his flock with the Bible and the Talmud as his guide."

It is Mordecai Tuska's son, Simon Tuska, however, who provides the most important evidence on the impact of the early years of Reform on a Rochester Jew. The youngest of the five sons of Mordecai and Rebecca Tuska, Simon Tuska was born in Veszprem, in western Hungary, in 1835, and came with his parents to the United States in 1848. While relatively little is known about Mordecai Tuska, Simon became one of the most significant figures in ante-bellum

Daguerrotype depicting Mordecai and Rebecca Tuska. From 1849 to 1856 Mordecai Tuska, a Hungarian immigrant, was rabbi of Temple B'rith Kodesh. (Courtesy American Jewish Archives)

American Judaism. An advocate of an English-speaking rabbinate, he helped shape the early Reform movement. He was the first rabbi to graduate from an American university, and, in the absence of a suitable institution in the United States, the first American to attend a European rabbinical seminary. Though he never held an official position at B'rith Kodesh, he was a spiritual leader of the congregation throughout the 1850s.

The newly opened University of Rochester awarded Tuska a full scholarship in 1851. At the university, Tuska concentrated on the classical languages, and when he graduated with honors, in 1856, he gave his commencement address in Greek. He was popular with his classmates and instructors, and as a Jew in an American university, a distinct novelty. Though he tried to avoid theological discussions at the university, apparently the temptation proved irresistible. He brought many of his acquaintances to services at B'rith Kodesh, and at their request prepared a short guide to Judaism, *The Stranger in the Synagogue, or the Rites and Ceremonies of Jewish Worship Described and Explained*, published in 1854. (He thereby earned another "first," as this was the first book published by either a student or alumnus of the University of Rochester.)

Though *Stranger in the Synagogue* is for the most part a generic account of Jewish worship practices, it does provide some information about services at B'rith Kodesh. From the temple's earliest days, a prayer for the United States was recited after the reading of the *Haftorah* (the weekly selection from the prophetic writings). By 1854, Rochester already had its share of Jews who stayed away from the synagogue for most of the year, coming only on the High Holy Days "most earnestly seeking pardon for their sins."

The volume provides evidence of the inroads of the Reform movement on Tuska's thinking. In the preface he noted that "In many synagogues some unsocial customs ordered by the Rabbins [sic] are reformed, and the vain traditions of the Talmud rejected." No doubt responding to incessant quizzing by his college mates, Tuska complained that the details of talmudic practice "are more interesting to Christians than they are approved of by the majority of the Jews." Judaism would be strengthened, he argued, if Jews devoted themselves more to the study of the Torah and the Prophets. Yet for all of its anti-talmudic bluster, *Stranger in the Synagogue* presents an entirely traditional view of Jewish ceremonies. It includes the blessings for donning tallit and tefillin, and ends with an explication of Maimonides' Thirteen Articles of Faith.

We do not know how Mordecai Tuska and other B'rith Kodesh members reacted to *The Stranger in the Synagogue*, but in the autumn of 1854 they asked Simon Tuska to preach on Rosh Hashanah, an extraordinary honor for a young man of nineteen years. The German-language text of Tuska's address was printed shortly thereafter. "Opfer und Reue" (Sacrifice and Repentance) is the oldest extant B'rith Kodesh sermon. In the sermon, delivered in an elegant German style, Tuska spoke on the nature of sacrifice, both in the Bible and for contemporary Jews. He cast Moses as a moderate reformer, trying to elevate his people—still following the barbaric excesses of Egyptian and Phoenician sacrificial rites—by recasting the rites as sacrifices to the true God. The prophets, Tuska said, taught that sacrifices alone cannot atone for sins without internal contrition, and with the destruction of the temple this became the basis of subsequent Jewish understandings of sacrifice. Throughout the sermon Tuska made pointed comparisons between Judaism and Christianity, and ended with praise for the United States and a call for the restoration of the Temple in Jerusalem.

*"**Sacrifice and Repentance:** A Sermon Given on New Year's Day 5615 to the Congregation Berith Kodesh in Rochester, New York"*

My dear Listeners! New Year's Day is upon us—with all its solemnity. On this day all the children of Israel gather (yes, even those who have become negligent during the year because they were pursuing idle and transient tasks)—all of them go to the place of Worship to ask the Almighty for mercy, and for a wonderful year. It is on this day that the shofar is blown in order to arouse us from our inertia, in order to have us acknowledge our sins and repent before the Judge of the whole world. For this is the day when we are examined like a herd of sheep, when our fate is recorded. Verily, it is not without a sense of profound anxiety do I take on the task to which I have been called. How could it be different when I can truly say as the prophet did: "Lo, I am not fit to preach, for I am too young?" And whereof shall I speak? Shall it be an essay on good habits and pious behavior? Then, with justification you would object loudly, "Look at him, he is only a beginner, and already he wants to sit in judgment!" Others may find pleasure in the thundering voice of criticism and reproach, or in sweet and flattering praises about virtue and piety. But there is a more sacred area of religious endeavor: seeking understanding of Holy Scripture and interpretation of its teachings—it is to that we turn when dreary doubt misleads our common sense. The wise Solomon says: "The fear of the Lord is the beginning of wisdom." It is only in Holy Scripture that we can obtain the kind of knowledge that leads to the fear of the Lord. Only Holy Scripture comforts the burdened soul, and fills it with sweet teachings.

My dear listeners: after these introductory remarks I ask most humbly that you pay attention to the ensuing words, which I believe to be of instructive value. And may the Lord who is the origin of all wisdom and enlightenment be with us; may He grant that my words contribute to the glorification of his holy name. Amen.

The enraptured King David sat, as he pleads with God for the forgiveness of his sins: "For Thou delightest not in sacrifice, else would I give it; Thou hast no pleasure in burnt offerings. The sacrifices of God are a broken spirit; a broken and contrite heart, O God, Thou wilt not despise." (Psalms 51: 18–19.)

In the time of the Holy Temple sacrifices were made, and through them God showed mercy to the penitent sinner. But now, when we are outside of the Holy Land, when the Temple in Jerusalem has been destroyed, where shall we offer our sacrifice? The land that was once so magnificent is desert now; the city where once we gathered to celebrate our holy days is desert now. But for how long have we been away from our homeland, scattered all over the world without king, without priest, without altar, without sacrifice! No more can we celebrate our feasts according to God's dictates, as we once did. How very different it was for our forefathers when they sacrificed burnt offerings for repentance, for gratitude, for sins. We are now not able, nor are we permitted, to make sacrifices. How then can we make our peace with God? . . .

Nearly all our prophets have declared that atonement is sufficient to obtain pardon for our sins. Thus the rabbinic word "repentance, prayer, and charity avert misfortune" is well supported. And with this conviction, my dear listeners, we are assembled today in this temple to seek Him who alone can forgive our sins. As always we reject the notion that our God cannot impart forgiveness, that we must seek an intermediary to protect us from the fiery arrows of Him who destroys and resurrects—He, who holds salvation in his right hand, who alone can redeem us, so that our soul—purely and joyfully—may be accepted into the kingdom of heaven with song and hallelujah of the hosts and angels. "Grass withers and flowers dry up, but the word of our God lasts forever." Earth and Heaven proclaim it: God's decrees are unalterable, irrevocable, and eternal, and the children of the covenant—it was made with our forebears, strengthened and sealed on Mount Sinai—they are the living proof of the truth that God's word is unchangeable. For what accounts for the wonderful continuance of our nationality and religion, other than the fact that God lasts forever. ...Israel cannot be annihilated, not can its faith and its worship be destroyed. For eighteen centuries we wandered in countries that never knew our domination; often we were persecuted; rarely we were protected; frequently we were put to the rack, our bodies were tortured with the cruelest tools in order to tear from our hearts the belief in the mercy and power of the Lord. In spite of all that—like burning logs snatched from the fire—we escaped annihilation; we held fast to our religion. For with outstretched wings the Almighty protected us and assisted us in our time of need. Recognizing that God has kept us alive, has watched over us, has permitted us to enjoy another new year, how could our heart ever cease to beat with gratitude, how could our mind ever cease to ponder devotedly on the compassion of the Lord? ...

Here where each of us can worship according to the dictates of his conscience, where detestable differences between sects are eliminated, where no one asks of our religious affiliation, but where the worth of each man and citizen is valued for its own sake—in this glorious land Israel does not deny its God and has not forgotten the saving hand that led it through great waters to a land of religious and civil freedom. The temples which are being built all over the length and breadth of the land bear witness to the loyalty and dedication of the children of Zion and give proof of devotion to her faith.

The past and present history of our nation is a sure sign of the glorious future still in store for Israel. Whether that future be distant or near, in either case it is incumbent on every Jew to pray for its coming. For only then, says the Holy Scripture, mankind will know peace for all, heavenly enlightenment, and eternal joy. But in order to renew the towers of Jerusalem, in order to rebuild the holy temple, we must first renew our soul, and with devotion we must learn to follow the ways of the Lord, and we must forget those

Simon Tuska preached this Rosh Hashanah sermon at B'rith Kodesh in 1854, when he was only nineteen years old. (Courtesy Library of Congress)

insignificant contentions and differences that have separated the house of Israel for so long. Then we shall fulfill the aim of our Father and became a nation of priests, a holy nation. Then the mercy of the Almighty will shine upon us eternally, and we shall rebuild the temple of Zion and convert the nations of the earth to revere one God, one King, one Savior, and one Father.

Amen.

By 1855 Tuska emerged in the pages of American Jewish periodicals as a strong voice for a distinctively American Judaism. He was a spokesperson for a new generation of American Jews, who wanted their sermons in English, and expected their rabbis to be familiar with the customs and intellectual traditions of the United States. His knowledge of contemporary Protestant theology was comprehensive, and he published articles in Baptist theological journals. For Tuska, the principles of Judaism were fully compatible with the ideals of American democracy. Ancient Israel, he wrote in 1856, was ultimately governed not by kings but by God and the voluntary acceptance by the people of the law of Moses. And this law was, Tuska argued, "eminently democratic—a society that adhered to the fundamental principles of republican government, with *"equal rights, equal claims* to civil promotion, *no superior, no inferior classes."*

Like many young college graduates, Tuska was unsure of what career path to follow. For several years he studied systematic theology at the Rochester Theological Seminary, taught at the Collegiate Institute in nearby Brockport, and preached occasionally at B'rith Kodesh. Though hired as a Hebrew instructor at Union Theological Seminary in New York City, the appointment was rescinded when some at the seminary felt that a Jew on the faculty was inappropriate. In his spare time Tuska completed a novel.

But eventually the pull of a rabbinic calling proved too strong. By 1855 Isaac Mayer Wise, the leading figure in nineteenth-century Reform Judaism in America, had adopted Tuska as a protégé, indeed,

Simon Tuska, looking rather dashing in this photograph, was a pioneering figure in the evolution of the American rabbinate. (Courtesy American Jewish Archives)

as the "future prospect" of American Judaism. Wise urged Tuska to raise the level of the American rabbinate by obtaining rabbinic ordination at a recognized European seminary. In June of 1858 Tuska left for Europe with the blessing of Rochester's Jewish community, which had helped raise money to defray his expenses, and sent him off with the wish that he would return one day to Rochester. Tuska too hoped that it would "be my lot hereafter to cultivate the field of Judaism on the soil of Berith Kodesh in the Flour City."

Tuska spent almost two years in Europe, studying at the rabbinic seminary in Breslau with such luminaries as Zechariah Frankel (one of the central figures in what later emerged as Conservative Judaism) and renowned Jewish historian Heinrich Graetz. Though he enjoyed those eminent teachers, he found the regular course of study somewhat confining. In addition to his study in Breslau he traveled throughout central Europe, reporting on his journeys for both local periodicals in western New York and American Jewish journals. He met with many prominent Jewish figures, including Abraham Geiger in Berlin, Isaac Noah Mannheimer and Adolf Jellinek in Vienna, and Solomon Judah Rapport in Prague. He also found time to go the opera and concerts, and was especially impressed by the performance of ten-year old violin prodigy Leopold Auer, like Tuska a native of Veszprem, Hungary. (Auer went on to become the father of the "Russian School" of violin playing, and the teacher of Mischa Elman, Jascha Heifetz, and Nathan Milstein, among others.) Many Europeans were surprised to meet an educated and pious American Jew. Solomon Sulzer, the famed cantor of the Vienna synagogue, was excited to have an American among his auditors, and seated Tuska in a front pew.

Tuska returned to the United States in the spring of 1860, but not to Rochester. B'rith Kodesh did not hire him as rabbi, despite an opening created by Ferdinand Sarner's resignation that July. B'rith Kodesh member Simon Hays said at the time of Tuska's death: "When he

The St. Paul Street Temple is beneath the number three in this 1882 panorama of downtown Rochester. In this, the only surviving image of the temple, its two spires and Moorish style can be clearly discerned. (Courtesy Division of Rare Books and Special Collections, Rush Rhees Library, University of Rochester)

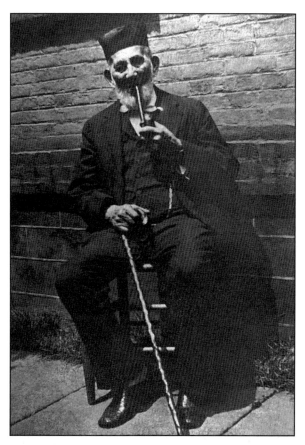

A founding member of B'rith Kodesh, Joseph Katz was the first Jew to settle in Rochester, possibly as early as 1834, the year the city was incorporated. In 1847 he went to his native Bavaria to marry Jeannette Friedman. The couple returned to Rochester, where they remained for the rest of their lives. The Katzes lived for many years on Elm Street in downtown Rochester; Joseph Katz survived into the twentieth century. (Courtesy American Jewish Archives)

returned [from Europe] it was expected that the Flour City would be his abiding place. But it is said that great men do not have honor at home." The explanation for the surprising decision not to hire Tuska probably lies in Sarner's short and unhappy tenure at B'rith Kodesh, which was characterized by bitter disputes between reformers and conservatives. The majority evidently felt that hiring a Reform advocate like Tuska would irrevocably rend the congregation. Tuska accepted a position at B'nai Israel in Memphis, Tennessee.

Tuska made one further attempt to return to Rochester. In late 1862 B'rith Kodesh had yet to fill the vacancy left by Sarner's departure, and Tuska applied for the position. This time the congregation elected Tuska rabbi, but when B'nai Israel offered him an extension on his contract, he stayed in Memphis. In his Memphis congregation Tuska introduced family pews and Isaac Mayer Wise's moderate Reform prayerbook, *Minhag America*. Tuska died suddenly of a heart attack in January 1871, aged thirty-five. Among the papers he left at his death were plans for a seminary for Reform Judaism. The B'rith Kodesh tribute to Tuska read in part, "Having known him almost from his infancy, we watched with pleasure the rapid strides to honor and renown of him who was the friend of all and beloved by all who knew him."

Growing Pains

Ideological ferment proved to be a sign of strength, not weakness at B'rith Kodesh in the 1850s. The congregation grew rapidly over the course of the decade. One observer in 1855 estimated that the congregation had 75 members, while a B'rith Kodesh member, writing only a year later, claimed that "the Hebrew congregation of Rochester numbers 100 men, all of them married." Isaac Mayer Wise wrote of seventy families in 1860; another visitor in 1862 of ninety. Whatever the size of the congregation in 1860, it was four or five times larger than it had been only ten years earlier.

Both men and women played active roles in the life of the congregation. Visiting lecturers were surprised by the number of women in the audience. Women sang in the choir after its organization in the early 1860s. In 1866 the congregation's young men and women formed a dramatic group, the Independent Literary Union. And girls as well as boys participated in the rite of Confirmation. B'rith Kodesh's first Confirmation class in 1857 included an equal number of boys and girls (five each). A female teacher was employed in the B'rith Kodesh school as early as 1859. Some women's activities in the congregation followed their domestic roles. They participated in the upkeep of the sanctuary through needlework projects, including the embroidery of a curtain for the Torah ark, and clerical robes.

In the 1850s and 1860s, many members of B'rith Kodesh achieved considerable economic success, especially in the men's clothing industry.

Before the 1920s, all B'rith Kodesh members purchased individual pews. This seat indenture predates the institution of family seating in 1869. In this agreement from 1863, Solomon Benjamin and his wife purchased separate seats in the male and female sections of the synagogue, for an outright fee of $60 and annual dues.

They expected their synagogue to reflect their success. B'rith Kodesh member Nathan Mayer crowed in 1856, "in a social point of view, our brethren of this city are far above many of their sister congregations." Mayer went on to praise B'rith Kodesh members for their exquisite taste—in the architecture of their houses and the layout of their gardens, the adornment of their walls with excellent oil paintings, and for placing fashionable books in conspicuous places on their coffee tables. Outsiders agreed. An article in the *Jewish Messenger* in 1862 praised the congregation "as one of the most prosperous in the Union," successful in business, politics, and in their social endeavors. In 1866 the pseudonymous "Ben Berith" epitomized the spirit of boosterism: "Rochester possesses, without exception, for her size, the most intelligent, liberal, and wealthy Israelites in this country."

With increasing size, wealth, and prestige, B'rith Kodesh soon outgrew its sanctuary on Front Street. A hotly contested election for president in 1855 turned on the issue of congregational expansion. Despite much jockeying between rival slates, the final election results were reported as unanimous victory for Elias Ettenheimer. The High Holy Days, especially, forced the renting of larger quarters, since the observance drew Jews from Brockport, Albion, Palmyra, and other surrounding communities. For the High Holy Days in 1855, B'rith Kodesh rented the Tabernacle Baptist Church on St. Paul Street. Services were split that year, probably at the behest of the younger men in the congregation. While Mordecai Tuska preached in German at Front Street, Mr. Barnard and Simon Tuska presented English-language sermons at St. Paul Street.

This temporary division hinted at deeper divisions in the congregation. There had been talk of purchasing the St. Paul Street building before the High Holy Days, but the church was unsure whether to sell the building, and some members of B'rith Kodesh did not want to worship in a former church, which lacked a proper gallery for the women. (As on Front Street, men and women sat separately at St. Paul Street, with men to the right and women to the left, divided by the center aisle.) In the fall the congregation bought a lot on the corner of Atwater and Chatham streets for $2,000, but the title to the land was questionable. In August 1856 the Tabernacle Baptist Church placed the St. Paul Street property on the market, and the members of B'rith Kodesh, overcoming their earlier doubts, unanimously decided to purchase it for $6,750. The new owners spent an additional thousand dollars to turn the former church into a synagogue. Among the other changes, the baptismal font found new use as a *mikveh*, a ritual bath. St. Paul Street would be the address of B'rith Kodesh for almost forty years.

With the move, the struggle over Reform began in earnest. In the fall of 1856 Isaac Mayer (not to be confused with Isaac Mayer Wise) was hired as the congregation's new rabbi. The reasons for the resignation of Mordecai Tuska are not known; perhaps he simply wished to retire. He remained in Rochester until his death in 1871, and though he remained active in the congregation, he never again held a rabbinical position. A native of Alsace, Isaac Mayer had been rabbi at K.K. Shearith Israel in Cincinnati for six years before coming to Rochester.

By later standards Mayer was a moderate Reformer. The touchstones of classic Reform—family seating, elimination of head coverings, and de-Hebraicizing the service—were not at issue during Mayer's years at B'rith Kodesh. Mayer sought to strip the Jewish service and theology of its harder-to-understand elements. One observer of Mayer's first High Holy Day services noted that "many prayers were not recited, others altered, and the service gone through in a manner more suited to the age than it ever has been here before." But more sweeping liturgical reform evidently came more slowly, for by the time of Mayer's first Shavuos service at B'rith Kodesh he was

Elias S. Ettenheimer, elected president of B'rith Kodesh in 1855, left the congregation in the late 1860s when he felt it was becoming too strongly identified with radical Reform.

21

still critiquing the "hyper-annuated and exceedingly ancient mode of service." Referring to the traditional European customs he found objectionable, Mayer suggested if the congregation continued to resist the proposed reforms, they might as well beat Haman on Purim, or throw nuts at each other on Simchat Torah.

Mayer's introduction of the Confirmation ceremony in 1857 provides other clues to the nature of his Reform views. The Confirmation service from the beginning primarily was conducted in English, and was a public catechism in which the candidates were called upon to profess the chief principles of Judaism. In Mayer's service there were three—not thirteen—Articles of Faith: the uniqueness and unity of God was the paramount principle; the two others were the eternal truth of the divine law of Moses, and the belief in divine providence. *The American Israelite* in 1858 criticized the last of Mayer's principles for being somewhat equivocal, and predicted correctly that traditionalists would be upset by Mayer's failure to explicitly include the fulfillment of messianic prophecies and the bodily resurrection of the dead among the core teachings of Judaism

Mayer introduced his reforms into a congregation that was already divided into traditionalists and modernists. In October 1855, *The Occident* reported that some members of B'rith Kodesh wished to introduce family seating, a policy the congregation did not adopt until 1869. Despite the strong feelings among members, B'rith Kodesh consistently tried to mute its internal ideological divisions in the interest of maintaining harmony. The frequent reports of unanimous votes on divisive issues indicates a will to reach a consensus. An article in December 1855 indicated that while some members wished to introduce changes to the service, "they will not desire to introduce any reform which might lead to disunion."

Five years later, reformers still encountered the same situation. Isaac Mayer Wise, who visited the congregation in 1860, claimed that the majority favored Reform, but held back to avoid

In 1859, and again in 1870, B'rith Kodesh advertised for a new rabbi in the pages of the Jewish Messenger *(1859, below) and the* American Israelite *(1870, top). Over the course of the decade, the congregation moved far along the path to radical Reform.*

giving offense to the minority. For many in B'rith Kodesh, ideological disputes were simply less important than keeping all of the Jews in the community worshipping together on good terms. Such unity could be maintained only if all parties were willing to compromise even as Reform principles were slowly introduced into the ritual. In December 1863 one writer claimed that half the members of the congregation were orthodox, and the rest divided between moderate and "ultra" reformers. But B'rith Kodesh remained united because all sides had "the same object in view, the mutual advancement of our religion."

Harmony came at a price, however, and on more than one occasion the congregation placated a minority by firing the rabbi. By the fall of 1858 Isaac Mayer was out of a job. His supporters claimed that this was the doing of "the mischievous intrigues of a small party who is his enemy." Apparently, a small group of members, who in letters to newspapers called themselves the "pious five," took to walking out every time Mayer started to preach. Even after his forced resignation, he retained close contacts with members of the congregation. Remaining in Rochester for a year after his ouster, Mayer opened a Hebrew school, and occasionally preached at B'rith Kodesh on a freelance basis. By 1859 he had moved to Hartford, Connecticut, where he was rabbi of Congregation Beth Israel. In another sign of internal dissension, some of Mayer's enemies established Adas Jeshrun in the fall of 1858, a short-lived breakaway congregation that followed the Polish rather than the German ritual, and was more traditional in its worship than B'rith Kodesh.

In the fall of 1859, the congregation had a new rabbi, Ferdinand Leopold Sarner. Born in East Prussia in the borderlands between Central and Eastern Europe, he was highly educated, with a doctorate from the University of Hesse (though the circumstances of his graduation are somewhat murky). He came strongly recommended to B'rith Kodesh by S. N. Isaacs, a traditionally minded New York City rabbi. Many members of B'rith Kodesh were delighted that with the hiring of Sarner, "the dark clouds" threatening the congregation had dissipated: "All troubles and misunderstandings have come to a happy and peaceful termination." This optimism was premature.

Hired as a moderate, Sarner at first was careful not to tip his hand in the Reform/anti-Reform controversies. But remaining above the fray is very difficult in such circumstances, and he soon weighed in as a reformer, cutting some prayers and indicating his intention to introduce a choir. In a further effort to change the quality of its services, the congregation hired a cantor, Elkan J. Herzman, from New York City—B'rith Kodesh's first and last cantor for over a century—but perhaps getting caught in the ideological crossfire, he only stayed two months before moving to Cleveland. The members of Adas Jeshrun, evidently lured back into B'rith Kodesh with

Nimrod Rosenfield was one of the most influential members of B'rith Kodesh in the 1860s and 1870s, and a leader in the movement for radical Reform. In 1862 he became the congregation's first music director.

promises that the reforms of the Mayer era were over, expressed outrage. Sarner, they said, "applied the knife to the prayer book of our ancestors, to make room for new light Theology." The traditionalists disliked Sarner even more than they did Mayer, perhaps because Sarner had been hired as a traditionalist. Aaron Parkes (or Park), the leader of the "pious five," wrote in June 1860 that while Isaac Mayer's talent had always commanded respect, Sarner had "little religious impulse."

Sarner had his admirers within the congregation. An article in the *American Israelite* in February 1860 claimed that "the Rev. Doctor Sarner won laurels as a minister and orator." Visiting Rochester in July 1860, Isaac Mayer Wise praised Sarner's "brilliant talents." It is difficult to determine the size of the respective factions, but Sarner had "some very severe opponents" in the congregation, who, one observer felt, would "surely will succeed in undermining him."

The "pious five" were not the only ones unhappy with Sarner. According to one account, the congregation unanimously offered to buy out his contract in early spring 1860. When Sarner declined, at least twenty members signed a petition to fire Sarner immediately. This dispute, conducted very publicly in the leading Jewish newspapers of the day, was an embarrassment for all involved. When Sarner finally resigned, in July 1860, the congregation tendered him a rather disingenuous testimonial, and let him go with a sterling recommendation. For his part, Sarner did not forget his treatment in Rochester. In 1864 he published a highly unflattering article about his successor in the B'rith Kodesh pulpit. The congregation condemned Sarner's "vile slanders" and accused him of sinking to the "lowest depth" in his journalism.

After Sarner's resignation, it would be three years before B'rith Kodesh hired another rabbi. During this period services were generally conducted by members of the congregation, assisted by visiting rabbis during the High Holy Days. (It was during this period that the congregation failed to hire Simon Tuska.) The congregation was fully in the hands of the laity, and it was during those years that it made its decisive move to Reform. Given the contentious fights of the late 1850s, the final move to Reform was almost anti-climactic. Perhaps without a rabbi to focus their animosities, the congregation found it easier to reach a consensus on reforms. In early 1862, Nimrod Rosenfield, a member of the congregation, became B'rith Kodesh's first choral director and also introduced an organ into the service.

In 1862 Rabbi Judah Kalisch officiated at the High Holy Day services. A persuasive advocate for reform, he apparently convinced the congregation to adopt Isaac Mayer Wise's reform prayer book, *Minhag America*, after several years of hesitation. Though this was a momentous step, Wise's efforts to fashion a ritual that would not be offensive to traditionalists no doubt smoothed the way to its acceptance. *Minhag America* contained two separate services, one entirely in Hebrew, one an English translation. It contained only small variations from the Orthodox *siddur*, and the changes were primarily limited to paraphrases of passages (such as those dealing with a personal messiah) that Wise found archaic. At about the same time, the congregation also ended the traditional practice of having individual congregants read publicly from the scriptures. Following a practice that had been adopted at Temple Emanuel in New York City, all Torah reading was conducted by the officiants at the service.

Joseph Cauffman, a leading garment manufacturer in Rochester, was a long-time secretary and one-time president of B'rith Kodesh.

The first generation of reformers viewed traditional worship as anarchic. Individual congregants prayed at their own pace, and the service lacked a pleasing sense of harmony. Reformers sought to infuse Judaism with a Romantic religious style that emphasized unison prayer and meditation as the necessary background to genuine religious feeling. What subsequent generations often found to be stifling and over-rehearsed, the first reformers found spiritually moving and uplifting. In 1855 the reformers in B'rith Kodesh claimed that what they wanted was "order in the worship" and "nothing beyond it." When Isaac Mayer returned to Rochester for Passover in 1862, he was delighted by the changes in the service. Now, he said, "the strictest order, quietness, and devotion ruled during the whole service." This left the worshippers "more elevated and edified than ever before." Writing in 1863, a member of B'rith Kodesh proclaimed that the mist of Orthodoxy had finally dissipated, "and behold we have a reformed congregation which entirely obliterates and does away with all those foolish customs and brings order and decorum (the first great principle of religion) into the house of God." More decorum would enable Jews to pray with greater "feeling and devotion."

Building a Congregation

Despite the incessant controversies over Reform, B'rith Kodesh prospered in the 1850s and 1860s because of the active involvement of its members. They organized several benevolent organizations including the Hebrew Benevolent Society (the Gemilos Chesed Society) in 1856, and the Zerubabel Lodge of the International Order of B'nai B'rith in 1864. As early

Bar Mitzvah in 1860

Then, as now, becoming a Bar Mitzvah (Son of Commandment) preented an occasion for a lavish party. When Henry Seligman, possibly the first Jewish male born in Rochester, became a Bar Mitzvah in 1860, his parents invited a hundred people to their house for dancing and card playing. Seligman's Bar Mitzvah speech has survived. It opened with an acknowledgment of the momentous nature of the event:

Almighty Father! Thou who art ever ready to listen to the prayers of the *young* as well as the old suffer me now to come before Thee, in childlike simplicity and reverence. The solemn hour has arrived, when I am to leave the frolicsome enjoyments of childhood, and enter into the religious communion with the

Elias Wolf, a founding member and early president of B'rith Kodesh, a prominent garment manufacturer, and one of the wealthiest members of the Jewish community.

as 1851 there had been a Ladies Benevolent Society. This functioned as a burial society for the Jewish women of Rochester, and like its male equivalents undertook to attend the sick, sit with the deceased between death and burial, and to raise money for poor and indigent Jews. A successor organization, the Hebrew Ladies Benevolent Society was formed in 1865 to assist in relief for the poor. Mrs. Henry Lempert was its first president.

A number of visitors commented that B'rith Kodesh members had unusual ties of friendship that triumphed over occasional animosities. Social activities of the members strengthened these bonds. Beginning in 1856, the Hebrew Benevolent Society sponsored an annual ball shortly after Yom Kippur. The first one set the pattern for the subsequent affairs: large numbers of non-Jews attended, the party lasted until dawn, and, as one observer rhapsodized, "the ladies of Rochester vindicated their fame for beauty, elegance, fashion, and joyous tempers."

Young Seligman doubtless attended the congregation's religious day school. Its establishment in 1856 was perhaps the most noteworthy communal undertaking of B'rith Kodesh in its early years. Before that date, Mordecai Tuska and Mr. Barnard had conducted private Hebrew instruction at home. The inadequacy of Rochester's public schools, which in the mid-1850s could accommodate only two-thirds of the children of school age provided one reason for the opening of a congregational school. (There had been a drastic cut in the city school budget in 1855.) Moreover, like the Roman Catholics, some Jews were suspicious of the overt Protestantism of the early public schools. Curiously, some B'rith Kodesh members sent their children to Catholic schools, presumably to take advantage of German-language instruction.

The B'rith Kodesh school opened June 15, 1856, in the basement of the synagogue on North St. Paul Street. By fall the school had eighty students. Isaac Mayer taught Hebrew, Nathan Mayer was the German instructor, and a Mr. Thomas taught English. Pleased with Isaac Mayer's work in the school, the congregation voted him a raise. At the same time it purchased a separate building for a schoolhouse, on Andrews Street, near North Clinton Avenue. The new schoolhouse opened in 1857. The same year, B'rith Kodesh established a semi-autonomous board, the Chevra Talmud Torah, to run the school, though all the members of the board were active in the congregation as well. The school offered scholarships to poorer families outside the congregation, financed by bequests from wealthy members.

Hebrew day schools were sufficiently popular in the late 1850s that Rochester comfortably supported two, for when Isaac Mayer was let go by B'rith Kodesh in the summer of 1858, he established his own school, which lasted at least through 1860. Mayer was one of the pioneers of Hebrew and Jewish education in the United States. Just before coming to Rochester he authored a Hebrew grammar, the first Hebrew book published west of the Alleghenies. The volume was designed to remedy the lack of suitable introductory Hebrew textbooks for English speakers. Not surprisingly, the school emphasized the teaching of Hebrew. Later in his career he published a Jewish catechism for children. Graduates of Rochester's Hebrew day schools remembered the liberal use of corporal punishment to keep the students in line. Favored students were sometimes allowed to go around to a corner store and purchase chewing tobacco for their teachers. By the late 1860s, however, Rochester Jews were increasingly comfortable with the city's public schools, and the need for a day school diminished. The congregational school closed in 1867, and B'rith Kodesh established its first Sunday school in 1869.

B'rith Kodesh also took an interest in Jews elsewhere in the world. The Mortara Affair of 1858 shocked Rochester Jews. Edgar Mortara, the child of Jewish parents in Bologna, in the Papal States, had been secretly baptized by his Catholic nurse, and then removed from his parents by the Vatican police. B'rith Kodesh passed a resolution condemning the incident, probably its first statement on international Jewish affairs. In 1865, Rochester Jews formed a local chapter of the Alliance Israelite Universelle, a French organization that was originally organized in response to the Mortara Affair. The congregation also gave—fairly generously—to traveling Palestinian *sh'lichim* (emissaries) who came to the United States in search of funds for poor Jews in Palestine. When in 1862 I. J. Benjamin found a full and attentive audience in Rochester for his lecture on Sephardic Jews, he took this as evidence that Jews, "no matter how far they are separated from each other and no matter how many seas and deserts divide them, still feel to be members of one family."

responsible sons of Israel. The day has come when it behooves me to take upon myself the solemn responsibilities resting upon every member of the synagogue.

After acknowledging the providential protection of God, Seligman thanked his parents, who had raised him without the thought of "pecuniary reward or temporal blessing, but to make me a true son of Israel." To the members of the synagogue, he affirmed the three principles of Judaism familiar from Isaac Mayer's Confirmation classes, the belief in God, the revelation of God to Moses and the prophets, and belief in the immortality of the soul and divine reward.

The grand vistas of Mt. Hope Cemetery often inspired romantic reveries by visitors.
(Courtesy Rochester Public Library)

Three Visitors to B'rith Kodesh

In its early decades B'rith Kodesh had a number of visitors who provide the best accounts of the congregation. Three stand out, Isaac Mayer Wise, I. J. Benjamin, and the editor of a leading Rochester newspaper.

Isaac Mayer Wise, American Israelite, *July 20, 1860*

Isaac Mayer Wise (1819–1900) was the central figure in nineteenth-century Reform Judaism in the United States. In the 1850s he used his friendships with both Simon Tuska and Isaac Mayer to try to nudge B'rith Kodesh into the Reform camp. His account of his first of many visits to the congregation gives no indication of the underlying tension that would, in a matter of weeks, lead to the resignation of Ferdinand Sarner.

July 11, 1860

Rochester is the Cincinnati of this part of the country, as far as our brethren are concerned. They are nearly the same class of people with the same religious views, display the same sensitivity in matters of religion and are like the Cincinnatians of the "go ahead" stamp. When I arrived at the depot there was the committee of reception consisting of Messrs A. Sloman, S. Stettheimer, D. Cohn, Joseph Beir, and Moses Hays. The latter being the president of the congregation welcomed me in a neat little address, and told me that every house was ready to receive me. Having thanked the congregation for their extended hospitality, I was escorted into the friendly home of my friend Martin Bier where cordial friends and brothers received me.

I spent a very happy day in Rochester. Martin Bier Esq., showed me the sights, among which I must notice Mount Hope, the city cemetery for all societies and religious denominations, a plot of ground which nature designated for this purpose. Its ups and downs, its hills and rivulets are the symbols of life's perpetual changes, and there the dead rest in silent repose and peace. We ascended the highest point of Mount Hope, and there we mounted the observatory. What a grand sight! To the north Lake Ontario bounds the horizon, below the city of Rochester with her fine buildings, and southward the fertile Genesee valley, with its numerous villages and hamlets stretches away for many miles. It is a panorama of nature and art grand enough to rouse every sensation of admiration, grandeur and piety in the heart. There the dead slumber, and the very spot elevated above the surrounding country, the Pisgah from which the holy land can be seen, is an expressive symbol of immortality. They see the valley of life, behind the details and totality of earthly existence and dwell in undisturbed peace.

Among the many interesting acquaintances I made here is that of Rev. Dr. Sarner, a young rabbi recently from Germany with a classical education and brilliant talents. He is the rabbi of the congregation.

Rochester has only one Hebrew congregation, one benevolent society and two Hebrew schools, one of which I visited and found it was in the best order. The vast majority of the congregation are in favor of reform and work for it. But they hold back out of respect to the minority, because the members of the congregation, being all of them personal friends they would not give offense or cause of complaint to the minority. This is laudable, but the gentlemen of the minority with due respect to their friends should certainly reciprocate, and I believe they are willing to do so. There is profound peace and very good spirit among the members of this congregation. It is very pleasing to hear that seventy families are joined together not only by the ties of religion but also by the ties of mutual friendship. Their synagogue is a splendid and large building. The sexes are divided on the floor of the house, as the building has no galleries.

In the evening I delivered a lecture to a crowded house of Jews and Gentiles. Rev. Dr. Sarner opened and concluded the occasion with prayers. I spoke with more fervency than I have for some time, for I see before me a highly intelligent community. The impression made must have been a highly favorable one. … It being the desire of the congregation to hear me again on the Minhag America, *I addressed them the next morning in the Synagogue. I am told that the congregation was inclined to adopt this ritual.*

I went from Rochester much pleased with my day's labor. I had seen many friends and took with me the most pleasing recollections. The Rochester congregation, we have no doubt, will soon rank among the foremost of our congregations in this country; for there is both the proper material and the good will to elevate the religion of Israel in the estimation of all. God bless them.

— *Isaac Mayer Wise*

I. J. Benjamin, Three Years in America, 1859-1862

I. J. Benjamin was a nineteenth century German Jewish adventurer, like his self-chosen namesake, the medieval Jewish traveler, Benjamin of Tudela, he had spent much time visiting the Jews of the Middle East and Asia. From 1860 to 1862 he went on an extended lecture tour of the United States, and his published account of his journey, containing descriptions of almost every synagogue and Jewish community in the country, is an invaluable resource for historians. Benjamin came to Rochester in early 1862. His portrait of Rochester's Jewish community differs in many details from other accounts from the same period:

On the evening of January twenty-eight [1862], I left Buffalo and reached Rochester at ten o'clock at night. The distance is about ninety miles. There is a Jewish congregation here. It has no particular name. It was founded in 1847 [5607]. The congregation has about ninety members. Mr. I. Katz is the president. The hazzan is Mr. Hiss. As yet the congregation has observed the old ritual but, for some time, several members have insisted upon the introduction of a new one. However, they have not yet succeeded in accomplishing this.

There is also a charitable society here: Chebarath Nashim Gomloth Chesed to assist the poor. The Jews of this city are in general very friendly and charitable.

On the evening of the twenty-eight of January, several members of the congregation invited me to the synagogue that I might tell a number of my fellow Jews about the Jews of the Orient. I did not decline the invitation and went to the synagogue. I was surprised, however, to find a great number of people, women as well as men, all eager to hear me. They wished to lead me to the pulpit, but I declined that place and spoke from where the hazzan stands, fully an hour about the Jews in Asia and Africa. All listened with great attention. All invited me to their homes and those I visited considered it a great honor. This is some evidence of the fact that Jews, no matter how far they are separated from each other and no matter how many seas and deserts divide them, still feel to be members of one family, and are glad to receive news of their brothers.

In May 1865, the editor of the *Rochester Daily Union and Advertiser* attended Saturday services at B'rith Kodesh. The account makes reference to the assassination of President Abraham Lincoln the month before:

"An Hour in the Synagogue," Rochester Daily Union and Advertiser, *May 22, 1865*

We had an opportunity last Saturday to visit the Synagogue of this city, and were agreeably surprised to notice the progress made by our Jewish fellow-citizens. A few years ago the Rochester Hebrew congregation was worshipping as a strictly Orthodox congregation. Since, however, the wheels of progress and reform have made some revolutions and the Israelites of Rochester are now among the foremost on this continent who, while in principle adhering to the fundamental laws of Judaism

Rabbi Isaac Mayer Wise, the leader of American Reform Judaism in the nineteenth century, and a frequent visitor to B'rith Kodesh.

reject non-essentials and follow the banner of progress. This was, we believe, the first congregation in the Empire State to adopt what is called the "Minhag America," that is prayers and other regulations for the Divine service selected and arranged by a few distinguished rabbis of this country in accordance with the spirit of the times.

In entering the synagogue in North St. Paul Street, formerly a Baptist church—a plain but handsome building—we discovered the holy ark, or the sanctum sanctorum draped in mourning on account of the national calamity.

One of the peculiarities that strikes the visitor as he enters is the appearance of the congregation divided—the gentlemen on the right of the centre aisle and the ladies on the left, and the former with their heads covered. In other respects the Synagogue is not unlike a church. The rabbi and reader are seated opposite the entrance, the choir occupying a gallery over the entrance facing the rabbi.

There would be no objection to families occupying the same slips, but we are told that it is because a satisfactory division of the slips cannot be made to please all, that the present method is adopted. The seats are owned by the congregation, and the members are taxed according to value to meet current expenses. The salaries paid the Rabbi, Reader, Choir, &c are liberal, and the tax upon the congregation is large.

The Jewish service is solemn and impressive, and is made so in part by the music. The choir of the Rochester Synagogue is said to be the best in any Synagogue in the State, not even excepting New York City. The principal singers belong to the Christian congregations. It speaks to the liberal spirit of the age when Christian ladies and gentlemen are seen in the choir of the synagogue, contributing by their voices to the beauty and solemnity of the Jewish worship. What would the Rabbis of ages gone by have said, had they seen their congregations inspired by the sacred songs from Gentile voices?

In the Choir at the Synagogue we noticed with

pleasure, besides the singers of the Jewish faith, Miss Jennie Bull, Miss Young, Miss Chapman, and Mr. Rhodes, all well known in musical circles and to the public as artists. The choir is led by Mr. N. Rosenfield, who acquits himself admirably in the position and is entitled to great credit, as is the congregation. Prof. Schultz is organist and teacher, and he composed many of the fine pieces executed by the choir. The brains and hands of the Professor contribute largely to the reputation of the choir.

The reader in the Synagogue is Mr. Abraham Schmidt, a gentleman who has a clear, well-toned voice, and distinct articulation. His reading in Hebrew is excellent.

The Rabbi, Rev. Dr. Gunzburg is no stranger to our readers, having contributed to our columns on a number of occasions interesting articles, showing, as they did, that he was a gentleman of great learning and research, and one admirably posted in the history and principles of his faith. He may be congratulated upon the fact that he has the esteem and affection of his congregation. It was not our good fortune to hear the Reverend Doctor preach, as he had no sermon on Saturday. A sermon from such a man to a progressive Jewish congregation would be interesting.

The general management of the affairs of the congregation is in the hands of a Board of Trustees chosen by the whole and to whom they are indebted very much for the success which has followed. The officers are S. Stettheimer, President; D. Rosenberg, Vice-President; W. Guggenheim, Secretary and Trustee; Joseph Bier, H. Michaels, N. Rosenfield, Trustees.

We are told the former President, Mr. Moses Hays, was active in the introduction of the reforms which have contributed to the prosperity of the congregation.

Our visit to the Synagogue was a source of much gratification, and we may assure our readers of whatever denomination that an hour spent in the Jewish place of worship will be profitable. It will give the visitor more respect for the people of that faith, and will gratify as it will convince all that our Jewish fellow-citizens are among the foremost in the United States to move forward with civilization and enlightened progress. We are proud of this congregation, as it does honor to our city.

B'rith Kodesh in the Civil War

In the spring of 1861, the dispute between reformers and traditionalists was crowded into insignificance by the impending crisis of the American Civil War. Before the election of Abraham Lincoln to the presidency in the fall of 1860, Rochester's Jews, like Jews elsewhere, were greatly troubled by the prospects of war. Most synagogues and many Jewish leaders avoided taking a position on the slavery and free soil controversies until the last possible moment. There were good reasons for this. Almost half of the American Jewish population in 1860 lived below the Mason-Dixon line, and there were often close ties between northern and southern Jews. (Simon Tuska, who was living in Confederate Memphis when the war began, is only one example of the connection between Rochester's Jews and the South.) And while most American Jews in 1860 were patriotic, they were also recent immigrants, without the sectional identities and animosities that played such a large role in fomenting the war.

We do not know much about the political views of B'rith Kodesh members as war approached, but it is likely that many were looking for a peaceful resolution of the sectional conflict. Rochester's Jews thus demonstrated a lack of sympathy with abolitionists and Republicans. The congregation's rabbi for most of the war, Rabbi Aaron Guinzberg, came to Rochester in June 1863 from Baltimore. Most Marylanders had a "border state" mentality, pro-Union but anti-Republican, and this was shared by Guinzberg. He felt that many abolitionists were anti-Semitic, and in 1865 accused the radical Republicans of being "more zealous for the half-civilized Negro" than for the Jews. Friends of the congregation shared similar views. Morris Raphall, the leading rabbinic exponent of the notion that southern slavery was sanctioned by the Bible, had close ties to B'rith Kodesh since its founding, and was given a silver trophy upon his 1859 visit to Rochester. Isaac Mayer Wise believed that the federal government had no power to interfere with slavery in the southern states, and called for a negotiated peace with the South.

At the outbreak of war in April 1861, B'rith Kodesh members—whatever their reservations—rallied round the flag. Support for Lincoln was no longer a political issue, but a civic duty. The patriotic activities of the congregation were widely praised. The war was also, it must be acknowledged, good for business. The Union Army's need for uniforms kept Rochester's clothing manufacturers very busy. A correspondent in the *American Israelite* in December 1863 wrote, almost sheepishly, "One would scarcely believe that we are in the midst of a civil war, all branches of business seem to thrive in the city." Rochester's Jews participated in many patriotic rallies and recruitment drives, offering enlistment bounties for new recruits. Relatively few Rochester area Jews served in the war, perhaps because the members of the founding "generation of 1848" were too old to serve, while their children were too young. Arndt Rosenthal, the city's only Jewish officer, was officially given his commission as 2nd lieutenant at the annual post-Yom Kippur ball in 1862, as visiting dignitaries lauded the patriotism of the city's Jews.

At the same time, Ferdinand Sarner, the former B'rith Kodesh rabbi, secured his special niche in American Jewish history as the first rabbi to serve as a regimental chaplain in the U.S. Army. Little is known of Sarner's career between 1860 and 1863, but on April 10, 1863, he enlisted in the army, and was immediately elected chaplain of the 54th New York Volunteer Infantry. Known as the Schwarze Yaeger (the "Black Hunters"), this regiment of German immigrants did not have a large Jewish component. Apparently Sarner's ability to preach in German and his educational attainments were more important to the regiment than his religious background.

Sarner soon saw action, first at the Battle of Chancellorsville in May 1863. Two months later, the 54th New York Volunteers fought fiercely at the Battle of Gettysburg, where they defended a position on Cemetery Hill. Sarner was badly wounded during the engagement, and the unit as a whole suffered heavy casualties. Of the 216 men in the regiment, 102 were either killed, wounded, or captured in the course of the fighting. According to a French Jewish magazine, Sarner's horse was shot out from underneath him, and he sustained a serious leg injury. In January 1864, the *Jewish Record* of New York, with patriotic hyperbole, claimed that Sarner was "probably the first Rabbi who voluntarily took part in a fight since Rabbi Akiba." Sarner served with his regiment until the end of July, 1864 when he left the service. After the war, he spent some time in New York as a journalist and author. Like Simon Tuska, he ended his days in Memphis, Tennessee, where from 1872 to 1878 he was rabbi to Beth El Emeth, the city's Orthodox congregation. Sarner established a path followed by his successors in the B'rith Kodesh pulpit; Horace J. Wolf was a chaplain during World War I, Judea Miller, an army chaplain in the 1950s, and Philip S. Bernstein was the supervisor of all Jewish

Ferdinand Sarner, rabbi of Temple B'rith Kodesh, 1859–1860; chaplain of the 54th New York Volunteers at the Battle of Gettysburg, July 1863. (Courtesy American Jewish Archives)

military chaplains during World War II.

In Rochester, B'rith Kodesh followed the war closely. In May 1864, heeding a proclamation of President Lincoln, it celebrated a day of prayer, and Rabbi Guinzberg took the occasion to offer a prayer that God bring an end to slavery and give victory and triumph to the Union cause. But an adolescent member of the congregation offered the most heartfelt statement of the wartime patriotism. On April 15, 1864, Henry Rice, probably speaking at the B'rith Kodesh day school, talked of America as a God-favored land of refuge. Its institutions and territory, Rice said, must be restored:

> Slavery that detestable cause of strife, envy, and partisanship and which produced this wicked rebellion itself and with which we were taunted by all the nations of Europe is now forever destroyed. Under all these free institutions of liberty, equality, and enlightenment and enterprise, by the blessings of Providence our county has prospered for over seventy years, and relying on the virtue and the courage and the patriotism and the strength of the people for the preservation and protection of our country and maintaining of our liberties, she will yet come out of this war with her dignity upheld and not a star erased from her banner, and when this awful war is crushed, we may yet expect that the time is not yet far distant when the proudest boast of man shall be—I am an American.

Chapter II

Rabbi Max Landsberg and the Triumph of Radical Reform, 1865–1894

Introduction

The adoption of Isaac Mayer Wise's prayerbook, *Minhag America,* in October 1862 was a triumph for the reformers in B'rith Kodesh. But real divisions still remained within the congregation. Though the vote was declared to be unanimous, this probably reflected the B'rith Kodesh practice of seeking a congregational consensus after a decision was reached on a controversial issue. It certainly did not mean that all opponents of reform had undergone a sudden change of opinion. Debate continued on many issues pertaining to the ritual. One particularly heated controversy was over whether the hazzan should face the ark (east, in the direction of Jerusalem) during the service, or turn toward the congregation. According to an account written in August 1863, nearly half the congregation was still "genuine Orthodox" while the remaining members were split into at least three distinct persuasions—moderate Reformers, adherents of Isaac Mayer Wise, and a party favoring "ultra Reform." Over the next

Elegant and imperious, Max Landsberg was senior rabbi of Temple B'rith Kodesh from 1871 to 1915. (Courtesy American Jewish Archives)

Dr. Guinzberg on the Liquor Question, **Rochester Union and Advertiser,** *September 5, 1867*

Your urgent request of the 2nd inst., to preach in behalf of the temperance cause I have received. Now permit me to say, that I am always willing to support any good cause, particularly if tending to the furtherance of morality, for I consider this one of my chief duties as a Rabbi.

Still must I beg to be excused for declining to preach about the topic suggested by you, for although we Israelites do not despise to partake occasionally of that which God's kind providence, or even human invention, has prepared for the comfort and benefit of man, still, as a nation, we live very moderately and

decade, while each of the factions maintained congregational harmony, they each advanced their own agendas, and that of the "ultras" prevailed. The subsequent arrival of Max Landsberg in 1871 solidified the triumph of radical Reform. B'rith Kodesh became its bastion for the next half century.

A Moderate Reformer: Rabbi Aaron Guinzberg

B'rith Kodesh made progress toward reform, despite the absence of clerical leadership following the departure of Ferdinand Sarner in 1860. After the adoption of *Minhag America*, and the introduction of an organ and choir, the leading reformers, especially Moses Hays and Sigmund Stettheimer, respectively the president and wealthiest member of the congregation, thought B'rith Kodesh "had everything but a rabbi." The task of Hays and Stettheimer was to find a moderate reformer who would strengthen the Reform direction of the congregation without alienating the conservatives. The religious day school, without a full-time director since the departure of Rabbi Sarner in 1860, was in particularly difficult circumstances. Sigmund Stettheimer, influential in both the school and the synagogue, advanced most of the funds to hire a new rabbi who would also direct the religious school. A Baltimore rabbi, Aaron Guinzberg, was invited to Rochester to deliver trial sermons in German and English, and was hired shortly thereafter in June 1863, for a five-year term, at an annual salary of $1500.

Guinzberg was a native of either Austria or Hungary. Before coming to the United States, he had been active in Austrian Jewish affairs, and was the author of a substantial work of talmudic scholarship. A Rochester correspondent wrote in the *American Israelite* that Guinzberg was not a "*radical* reformer but a man of progress." Guinzberg approved of *Minhag America* and the other B'rith Kodesh ritual innovations of 1862, but had little inclination to push for other reforms, such as family seating, which was becoming increasingly common in American synagogues at the time. Although not a remarkable orator, Guinzberg was generally viewed as a good lecturer, a man of great learning, and an excellent teacher. Within a few months he received the highest accolade any rabbi can receive upon assuming the pulpit of a divided congregation. Since his arrival, one correspondent noted, "peace and concord prevail," and "all parties are well satisfied." Indeed, there seems to have been little internal contention in B'rith Kodesh during Guinzberg's five-year tenure.

As with many American rabbis of the era, Guinzberg saw as one of his main tasks the defense of Judaism against the aspersions of Christian divines and the casual anti-Jewish slurs common in the public discourse of the day. While still in Baltimore, he had defended the Talmud against the charge that it contained numerous incitements to violence against Gentiles. In 1865, when an article in the *Rochester Union and Advertiser* claimed that it was a Jewish precept to hate one's neighbor, Guinzburg replied with a learned essay that traced the accusation from the Gospel of Matthew to Shakepeare's *The Merchant of Venice*. To view Judaism as an exclusive and tribal religion, as opposed to the supposed universality of Christianity, Guinzberg argued, was to make the Jews responsible for all that was narrow and parochial in Christianity, including its anti-Judaism.

Guinzberg worried about an upsurge of anti-Semitism during the Civil War years. He wrote in 1865 that in recent years, "many ignoramuses and fanatics, vile politicians and mean spirited stump speakers have assailed the Jews and their religion in all shapes and forms." Guinzberg was especially concerned about the tendency of many evangelical supporters of the Union cause to see the United States as a holy, Christian nation, though Guinzberg himself was not averse to invoking the Jewish God for the Union side. He denounced efforts by evangelical ministers to pass a constitutional amendment to have the United States officially declared a Christian nation; in addition he strenuously opposed all such attempts to erode America's separation of church and state, which had been such a beacon of hope for Jews in Europe.

Guinzberg's opposition to the creeping Christianization of public discourse led him to be suspicious of such Christian-inspired reform movements as abolitionism and temperance. In 1867, a group of Rochester clergymen requested that Guinzberg join them in preaching to their congregations on the importance of closing the city's liquor stores on Sunday. Though this invitation may have indicated a growing willingness on the part of the local clergy to include B'rith Kodesh in interdenominational appeals, Guinzberg was disinclined to accept it. He disagreed with many of its assumptions, including the primacy of the Christian over the Jewish Sabbath, the evangelical intrusiveness into everyday life, and the presumption that the Jews had a drinking problem. Guinzberg's response was published in the *Union and Advertiser*, where it created something of a stir.

But if Guinzberg continued to defend the Jewish "nation" against its detractors, an increasingly influential segment of Rochester Jewish opinion denied that there was any ethnic or extra-religious dimension to Judaism at all. In 1864, a seemingly innocuous invitation to the Hebrew Ladies' Benevolent Society to participate in a charity bazaar appeared to Sigmund Stettheimer to perpetuate the notion that the Jews were a people separate from other Americans. The "only national character in which they wish to appear," Stettheimer insisted on the ladies' behalf, "would be under the Star Spangled Banner." To take part in a city-wide charity bazaar as Jews would confirm the suspicions of many Gentiles that Jews were different and not fully American.

soberly. Drunkenness and intoxication are something unheard of among our people. I have been here in my congregation for more than four years, and I have yet to hear of the first case where a Jew here has disgraced our community by appearing as a drunkard or tippler, and I refer in this respect to the records of the Police Court. Drunkenness is a vice on any day of the week not less on Sunday, or even our Sabbath day. I cannot see any difference in the time. Should I, therefore exhort my congregation to abstain from a vice of which they are not guilty, I would not only offend their feelings, but do them great injustice— either of which I have no right to do.

— Aaron Guinzberg
Rochester, September 4, 1867

No doubt the frequent use of "Jew" as an adjective associated with disreputable behavior encouraged the insistence of many Rochester Jews that the Jews were a religious group, not a people. In 1866 B'rith Kodesh members objected to a description in the *Rochester Daily Democrat* of a stolen coat found in a "Jew store." The newspaper offered a grudging apology: "If our Hebrew friends insist upon applying the Jewish name to their religion rather than their race, we do not wish to run counter to their wishes, mistaken as we think them to be." The denial of Jewish ethnicity would be central to Judaism at B'rith Kodesh for the rest of the nineteenth century.

The Arrival of Max Landsberg

B'rith Kodesh did not renew Aaron Guinzberg's contract in 1868, and he moved on to Ohabei Shalom in Boston. Without a rabbi, B'rith Kodesh made do with several hazzanim, including founding member Gabriel Wile, and Abraham Schmidt (or Smith) who served as hazzan from 1860 through 1874. The Guinzberg years had been a time of quiet in the congregation; in the minds of some, probably too quiet. Rumblings now came from an influential group of members who felt that B'rith Kodesh had taken up "an abode in the valley of inactivity." New reforms were needed, especially the introduction of family seating and the use of *Minhag America* for the High Holy Days. In 1868, The Board of Trustees approved family seating, pending the vote of the congregation, which apparently turned down the idea. The following year, a congregational faction ran for office on the platform of "Rochester Wants Radical Reform! Slips! School! Religion! Education!" ("Slips" was an alternative term for family pews.) Though the slate's candidate for president, choir director Nimrod Rosenfield, did not win, three of its eight candidates were elected. Despite the radical ticket's equivocal results, the congregation introduced family seating in late 1869.

The decision in favor of family seating prompted a number of members to leave B'rith Kodesh. A Mr. Salomon told the board in early 1870 that the "mode of divine service" had created "a feeling of hostility in him so that he could not remain a member of the Congregation." The largest exodus from B'rith Kodesh was led by Meyer Greentree, one of the wealthiest Jews in Rochester. We do not have any contemporary comments from Greentree on the reasons for his leaving, but his earlier history made him a somewhat unlikely candidate to lead a conservative secession from B'rith Kodesh. Greentree had arrived in Rochester by the early 1840s, and married a non-Jewish woman in a Protestant ceremony shortly thereafter. Though he was the first significant Jewish figure in the city's garment industry, he was conspicuously absent from the names of the founders of B'rith Kodesh, and the intervening decades do not indicate much involvement in the

A silver Kiddush cup, inscribed "Presented to N. Rosenfield by the Congregation Berith Kodesh 1870." (Photo by Jennifer Alrutz)

congregation. Whatever prompted his departure, he helped to organize a new congregation, Elon Yerek, in April 1870, and served as its first president. Later known as Aitz Ra-Non, the new congregation had its sanctuary on St. Joseph Street. (St. Joseph Street, soon to be elevated to the status of an avenue, and, at Jewish insistence, decanonized, became the primary thoroughfare in Rochester's main Russian-Jewish neighborhood.)

Aitz Rah-Non had a short and curious history. At first it followed a traditional liturgy, and did away with the organ during the service. But by 1873 it had adopted a pattern of worship closely resembling that of B'rith Kodesh. And though the question of seating had been the main cause of the break with B'rith Kodesh, Aitz Rah-Non had family pews from the beginning. Was the "Greentree schule," as it was popularly known, an early attempt to establish a form of Conservative Judaism? Perhaps, but it is hard not to conclude that Meyer Greentree's vanity had as much to do with the founding of the new congregation as did ideological differences with B'rith Kodesh over the pace of reform. Both Elon Yerek and Aitz Ra-Non are Hebrew versions of "green tree." Moreover, the founding officers included a man who was both Greentree's business partner and brother-in-law, as well as the son of another business partner. Certainly within a few years of its founding, the congregation had largely lost whatever "Conservative" direction it once had.

Aitz Ra-Non was soon divided between conservatives and moderates. Rabbi Victor Rundbacken served the congregation for eight years, to be replaced in 1878 by Rabbi Max Moll. Moll was born in the Poznan region of eastern Prussia, but was thoroughly Germanified, and later published a manual on German language instruction. Moll was at Aitz Ra-Non from 1878 through the congregation's dissolution in 1886, when most of its members rejoined B'rith Kodesh. They left behind a small Orthodox remnant, the nucleus of the Orthodox congregation Berith Oulum. Moll became an assistant rabbi at B'rith Kodesh, remaining with the congregation for twenty years. Always in the shadow of Max Landsberg, Moll was primarily responsible for the temple's Sunday School, and for delivering an occasional sermon in German.

The exit of the Greentree faction did little to slacken the pace of reform at B'rith Kodesh. In April 1870, Isaac and Solomon Wile, two teenaged members of the congregation, invited the pastor of the Unitarian Church of Rochester, the Rev. Newton Mann, to speak at B'rith Kodesh. Among the earliest instances of a Christian minister speaking in an American Jewish pulpit, the event was quite successful, and the sanctuary was filled to capacity. The two congregations thus initiated a close and long-standing relationship.

In the fall of 1869, the decision was made to hire a new rabbi, one who could preach in both German and English, and who would be, as the advertisement in the *American Israelite* stated, a "gentleman of advanced

The Wiles were among the most prominent Jewish families in 19th century Rochester. The brothers Joseph and Gabriel Wile were founding members of B'rith Kodesh. Sol Wile, not pictured here, helped found the Clothier's Exchange of Rochester, the garment manufacturers' trade association. Isaac Wile was the first historian of the city's Jews. From left, brothers Gabriel, Joseph, Abram, and Isaac Wile, and an unidentified sister.

ideas and reformed religious views." After none of the applicants seemed suitable, the congregation turned to Europe to find a rabbi. Joseph Wile, the president of B'rith Kodesh, contacted Abraham Geiger, the leader of radical Reform in Europe, asking for suggestions for a suitable candidate. Geiger encouraged one of his protégés, Max Landsberg, to apply. As Landsberg later recalled, he hesitated to try for the position, probably because he felt that America was an intellectual backwater. Geiger tried to sway him by speaking warmly of the future prospects of American Judaism, telling him that if he, Geiger, were twenty years younger he too would go to America. After several months of reflection, Landsberg took his mentor's advice and in December 1870 applied for the job in Rochester. B'rith Kodesh invited Landsberg to come, and he arrived in time for Pesach in 1871. He would remain the temple's senior rabbi until 1915.

Landsberg's radical Reform principles found a receptive audience in Rochester. A series of written queries prepared by the congregation in April 1871 provide a good sense of where they stood on liturgical matters on the eve of Landsberg's arrival. Some of the requests fall within the boundaries of moderate Reform Judaism of the 1870s. The congregation asked Landsberg to offer a weekly prayer service late on Friday night, a new but increasingly popular custom in American synagogues. Following a common Reform practice, they asked for the Torah to be read on a three-year cycle, thereby cutting down on the length of the weekly portion. The congregation thought a weekly commentary on the Torah portion would be an "important improvement" in its spiritual life, as would a benediction by the rabbi at the conclusion of the service. Other requests speak specifically to more radical innovations. One query asked whether the abolition of the wearing of tallises and yarmulkes would be in accordance with "Mosaic Law." Another asked if it would be permissible to forego the observance of the second days of holidays, including Rosh Hashanah and Passover.

During the first decade of Landsberg's tenure in Rochester, the pace of radical Reform proceeded slowly, no doubt because of the opposition of the more traditionally minded members. In 1874, members were permitted to attend services with uncovered heads. However, neither Landsberg, nor the president or vice president of the congregation (who at the time sat on the *bimah* with the rabbi), left their heads uncovered at this

Moses Hays, a leading advocate for reform and president of B'rith Kodesh, was born in Germany in 1825, and lived in Rochester until his death in 1892. His son, David Hays, was a leading lawyer.

time. In 1878 the congregation asked Landsberg to deliver a sermon on their concern about head coverings. The next year David Rosenberg was elected president in part because of his pledge to sit hatless during services. He was true to his word, causing much consternation among the more traditional members. The radicals soon pressed their advantage. By 1883, uncovered heads would become mandatory for all new members and guests, and there would be no hats worn at B'rith Kodesh worship until well after World War II.

Principles of a Radical Reformer

Max Landsberg, like his two immediate successors, Horace Wolf and Philip Bernstein, was named senior rabbi of B'rith Kodesh while still in his late twenties. Landsberg was born in Hildesheim in the German state of Hanover in 1845, where his father, Meyer Landsberg, was a prominent rabbi, with an inclination to Reform. The younger Landsberg was educated at the universities of Göttingen, Breslau, Berlin, and Halle, which awarded him a doctorate in 1866, and shortly thereafter he obtained his rabbinic ordination from the Jewish Theological Seminary in Breslau. (He would become one of a handful of American rabbis with a doctorate.) After graduation he taught for several years at the Jewish Theological Seminary in Hanover. His early publications include a study of Judaism in the twelfth and thirteenth centuries.

Throughout his career Landsberg unflinchingly defended the principles of radical Reform. In an article written in 1910 for the centenary of Abraham Geiger's birth, he argued that his mentor's great contribution to Judaism was the introduction of historical criticism to the study of scripture and Talmud. Geiger, said Landsberg, taught that "Judaism was not brought into existence by the Bible, but that the Bible was produced by Judaism." The religious civilization of Judaism reached its finest flower during the biblical period, with the ethical monotheism of the prophets. The talmudic elaboration of a strict code of rituals, laws, and ceremonies was a diversion from the true purpose of Judaism:

> Ceremonies are means of sanctification. They are not religion, but are intended to make men religious; they have no value in themselves, but are only a means by which this end is to be accomplished. They are needed to remind us of our duties and to save us from being seduced by the evil inclinations of our heart. If they have this effect, they are good; if not, they are harmful.

Landsberg hoped for a revival of true biblical Judaism everywhere but in the land of Israel. The Jewish connection to Israel ended with the destruction of the Second Temple, and it was the Jewish mission to spread the truth of its ideas to all the world. As he wrote in 1891, "The Hebrew nationality is dead, has been dead for eighteen centuries, never to be revived." For Landsberg, this was not an occasion for lamentation. The truths of Judaism needed to be spread among the nations, and not bottled up in an insignificant corner of Asia.

It appeared that nothing now stood in the way of the entrance and complete acceptance of Jews into polite society, save their own reluctance to discard some of their peculiar customs. Landsberg did recognize that occasional intolerance among Christians also constituted an obstacle. When *The Nation* in 1877 condoned the exclusion of Jews from fashionable Saratoga resorts on the grounds that wealthy Jews tended to dress in flashy clothes and were impolite in their manners, Landsberg fired off an angry letter to the editor, defending the intellectual attainments and social accomplishments of Jews throughout the ages.

For Landsberg, however, the main responsibility for adjusting to American society fell to the Jews. They had to be ever vigilant, he argued, against the temptation to unearned ethnic pride. Landsberg attacked an annual Jewish periodical for publishing a list of American Jewish officeholders. He wondered what the Jewish reaction would be if a non-Jewish journal published a list of Jewish felons. Jewish clannishness will not die out, Landsberg argued, "until the Jews themselves cease to show symptoms of it, until by their practice they prove how they appreciate living in a country where civil rights have nothing to do with religious affairs, and recognize, with regard to political affairs, they are only Americans."

Landsberg loathed Zionism. From the time of its emergence in the late nineteenth century he saw it as a threat to his most cherished beliefs. Its popularity among assimilated Jews alienated from Jewish Orthodoxy he viewed as a serious challenge to Reform Judaism. Even among the anti-nationalists and anti-Zionists who dominated Reform Judaism in the late nineteenth century, Landsberg stands out for the fierceness of his opposition to Zionism. "Quixotic" was perhaps the mildest term he applied to it; "insanity" was more common. He regularly spoke to Rochester's Fortnightly Club, an elite debating society, on the dangers of Zionism. There in the waning months of World War I he delivered one of his last public statements. It can serve as his final word on a subject that consumed the second half of his career.

Max Landsberg "Zionism Again," *Fortnightly Club, Rochester, New York, 1918*

If after this terrible war is over there be anywhere Jews who may deem their stay in the land where they live impossible because their rights as citizens are denied them, or because they are too sensitive to endure the pinpricks of vulgar or fashionable Antisemitism, and others for other reasons consider immigration into Canaan as the desirable step to take, let them by all means act upon their impulse or intention. But the nation which they there may found is not my nation. I shall stay in this country of God, the United States, and propose to do my part as a loyal American and a convinced devotee to my religion. If others prefer to live in Jerusalem, that is their business. But over there, as citizens of the Palestinian state they are not my compatriots, and from present indications I have reason to fear that they will not be my co-religionists.

One of the many reasons Landsberg detested Zionism was the secularism of such early Zionist leaders as Theodore Herzl and Max

Nordau. Despite Landsberg's radical assimilationism, he remained deeply committed to religious Judaism. Though he was close to local Unitarians, he had no interest in exploring possible mergers of the two religions. In this he differed from some of his colleagues in radical Reform. Unlike Felix Adler, who left the Reform movement to found Ethical Culture, Landsberg never felt that realizing the universal truths of Judaism required the abandonment of the Jewish religion. Indeed, Landsberg was convinced that as the universal principles of liberal religion became more widespread, increasing numbers would turn to Judaism as the liberal "mother religion." Jews should be proud of their heritage, Landsberg believed, and always remember that their religion was "the immortal root from which has grown all that is of good and noble and lasting value in the life of civilized man." It was the evolving and progressive nature of Judaism that made it superior to Christianity. Liberal Christians and Unitarians could adopt liberal principles only by breaking decisively with their Christian heritage and abandoning the core dogmas of their religion. Jews had no such problem since Judaism had no core of dogmatic principles. Judaism had evolved organically from its origins, taken a detour through medieval backwardness, and recently arrived at its present flourishing state.

Ironically, despite their notions of the inevitability of progress unfolding over time, many advocates of radical Reform were deeply pessimistic about the immediate prospects of Reform Judaism in America. Landsberg saw the late nineteenth century as an irreligious and skeptical era, one in which there had been a radical decline among Jews in their interest in Judaism. Many of the most controversial reforms he introduced, such as dropping Bar Mitzvah and near elimination of Hebrew from the service, were intended to keep wavering Jews within the fold. Judaism had to adopt to the new circumstances of American Jews, who simply had less time and less interest in Judaism than before. Reform had to adjust to the new lessened importance of Judaism in the lives of its adherents. The alternatives of a return to Orthodoxy, or the extinction of Judaism, were equally unthinkable.

Landsberg expounded his views on Judaism in a manner typical of most Reform rabbis of his era. Not a person of great personal warmth, he apparently lacked a sense of humor. His sermons were serious and didactic. His personal manner was proper and dignified. With his pointed goatee and elegant dress he represented, well into the twentieth century, the ideal of a nineteenth-century gentleman. Sophy Bernstein, the wife of Philip Bernstein, remembers Landsberg as a "very, very precise gentleman of the old school." He gallantly kissed the hand of the wife of the young assistant rabbi at their only meeting, about a year before Landsberg died in 1928.

But despite his good manners, Landsberg possessed a streak of arrogance that was never far from the surface. He never disguised his contempt for those who disagreed with him. He had learned from Abraham Geiger not to temporize or compromise his Reform principles for the sake of surface harmony. He learned his lesson well. Speaking of one rare attempt to find the middle ground during a controversy in the temple in the 1880s, Landsberg drew an appropriate radical Reform conclusion. "Like most compromises, this one failed to give satisfaction to either party." In a tribute to another early reformer, Leopold Zunz, Landsberg made a similar point: "No reform is of any value in any department unless it be radical. Radical means going to the root—not satisfied with superficial improvements, with smoothing over the surface... [but to] intelligently and conscientiously discard what is dead and to cling to that which is of lasting value." In his own way, Landsberg was as consistent, rigorous, and unsentimental in defending his own conception of Judaism as any Orthodox rabbi. Elements of Judaism that did not contribute to the growth of the religion, whatever emotional attachment anyone might have to them, had to be discarded. Landsberg's version of radical Reform dominated B'rith Kodesh for almost half a century.

Religious Education

One of the most important aspects of the religious life of B'rith Kodesh was its religious school. With the closing of the day school in 1867, efforts began to establish a Sunday school for the congregation. The Radical slate in the 1869 congregational elections made the opening of a Sunday school a top priority, and one opened that fall. It was an immediate success, and maintained high enrollments for the rest of the century. In 1890, for example, the school had 224 children, a quite respectable total for a congregation with about 150 families. From the outset, the religious school was one area of the temple's life that encouraged the participation of women. In 1888, of the eight teachers in the religious school, six were female.

At the turn of the century, the B'rith Kodesh Sunday school was divided into eight grades. Students were expected to begin at about age seven or eight, and continue in the school until Confirmation. Typically, more girls than boys were enrolled in the religious school, as in 1902, when there were 83 girls and only 59 boys. Sunday school classes began at 9:30. After meeting individually with their classmates, the Sunday school came together for hymn singing and a lecture by the superintendent of the religious school on a religious or ethical topic. The focus of early

B'rith Kodesh Sunday School students at the turn of the twentieth century. Education has always been a top priority at the temple. (Courtesy Department of Rare Books and Special Collections, Rush Rhees Library, University of Rochester)

childhood education in the religious school was on the Bible, and the history of the Jewish people through the Bar Kochba rebellion. Exilic history was reserved for the post-Confirmation classes. Landsberg strove for an approach that stressed the "science of comparative religion," while being sure to impart to the students "a clear idea of the advantages and superiority of Judaism above other faiths."

The B'rith Kodesh religious school, and Jewish education in general, was a topic close to Landsberg's heart. In 1885 Landsberg discussed at length his ideas on religious education. Formal instruction should begin early in childhood, he argued, for it was from ages seven to nine that "the best and most lasting impression can be made upon the hearts of the little ones." He was absolutely opposed to corporal punishment as a means of discipline in the religious school. (This was in contrast to the policy in the B'rith Kodesh day school, in which alumni remembered—somewhat fondly—the instructors exercising the rod and "warming the jackets" of wayward students.)

Landsberg favored making Hebrew instruction optional in the

religious school. Ironically, Landsberg himself was a superb Hebrew scholar, and late in his life he was given the signal honor of translating the book of Genesis in the first English-language Bible published by the Jewish Publication Society. He argued, however, that it was wrong to force "unwilling children to take part unwillingly in an instruction about which they care nothing," which could only result "in parents choosing not to send their children to religious school."

Though noncompulsory, Hebrew-language instruction remained fairly vigorous at B'rith Kodesh. Hebrew remained in the curriculum, and at graduation ceremonies of the religious school, prizes were awarded in Hebrew proficiency. In 1902 out of a total enrollment of 141, there were 27 students in Hebrew classes. Rabbi Max Moll, the superintendent of the religious school, taught three levels of Hebrew classes, which met four times a week. Some went for further instruction, as in 1906, when Clara Weil and Lillie Schifrin studied Leviticus and Deuteronomy in Hebrew with Moll. Landsberg also offered private Hebrew classes to interested students.

A distinguished educator who wrote extensively on pedagogic issues, Prussian-born Max Moll came to America in 1866. Before coming to Rochester in 1878, he was rabbi in New York City, and Paterson, New Jersey. During his two decades at the temple, he strengthened its Sunday School.

But since Hebrew was largely excluded from the B'rith Kodesh service, some argued for the elimination of all teaching of Hebrew. In a 1906 letter to the School Board, Landsberg strongly protested against such efforts. Though, as he noted, only about a sixth of the students in the religious school were enrolled in Hebrew classes, it was too important to be entirely eliminated from religious instruction at B'rith Kodesh:

> While there remains some Hebrew in our Ritual, it seems imperative that opportunity should be given to learn enough of the language to understand it. Besides, those who wish to learn more and to prepare themselves for the study of Jewish theology ought not to be deprived of the elementary instruction which is the foundation that should be laid in childhood.

"The training of the heart" and ethical teaching were integral to Landsberg's conception of Judaism. The public examinations at the end of the 1891-92 school year give a sense of the curriculum. The theme that

Confirmation Speech of Lilli Savage,
May 22, 1876

Heavenly Father, not from zeal or anxiety do I place myself before thy throne to offer up a prayer to thee. O heavenly father, but the dictation of my heart bids me thank thee for all the kindness and grace thou hast bestowed on me and provided me with all I stand in need of, and I feel it more than ever on this day. Hear my supplications and accept my fervent prayer, thou hast given me such kind parents who have always loved me, who have done all in their power to instruct me with the knowledge of the true and good. Oh spare them unto me, these guardian angels of mine [sic] existence, to whom I am so much indebted

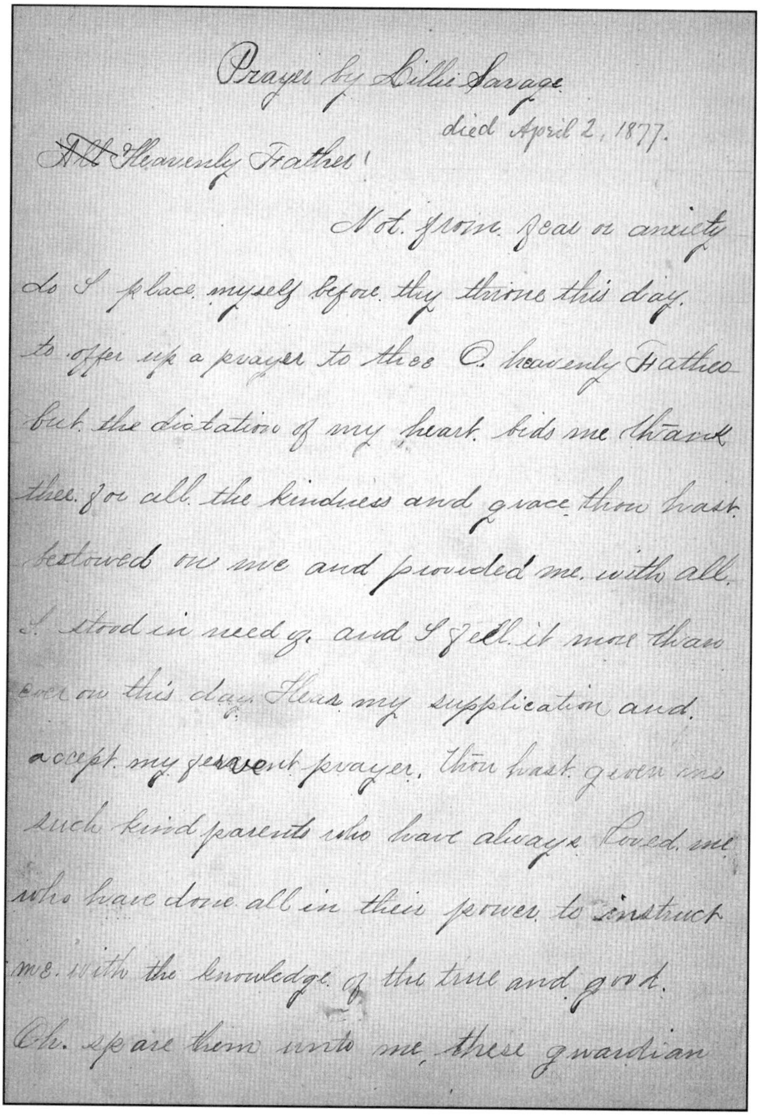

Prayer by Lilli Savage
died April 2, 1877.
~~All~~ Heavenly Father!
Not from zeal or anxiety
do I place myself before thy throne this day
to offer up a prayer to thee O heavenly Father
but the dictation of my heart bids me thank
thee for all the kindness and grace thou hast
bestowed on me and provided me with all
I stood in need of. and I feel it more than
ever on this day. Hear my supplication and
accept my fervent prayer, thou hast given me
such kind parents who have always loved me
who have done all in their power to instruct
me with the knowledge of the true and good.
Oh. spare them unto me, these guardian

year had been ethical living at home. Landsberg questioned the pupils on the proper behavior to adopt toward parents, siblings, grandparents, servants, and pets. At the conclusion of the assembly, one of the students sang, appropriately enough, "Home, Sweet Home."

The cornerstone of religious education at B'rith Kodesh was the ritual of Confirmation. In 1882, at Landsberg's urging, the temple dropped Bar Mitzvah for thirteen-year-old boys. This merely made official the congregation's emphasis on Confirmation as its primary coming of age ritual. Whatever the wisdom of terminating the practice of Bar Mitzvah, Confirmation was a ceremony that was open to girls as well as boys, and from the earliest years there was a gender balance among confirmands.

angles of mine existence to whom I am so much
indebted for. How earnestly do they work for the
welfare of their children. every moment of their lives
is devoted to them and all their thoughts are
directed to the aim of giving us every advantage
of an good education. And how with anxious hearts
have they awaited the advent of this day.
Bestow thy heavenly blessing on them grant that
they may realize the hopes and joyful expectation
which fills their loving hearts in this moment.
Assist me with thy help and led by their kind
hands I may grow up to show my gratitude more
dearly and be an honor and a comfort to
them, Bless my dear brother and sisters

for....Grant mercy, peace, and happiness to my beloved classmates who trembling stand before thee awaiting thy heavenly blessing. Oh! Do thou direct my heart unto all that is good. Oh! May these thoughts continually be in my mind. That I may never allow myself to be influenced or led astray that I may never deny assistance to anyone in need thereof. Grant O merciful one that the experience of this day may never be forgotten that the spirit of righteousness which inspires me this day may never depart for me:

***Guide O guide
this hopeful land.***

***Father in thy
truth and light.***

***May we children
ever stand.***

***Firm in virtue
and in right.***

Perhaps to make Confirmation a truer replacement for the more traditional ceremony, Landsberg reduced the age of Confirmation from sixteen or even older to fourteen. Confirmation services were held on the morning of Shavuos. Each of the confirmands offered an English-language prayer of his or her own devising, and the parents of each of the children held an afternoon reception in their home. In the evening the confirmands gathered with friends and family at the religious school. After presenting Landsberg with a gift, they held a lawn party, with refreshments and dancing.

Surviving Confirmation addresses from the Landsberg years have the clichés appropriate to such occasions. But beneath the formulaic

Organ Prelude, - - - - - - PROF. HENRY GREINER

"Hallel:" PSALM CXVI.

Choir: "BORUCH HABBO:"

> Blessed be he that cometh in the name of the Lord ;
> We bless you from the house of the Lord.
>
> [During this song the class is conducted into the Temple.]

Prayer : - - - - - - - DR. MAX LANDSBERG

Choir : AMEN.

Prayers :

ABR. BLACK.	HATTIE LEVI.
ALBERT GOLDSTEIN.	ISIDOR HECHINGER.
JOHANNA LESERITZ.	STELLA KOCHENTHAL.
SAMUEL MEYER.	BELLA GOLDWATER.
MILTON ADLER.	

Morning Service :

Reading from the Thora : The Ten Proclamations.

HATTIE LEVI. SAM MEYER. MAX MEIER. MARTIN MOLL.

Opening Remarks : - - - - - - DR. MAX LANDSBERG

Hymn 116, Tune 13.

> Hear, O my people ; to My law
> Devout attention lend;
> Let the instruction of My mouth
> Deep in your hearts descend.
>
> We will not hide it from our sons,
> Our offspring shall be taught
> The praises of the Lord, whose strength
> Has works of wonder wrought.
>
> For Jacob He His law ordain'd,
> His league with Israel made ;
> With charge to be from age to age,
> From race to race convey'd:
>
> That generations yet to come
> Should to their unborn heirs
> Religiously transmit the same.
> And they again to theirs.
>
> To teach them that in God alone
> Their hope securely stands :
> That they should ne'er His works forget,
> But keep His just commands.

Opening Prayer : - - - - - - FLORENCE MILLER

Prayers :

STELLA ROSENBAUM.	ELMER SCHWARZ.
NETTIE GOLDSMITH.	BLANCHE HAYS.

Choir : "Father, we pray to Thee," by Himmel.

Original Essays :

Religion, What it is, - - - - -	FLORENCE SHATZ
Jewish Religion, What it is, - - - -	JULIA SELIGMAN
Revelation, - - - - - -	MAX MEIER
The Bible, - - - - - -	BERTHA DAVIS
The Talmud, - - - - - -	FRED OETTINGER
Man, the Image of God, - - - -	NETTE ROSENBERG
The Messiah, - - - - - -	CARRIE ROSENBERG

The program for the 1894 Confirmation class is the oldest surviving program for a B'rith Kodesh service.

Alto Solo : - - - - Mrs. Sara Hays Taylor

Original Essays :

Prayer, - - - - - Hortense Levi
The Sabbath, - - - - Aimee Mock
The Historical Festivals, - - - Matilda Meyer
The Purely Religious Festivals, - - - Stella Geismar
Confirmation, - - - Milton Guggenheimer
Duties to Ourselves, - - - Frances Louise Weinberg
Dignity and Humility, - - - Jesse Kochenthal
Duties to Our Fellowmen, - - - Martin Moll
Duties to Parents, - - - Grace Lillian Landsberg
Charity, - - - - Etta Goldsmith

Prayer : - - - - Miriam Seligman

Address to Parents, - - - Blanche Goodman
Address to Congregation, - - - Mortimer Adler
Statement of Principles, - - - Rose Kraker

Choir : "Hark, Hark, my soul."

Address to Children : - - - Dr. Max Landsberg

Confession of Faith.

Organ Voluntary : - - - - Prof. Henry Greiner

Hymn 72 : Chanted.

Father, see Thy suppliant children
  Trembling stand before Thy throne,
To confirm the vow of Horeb :
  "We will serve the Lord alone."

Thy command shall be engraven
  On the tables of our heart,
Till the heart in death be broken
  And the cord of life shall part.

When dark tempests lowering gather
  It will be our strength and stay,
It will be our guardian angel
  Upon life's laborious way.

As a sheltering cloud at noon-tide,
  As a flaming fire by night.
Through prosperity and sorrow
  It will guide our steps aright.

Till we reach the land of promise,
  When the toils of earth are past,
Till we sleep the sleep eternal
  In the realms of peace at last.

Closing Prayer.

Choir : Amen.

[The class leaves the Temple.]

Memorial Prayer.

Hymn 240, Tune 26.

God is our Refuge, tried and proved,
  Amid a stormy world ;
We will not fear, though earth be moved,
  And hills in ocean hurled.

The waves may roar, the mountains shake,
  Our comforts shall not cease ;
His children will He ne'er forsake,
  The Lord will give us peace.

Benediction.

It is requested that nobody will leave the Temple before the close of the services.

Confirmation Class.

❖ ❖ ❖ ❖

BLANCHE BLOCH,	HATTIE LEVI,
BERTHA DAVIS,	AUGUSTA LICHTMAN,
STELLA GEISMAR,	MATILDA MEYER,
ETTA GOLDSMITH,	FLORENCE MILLER,
NETTIE GOLDSMITH,	AIMEE MOCK,
BELLA GOLDWATER,	STELLA ROSENBAUM,
BLANCHE GOODMAN,	CARRIE S. ROSENBERG,
BLANCHE HAYS,	NETTE ROSENBERG,
STELLA KOCHENTHAL,	ALICE ROTHSCHILD,
ROSE KRAKER,	JULIA SELIGMAN,
GRACE LILLIAN LANDSBERG,	MIRIAM SELIGMAN,
JOHANNA LESERITZ,	FLORENCE SHATZ,
HORTENSE LEVI,	FRANCES LOUISE WEINBERG.

❖ ❖ ❖ ❖

MILTON ADLER,	JESSE KOCHENTHAL,
MORTIMER ADLER,	MAX MEIER,
ABRAM BLACK,	SAM MEYER,
ALBERT GOLDSTEIN,	MARTIN MOLL,
MILTON GUGGENHEIMER,	FRED OETTINGER,
ISIDOR HECHINGER,	ELMER SCHWARZ.

Post Express Print.

54

invocation of blessings on parents, congregation, and country, one finds hints of individual priorities and personalities, as well as some evidence of genuine religious feeling. Typical was the prayer of David Kays, confirmed in 1872, who said, "As I now enter into a state of manliness I pray thee to lead me in the path of virtue and goodness, and let me not either stray from it or fall back." Mollie Stein, a member of the 1876 Confirmation class, prayed for "my dear old grandma whom thou hast blest with such a good old age." Perhaps the most moving of the surviving speeches was that of Lilli Savage, also a member of the 1876 Confirmation class, whose speech conveys an awe-filled sense of the occasion. It is also the saddest. The book which records the speech also notes that young Lilli passed away within a year of her Confirmation.

The New Prayerbook

Landsberg's arrival in 1871 shifted the balance in the congregation toward more comprehensive liturgical change. Like many radical reformers, Landsberg found Isaac Mayer Wise's *Minhag America* to be an overly cautious half-step, conceding far too much to the traditionalists. The model for a more radical ritual already existed. In 1858, an influential Baltimore rabbi, David Einhorn, published *Olat Tamid*, a far more dramatic altering of the traditional service than *Minhag America*. Opening from the left, *Olat Tamid* had about half of the service in the vernacular (German, not English): though it kept the basic form of the traditional service, it shortened many standard prayers.

One of Landsberg's first tasks as rabbi of B'rith Kodesh was to travel to New York City, observe Reform services, and make recommendations on what changes to make in B'rith Kodesh ritual practices. Einhorn, by then rabbi of Temple Beth-El in New York, and Landsberg soon became close associates in the cause of radical reform. After an English translation of *Olat Tamid* appeared, Landsberg recommended its introduction at B'rith Kodesh, and the board approved its adoption on April 27, 1873. This action proved to be extremely controversial. Ten days later, twenty members of the congregation petitioned for a reconsideration of the move, claiming that the adoption of Einhorn's ritual had been contrary to the temple's constitution.

Because of the protests it provoked, Landsberg and the leaders of the congregation backed away from *Olat Tamid*, and started to use a somewhat older and somewhat more traditional Reform liturgy, one published by Temple Emanuel in New York City. But the English of both *Olat Tamid* and the Temple Emanu-El liturgy was stilted and artificial. As a result, Landsberg claimed, while the services were shortened, "they were made neither more intelligible nor more attractive to the young than they had been before."

The need remained for a radical Reform liturgy in idiomatic English. The late nineteenth century was a time of unparalleled experimentation with the Jewish liturgy. Many congregations developed and published their own prayer books, following European custom, where each rabbi developed his own prayer book. Some prominent Jewish leaders thought this was too much of a good thing. Isaac Mayer Wise, the author of the now supplanted *Minhag America*, complained in 1891 that there were so many prayerbooks that "people can scarcely tell what Judaism is." Nevertheless individual congregations, such as B'rith Kodesh, could exert a major role in shaping the Reform liturgy.

Whatever the inadequacies of the Temple Emanu-El ritual, B'rith Kodesh used it for almost a decade, almost as long as it had used *Minhag America*. Almost from its adoption, Landsberg tinkered with it extensively, rearranging it and adding new English versions of different parts of the service. Among the first fruits of Landsberg's liturgical revision was the congregational hymnal, prepared by Landsberg and Sol Wile, and first published in 1880. The *Hymn Book for Jewish Worship* contained about 300 hymns, primarily psalm settings and contemporary religious verse. About two-thirds were in English, with the remainder in German. The choice of melodies reflected the influence of the Lutheran chorale tradition. In the back of the volume was a small set of standard Hebrew prayers, along with a German text "Tag des Herrn" [Day of the Lord] set to the traditional Kol Nidre melody. In his introduction to the hymnal, Landsberg complained that the tendency of

---

MORNING SERVICE.   19

M. Praised be the Lord, who is praised through eternity.

[The Congregation resume their seats.]

BE praised, O Lord our God, Ruler of the Universe, Creator of light and darkness! Wisdom and might are thine. Thou changest the times and seasons. Thou pourest the light of thy sun over the earth and shinest in every star. Thou givest wisdom unto the wise and knowledge to them that have understanding. Thou revealest the deep and secret things. Thou knowest what is in the darkness; and the light dwelleth with thee.

With great love hast thou loved us. We thank thee that thou didst teach our fathers the laws of life. O enlighten our eyes also, make our hearts cling to thy precepts, and grant that we may never forget the holy mission for which our fathers were set apart, to acknowledge thee and thy unity before all the nations on earth.

Happy are we; how beautiful is our portion, how pleasant our lot, how blissful our inheritance! Happy are we who proclaim:

Hear, O Israel, the Lord our God, the Lord is One!

שְׁמַע יִשְׂרָאֵל יְיָ אֱלֹהֵינוּ יְיָ אֶחָד׃

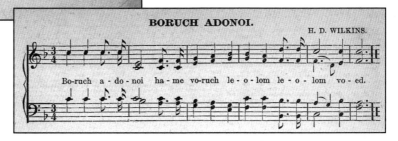

modern Jewish rituals to delegate all responsibility for prayer to the officiants and the choir tended to breed monotony in the service and boredom among congregants. He hoped that increased vernacular congregational singing would remedy this problem.

But it was the B'rith Kodesh prayer book, *Ritual for Jewish Worship*, introduced in 1884, that really placed the temple on the map as a center of radical Reform. According to Landsberg's overly modest account, he reluctantly agreed after years of urging by his congregants to prepare a new ritual that would "conform to the sentiments of the living generation." Since the majority of the new generation did not know Hebrew, drastic measures were needed to keep them from abandoning the faith. To a critic who missed in the new ritual the "soul stirring poetry and warmth of the old typical prayers," Landsberg acknowledged that learned Hebraists might find the ritual wanting, but "to those who neither understand nor

The B'rith Kodesh Ritual for Jewish Worship *of 1884 eliminated the bulk of the traditional service in favor of a largely English liturgy, but did retain some of the core Hebrew prayers. The main service included the Sh'ma, an abbreviated version of V'ahavta, and Michamocha. The 1880 hymn book included four-part choral settings. Congregational singing of English and German hymns was common throughout this period, constituting the main form of participation by the congregation in temple services.*

take the least interest in the Hebrew prayers, some form of this kind is a great improvement." Landsberg acknowledged the assistance of his long-time friend, Unitarian Minister Newton M. Mann, in rendering the prayers of the liturgy into fully idiomatic English.

From Landsberg's perspective, the new ritual had retained the essence of the traditional service, though in an admittedly much abridged and altered fashion. The Friday evening service was twelve pages long, the morning service only twenty-two pages. The service was almost entirely in English. A trial version of the ritual, distributed at the end of 1883, contained no Hebrew characters at all, though it did offer transliterations for a few of the major prayers. Landsberg saw the ritual as a careful balancing of the old and new:

> It is in the very nature of a Jewish ritual that it should contain as much old and familiar material as possible. Therefore it has not been attempted to change the frame-work of the ancient liturgy, and besides a liberal advantage has been taken of all the Rituals that were available to me. The object was not to create something new—which would be a decided mistake—but to furnish a liturgy which, by suggesting everywhere reminiscences of what is familiarly known, would prove most satisfactory to the congregation.

Though some rabbis applauded the new prayer book, most critics—such as those in the *American Israelite, Hebrew Standard*, and *Jewish Messenger*—reacted negatively, attacking it for its radical abbreviation and expurgation of the traditional service. The *American Israelite* quipped that B'rith Kodesh was changing "its ritual for the fourth time within one man's memory. That is progressive reform undoubtedly." A review of the new liturgy in *American Israelite*, probably by Isaac Mayer Wise, criticized the liturgy for its "Karaitism," by which he meant its reliance on the psalms and biblical excerpts rather than traditional prayers. The review also charged that the doctrinal passages of the volume were not specifically or sufficiently Jewish, particularly in that they lacked almost any trace of collective national aspiration, so the ritual could be too easily mistaken for a Unitarian or Universalist worship service.

Similar charges were heard at B'rith Kodesh. Though the Board of Trustees had approved the new prayerbook, the membership was deeply divided. The ritual was first used on December 13, 1883. A meeting held on December 16 to approve the prayerbook proved stormy. The congregation's hazzan, Sigmund Mannheimer, led the opposition. (Mannheimer would resign from B'rith Kodesh a month later, taking a position at the Hebrew Union College.) The congregation came close to rebuffing Landsberg and the Board of Trustees, narrowly ratifying the prayerbook by a vote of 22 to 19. Given this underwhelming vote of confidence, Landsberg and his allies made several concessions to the opponents of the ritual, agreeing to postpone the final decision for an additional month, and to use Hebrew characters rather than transliterations for the main prayers. The final version of the ritual, published the next year, did contain Hebrew versions of the Sh'ma, Bar'chu, Michamocha, the Torah blessings, the Kaddish, and from the High Holy Day liturgy, Avinu Malkeinu.

With Mannheimer gone, Max L. Gutman became the leader of the opposition to the prayerbook. Little is known about Gutman, but he was sympathetic to the aims of the emerging "historical," or Conservative, movement, and in his comments tried to strike a more moderate balance between tradition and modernity than did Landsberg. His writings speak to the high level of Jewish education, and the wide diversity of opinion, among the B'rith Kodesh laity in the 1880s. In the summer of 1884, Gutman complained, no doubt with B'rith Kodesh in mind, that "as *Jews prosper*, they are apt to be misled into *extreme notions of reform*, partly on account of inattention to, or of their indifferent ideas about religion." Elsewhere he complained about modern prayerbooks that contain neither "Torah nor Law." Quoting Philadelphia rabbi Joseph Krauskopf, Gutman expressed his views on the appropriate role of the synagogue:

> The temple is not a university class-room. It is neither a laboratory nor an observatory, nor a dissecting room. It has not been dedicated to the promotion of philosophy, or archeology, or philology, or mythology. The people gather there, according to our very text, not for *"secular knowledge,"* but for *the Law of God*; for the former, they have their various schools, for the latter they have their synagogue only, and where the synagogue attempts to accomplish both within its precincts it does the work of neither.

Both Landsberg and Gutman tried to rally their forces for the crucial meeting on January 20, 1884. Though this second meeting was better attended, the result was much the same as in December 1883: a bitterly divided congregation. Gutman argued that a decision of this magnitude demanded a two-thirds majority vote, no doubt hoping for a repeat of the percentages of the vote a month before. After discussion, Gutman's parliamentary maneuver was rejected 28 to 26, thus by the slenderest of margins assuring the eventual adoption of the new ritual.

But the debate over the ritual had just begun. The congregation split

Rabbi Landsberg was held in high esteem by the members of B'rith Kodesh, as seen in this 1882 testimonial from the Board of Trustees. (Courtesy Department of Rare Books and Special Collections, Rush Rhees Library, University of Rochester)

mostly along generational lines, with the older generation of B'rith Kodesh opposed to the English-language service. Ignatz Thallheimer complained that the ritual took away everything of value from the traditional service. Gabriel Wile, one of the founders of the congregation, said that he had agreed to much for the sake of maintaining congregational harmony, but would draw the line here, and resign his membership if the new prayerbook were adopted. Wile, Nathan Levi, and Max Gutman all argued for caution in adopting such a potentially divisive change.

The new liturgy's defenders were equally vociferous. Sol Wile argued that the temple's main responsibility was to transmit Judaism to the next generation, which could only be accomplished if the service were intelligible. To this end, it mattered not if "the congregation prayed in English, Hebrew, or Greek." Others came to the defense of Landsberg, who was not present during the meeting, and expressed resentment at what they saw as attacks on his character and motives. Simon Hays said the opposition to the new ritual was based on mere prejudice. Max Gutman tried to postpone the final decision until the fall, but this rather desperate move was quickly rejected. When the vote finally came, some members switched their votes, and the new ritual passed by forty to fifteen.

The Landsberg ritual remained in use at B'rith Kodesh for over fifty years. An 1890 visitor provided a concise description of the new pattern of worship. "The services are conducted in the vernacular—only a few Hebrew responses, alternatively spoken by the minister and sung by the choir, remind us of the ancient ritual." If anything, the Landsberg prayerbook is unrepresentative of the amount of Hebrew actually used in B'rith Kodesh services in the late nineteenth century. It seems that much of the rather scanty Hebrew material in the service was dropped over time. In 1887, a congregant complained that the aleinu was being omitted from Sabbath services. Landsberg, thinking it a superstition, regularly skipped the Kaddish.

Despite the criticism, Landsberg had largely succeeded in his intention to produce the first fully idiomatic, English-language radical Reform service. It was widely adopted by other congregations with similar inclinations, and went through three editions by 1911. Its innovations went beyond the translation and revision of the service. Critics noted that it was among the most choreographed services produced up to that time, with very precise instructions on when to stand, sit, and speak. The new ritual helped to popularize responsive reading in the vernacular as an important part of the Reform service. Other innovative elements included the use of biblical quotations as the heading for each section of the liturgy, and the heavy incorporation of

Rabbi Max Landsberg

psalms into the service, both elements common in contemporary Protestant prayer manuals.

Among those impressed with Landsberg's *Ritual* was Milwaukee Rabbi Isaac Moses, whose 1884 liturgy, *Tefillah Le-Moshe*, borrowed extensively from Landsberg's service. In 1896 Moses was the chief compiler and editor of the first edition of the *Union Prayer Book*, which was intended to provide a liturgical standard for the Reform movement. The new volume relied heavily on Moses' earlier efforts, and incorporated a number of Landsberg's prayer settings into the new *Union Prayer Book*. The *Union Prayer Book* had more Hebrew than Landsberg's ritual, though both prayerbooks took their ultimate inspiration from David Einhorn's *Olat Tamid*. *Ritual for Jewish Worship* was thus one of the most important steps toward making Einhorn's radical liturgical notions the standard for the Reform movement.

The *Jewish Tidings* and Sunday Services

Through all of the controversy, Landsberg remained confident that the introduction of the new prayerbook would not lead to a split, and that its

The Jewish Tidings.

A WEEKLY JOURNAL.

Louis Wiley, . . . , Editor and Publisher

Rochester, N. Y., Jan. 13, 1893

Entered as second-class mail matter.

TWO DOLLARS PER YEAR.
Office 301-303 Cox Building.

The Tidings may always be found on sale at the
following Rochester news-stands :
  C. E. Morris, Powers' Block;
  W. Merk, Washington Hall Block;
  E. Darrow & Co., 214 East Main Street;
  A. Jackson, Arcade.

The Jewish Tidings has the largest circulation
of the Jewish journals of the country.

There is No Jewish Race.

Even the masthead of the Jewish Tidings *proclaimed its stalwart commitment to radical Reform, and its detestation of any ethnic component to Judiasm.*

critics would eventually assent to its introduction. He proved to be a shrewd judge of his congregants, and most of the strongest objectors, including Gabriel Wile, remained members of B'rith Kodesh. Landsberg's victory marked the full emergence of the temple's second generation, the American-born, English-speaking children of the founders. Unlike some radical Reform rabbis, such as David Einhorn, Landsberg felt no special connection to the German language. After his arrival in Rochester, the temple gave Landsberg a chance to acquire fluency in English, and by 1874 Landsberg preached alternately in English and German. Landsberg's English was soon quite idiomatic, and by 1883, he reduced the frequency of German sermons to no more than once a month, angering some die-hard Germanists.

B'rith Kodesh's second generation, far more than its parents, was committed to the assimilationist implications of radical Reform. The most representative voice of the new generation could be found in the weekly Rochester journal, the *Jewish Tidings*, published from 1887 to 1894. This lively, well-written magazine soon found a following outside of Rochester. Within a year of its founding it claimed a circulation of 5,500, far more subscribers than it could possibly have had in Rochester alone. By 1890, it boasted the highest circulation of any weekly Jewish periodical in the country. Despite its national ambitions, the *Jewish Tidings* was in many ways a glorified house organ for B'rith Kodesh, whose activities were always the central focus of the magazine. Though a mouthpiece for its editors, it also was broadly representative of the generation of Rochester Jews that came of age of 1880s.

The *Jewish Tidings* was definitely a young person's journal, brash and outspoken, committed to correcting the mistakes of past generations, convinced of the rightness of its positions, and impatient of alternatives. It was the brainchild of two men in their late teens, Samuel Brickner and Louis Wiley. Born in 1867, Brickner graduated from the University of Rochester in 1888, and after a brief career in journalism, became a physician, associated with Mt. Sinai Hospital in New York City. But the dominant figure in the *Jewish Tidings* was Wiley, who by 1890 was the journal's editor and publisher. Born in 1869 in New York State's Southern Tier, he first came to Rochester in 1886. In 1893 he left the *Jewish Tidings* to become editor of the *Rochester Post-Express*. He soon left Rochester and ascended to that high citadel of German-Jewish assimilation, the *New York Times,* where he eventually became business manager.

The *Jewish Tidings* made clear its assimilationist commitments by its masthead slogan, "There is no Jewish Race." The editors believed that radical Reform had not yet completed its work. They approved of Landsberg's ritual, but felt that even its retention of Hebrew conceded too much to the enemies of progress. "Hebrew is a dead language," the journal claimed. "Civilization has pushed it to the rear. Judaism must keep pace with civilization." Neither did the *Jewish Tidings* shrink from the ultimate implications of its radical assimilationist position, actively encouraging marriage between Jews and non-Jews. Only by marrying Gentiles could Jews refute the ancient canard about their clannishness. As for the argument that intermarriage would have deleterious effects on the future of Judaism, the *Jewish Tidings* was unimpressed. "We give no support to the claim of some that the fate of Judaism depends upon the marriage of the present believers in the religion to each other. There is too much strength and merit in the doctrines of the Jews for that." Landsberg agreed with the *Jewish Tidings* on this matter, and was one of a handful of Reform rabbis in the nineteenth century who officiated at mixed marriages. He also agreed with the Tidings that male converts to Judaism did not need to undergo the ritual of circumcision.

But the main religious cause of the *Jewish Tidings*, pursued with a tenacity and fervor that perhaps could have been put to a better purpose, was the instituting of Sunday services at B'rith Kodesh. This was among the most divisive issues in late nineteenth-century Reform Judaism. Because most municipalities required businesses to close on Sunday, observing a Saturday Sabbath posed a considerable financial hardship for Jewish merchants. In response, many synagogues instituted late Friday evening services as an alternative to Saturday attendance. Isaac Mayer Wise first adopted regular Friday evening services in Cincinnati in 1869; B'rith Kodesh followed suit in October 1874. But some Jews expressed an interest in Sunday services, and in 1874 Rabbi Kaufmann Kohler's Temple Sinai in Chicago became the first Jewish congregation to institute Sunday services. The practice grew slowly. By 1880 only four temples had followed Sinai's lead.

There seems to have been little interest at B'rith Kodesh in Sunday services until the *Jewish Tidings* pressed the issue. By 1890, almost every issue of the paper agitated for Sunday services, through such articles as "Let Us Have Sunday Lectures," and "A Unanimous Sentiment in Favor of Sunday Lectures." The *Tidings* distinguished between lectures and services, and did not call for a Torah service on Sunday. Indeed, it wanted such gatherings to be devoid of most explicit Jewish references. The lecture—preferably on a topic of general and not specifically Jewish interest—was to be accompanied by a minimal prayer service at most.

The *Jewish Tidings* saw Sunday lectures as the only way to reverse the decline of interest in religious life at the temple. In addition to the decrease in attendance, the *Tidings* worried about the feminization of Saturday morning temple services, which were primarily attended by women, children, and old men. While the *Tidings* had no objections to Friday night services in principle, it felt that they would not work because most men were too tired after a full day of work and a hearty dinner to drag themselves to the temple. Only Sunday lectures would restore men to the temple, and only Sunday lectures would demonstrate the willingness of the Jews to abandon an arbitrary and economically disadvantageous peculiarity. In a Christian country, in which Jews served mostly Christian customers, Sunday was the only appropriate day for services.

The editors of the *Jewish Tidings* extended their campaign for Sunday services well beyond Rochester. They tried to stir national interest in the question, and looked forward to the day when "every Jewish temple in the country is open on Sunday." Other Jewish periodicals throughout the country frequently cited the paper on the Sunday service question. The *Tidings* polled thirty-five nationally known Jewish figures, who divided equally on the issue. If Isaac Mayer Wise was strongly opposed to the innovation, other Jewish leaders, such as Rabbis Emil Hirsch of Chicago, David Phillipson of Cincinnati, and Louis Marshall of Syracuse, supported the call for Sunday services. But Rochester was the main focus of the *Tidings'* campaign, which reached its crescendo in 1890 when the paper started a petition campaign to pressure B'rith Kodesh to introduce Sunday services.

The *Jewish Tidings* exerted itself especially to convince Rabbi Max Landsberg of both the need for Sunday services in Rochester, and of the popular support for them. In the beginning of the controversy the *Tidings* assumed that Landsberg would be a natural ally on the Sunday question. This proved not to be the case, and for perhaps the only time in his career, Landsberg found himself upholding the traditionalist side in a liturgical controversy.

Landsberg objected to Sunday services on both practical and religious grounds. He felt their introduction would be a divisive move, and one that was unlikely to substantially increase attendance. He resisted the implication that changes were needed because services were poorly attended, and insisted that attendance on Saturday morning was "large and satisfactory." Moreover, though he was not satisfied with the attendance at his Friday night lectures, he disagreed with the *Tidings* concerning the reason for the sparse turnouts. Attendance varied between twenty and forty persons, while many congregants evidently had enough energy to go to the theater or parties on Friday night. He questioned whether "those who stay away on Friday for such trivial reasons, would come on Sunday in large numbers."

But Landsberg also had religious objections to Sunday services. Though he agreed with the *Jewish Tidings* that in principle there was no religious reason precluding services on Sunday morning, he felt that the emotional attachment of Jews to the traditional Friday night Sabbath would doom any attempt to move it. Radical reformers often based their call for drastic changes on the need to reawaken interest in organized religion in an era of skepticism and indifference. There were limits, however, to how far they would go. In the 1890s Kaufmann Kohler, Landsberg's friend and the future president of Hebrew Union College, for example, recanted his previous enthusiasm for Sunday services, offering arguments similar to Landsberg's. Even a staunch supporter of Sunday services, such as Emil Hirsch of Chicago, rejected calls from his congregation to move High Holy Day services to the nearest Sunday. For Landsberg, the move to Sunday, and the call for the Sunday lecture to be devoid of specifically Jewish content, would be to remove the core of historic Judaism from the worship service. Landsberg's somewhat surprising position moved him to offer his most heartfelt defense of Jewish tradition.

Excerpt from Max Landsberg, "Friday or Sunday, Which?," Jewish Tidings, *November 28, 1890*

Those who habitually absent themselves from our Saturday and Friday Night services demand that the Sunday lectures should be made interesting and attractive by excluding as much as possible religious discussions and limiting them to topics of the day, of social and scientific matters, in a word by secularizing them completely.

Do you really expect that by such procedure religious indifferentism could be cured? Is it not rather obvious that the last remnant of religious fervor would be chilled, and our children and young people be taught the most effective object lesson that religion is something obsolete, only tolerated nominally, to satisfy those who have not yet lost all piety and devotion? You want to supply the religious wants of those who cannot be reached on Saturday morning, and you wish to do it by religiously excluding every vestige of formal religion from them, just that which feeds the spiritual hunger and quenches the spiritual thirst? Would it not be more advisable to dispense with the lecture and teach those cold with indifferentism how to pray, and give an impressive religious service, to arouse the dormant sentiment for ideal goods in them? Do they not need exactly what you want to eliminate? Do they not need sermons by which their religious sentiment is stirred up more than those who attend our services regularly every Sabbath? You cannot furnish all this as yet on Sunday, as nearly every one admits.

Much as it may be argued that in itself one day of the week is not endowed with any greater sanctity than the other, it cannot be denied that in spite of the poor observance all Jews still consider Saturday the Sabbath, while Sunday is a purely secular day for them which every one spends in such a manner as his instincts and inclinations lead them to do. Holy days, like holy places, cannot be manufactured in a day by decree of majority resolution. Their sacredness is of long growth and slow development. The traditions of many ages endow them with peculiar importance, and sweet reminiscences endear them to the heart. The practice of Christendom, continued through eighteen centuries, of considering only the day of Sabbath holy, could not wean the small minority of Jews from the sensation of regarding the eve of Sabbath, the Friday night after the night fall, as an intrinsic part of the day, and indeed it has always been the most important part. It is owing to the custom of celebrating it, that Jewish family life has assumed its characteristic intensity. It infused brightness and cheer into every home even in the most unfortunate times. It made the unhappy forget their troubles, the poor their want, the laborer his drudgery and furnished a touch of poetry to even the most prosaic life.

On this night the Sabbath is greeted like a beloved bride by the bridegroom, as a long expected guest. It is welcomed in the temple and holds its entrance in the homes made ready and beautified for its reception. On this night nobody would be satisfied with a mere lecture. All who have a Jewish heart in their bosoms, come

*prepared to attend an impressive divine service which
gives expression to sentiments, endeared by tradition,
which, as a magic wand conjures before us the sweetest
recollections of our childhood; the pious blessing of a
father, the anxious care of a mother who, though long
entered to their eternal reward, remain with us as the
strongest safeguard against temptation and the most
forcible motive power for a pure and unblemished life.
How small an argument over against such immeasurable
gain is the claim of a little fatigue after the day's labor
and some inconvenience resulting from the necessity of
reaching the temple directly after the evening meal?*

In the 1890s, Landsberg's opposition was sufficient to quash the movement for Sunday lectures. He was aided by a congregation strongly divided over the issue. An 1892 petition for making Sunday the primary day of worship—engineered by the *Jewish Tidings*—obtained the signatures of only 37 of B'rith Kodesh's 200 or so families. There was, however, considerable sentiment for experimenting with Sunday lectures to supplement rather than supplant Saturday services. In 1890 interviews in the *Tidings*, the president of the congregation, Leopold Garson, and most of the trustees expressed varying degrees of enthusiasm for trying Sunday lectures.

If the *Jewish Tidings* lost the initial battle over Sunday lectures, over time it won the war. As the years passed, Landsberg found fewer and fewer supporters for his position, and he proved as obstinate in his opposition to Sunday services as he was stubborn in his defense of his other radical reforms. After 1892, his compliance with the occasional demands of the trustees to experiment with Sunday services was at best half-hearted. (Over time, the distinction between Sunday lectures and Sunday services became fuzzy.) After 1900, Landsberg's reluctance to start Sunday services was a major factor in his growing alienation from the congregation. It was not until 1911, after Landsberg's hold on the congregation waned, that Sunday services became a regular part of B'rith Kodesh worship.

German-Jewish Social Life

The outlook wasn't brilliant for the Rochester nine on a late summer's day in Buffalo in 1890. The baseball team of the Eureka Club, the most prominent Jewish social organization in Rochester, took the field against their archrivals from Buffalo's Phoenix Club. The Rochester team was thoroughly outmatched. One surviving account of the game acknowledged that when the Eureka team "appeared on the field in natty uniforms they presented a very creditable appearance, but as soon as they attempted to play ball, they were pronounced meat by the Buffalo men." Rochester's starting pitcher, Allie Guggenheimer, gave up seventeen runs in the first four innings, en route to a 34 to 16 drubbing by Buffalo. Rochester's first baseman, Barry Cohn, was forced to use his feet to stop several widely thrown tosses, while the left fielder proved himself an excellent runner because "he would rather chase a ball than catch it." The *Jewish Tidings*, which had as little tolerance for baseball mediocrity as it did for religious Orthodoxy, complained that if the Rochester team changed "their first, second, and third basemen, their shortstop, pitcher, and catcher, to say nothing of their outfield, which did not make a single assist or put-out" they might make a better show in future games.

Despite this disappointing outing, Rochester's German Jews continued to play baseball, and to participate in other sports and activities. The members of B'rith Kodesh were active in such German-Jewish social organizations as the Eureka Club. For all of their pride in their acceptance as equals by local non-Jews, the Jews of Rochester still tended to go into business together and marry one another, and often lived both their professional and social lives within their little tightly knit community.

In all of this, Temple B'rith Kodesh served as an anchor of German-Jewish life in Rochester. If the Sunday service controversy raised questions about the temple's effectiveness as a transmitter of Jewish tradition, there were none concerning its central role as a source of cultural identity for Rochester's socially prominent Jews. Few remarked on the irony of a community of assimilated Jews spending almost all of their free time together, though some expressed anger at the genteel anti-Semitism that placed limits on the social acceptance of Jews, whatever their level of economic success. One suspects, however, that many agreed with the recommendation of the *Jewish Tidings*; Jews should go where they were welcome, and not make too great a fuss about those places where they were not. The temple was one of the places where Jews were always welcome.

B'rith Kodesh was at the center of a network of fraternal organizations. The oldest men's association was the Zerubbabel Lodge of the Independent Order of B'nai Brith, formed in March 1864. Often holding its meetings at the temple, the lodge became the premier, and most prestigious, Jewish fraternal organization in Rochester. Unlike the men's associations, the women's societies in Rochester were generally organized around clear philanthropic purposes. The elite female clubs in Rochester included the Hebrew Ladies' Benevolent Society and the Jewish Ladies' Aid Hospital Society. Other German-Jewish fraternal organizations in Rochester included the Ancient Jewish Order Kesher Shel Barzel, founded in 1873. The

Independent Order Free Sons of Israel, and the Independent Order B'rith Abraham appealed primarily to poorer German Jews and, increasingly, to Eastern European Jews. For some, especially those who could not afford the high price of joining B'rith Kodesh, lodge membership, with its provisions for sickness and death benefits, made an attractive alternative to temple membership.

In the hierarchy of Rochester's Jewish society, the pinnacle was the Eureka Club. This prestigious men's club opened on North Clinton Street in 1881. This was its third incarnation; it had been the successor to

EUREKA'S FAIRY PALACE.

MAGNIFICENT NEW HOME OF ROCHESTER'S FAMOUS ORGANIZATION.

The Eureka Club, the site of numerous weddings and parties, was at the apex of Rochester's German-Jewish society in the 1880s and 1890s.

the Harmony Club of the late 1860s, and the Phoenix Club, organized in 1873. Unlike its predecessors, it admitted women to its premises. But the Eureka Club surpassed its predecessors, both in opulence—its quarters had been refurbished at great expense—and in social prestige. Its over 125 members and their families could make use of its dining facilities, its card rooms, and its billiard parlor. Or they could attend Purim balls and other dances in what was reputed to be the largest ballroom in Rochester. Among the club's other activities were bowling parties (for both men and women), and harness races, in which Jews were active as owners and drivers as well as bettors.

B'rith Kodesh served as a meeting place, auditorium, and theater for Rochester's German Jews. An early attempt at adult Jewish education started in 1889 when the temple introduced a Sunday night Bible class, in which members of the congregation offered talks—usually on biblical themes— with comments by Landsberg. Unmarried women and men apparently attended the class in large numbers. Wedding ceremonies often took place at the temple, with the receptions at halls such as the Eureka Club. For lavish nuptials, such as the 1891 marriage between Dr. Simon Elsner and Miss Minnie Wolff, all of Rochester's Jewish society turned out, well over one

A list of the presents received by the bride and groom follows:

Martin E. Wollf, check for $500; Abram E. Wollf, check for $500; Jacob Wollf, check for $25; Mrs. H. Elsner, solid silver set, 4 dozen pieces, and pearl-handled carving set; J. Bier, solid silver salad set; Mrs. A. Bier, solid silver salad fork and spoon 2; Miss Emma Elsner, solid silver gravy spoon; Mr. and Mrs. L. Moore, solid silver salad fork and ladle 2; Carrie E. Hymen, solid silver salt, pepper and spoon 3; Mrs. M. S. Hymen, solid silver soup, berry and cream ladles 3; Mrs. Sol Goldsmith, solid silver berry spoon; Harry Hanauer, solid silver sugar ladle; Mrs. I. S. Frankel, solid silver napkin rings; Mrs. A. Siebel, solid silver pie knife; Mrs. Herman Mendel, solid silver smoking set; Mrs. L. Waterman, solid silver fish spoon; Mr. and Mrs. G. Wile, solid silver sugar and cream; Mr. and Mrs. I. Hanauer, solid silver after-dinners 12; Mr. and Mrs. I. J. Beir, solid silver soup ladle; Mrs. and Elks Hochstetter, solid silver sugar ladles 2; Mrs. A. S. Bigelow, solid silver berry spoon; Mr. and Mrs. T. Oberfelder, solid silver oyster and after dinners; Mr. and Mrs. N. and Louis S. Stein, solid silver salad fork and spoon;

The opening portion of a detailed list of the wedding presents for the 1891 nuptials of Simon Leopold Elsner and Minnie Wolff, as printed in the Jewish Tidings, *provided the German Jews of Rochester with a convenient gauge of the generosity of their neighbors. Simon Elsner (1863–1910) was a well-regarded physician, who spent much of his time ministering to the poor of Rochester before his death in 1910. Minnie Wolff (1863–1901), was the daughter of Elias Wolff, a prominent real estate and insurance broker. Her brother, Martin L. Wolff, operated some of the leading legitimate and vaudeville theaters in Rochester and Syracuse.*

hundred couples. (In June of 1901 Dr. Elsner delivered a self-described "squalling brat" into the world, Philip S. Bernstein.) The *Jewish Tidings* printed the guest list, along with a description of each guest's wedding present, a custom that no doubt encouraged conspicuous generosity.

Not all the social activities of B'rith Kodesh involved such prodigal consumption. Theatrical productions were important events, and congregation members participated both as performers and audience. At a time when Americans were still willing to entertain themselves, the Jews of B'rith Kodesh loved to don costumes and greasepaint and put on a show. One of the highlights of the year was the annual Purim masquerade at the Eureka Club. In 1891 the Purimspielers dressed as clowns, convicts, frogs, waffle vendors, nuns, washerwomen, and even Knights of Labor activists—though some thought the last in poor taste, because of ongoing labor problems in the city's garment industry.

In the fall of 1890, B'rith Kodesh opened a new Assembly Hall on Gibbs Street, in downtown Rochester, a prelude to the move of the sanctuary to Gibbs Street four years later. The primary purpose of the hall was to expand space for the religious school, but it also contained an auditorium for theatrical performances, with a seating capacity of 450. For the inaugural performance in 1890 an original comedy, both written and acted by B'rith Kodesh members, filled the hall to capacity. The audience evidently enjoyed Ralph Stadeker's *Yomtofick Gaensefett* (Holiday Goosefat), on the theme of the conflict between Reform and traditional Judaism. In the play, to the surprise of no one in the audience, the broadmindedness of Reform triumphed over the narrowness of Orthodoxy. To further stack the production against religious traditionalism, a woman portrayed the Orthodox Jewish male character, no doubt heightening the sense of the ridiculousness of the Orthodox position.

Jewish Tidings, *October 3, 1890*

The handsome new hall of the Berith Kodesh congregation was brilliantly lighted Wednesday evening and every seat in the spacious auditorium was occupied. There was an air of expectance and interest among the auditors, for the comedy "Yomtofick Gaensefett" written by Ralph Staedeker, was to be presented. It was a brilliant audience. The handsome dresses of the ladies and the decorations of the hall added a wealth of attractiveness to the scene.

It may be well to briefly review the story of "Yomtofick Gaensefett" before proceeding to a review of the performance. Jacob Goldstein, an Orthodox Jew of the strictest variety, whose devotion to the ceremonies of his religion exceeds the bounds of reason, has a charming daughter named Deborah for whose hand one Felix Stonehill is a claimant. Felix loves Deborah deeply and the young lady warmly reciprocates the affection. But a seemingly insurmountable objection to marriage is the opposition of the young girl's father who objects to the young man's views on religious rites. In fact the young man is so liberal in his opinions that he expresses himself in hearty agreement with the Tidings *on the issues of the hour. A sad accident in the Goldstein household is the turning point in Mr. Stonehill's favor. Mrs. Goldstein discovers on Pesach Eve that there is no gaensefett in the house. There is bitter wailing and gnashing of teeth, and Mr. Stonehill, who is present, relieves the distress by promising to secure some of the sacred food. He boards a train for Buffalo, gets a quantity of gaensefett and returns with it to the bosom of a family happy once more. From that time forward Mr. Goldstein becomes reconciled toward Stonehill and he secures Mr. Goldstein's warm friendship by narrating a rather incredulous tale about being the possessor of another sacred item—the basket in which Moses was found in the bullrushes. The reconciliation is complete and the wedding follows.*

The play is an excellent piece of literary work. A vein of pronounced but refined humor runs through it. The satire in the comedy is delightful and the whole work is a credit to its brilliant author. The lines fairly ripple with mirth, yet there is much of wholesome sentiment and moral truth in them. The principal idea of the play is to furnish an amusement, but it does more than that—it illustrates the absurdity of some of the notions of our co-religionists.

A New Temple Building

After the B'rith Kodesh congregation moved into the former church on St. Paul Street in 1855, early visitors were unanimous in praising the sanctuary for its space and airy quality. At the time, the temple nearly had the block to itself. Over the course of two decades, however, considerable industrial development took place in the area. Factories arose, many of them owned by Jewish garment manufacturers. The factory buildings crowded the temple, blocked out sunlight, created noise on Saturday mornings, and contributed to a general dreariness and sense that St. Paul Street was no longer a particularly fashionable address.

By the mid-1870s, many in the congregation wanted to move from St. Paul Street. The classroom space was particularly inadequate. A resolution in early 1876 stated that "our Sunday school rooms are in an exceedingly unhealthy condition thereby rendering the teachers and pupils attending there liable to sickness and disease." Not surprisingly, this tended to keep down enrollments at the Sunday school. The relatively small size of the sanctuary, the resolution complained, made it impossible to add new members to the congregation. In response, B'rith Kodesh decided to rebuild the sanctuary entirely. This was done rapidly, at a cost of $25,000, and the temple was rededicated on September 15, 1876.

The renovations apparently succeeded for a while in curbing complaints, but by the late 1880s, many of the same issues returned. During the controversy over Sunday services, when the question of poor attendance at Saturday morning services was raised, Rabbi Landsberg

Dedicated in 1894, the Gibbs Street Temple was a fine example of neo-Romanesque synagogue design, with its pitched roof, rusticated stonework, high arched windows, and corner tower. Designed by Leon Stern, a member of the congregation, its likely inspiration was Temple Beth Emeth in Albany, N.Y., built in 1887.

argued that the real problem was not the liturgy, the quality of the preaching, or any purely religious matter, but the temple sanctuary itself. In 1889 he painted a description of the sanctuary that made it sound more like a dungeon than a house of worship:

> We have no sunlight. Whatever good air there is, is rapidly absorbed by the many gaslights we are compelled to burn on the brightest days. We have no means of renewing the vitiated air by ventilation, and consequently many find it distressing to be in the temple when it is but moderately crowded. Under the present condition we have not as much right to blame those who stay away as to bestow particular praise upon those who do not allow such discomfort to interfere with their regular attendance.

Few defended the St. Paul Street sanctuary, but a number of prominent members felt that the low level of attendance and meager interest in religious affairs did not warrant a new building. They also worried whether the old building could be sold for enough money to justify a move. Those in support of a move recognized the need to generate more congregational enthusiasm for the project. They conceded that this would entail considerable expense, but argued that it was essential for the continued health and prosperity of the congregation. There was much discussion about whether the seating requirements for the High Holy Day services—when the temple was filled to capacity and non-members were often turned away at the door—warranted enlarging a sanctuary that was more than adequate for the rest of the year.

Those opposed to a move argued that it would be certain to lead to an increase in the level of dues, which were already quite high. Indeed, it required a considerable financial commitment to become a member of B'rith Kodesh. Once an applicant passed the hurdle of the admissions committee—a two-thirds vote was required, and blackballing prospective members was not uncommon—he faced an initiation fee, as well as pew rental that could cost over $300 a year. (The more desirable pews had higher rent.) The high price of membership created two classes within the

A Suggestion for the Proposed New Temple in Rochester.

Moorish architecture was a fashionable style of synagogue construction in the late nineteenth century. This striking rendering for the proposed new temple on Gibbs Street, though ultimately not selected, appeared in the Jewish Tidings *in 1892.*

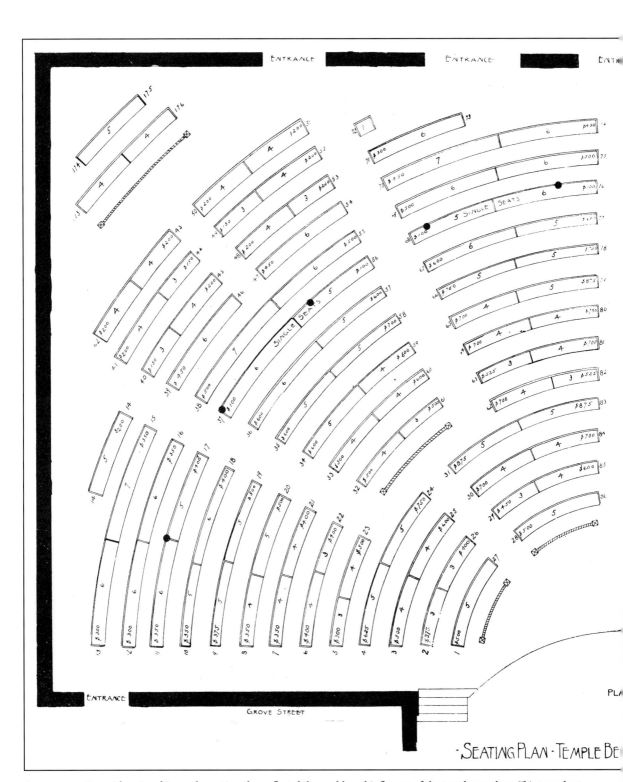

In a congregation with assigned pews, the seating plan reflected the wealth and influence of the temple members. This pew chart dates from around 1900.

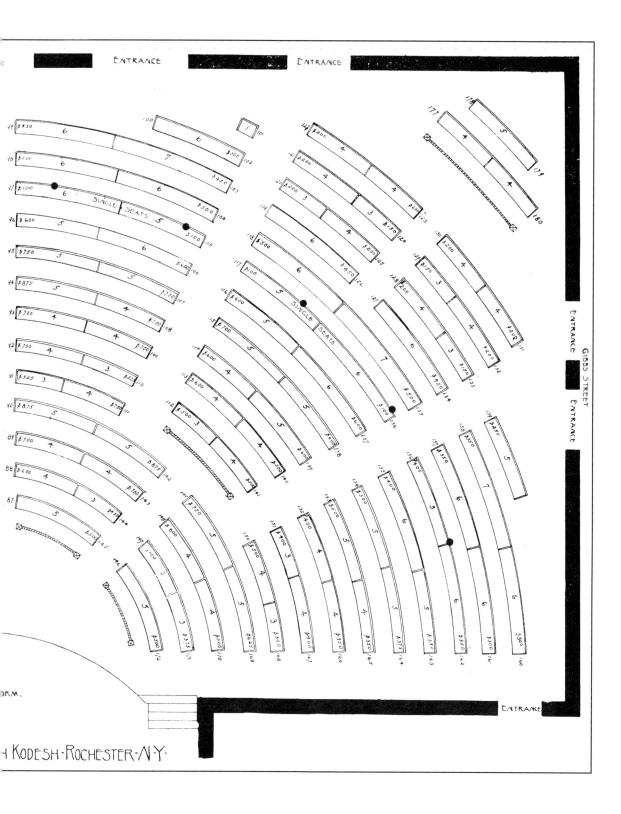

Henry Michaels, born in England in 1822, founded Michaels & Stern in 1873, soon one of the most prominent garment manufacturing companies in Rochester. He was a driving force behind the building of the Gibbs Street sanctuary.

Max Lowenthal, president of B'rith Kodesh from 1894 to 1901, and again from 1912 to 1915, was born in Silesia in 1843, coming to the United States in 1853, and to Rochester a decade later. In 1873 he founded the Rochester Knitting Works, which manufactured woolen mittens, vests, and other knitted products. By 1911 his family's factory on South Clinton Avenue did half a million dollars of business annually.

congregation. Full membership included the additional benefits of free tuition for the religious school, the right to have the rabbi officiate at weddings and funerals, certain death benefits, and the right to vote in congregational elections. Those unable or unwilling to spend that sort of money could rent a seat from the congregation, but "seatholders" were definitely second-class citizens, unable to vote in temple elections. Between 15 and 25 percent of B'rith Kodesh members were seat holders. In 1884, according to one source, B'rith Kodesh had ninety-six full members and fifteen seat-holders.

The final decision to leave St. Paul Street took place in three separate steps. At the end of 1887, the congregation decided to build a new house of worship. In September 1888, after considering three lots, one on the east side of Franklin Street, one at Williams Street and Chestnut Park, and one at the corner of Gibbs and Grove streets, the temple opted for the latter most lot. This was the most expensive of the three, costing $21,000, but in the opinion of the committee it was the best situated. East of the Genesee River, it was near East Avenue, rapidly becoming the most fashionable residential district in the city. The new lot remained vacant for a while, however, as many members still hesitated to build a new temple, and the congregation debated over what price to set for the site on St. Paul Street. In October 1890, the Assembly Hall opened on part of the Gibbs Street lot. There was general agreement on the success of the new building, designed by Leon Stern of Rogers, Sturges & Stern, and a member of the congregation.

Nonetheless, the members made no move to build a new sanctuary. In October 1892, the *Jewish Tidings* was still editorializing on the need for a new building, complaining that the Eureka Club raised funds more easily for a new building than the temple did for a new sanctuary. It required the enthusiastic backing of Henry Michaels, president of B'rith Kodesh from 1892 to 1894, to kindle support for the erection of the new temple building. Born in England in 1822, Michaels became the first non-German president of B'rith Kodesh during an earlier term as temple president from 1886 to 1888. President of Michaels, Stern & Co., he was a leading manufacturer of men's ready-made clothing, and in 1890 became the first president of the Clothier's Exchange, a trade group of the city's garment manufacturers. Michaels managed to raise the necessary funds for the new temple in only a few months in 1893, despite the serious financial recession that year—a tribute, an obituary note observed, to his "indomitable will power."

The groundbreaking ceremony took place on July 5, 1893. At

the ceremony, Max Lowenthal, chairman of the building committee, expressed the hope that the new temple would be dedicated to the proposition that "to be a good Jew is nothing else than to be a good man." Built at a cost of $85,000, the temple was dedicated less than a year later, on June 1, 1894. Sadly, Henry Michaels did not live to see the temple building completed; he had died on March 2, 1894. Emil Hirsch, Rabbi of Chicago's Temple Sinai and a leader of radical Reform, and Dr. David Hill, president of the University of Rochester, were the two main speakers. Hill praised the congregation and its achievements, and, echoing Lowenthal's comments of a year earlier, hoped that the congregation would continue to exemplify the truth that "all men are brothers." Admiring the new edifice on Gibbs Street, the members of B'rith Kodesh had good reason to be proud of what they had accomplished in Rochester, both as Jews and as Americans, in fewer than fifty years.

Two of the four seasons at B'rith Kodesh. The temple in spring and in a Rochester winter. (Courtesy Carol Yunker)

Chapter III

The Progressive Era and Rabbi Horace J. Wolf, 1894–1927

Horace J. Wolf, senior rabbi of Temple B'rith Kodesh from 1915 to 1927, was the temple's first rabbi born in the United States. His vigor and concern with urban problems revived the congregation. (Courtesy American Jewish Archives)

Introduction

By the end of the nineteenth century, B'rith Kodesh was one of the most influential congregations within the Reform movement. The congregation was an early member of the major organization of Reform Judaism, the Union of American Hebrew Congregations (UAHC), which was founded in Cincinnati in July 1873. B'rith Kodesh joined the UAHC in April 1874, but perhaps because of Rabbi Max Landsberg's misgivings about the UAHC President Isaac Mayer Wise's ambitions for control of American Judaism, the temple soon withdrew from membership. B'rith Kodesh was not alone in its suspicions about Wise, and many prominent East Coast synagogues refused to join the UAHC until around 1880. In any event, B'rith Kodesh rejoined in April 1879 and has been an active member ever since.

Landsberg was active in the Central Conference of American Rabbis (CCAR) from the time of its founding in 1889. In 1895, one year after the opening of the Gibbs Street sanctuary, Rochester and Temple B'rith Kodesh hosted the CCAR annual meeting. In his opening address at the temple, Isaac Mayer Wise praised the gathering in "beautiful and generous Rochester" as one of the most important in Jewish history. The turnout—with more rabbis in attendance than at the ancient Sanhedrin—was proof to Wise that Judaism was "the universal religion, progressive like reason...and like God's sun, radiating

Thirty-First

ANNUAL CONVENTION

of the

Central Conference
of American Rabbis

TEMPLE BERITH KODESH
Rochester, N. Y.

JUNE 29th — JULY 6th, 1920

OFFICERS 1919-20

KAUFMAN KOHLER, *Honorary President*, Cincinnati, Ohio
LEO M. FRANKLIN, *President*, Detroit, Mich.
EDWARD N. CALISCH, *Vice-President*, Richmond, Va.
ABRAM SIMON, *Treasurer*, Washington, D. C.
ISAAC E. MARCUSON, *Recording Secretary*, Macon, Ga.
FELIX A. LEVY, *Corresponding Secretary*, Chicago, Ill.

EXECUTIVE BOARD

HENRY BERKOWITZ, Philadelphia, Pa.   DAVID LEFKOWITZ, Dallas, Texas
MAX C. CURRICK, Erie, Pa.   MARTIN A. MEYER, San Francisco, Cal.
HENRY ENGLANDER, Cincinnati, Ohio   MARCUS SALZMAN, Wilkesbarre, Pa.
LOUIS GROSSMAN, Cincinnati, Ohio   GEORGE SOLOMON, Savannah, Ga.
SAMUEL HIRSHBERG, Milwaukee, Wis.   LOUIS WOLSEY, Cleveland, Ohio
            CLIFTON H. LEVY, New York City

Proceedings OF THE

Sixth Annual Convention

OF THE

Central Conference of American Rabbis.

ROCHESTER, N. Y., July 10, 1895,}
TEMPLE B'RITH KODESH. ∫

The Sixth Annual Convention of the Central Conference of American Rabbis began its sessions in the city of Rochester, New York, in Temple B'rith Kodesh, on Wednesday evening, July 10th, at 7:30 o'clock. The Conference was called to order by the honorable President, Dr. I. M. Wise, after which the Temple Choir sang a beautiful anthem.

Dr. I. Aaron, of Buffalo, delivered the invocation.

Dr. Max Landsberg, Chairman of the Local Committee of Arrangements, extended hearty greetings to the Conference in an Address of Welcome, which was responded to by Dr. G. Gottheil, of New York, Vice-President of the Conference.

A hymn was then sung by the whole congregation, when, amid hearty greetings, the venerable President, Dr. I. M. Wise, arose and delivered his annual address and message, which he concluded by declaring the Sixth Annual Conference duly opened and ready for the transaction of business.

In 1895, and again in 1920, the Central Conference of American Rabbis held their annual convention at B'rith Kodesh.

light and life to all pilgrims of this sublunar sphere."

Whatever their other differences, Wise and Landsberg were in complete agreement that the liberation of Judaism from its ceremonial encumbrances was one of the great triumphs of the nineteenth century. Landsberg had little doubt that by rejecting superfluous ritual, Reform Jews had demonstrated their insistence on being accepted as full citizens of the United States, and had set an example for Christians in their adherence to non-dogmatic religion. A plaque in the Gibbs Street Temple honored Landsberg for leading the congregation out of "orientalism," his disdainful term for traditional Jewish ritual. Throughout his near half-century at B'rith Kodesh, Landsberg assumed that the Reform movement would continue to discard the chaff of Jewish ritual until all that had kept Jews apart and different from their neighbors during the long centuries of exile would be no more.

But by the time Landsberg retired in 1915, growth at B'rith Kodesh was not proceeding according to his plan. New forces had shifted the congregation away from Landsberg's vision of a Judaism characterized by radical assimilation and anti-ceremonialism. Most notable among these changes were the more active participation of women in temple affairs, the massive emigration of Eastern European Jews to the United States, the gathering strength of Zionism, and the engulfing catastrophe of World War I. Under Landsberg's successor, Horace J. Wolf, the pace of change rapidly increased, and by the end of Wolf's all-too-short tenure at B'rith Kodesh in 1927, the congregation had forged a new, and in many ways quite distinct, understanding of the meaning of Reform Judaism.

The Power of Sisterhood

By the late nineteenth century most of the regular attendees at B'rith Kodesh services were women. The "feminization" of religious worship within Reform Judaism was widely observed and occasioned much debate. Low male attendance at religious services was an important subtext to the "Sunday Service" controversy at the temple. The primary advocate of Sunday services, the *Jewish Tidings*, complained in 1890 that "the empty benches at the temple at each recurring service testify, in no uncertain way, either the unwillingness or the inability of the male members of the congregation to enter the synagogue's portals." In his response, Landsberg could do little else but acknowledge that B'rith Kodesh was indeed a "congregation of women and children with a slight sprinkling of mostly elderly men."

But the statistical dominance of women in congregational life at B'rith Kodesh did not translate into a commensurate influence on temple affairs. Women played little role in the service, did not serve as temple officers, and could not vote in congregational elections.

A NOBLE UNDERTAKING.

THE BERITH KODESH SISTERHOOD FORMED

Officers Elected and Constitution and By Laws Adopted Plan of Work of the Society Commendable Objects.

The Berith Kodesh Sisterhood was formed at the Assembly hall last Monday evening. There was a large and enthusiastic attendance. The objects of the society are to develop among its members a warmer and more active interest in the prosperity of the temple; to promote social and friendly intercourse, the higher purposes of life, and mutual improvement among its members, to further works of charity, philanthrophy and education in co-operation with the United Jewish Charities; and to lend a helping hand wherever anyone may be in need of material or spiritual assistance.

The officers of the sisterhood shall consist of a managing board of twenty. The following named ladies have been chosen: President, Mrs. R Stntz; first vice president, Mrs. Joseph Michaels; second vice-president, Mrs. D. M. Garson; recording secretary, Mrs. M. Meyer; corresponding secretary, Miss Stella Levi; treasurer, Mrs. S. L. Ebner; trustees, Mrs. J. Solomon, Mrs. H. Seligman. Mrs. M. Landsberg, Mrs. M. M. Meyers, Mrs. L. A. Baum, Mrs. Max Lowenthal, Mrs. S L. Ettenheimer, Mrs. H. Pincus, Mrs. S. Stern, Mrs. B. Rothschild, Mrs. H. C. Cohn, Mrs. I. J. Brir, Mrs. M. Dinkelspiel and Mrs. J. M. Wile. Rev. Dr. Max Landsberg was chosen Honorary President.

Announcing the formation of the B'rith Kodesh Sisterhood in the Jewish Tidings.

Nevertheless, they did help shape religious life within the congregation, and this role dramatically increased in the late decades of the nineteenth century. Women's new position in Judaism was rooted in their traditional domestic roles; the care of children, upkeep of the household (and, by extension, the sanctuary), and the assistance of other women to meet these obligations. But women soon expanded their sphere beyond these limits to forge a new understanding of their place in the synagogue.

Since the founding of the congregation, women had been active in charitable work, sometimes with men, sometimes by themselves. A desire to form their own organization lead to the foundation of the Hebrew Ladies' Benevolent Society in 1865. Another charitable group, the Hebrew Ladies' Aid Society, formed in March 1870, to assist poor women and orphans at Rochester City Hospital. A large component of its work consisted of distributing fabric and clothing to the poor in Rochester and elsewhere. The society helped clothe those left homeless after the Great Chicago Fire of 1872. Their first annual report from January 1871 indicates a substantial store of goods on hand: 9 rolls of cotton, 179 yards of calico, 91 yards of muslin, 4 comforters, 4 sheets, 4 pairs of gloves, 4 chemises, 2 skirts, and 2 aprons.

The Ladies' Aid society existed for over fifty years, gathering frequently for kaffee klatsches and communal sewing sessions. As a long-time member reminisced in a poem from the 1920s:

> *It was not like this in the Olden Days (no)*
> *It was not like this in the olden days*
> *Fifty years is long ago*
> *For then we had our coffee-cake*
> *When e'er we met to sew*
> *But nowadays we don't eat at all*
> *Our work can't be delayed*
> *We rip and baste with feverish haste*
> *For the Ladies' Aid.*

Though charity, or *tzedekah*, remained central to women's work within the congregation, there were other venues open to them. The founding of the choir in 1862 provided a way for women to participate directly in the service. Many female members did so, and the congregation often acknowledged their contribution, as it did in 1863 to Rachel Moerell, by giving her a gold chain in appreciation for her services in the choir.

Teaching in the religious school was another area of temple life in which women participated. The B'rith Kodesh day school employed a female teacher as early as 1859. In 1888, six of the ten teachers in the religious

Susan B. Anthony,

"The Women's
Movement,"
Jewish Tidings
December 4, 1891

---

*Ralph Waldo
Emerson a half century
ago said, "A wholesome
discontent is the first
step toward progress." I
think most would agree
with that sentiment.
First we will consider the
unrest caused by the
greed of the capital that
compels it to seek the
most work for the least
money. Women should
indeed be thankful for
this unrest and greed of
capital because it has
opened to them the
doors of every bread
winning industry and
trade; and because
millions of women have,
as a result, they are
reaping the benefit and
living in honorable,
independent homes, no
longer compelled to*

Susan B. Anthony (1820–1906), the nation's foremost suffragist, was a long-time friend of Temple B'rith Kodesh. Anthony's church, the First Unitarian Church of Rochester, had close connections to the temple in the second half of the nineteenth century. Anthony became a friend of both Max and Miriam Landsberg, and for some women in the congregation, an inspiration. (Courtesy First Unitarian Church of Rochester)

school were women. All of the female teachers were unmarried, and presumably had responsibility for teaching the younger grades. By the 1880s, women began to take direct responsibility for running the religious school. In 1888, the Board of Trustees authorized the president of the congregation to appoint three women as honorary members of the school board. It is not clear when women became full members of the school board, but by 1895 Landsberg wrote that they been serving in that position for a number of years.

The successful efforts of women to gain representation on the school board were evidence of their new assertiveness. Women were the majority of the regular attendees at the Bible Study group which met on Sunday nights, and Sarah Wile was on the three-person committee established in 1890 to supervise the meetings.

Men in the congregation divided over the propriety of increasing the role of women in congregational governance. In April 1891, Joseph Caufmann, the president of B'rith Kodesh, introduced a resolution that would have given voting rights to two groups of second-class members: seat-holders (those who rented rather than purchased seats) and women, to participate in congregational elections. "Wives of members and seatholders in good standing, while remaining so," the resolution read, "shall have the privilege of voting and holding office, except President and Vice President, upon the payment of $12 p.a." A second resolution would have granted seatholders and women the right to vote without a fee. There apparently was some support for these changes; *Jewish Tidings* attacked the current policy as "taxation without representation." When the proposal was put to a vote at the end of May 1891, it was decisively defeated by a vote of twenty to four.

If the majority of the men in B'rith Kodesh opposed the expansion of women's influence in the congregation, Rabbi Landsberg was an outspoken defender of women's rights. The question of "women's suffrage" in the temple, Landsberg argued, reflected the broader question of rights of women in American society. The home of Susan B. Anthony, Rochester had been a center of the feminist movement since the Seneca Falls convention in 1848. Anthony's church, the First Unitarian Church of Rochester, had extremely close ties with both the women's rights movement and with B'rith Kodesh. The annual Union Thanksgiving service between the two congregations started in 1871, and Landsberg often exchanged pulpits with the Unitarian minister. Landsberg and Anthony became good friends, and she would from time to time drop him notes to remind the rabbi to mention women's suffrage in his sermons and speeches. In 1901, for example, she wrote to Landsberg the following:

> I notice that at the Union Thanksgiving Service you are to speak on the subject of "the City Beautiful." I expect to be present on this occasion, and shall be disappointed if you do not find a prominent place in the "City Beautiful" for *enfranchised womanhood*, and do not take the ground that she *cannot utilize* her *full resources* without the power of the ballot.

For at least one Union Thanksgiving service, Anthony and Landsberg

marry men they neither love nor respect simply in order to procure for themselves bread and shelter. Second, all married women should be thankful because of the unrest of self-interest, not to say selfishness of a few rich men who secured the property law of 1848 by which all wives enjoy the unspeakable blessing of owning and controlling the money they inherit from their fathers and friends. And yet more thankful shall we be when the great unrest of to-day shall have secured to the wife enjoyment in the joint earnings of the marriage copartnership, making two financial heads in the household instead of one. And how thankful should we be for the unrest of yesterday that has given to women school suffrage, a controlling voice in the educational interests of twenty-three states, municipal suffrage in Kansas, and full and complete suffrage in that mountain state of Wyoming.

shared the pulpit. In 1891, the service had the provocative theme "The Unrest of Our Times, A Cause for Thankfulness." Anthony spoke on how a "wholesome" discontent had provided the impetus for the progress of women.

Landsberg was among the first American rabbis to explore the theological implications of the emancipation of women. This examination culminated in his 1893 Chicago address, "The Position of Women Among the Jews. Landsberg presents a rather idealized view of women and emphasizes their maternal qualities, as did most prominent Jewish women of the era. When it came to specific recommendations, he was rather cautious. Nonetheless, he recognized the changing role of women in Reform Judaism. The address, reprinted in the *Jewish Tidings* article is also an excellent introduction to Landsberg's general religious views on Judaism, which he believed had reached a high point of development in biblical times, had slid backwards into obscurantism during the Middle Ages, and re-emerged triumphant in western Europe and America in the nineteenth century. Landsberg saw the status of women as a bellwether of the health of Judaism throughout history.

Max Landsberg, *"The Position of Women Among the Jews,"* Jewish Tidings, *September 8, 1893*

The consideration of Woman's position among the Jews must naturally be divided into three parts coincident with the three great periods of Jewish history…

The first period embraces the biblical time down to the destruction of the Jewish nationality by the Romans…The duties to father and mother were perfectly alike. The women were not excluded from the company of men. They were not confined to the innermost part of the house and kept there in utter ignorance of every thing except their household duties, but freely took part in all that concerned their husbands and fathers, and were benefited by the education and training gained by such free intercourse. Choruses of women were admitted to public celebrations. Evidence for this is not wanting. Miriam is reported to have celebrated escape from Egypt at the head of a host of women with music and song; David, after his victory, received the laurel wreath from the maidens of his people [I Samuel, 2], and religious processions were conducted by women [Psalms 68:26]. On Sabbaths and New Moons they

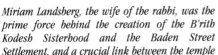

Miriam Landsberg, the wife of the rabbi, was the prime force behind the creation of the B'rith Kodesh Sisterhood and the Baden Street Settlement, and a crucial link between the temple and the wider circles of female social reform and suffragism in Rochester. Her elegant Sabbath dress, black with an ecru neck ruff, was typical of the couture of B'rith Kodesh women. (Courtesy Rochester Museum and Science Center, photo by Paul Porell)

appeared at the places of worship "to seek God" and went to the schools of the prophets to seek their religious instruction [II Kings 4: 23].

Thus, far from being unconditionally subject to man, shut up in the harem and protected by isolation, they could move freely and unsuspected by men, participate in public affairs and were not excluded from the highest positions. One of the oldest songs was by a woman, and one of the finest prayers on record was placed in the mouth of the mother of Samuel.

Upon the basis of the practical equality between man and wife grew up that chastity, continency and temperance which are never promoted by legislation, but by the moral self-government of man, brought about by the recognized dignity of woman...

The second period [of Jewish history] includes the long time of suffering from the fall of Jerusalem to the

Miriam Landsberg,
"Woman in the Synagogue,"
Reform Advocate
February 20, 1897

Q: How can [a woman] best serve its interests?

A: By taking an interest in all of the affairs of the congregation, by attending divine service regularly, not alone, but with her whole family, may it be on Saturday or Sunday.

Q: Should she take an active role in the administration of its affairs? If so, in what capacity?

A: Jewish women should take an active part in the administration of the affairs of the congregation. Every Sunday-school board should consist of an equal number of men and women, and in every board of trustees there should be at least two women. Nobody can deny that our women know at least as much about the needs of the congregation, and are as much interested in its welfare as the men. Besides there should be a house committee, consisting of one man and two women, whose duty it should be to see that the temple is kept in good repair, and that every part of the building is kept clean.

Q: How can she best cooperate with the Sabbath School?

A: She can best cooperate with the Sabbath School, first, by becoming a member of the school board, and then doing her duty faithfully by attending as often as possible at the school. She is not expected to make speeches to the children, but she should silently observe, and

removal of political disabilities of the Jews which in France and the United States begin at the end of the last century…In the long period which succeeded the blotting out forever of the Jewish nationality, the natural development of Jewish religion and ethics was rudely interrupted, its stream led into a new channel and exposed in a great variety of unfortunate conditions. Hated, persecuted, and tempest-tossed, the only preventative against the total dissolution and loss of identity was found in the minute elaboration of the formal and ceremonial part of religion, with which the Jews surrounded themselves as with a protecting wall.

The Talmud, representing a development especially in Babylon under oriental influences, became the power ruling supreme. Rigid conservatism, a result of terrible oppression continued through centuries, furthered isolation and preserved isolation even in occidental countries. If, indeed, Judea had seemed like a piece of Occident in the midst of the oriental countries, now the Jews represented orientalism in the midst of the Occident. Every deportment of life was so influenced, and the position of woman was materially altered. Women were excluded from the participation in all those ceremonies which to the popular mind were the principal expression of religion [Tractate Menahot 43:6]. Women were gradually placed on a level with children and slaves, their testimony was not admitted on the witness stand, not even to testify for the appearance of the moon. [Tractate Rosh Hashanah 22a]…Excluded as she was from most of the ceremonial parts of religion, so excessively developed, and exempt from the practice of those manifold duties which lent to the Jews their peculiar oriental aspect, she was largely saved from the dangers of that formalism which so easily crushes under its weight all truly religious sentiment. She was led to concentrate her efforts upon the essential part of religion, upon that which is alike the true end and aim of all religions independent of creed and denomination …

As far removed from the unhealthy worship of feudal chivalry which made women an object of a playful cult, as from the extreme views of those who, clamoring for women's rights, wish to obliterate all the natural distinctions between the two sexes, the Jews always and everywhere appreciated the high significance of woman's work for the noblest goods, the gain of true liberty, and the conservation of religious sentiments... They found their noblest work in faithfully discharging their duties as wives and mothers; they were the priestesses at the sacred hearth of the home, gave the family a religious atmosphere, and infused it with that affection, sincerity, and holiness by which it is proverbially distinguished; they saved Judaism from becoming a church religion, and made it most emphatically a religion of life...

As soon as the spirit of liberty began to purify the air, and the nations were delivered from the undisputed sway of intolerance, the Jews were roused from their lethargy, and their leading men began with energy to demand the emancipation of the Jewish wives and mothers and daughters...In all our progressive Jewish congregations, women render the most valuable service as teachers at the schools of religious instruction, and it is well-known that they furnish the largest contingent in the attendance at religious services.

Nevertheless, it cannot be denied that the work has been only begun, that much remains to be done, and that it will not be completed until perfect religious equality has been established between men and women. There is no conceivable reason why our women should not have a voice in the management of our congregations, why they should not enjoy all the privileges of active membership, why they should not be elected to lend their aid, their wisdom and enthusiasm, as trustees and members of the school boards...[Women] will restore to Judaism, purified from the dross of former ages, its fire and inwardness which inspire all to make noble sacrifices, not only of their substance, but of their personal service. From our magnificent temples they will again transplant genuine religious spirit into the bosom of families, they will cause Judaism to be placed in its proper light before the world, they will be instrumental in bringing its influence to bear among the people at large by educating a generation, which, with the old fidelity and enthusiasm will exclaim: "All that God has spoken we will do."

confer on all matters with the superintendent of the Sabbath school. She should see that her children consider that the Sabbath School is just as important as the daily school, that they attend with the same regularity, that no dancing, music, or other lessons take the precedence. That the mother does not sleep so long on Sunday morning, that it is impossible for the children to have their breakfast and be on time for the Sabbath school; and that the mother impresses upon her child that it is even a greater disgrace not to behave well in the Sabbath School than in the daily school, because the teacher sacrifices his time and convenience in most cases, without any compensation, to come and give the children religious instruction.

Q: Should she occupy the pulpit?

A: I do not believe that Jewish women should occupy the pulpit. There are so many ways in which she can do good in the congregation, that she may leave the pulpit to men.

Q: How can societies composed of Jewish women be made of greater benefit to the synagogue?

A: All Jewish women should belong to the Council of Jewish Women, and if possible to a study circle, thereby growing in knowledge and understanding of their religion, and becoming more intelligent members of the congregation. They should make a study of philanthropy, and volunteer to do practical work such as visiting among the poor, thus helping to make the

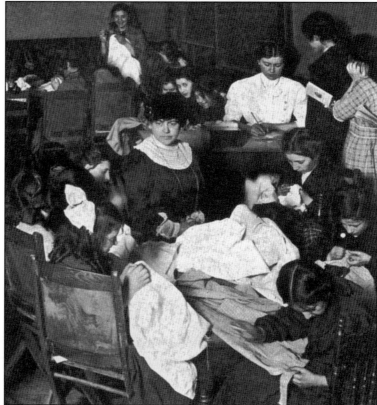

Rochester's early social service agencies made great efforts to channel potentially wayward youthful energies of Russian Jewish children into supervised and productive pursuits. The Boy's Evening Home, founded in 1887 by the First Unitarian Church, sponsored woodworking and other classes for boys. The founding of the Baden Street Settlement in 1901 by the temple Sisterhood marked a turning point in the involvement of B'rith Kodesh with social reform. It sponsored many educational and recreational programs for girls and boys in the Joseph Avenue area, such as this 1915 sewing class. (Courtesy Department of Rare Books and Special Collections, Rush Rhees Library, University of Rochester)

But if Max Landsberg favored advancing the status of women in B'rith Kodesh, his wife, Miriam, took a greater and more direct role in this process. We know relatively little of Miriam Landsberg's background. Born in Germany, she married Landsberg on February 26, 1871, shortly before their departure from Europe. Once in Rochester, she soon became active in philanthropic and women's club circles. In 1889, she became active in the Ethical Club, a women's forum for the discussion of social issues. This was a forerunner of the Women's Educational and Industrial Union, which she served as a vice president. Miriam Landsberg was also a good friend of Susan B. Anthony, and was active with her in the national suffrage campaign. In addition, her numerous philanthropic involvements included service as vice president of the Rochester chapter of the Society for the Prevention of Cruelty to Children as well as of the New York State Conference on Charities and Hospitals. She was also a member of the board of managers of Rochester City Hospital.

Miriam Landsberg was quite active in Jewish affairs. As the first female delegate to a council of the Union of American Hebrew Congregations, she was the first woman to be an accredited delegate at the national convention of any Jewish organization. She addressed the Jewish Women's Congress held in Chicago in 1893, which served as the founding convention of the National Council of Jewish Women. One of the few writings of Miriam Landsberg that has survived is an 1897 interview in the *Reform Advocate* in which she sets forth her views on women in Reform Judaism. Landsberg did not directly challenge male dominance of the lay leadership of congregational life or of the rabbinate. But she insisted that Jewish women needed to amplify and expand on their accustomed roles in Jewish life.

The founding of the B'rith Kodesh Sisterhood in 1892 was Miriam Landsberg's crowning achievement. Not only was she its prime initiator, but she also served as its "moving spirit" during her lifetime. Perhaps the rebuff to women's suffrage within the congregation in May 1891 provided the final impetus to the organization of a broadly organized women's organization within the temple. The Sisterhood had an initial membership of 106, which included almost all of the women in the congregation. Dues were set at ten cents a meeting. Mrs. R. Schatz was the first president, and Miriam Landsberg served as the honorary president. The new organization established committees in the following areas; Prosperity, Maternity, Membership, Visiting, Library, School Books, Sewing School, and School Entertainment. The *Jewish Tidings* of January 27, 1892, announced its formation under the heading, "A Noble Undertaking: The Berith Kodesh Sisterhood Formed":

benevolent institutions of the congregation more effective. They should assist not only with the money, but by trying to educate and elevate the poor, thus avoiding the danger of pauperization.

Ruth Kolko Lebovics as a young woman. (Courtesy Morton Kolko)

Ruth Lebovics,

Memories of the Baden Street Settlement

Ruth Lebovics, born in Rochester to Eastern European Jewish parents in 1903, remembered her early involvement with the Baden Street Settlement and settlement projects at the Gibbs Street Temple in a 1976 interview.

I used to go to the Baden Street Settlement for clubs when I was a very young girl. I used to go to sewing classes over there. And then one day a week we used to walk over the way to B'rith Kodesh for sewing classes. And then we felt we were in a different

Members of an early twentieth-century Sunday school class at Congregation Beth Israel, commonly known as the Leopold Street Shule. Founded in 1874, it was the oldest and one of the most prestigious Orthodox congregations in Rochester. Rabbi Philip S. Bernstein was raised and became Bar Mitzvah in the congregation, and maintained a spiritual and sentimental connection to the Leopold Street Shule until it closed its doors as a Jewish house of worship in 1973. He would regularly take Confirmation classes there to participate in services. The building, which has landmark status, is still standing in downtown Rochester.

The Berith Kodesh Sisterhood was formed at the Assembly Hall last Monday evening. There was a large and enthusiastic attendance. The objects of the society are to develop among its members a warmer and more active interest in the prosperity of the temple, to promote social and friendly intercourse, the higher purposes of life, and mutual improvement among its members, to further works of charity, philanthropy and education in cooperation with the United Jewish Charities, and to lend a helping hand wherever anyone may be in need of material or spiritual assistance.

From the outset, the Sisterhood's activities were many and varied. By 1893, they included distributing schoolbooks, a monthly cultural program, a musical society, and a Shakespeare class. But it was the growing presence of Eastern European Jews in Rochester that provided an impetus for the Sisterhood's most enduring achievement, organizing the Baden Street Settlement, the first settlement house in Rochester. This grew out of the Sewing Club, an activity that prepared young Jewish girls for the duties of motherhood, and children of both sexes for potential future careers as garment workers. But since the classes were held in the temple's Assembly Hall on Gibbs Street, the Sisterhood began to worry when children made their way home to the Joseph Avenue area (the heart of the Russian Jewish community) after dark.

To make its services and classes more accessible to the immigrant community, in April 1901 the B'rith Kodesh Sisterhood established the Social Settlement of Rochester, more commonly known as the Baden Street Settlement, after its headquarters at 152 Baden Street. Though the settlement house had no denominational affiliation, and in time its board would include some of the leading Christian social reformers in the city, its leadership was dominated by the women of B'rith Kodesh. Fannie Garson was its first and long-time president, and all the other officers were prominent members of the B'rith Kodesh Sisterhood. In its first year 150 persons, almost all members of B'rith Kodesh, contributed to the settlement house and its $4000 budget.

Its facilities were open to all, but the overwhelming majority of those who attended the Baden Street Settlement were Jews. As Blake McKelvey, the leading historian of Rochester, has suggested, the first important example of what became known as the "Social Gospel" in Rochester was founded by the women of B'rith Kodesh. Mrs. A. J. "Ray" Wile, the secretary and treasurer of the Baden Street Settlement, expressed the ideals of the organization in its first annual report in 1902:

> We are absolutely non-sectarian. Our desire is to touch the lives of those about us closely, regardless of race, creed, or sex; to devote time and thought to the education and environments of the children of the most congested district of the city; to keep them off the streets and to shorten their idle moments. By teaching them something useful and beautiful we lessen their chances for vice and immorality, and cultivate in them a love and respect for work, which shall make them useful and honest citizens.

In its first year of operations, 300 girls and 60 volunteer teachers participated in the activities of the Baden Street Settlement, which included a daily kindergarten and social hour, as well as classes in sewing, crocheting, basketweaving, darning, buttonholing, shirtwaist making, and several classes in housekeeping. In addition to these practical classes, there were also weekly sessions on elocution and current events, Shakespeare recitations, and even a Hebrew class. There was a penny provident bank, where girls learned lessons on the value of thrift by depositing their spare change. Weekly "heart to heart classes," led by Rochester's female physicians, instructed the girls in the facts of life. A "home art gallery" allowed students to take pictures home to brighten their drab tenements.

By 1904 the facilities were expanded, with shower facilities and more room for sports. Now boys as well as girls participated in the programs of

world. You went there and you felt you were among goyim. I felt very different when I came, but I liked to go, and they taught us sewing. I remember once they took us all to Seabreeze. I went with my friends; I never went alone. There was a whole group of girls and it was a very, very big walk to Gibbs Street. We were poor kids, and we didn't have many privileges, and so we came here and the teachers were very nice to us. And sweet and pleasant, and one year we got this lovely picnic, which was a very big treat. The building was different. It was austere; it was very clean. It had big, high rooms. And the ladies who were there were all dressed up like rich ladies. You felt like you were going to another world. It was nice, but then we came back home again.

the settlement house. From the beginning, the Baden Street Settlement had a milk station to distribute milk to mothers, and it soon hired a visiting nurse to instruct them on proper hygiene. In 1908, the Baden Street Dispensary opened, providing free medical care services to the neighborhood. The next year the settlement opened a day nursery at 13 Vienna Street, where, for five cents a day, young children received baths, meals, naps, and play periods. A music class, which would evolve into the Hochstein Music School, opened in the years before 1915. By that year there were over two thousand visits to the dispensary, and over one hundred young children in the day nursery. The Baden Street Settlement had become a permanent feature of Rochester's social service network. It will celebrate its centennial in 2001, and if the ethnic background of its clientele has changed over the years, its basic purpose of assisting the needy in the northwest area of Rochester has not. It remains the most lasting monument of the commitment of the B'rith Kodesh Sisterhood to social involvement.

The importance of the founding of the B'rith Kodesh Sisterhood and the Baden Street Settlement went beyond their significance in the advancement of the role of women in the congregation. In many ways, they were the initial moves in an expansion of the spiritual life of the temple beyond the bounds of Rochester's German-Jewish community. They represented the beginning of a redefinition of the meaning of Reform Judaism as fellowship with the wider Jewish world. But before these attitudes were more widely accepted within B'rith Kodesh, there would be a difficult period of adjustment between Rochester's German and Russian Jews.

B'rith Kodesh and the New Immigration

The organization of the Baden Street Settlement was just one sign of how rapidly the ethnic composition of Rochester's Jewish population was changing. Eastern European Jews started to arrive in the United States in large numbers in 1880. In Rochester and elsewhere they soon outnumbered the older Jewish communities several-fold. In 1875 there were probably 3,000 Jews in the city. There were 5,000 by 1890, and by 1910, 11,000. B'rith Kodesh, which for many decades had been the only strong congregation in the city, found itself with numerous rivals. Congregation Beth Israel, also known as the

Leopold Garson, born in Dutweiler in Alsace in 1824, came to America in 1838 and to Rochester in 1866. President of B'rith Kodesh from 1880-82, and again from 1888–91, he was also president of the Jewish Orphan Asylum of Western New York, and of the United Jewish Charities of Rochester. At his death in 1892 he was eulogized as one of the most respected and honored men in Rochester's Jewish community.

Leopold Street Shule, was founded in 1874. Many other Orthodox Eastern European congregations followed, at least six by 1900, and ten by the early 1920s.

From the vantage of many B'rith Kodesh members in the 1880s, the Eastern European Jewish immigration was troubling. The newcomers were poor. They were overwhelmingly Orthodox in their religious practices. And if they had drifted away from religious observance, they were likely to adhere to the socialist, anarchist or labor movements, all attachments perhaps even more objectionable than religious traditionalism in the eyes of many B'rith Kodesh members. Finally, because they arrived in far greater numbers than did the earlier generation of German Jews, they were able to form their own more or less self-contained communities, where pressures to assimilate to American life could be mediated through a network of communal institutions.

Many B'rith Kodesh members found the presence of Eastern European Jews an affront and an embarrassment. A remarkably ignorant and disparaging 1888 article in the *Jewish Tidings* described Yiddish as a "very queer Hebrew" jargon, and the Lower East Side of Manhattan as Hell's Half-Acre:

> Hester Street should certainly have one word in common for dirt, for they have the thing in common. It is no exaggeration to say that in dirt they live, in dirt they move, in dirt they have their being. Dirty babies, clad in a single garment, crawl over the pavements, dirty children play in the dirty street, and dirty men walk into dirty houses with very dirty shoes. All the people are smoky looking, all the houses grimy, all the cellars "gummy" and nearly all the people look as if they had not changed their clothes in months…To an American it is a mystery that people can be contented with such dirt. Yet they are. Cleanliness is no necessity to them as it is to Americans and the people of Western Europe. In all the thousands that crowd Hester Street of a mild evening, you will not see twenty in clean clothing. They do not feel the need of it.

Given these sentiments, it is not surprising that the *Jewish Tidings* opposed Eastern European immigration. When Louis Wiley, the paper's editor, spoke at B'rith Kodesh in late 1890, he stated that the influx of Russian immigrants was a "serious embarrassment" that retarded the progress of American Jews and their acceptance within the best circles of American society. Wiley felt that he and most other American Jews had nothing in common with Eastern European Jews save their religion. (Though given Wiley's ultra-Reform stance, there was likely no topic on

Emma Goldman came to Rochester from St. Petersburg in the 1880s as a teenager. Her years in the city included a memorable confrontation with B'rith Kodesh president Leopold Garson. (Courtesy International Institute of Social History, Amsterdam, Holland, and Candace Falk, Emma Goldman Papers)

which he and the majority of the Jewish immigrants would have disagreed more vehemently than their respective understandings of Judaism.) Wiley called on B'rith Kodesh members to "exert ourselves to prevent their coming here." While the *Tidings* was predictably hostile toward suggestions to settle Russian Jews in Palestine, the journal was enthusiastic about the plan of French philanthropist Baron Maurice de Hirsch to resettle Eastern European Jews in South American agricultural colonies.

Only a minority of B'rith Kodesh members supported the exclusion of Eastern European Jews from the United States. Even those most hostile to the influx of Russian Jews to America were shocked and outraged by the pogroms and restrictive decrees promulgated against Jews after 1881. The *Jewish Tidings* acknowledged that if their best efforts to prevent Russian Jews from entering the United States failed, American Jews had the responsibility to "care for them, to educate them, to bring them if possible up to our own standard."

Most B'rith Kodesh members saw the United States as the natural haven for their persecuted brethren. Rabbi Landsberg spoke frequently and eloquently on the persecution of Jews in Russia, and argued that American Jews had a deep religious obligation to help the new arrivals become "a credit to our religion and our country." Impressed by the intelligence of the recent immigrants, he reported favorably on the work of the Educational Alliance to produce newly minted Americans on New York City's Lower East Side. The temple also contributed to relief funds for Russian Jews, especially in the aftermath of the Kishinev pogrom of 1903.

By 1890, the primary social connection between German and Russian Jews in Rochester was respectively, as the dispensers and recipients of tzedekah. Before the 1920s, churches, synagogues, and individual ethnic organizations often assumed the major responsibility for providing aid to the newly arrived, the indigent, the ill, and the aged. B'rith Kodesh took its obligations to the new immigrants very seriously. Caring for the less fortunate members of the community had been an important part of the congregation's work since its founding. But by the late 1880s Rochester's Jewish charities were becoming increasingly institutionalized. In 1879, a meeting at B'rith Kodesh founded the Jewish Orphan Asylum

The Stein-Bloch Company at 140 North St. Paul Street was one of the largest garment factories in Rochester at the turn of the twentieth century. The Stein-Bloch Company was organized in 1883, a successor to the firms of G.& J. Wile, Cauffman & Co., Stein & Adler, and Stein & Solomon, all associated with families active in B'rith Kodesh. The principal partner of the Stein-Bloch Company, Nathan Stein (1828–1908), was a longtime member of B'rith Kodesh.

Association of New York, serving all of western New York. In 1884 the association opened an orphanage that could accommodate up to forty children on St. Paul Street in 1884, with Rabbi Landsberg serving as its president.

With the establishment of the United Jewish Charities in 1882, B'rith Kodesh created an umbrella organization to coordinate the activities of the Hebrew Benevolent Society, the Hebrew Ladies' Benevolent Society, and the Jewish Ladies' Aid Hospital Society. Under the leadership of Leopold Garson, who also served two terms as president of B'rith Kodesh, the United Hebrew Charities increasingly focused on the problems of recent arrivals from Eastern Europe, generally by finding them work in Rochester's booming garment industry, and providing them with financial support, clothing, and free coal.

The work of the United Jewish Charities involved a great deal of careful sifting through of requests for assistance. In the late 1880s the outlay of funds approached $3,000 per annum. Between October 1 and March 1, 1892, 106 families, containing 262 individuals, approached the organization for assistance. Eighty-five were given help. One typical case concerned a recently arrived family of ten, which received $130 and three and a half tons of coal over the six-month period. Well over half this money,

$77, was given to the family in the first month of eligibility. By the end of the six-month period, the head of the household had been retrained from a fish-packer to a garment worker, and was well on the way to economic independence. The charities refused assistance, however, to nineteen families, often "warning them out"—strongly encouraging them to leave the city. This was the case with a family of eight in 1903. Having found them "very shiftless and unwilling to work," the president of the charities suggested "that they be sent back to New York, whence they came."

The work of the United Jewish Charities often emphasized the gap between B'rith Kodesh members and the new immigrants. Although most charity workers undoubtedly derived their motivation from a sense of Jewish obligation and a genuine sympathy for those less fortunate, much of their philanthropy still struck its beneficiaries as being somewhat chilly. Landsberg complained that many Russian Jews failed "to understand this sensible mode of assistance and become dissatisfied with the scientific application of help which is often compelled to seem cruel rather than kind."

Relations between B'rith Kodesh members and the Russian Jews were complicated by their workplace interactions. The German Jews owned the garment factories, while the Russian Jews often worked as laborers in the same factories. Leopold Garson, the first president of the United Jewish Charities, had a reputation as a considerable philanthropist, tireless in his efforts to aid the Russian Jews. As one tribute put it, when Garson was determined to dispense his largess, no dwelling place "was too filthy to keep him out." But Garson was also one of the most successful garment manufacturers in Rochester, and he kept his distance from his workers.

Garson's most famous employee was the future anarchist Emma Goldman, who came to Rochester from Russia as a teenager in 1885. Securing a position with Garson, she found the work harder and the conditions more oppressive than those she had encountered in St. Petersburg. Her boss did not allow his workers to leave the shop without permission, not even to go to the toilet. When she asked Garson for a raise, she found him predictably officious and dismissive. Without even asking her to sit down, he told her she that had "rather extravagant tastes" and ordered her to return to work. She quit his employ shortly thereafter. One did not need to be as radical as Goldman to feel that the German Jewish garment entrepreneurs of Rochester treated their Russian brethren with disdain. Another Rochester Jew, the Russian-born Louis Lipsky, later a prominent Zionist leader, wrote in 1899 that "The sympathy which formerly existed between the rich and the poor Jew owing to their persecution by the common enemy is now almost entirely supplanted by cold charity and colder philanthropy."

By 1890 labor problems were growing in Rochester's garment industry. Rochester's garment manufacturers generally believed that their obligations to their workers ended with the payment of wages. They gave little attention to working conditions, especially within the dense network of subcontractors' sweat shops that flourished in Rochester, as in all other centers of garment manufacture. The hard working conditions gave disgruntled workers ample reason to organize unions, and the Knights of Labor gathered strength in the city's garment factories during the 1880s. To combat the Knights of Labor, twenty-one major garment firms in the city banded together in 1890 to form the Rochester Clothier's Exchange. Sol Wile, a lawyer, was the principal organizer of the exchange. Henry Michaels was its first president, and Joseph Caufmann its treasurer. Other officials included Abram Adler, Max Brickner, Bernard Rothschild, and Nathan Stein. All were prominent members of B'rith Kodesh.

The *Jewish Tidings* applauded the efforts of the Clothier's Exchange and their success in shattering the influence of the Knights of Labor in Rochester. The journal was strongly opposed to organized labor, and regularly linked anarchism, atheism, labor unions, and the immigration of foreigners. In 1891 the *American Hebrew* quoted a Baltimore rabbi who spoke of a Jewish obligation to right wrongs, and more specifically, to limit the power of business over politics. The *Jewish Tidings* rejected this as the "purest bosh," arguing that it wasn't "the business of Jews to right social wrongs. They should aid all good citizens in this object, not as Jews but as citizens. The journal asked, "What has Judaism as such to do with 'personal ends and the gains of corporations?'"

In the late nineteenth century B'rith Kodesh was strongly identified with the wealthy German Jewish garment manufacturers that dominated its affairs. They did not welcome overtly political sermons that challenged their interests. Landsberg gave little offense in this regard. As a "mugwump" with liberal Republican politics, his concern with social issues was largely limited to such questions as municipal corruption and prison reform. When he did comment on economic problems, he mainly offered a critique of the moral failings of paupers and their inability to adjust to the new world of industrial capitalism. Both the religious implications of radical Reform and the social standing of the congregation acted to distance B'rith Kodesh from the larger Jewish community of Rochester.

Landsberg in Twilight

By 1901 Max Landsberg had been rabbi at B'rith Kodesh for thirty years. Though many members still greatly respected him, an increasingly influential segment of the congregation felt that Landsberg stood in the way of its spiritual and demographic growth. Landsberg was never offered

Senior rabbi at B'rith Kodesh until 1915, Rabbi Max Landsberg remained ever resolute in his support of radical Reform.

lifetime tenure, and periodically went before the board to have his contract renewed. (By the turn of the century, Landsberg felt these supplications to be increasingly humiliating.) Some found him out of touch, and prone to repeating himself. Landsberg preached the same sermon on more than one occasion.

Time had done little to moderate his radical Reform convictions. The emergence of Zionism seemed to confirm all of his worst fears about the direction of Judaism. Despite the burgeoning Jewish population in Rochester, the congregation's membership in the decades near the turn of the century remained fixed at around 180 to 200 families.

Some members began to blame B'rith Kodesh's stagnation on Landsberg's hostility, or at least his lack of enthusiasm, toward welcoming Russian Jews into the congregation.

Landsberg based his generally hostile attitude toward Eastern European Jews on his conviction that their religious views would retard the progress of Judaism. However, he welcomed into the congregation those Russian Jews who were willing to adopt radical Reform. For example, Landsberg praised as a "man of enlightened religious views" Solomon Schifrin, a leader of the city's small circle of *maskilim*, exponents of the Russian *Haskalah* (enlightenment). In the 1890s Schifrin served as the liaison between B'rith Kodesh and the United Jewish Charities and the Yiddish-speaking Jews of Rochester. Rabbi Landsberg's most important protégé, Samuel Goldensohn, was born in Kalwaria, Poland, in 1878. After arriving in Rochester in 1890, his family joined B'rith Kodesh. Tutored by Landsberg, Goldensohn entered Hebrew Union College in 1904. After his graduation he enjoyed a distinguished rabbinic career, capped by his appointment as senior rabbi at Temple Emanu-El in New York in 1934. Goldensohn's mentor would have been proud of his pupil's support of the anti-Zionist American Council for Judaism in the mid 1940s.

Philip Present, the first Eastern European Jew to exert a major influence in B'rith Kodesh, was born in Russian Poland in 1856, and arrived in Rochester in 1884. Present long tried to bridge the gap between Russian and German Jews by working at such institutions as the Judean Club, a cultural organization formed in 1895. In 1907, Present, by this time a member of the B'rith Kodesh Board of Trustees, was the major benefactor and first president of the successor to the Judean Club, the Young Men's Jewish Association, commonly known as the "JY." (Because of Landsberg's steadfast opposition to the use of the term "Hebrew" to describe Jews, the organization in Rochester did not adopt

Born in the Russian section of Poland in 1856, Philip Present was the first Jew of Eastern European background to play a significant role at B'rith Kodesh. He came to Rochester in 1884, and became a successful jeweler. He was active in the formation of the Baden Street Settlement. As the local secretary of the Industrial Removal Office he helped to resettle hundreds of New York City Jews in Rochester and assisted them in finding housing and employment. As a member of the B'rith Kodesh Board of Trustees, he was an influential advocate for increased assistance and better relations with the Russian Jews of Rochester.

The JY's headquarters at 3 Franklin Square. Organized in 1907, the JY was among the first institutions in the city to bridge the gap between Reform and Orthodox Jews. From the beginning, the JY had a girls' auxiliary, and in 1936 became the Jewish Young Men's and Women's Association.

the more common "YMHA.")

After 1900 Landsberg and the congregation became increasingly estranged. This first manifested itself in a renewed quarrel over Sunday services. Landsberg resisted a request from the board to start Sunday services during the religious year of 1898–1899. The board complained in March 1899 that "they cannot help stating that the complete ignoring of their request in the matter…has been a painful surprise to them, the members feeling that personally and as officers representing the Congregation, they are entitled to more consideration on the part of their minister than this treatment has shown." They went on to add that Landsberg was not to assume that the temple was his property.

Landsberg had been so effective in teaching his determinedly anti-ceremonial brand of Judaism to several generations at B'rith Kodesh that his opposition to Sunday services must have struck many as little more than a personal eccentricity. At the same time, a lack of vitality in the spiritual life of the congregation no doubt convinced many members that something dramatic had to be done. In a congregational letter of 1901, Landsberg pleaded with the congregation for more participation, "if you, my friends, could be induced to be a little more interested in our religious affairs, we could not help being successful in *every* respect." For many, Sunday services remained the answer.

Another experiment with services on Sunday started in the fall of 1900, but by January 1901 they were discontinued due to unsatisfactory attendance. Landsberg's lack of enthusiasm was widely seen as the reason for the failure of the experiment. In June 1901, a committee appointed to bring "more life into Congregation affairs" recommended that an assistant rabbi be hired to deliver lectures on Sunday, with Landsberg's salary to be adjusted downward to cover the additional expense. What happened next was not clear, but dissatisfaction continued. In the fall of 1902, the congregation held a special meeting on "the indifference of the members of the congregation and their families to the purpose of the congregation" and how to arouse "a living interest" in temple affairs.

Landsberg's stubborn refusal to be dictated to by the congregation could at times be admirable, especially in his defense of the freedom of the pulpit. Among Landsberg's closest clerical associates in Rochester was the Rev. William T. Brown of Plymouth Congregational Church. After Brown preached at B'rith Kodesh on February 25, 1900, he wrote to the B'rith Kodesh Board of Trustees, claiming that he had never "met a minister in any religious fold with whom I felt so fully in accord as I do your eminent and gracious rabbi." Brown agreed so fully with Landsberg's view of the Higher Criticism and the social function of religion that he effused "there is every good reason" that the two congregations "should recognize a common faith." (A merger of liberal Christianity and Judaism was never a concern of Landsberg, who felt that attempts to construct a non-dogmatic Christianity were doomed to failure, and that genuine religious liberals should simply adopt Reform Judaism.)

Unfortunately for his good relations with B'rith Kodesh, Brown was a Christian Socialist, who actively called for the destruction of capitalism and supported an American Federation of Labor boycott against Rochester's garment manufacturers. This did not sit well with the B'rith Kodesh Board of Trustees. In May 1901, they banned Brown from the temple and from future appearances with Landsberg. In response, Landsberg wrote to the trustees asking them to reconsider their "hasty" resolution. While he acknowledged that he too was "diametrically opposed" to many of Rev. Brown's teachings, he argued that appearing with Brown in public forums did not imply an endorsement of his views:

It is the glory of our Country that it allows freedom of speech to all; and this is certainly the best safety valve for society. The most violent explosions of "socialistic-temper" are not by far as dangerous as repression. The truth will certainly best be served by free discussion…I am diametrically opposed to many of his teachings: but why should we set ourselves up as judges of the opinions of our fellow men?… We Jews ought to be particularly careful, for more than any other class of men, we had to suffer from just such prejudice and intolerance; and we are still suffering from it.

The Board of Trustees backed down, and Brown appeared at the 1901 Union Thanksgiving service. This was surely one of Landsberg's finest moments.

Landsberg won the battle over Rev. Brown, but he was losing the war to control the destiny of the congregation. The effort to find a younger, American-raised rabbi to replace, or at least supplement, Landsberg gathered strength after 1905. That year, the Prussian-born Max Moll, the assistant rabbi since 1886, was let go. In June 1906, the Board of Trustees ordered Landsberg to hire a young Hebrew Union College (HUC) graduate as an assistant, but he was unable to reach an agreement with the prime candidate, Rabbi Louis Mendoza.

The following year, B'rith Kodesh hired Felix Levy, a recent HUC graduate, as the new assistant rabbi. Levy's hiring, coming several months after the congregation passed a resolution deploring the creeping Zionist influence at Hebrew Union College, is somewhat surprising. Born in New York City to Russian immigrant parents, Levy was one of the earliest Reform rabbis to support Zionism. Caught between pro- and anti-Landsberg factions in the congregation, his one-year contract was not renewed. After leaving B'rith Kodesh, Levy had a distinguished career at Congregation Emanu-El in Chicago, and served a term as president of the CCAR in the mid-1930s.

In the fall of 1908, B'rith Kodesh hired another HUC graduate as assistant rabbi, the Odessa-born Nathan Krass. If Krass stayed clear of Zionism, he was extremely active in the Baden Street Settlement and other outreach programs serving Eastern European Jews, as well as social reform efforts in general. Krass was clearly the sort

Nathan Krass in a 1912 photograph. Social justice was a primary concern of Krass, assistant rabbi at B'rith Kodesh from 1908–1909. He later became senior rabbi at Temple Emanu-El in New York City. (Courtesy American Jewish Archives)

of young and socially progressive rabbi the congregation now wanted. But when B'rith Kodesh tried to extend his contract in November 1909, he left for a position with Temple Emanu-El in New York, where he was senior rabbi from 1923 to 1934.

Krass was active in the growing circle of liberal clergy in Rochester who were interested in social change. A national center of the "Social Gospel," Rochester was home to one of its best-known figures, the Protestant theologian Walter Rauschenbusch. Rauschenbusch spoke at B'rith Kodesh on at least one occasion, a 1913 conference on liberal religion.

The Baden Street Settlement was the link between B'rith Kodesh and Rochester's other social reformers, many of whom also became active in the settlement house. In 1906, the settlement house started to publish a bulletin. In 1908, its editorial board expanded beyond the B'rith Kodesh Sisterhood and, renamed *Common Good*, it emerged as Rochester's leading journal of progressive reform.

As the ambitions of the Baden Street Settlement grew in scope, the women of the Sisterhood and their male supporters became advocates for, as well as benefactors of, Rochester's poor Jews. The work in the settlement house grew beyond the mere distribution of clothing, holding of English language classes, or encouraging providence and thrift among the new immigrants. Settlement workers now addressed such issues as the inadequate housing and diet of the immigrants, the evil of child labor, the conditions of work, and the rights of working people.

Rabbi Krass touched on many on these questions in a 1908 article in *Common Good*. He called for curbing the power of trusts and monopolies, and offered a ringing condemnation of the excesses of unfettered capitalism, "the mighty monster, that powerful Moloch that swallows up in his industrial maw the children of the immigrant." In a 1909 sermon at the temple, Krass also criticized the lax morals of Rochester's wealthy Jews, who all too often, he said, "disregarded the common tenets of humanity" and often showed little regard for ethical standards. In contrast, Krass argued, Eastern European Jews might have rough exteriors, but they were deeply moral. As Jews, the members of B'rith Kodesh had an obligation to associate with their Jewish brethren and to rediscover an authentically religious way of life. This was dramatically new language for a B'rith Kodesh rabbi.

In July 1910 B'rith Kodesh hired Horace J. Wolf as assistant rabbi. His contract was extended several times, and in 1915 Wolf succeeded Landsberg as senior rabbi of B'rith Kodesh. It seems that Landsberg's resignation was forced. A committee appointed in March 1913 to remedy the "lack of interest in the religious life of the congregation" issued its recommendations in October of that year. Though its suggestions are not revealed in the minutes, within a month Landsberg offered his resignation (unanimously accepted by the board) to take effect March 1, 1915. Though Wolf was the obvious candidate to succeed Landsberg, he was not officially named Landsberg's successor until December 1914, the delay probably an effort not to ruffle the lame duck's feathers any more than was necessary.

Landsberg's last years were embittered. The death of Miriam Landsberg in 1912 was a severe blow. He later wrote to his children that for some time after her passing he did not think that he could continue to go on living. Though he remained in Rochester, he largely severed his connection to B'rith Kodesh after 1915. Indeed, his retreat from the congregation probably started right after he handed in his resignation in late 1913. As rabbi emeritus, Landsberg refused to sit on the bimah when his successor presided at services. Instead, sitting in the congregation, he often ostentatiously read a newspaper during Wolf's sermons. When Wolf's attempt to establish an eternal light in the sanctuary was challenged by some influential B'rith Kodesh members, Landsberg evidently took it upon himself to switch it off whenever he could, so the B'rith Kodesh sanctuary had the odd spectacle of an eternal light that regularly was turned off and on.

Landsberg's final years were burdened with the knowledge that he had lost the major battle of his life, the struggle to purge Judaism of its national and ceremonial elements. In 1922 he wrote HUC President Emeritus Kaufmann Kohler that he was "very disgusted by the present condition of Judaism." Reform Judaism, he believed, had reached its height during the heyday of David Einhorn and Emil Hirsch, and had been in retreat ever since. Landsberg wanted nothing to do with a Reform movement whose leaders were willing to tolerate Zionism.

Landsberg instructed his children that his entire funeral service should consist of a recitation of the 91st and 23rd psalms. Above all, he did not want it to include the Kaddish, which he considered a "base superstition," and regretted having included it in his prayerbook. Neither did he want his Yahrzeit (anniversary of his death) to be observed. He called on his children to burn his lectures and sermons, and he requested a small, private funeral, in a place other than the temple where he had been rabbi for almost half a century. When Max Landsberg died in December 1927, this final request was not honored.

The Great Fire

The most traumatic event that can occur in the life of any religious congregation is the destruction of its sanctuary. On April 13, 1909, a large fire, spread by high wind, whipped through several blocks in the area of Main and Gibbs streets. About noon, sparks from the Palmer Building, at the corner of Gibbs and Main, spread to the temple building. Within minutes, the temple was a complete loss, a burnt-out hulk from which little could be

In this remarkable sequence of photographs, Alfred Stone, photographer for the Rochester Herald, *captured the devastating 1909 fire that destroyed the Gibbs Street temple. (Courtesy Stone Negative Collection, Rochester Museum and Science Center, Rochester, New York)*

salvaged. In an emergency meeting held that day in the law offices of Wile & Oviati, the Board of Trustees agreed to hold temporary services at the Unitarian Church, a congregation with a long-standing relationship with B'rith Kodesh. The trustees were also deeply grateful that a total of twelve Rochester churches offered the use of their premises until B'rith Kodesh could find permanent quarters; these helpful churches included the Unitarian Church, St. Peter's Church, Central Church, First Presbyterian, Asbury Methodist, First Universalist, Evangelical German Lutheran Church, First Baptist, and the Second Baptist Church of Rochester. Some large congregational meetings were held at the Universalist Church, while the religious school met temporarily at the house of Louis Stein, at 50 Gibbs Street. In May 1909, the Board of Trustees agreed to rebuild on the same spot, aided by $70,000 they collected in fire insurance. If the architectural style of the new building was broadly similar to its predecessor, there were also significant differences. The tower on the left side of the facade was lower and less pointed. A new high tower was added to the right side. The windows and the doors of the facade also underwent changes in their shape and number. In October 1910, the new sanctuary was dedicated.

Horace Wolf: The Rabbi as Progressive

Horace Wolf, the new senior rabbi of B'rith Kodesh, was born in Cincinnati, Ohio on June 15, 1885, the youngest of ten sons of Moses and Jeanette Mass Wolf. Wolf was the first American-born senior rabbi of B'rith Kodesh. He was probably also the first of eastern European background. Wolf jointly attended the University of Cincinnati and Hebrew Union College, and was ordained a rabbi in 1908. After one year as an assistant rabbi in West Lafayette, Indiana, he came to Rochester in the summer of 1910. Wolf lettered in football while at the University of Cincinnati, an accomplishment remembered with considerable awe by his successor, Philip Bernstein, as a successful accommodation to American society beyond the wildest dreams of most Jewish boys. Indeed Wolf displayed a Teddy Roosevelt-like robustness. He was an exemplar of the "muscular Judaism" that in the early twentieth century replaced the somewhat forbidding and austere countenance of classical Reform.

Young, outgoing, and American-born, Wolf seemed to be the antithesis of Landsberg. Wolf's religious views represent a modest reaction against the deritualized Judaism of classical Reform. In one of Wolf's first articles, published in the *American Hebrew* in 1909, he criticized the "hyper-rationalism" of radicals who called for the abandonment of all Jewish ceremonies. "When a religion is reduced to a mere theology," Wolf warned, "its death-knell is sounded." But if

For Horace Wolf, the continued relevance of Reform Judaism required a grounding in the social realities of urban life in the early twentieth century. His commitments to the agenda of progressive reform, and to expanding the membership of the congregation beyond wealthy German-Jewish families, were two related means toward reaching this goal.

105

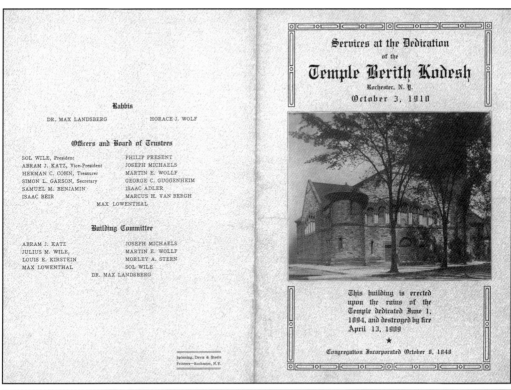

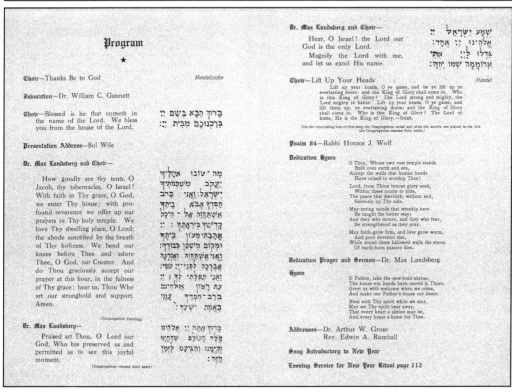

To the strains of Mendelssohn and Handel, the rebuilt Gibbs Street Temple was dedicated on Erev Rosh Hashanah, October 3, 1910.

The Gibbs Street Temple, home of B'rith Kodesh from 1894 to 1962. Though the reconstruction of the temple retained the neo-Romanesque style of the building destroyed in the fire, there were significant differences in some important details; a gentler slope in the roof, an expanded number of second-story windows, an elimination of the foyer entrance, and a flatter and more rounded cupola on the left tower.

Wolf wished to inject an element of ritualism into religious services, he remained loyal to the non-Talmudic and prophetic tenets of classical Reform. Where Landsberg's version of classical Reform was severe and critical, Wolf's Judaism was positive, hearty, and largely non-polemical. Landsberg was generally remembered for his arrogance and distance from the congregation, while Wolf was seen as a person of great warmth and charismatic gifts who worked hard to attract new members and constituencies to B'rith Kodesh.

Wolf wasted little time in trying to implement a new vision of the Reform temple as a community center. In early 1912, barely two years after his arrival in Rochester, Wolf was a member of a committee that recommended setting up a civics class, a reading room, a nursery, and a monthly congregational bulletin. (A bulletin appeared for a time, but was abandoned after a few months.) Wolf next called for the establishment of a class for the blind, the building of a playground on temple premises, and the holding of dances two nights a week in the Assembly Hall. The committee that proposed these changes was itself an indication of the changes underway at B'rith Kodesh. It was chaired by Sara Wile Hays, who several months earlier, on December 3, 1911, had become the first woman appointed to the Board of Trustees. Another member of the committee was Philip Present, the first Russian Jew to play a prominent role in B'rith Kodesh affairs. Drawing on these new constituencies was critical to Wolf's success in changing the established way of doing things at B'rith Kodesh.

Horace J. Wolf,
"Democracy and the
Reform Temple,"
American Hebrew,
February 12, 1915

The most cursory study of the Prophets, so frequently described by Reform Rabbis as their "spiritual ancestors," reveals their close relationship with the poor, the burden-bearers and the toilers…But the most significant fact about the latter-day "descendants" of the ancient prophets is that their preachments are delivered to the ears of those who are not poor, that the institution in which they labor is the meeting-place of the rich. Is it purely a matter of accident that every Reform Congregation is made up of people in comfortable circumstances? The Orthodox Synagogue, on the other hand, whatever else it was, or is, represented and still represents the democratic spirit; but the Reform Temple, with the rarest of exceptions has become a class institution...

Has your Temple ever made a systematic attempt to link the Jewish factory hands, the Jewish servant-girls (a startling idea, this last, is it not?) with the synagogue? There are hundreds of young men and women in every large city who have drifted away, or become alienated from the Orthodox Synagogue—and who are not sought out by the Temple...In this respect the Temple lags far behind the churches; many Jewish housewives can tell of personal visits to their new maids by ministers and priests, with hearty invitations to join the church; but who

108

Neighborhood Dance Committee

In January, 1914, the Neighborhood Dance was inaugurated to give young people the opportunity to dance in a clean, decent environment under proper supervision. The Committee which launched the experiment consisted of Mrs. J. M. Garson, Mrs. S. L. Garson, Mrs. G. Steinfeld and Rabbi Horace Wolf. The institution became an immediate success. The dance is held every Saturday night, in the Assembly Hall, from October to May. This year the attendance to January first averaged one hundred and eighty-five; for a few weeks the number fell below that average because of the conflicting attraction of the basket-ball season. With the close of the latter season, however, each Saturday night has seen the Assembly Hall crowded beyond capacity. The boys and girls have requested the Committee to continue the dances through the summer.

A rest room for the use of the girls was furnished out of a fund accumulated from the nominal admission fee of fifteen cents; this room has been very much appreciated. The pleasant surroundings afford an excellent opportunity for the chaperones to become better acquainted with the girls.

The B'rith Kodesh Sisterhood regularly sponsored chaperoned socials, such as this dance party depicted in the 1918–1919 Sisterhood Annual Report.

Wolf found the social commitments of Reform Judaism to be out of date. He believed that the movement's message and audience needed to be renewed. Reform Judaism could only regain its relevance if the temple stood once again at the center of Jewish community life. Instead, Wolf argued, Reform Judaism had built splendid edifices that were shuttered six days out of seven. Wolf recommended taking a page from the institutional church

A playground at School No. 9, a largely Jewish public school in the Joseph Avenue area. The establishment of playgrounds for immigrant children was a prime concern of Rabbi Horace Wolf, a strong believer in the educational and moral value of supervised recreation. (Courtesy Stone Negative Collection, Rochester Museum and Science Center, Rochester, New York)

movement of the early twentieth century, by providing an array of social services to expand the reach of the congregation. He advocated the temple as community house, offering a range of classes, lectures, and sporting activities to the entire Jewish community.

The Reform temple had become "a class institution," according to Wolf, run by wealthy Jews for wealthy Jews. With its high membership fees, it was "a luxury beyond the reach of the masses." Wolf decried the growing suburbanization of Reform Judaism as another means of distancing the temple from Russian Jews. The annual Confirmation service, he charged in a very controversial article in *American Hebrew*, had become another instance of the combination of religious laxness and conspicuous consumption all too characteristic of Reform Judaism. Too many congregations, he said, confused their fiscal strength with their spiritual health.

Somewhat ironically, the first lasting practical consequence of Wolf's rabbinate was the introduction of Sunday services on a permanent basis. Landsberg's diminished power after 1910 removed the last significant impediment to Sunday services. Rabbi Wolf evidently had no strong feelings about the issue, and on November 5, 1911, the Board of Trustees voted to experiment with having the main service on Sunday.

Three services on the weekend—Friday night, Saturday morning, and Sunday morning—stretched thin the resources of the congregation, and Friday services were suspended in December 1912. The 5–3 vote of the trustees, however, reveals the extent to which the Sunday service question divided the membership. In December 1913, the congregation was tallied on which combination of services they preferred—Friday and Saturday, Saturday and Sunday, or Friday and Sunday. Though the combination of Saturday and Sunday won a fairly thin plurality of 44 percent in the three-way race, opposition to Sunday services remained strong. While 80 percent

ever heard of a Reform Rabbi following this practice?...

Any minister who has come into contact with organized labor or with socialistic societies knows how severe is their arraignment of the church as a class organization, and of the clergy as mouthpieces of capital. The Temple and the Rabbi must beware lest they too come to be included in this indictment. In view of the growing number of Jews in these organizations, if the Rabbis are to combat the extension of this indictment to the Temple, they must concern themselves more than they have in the past with the social and industrial questions of their communities...

Judaism has always stood for democracy and an institution which is organized to further the faith must overcome class-consciousness in itself and its agent. For class-consciousness is like a stoppage of the arteries. It always means an atrophy of the part affected and its isolation from the common life…The motto I would like to offer to every Reform Temple, which I would urge it to chisel over its doors and the spirit which I would insist should animate its every purpose is: "Here let no Jew feel himself strange."

A. M. BERINSTEIN

Artistic Designer of

Ladies' Fine Tailor-Made Garments

Suites 317-324 Mercantile Building
Main, cor. North St.

ROCHESTER, N. Y.

A. M. BERINSTEIN

THE original of the illustration shown above is well and favorably known to the ladies of the social set in Rochester as a designer and modeller of "smart garments." Mr. Berinstein came to this country at the age of 16 years from Russia, where he was born and educated.

Starting in the "Ladies' Tailoring" business on East Main Street in 1891, Mr. Berinstein during the next seven years built up such a large clientele that a more suitable location was necessary, and the recently vacated home at 119 East Avenue was occupied in 1898.

Mr. Berinstein has recently removed to suites 317 to 324 Mercantile Building where every facility and convenience is afforded his patrons, both in the way of amply lighted reception and exhibit rooms and work rooms where the choicest creations of ladies' garments are designed. Twenty-five expert tailors and designers are employed all the year around.

Mr. Berinstein and wife, who was Miss Augusta Nusbaum, and son William A., are members of Berith Kodish congregation.

cxx

An upwardly-mobile garment trade entrepreneur, A. M. Berinstein was typical of the Russian Jews that joined B'rith Kodesh in the early years of the twentieth century.

of those voting favored some kind of Saturday worship, only 64 percent voted for regular worship on Sunday, leaving the substantial minority of 36 percent still opposed to any Sunday services in any form. Despite these less than overwhelming results, Sunday services remained the primary service at B'rith Kodesh for the next thirty years (see Table 3).

Whether because of the introduction of Sunday services, or in spite of them, Wolf was quite successful in attracting larger numbers of Russian and

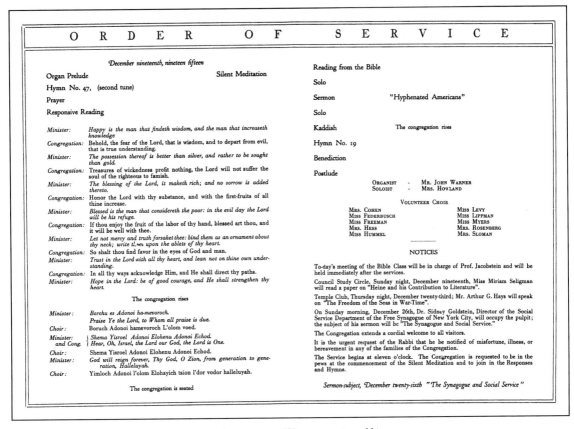

A typical Sunday service at B'rith Kodesh, soon after Horace Wolf became senior rabbi.

Polish Jews to the congregation. Wolf believed that one of the major purposes of expanding the temple's social services was to attract the "un-synagogued, " those Eastern European Jews and their children who had drifted away from Orthodoxy, and were looking for new forms of Jewish expression. To be sure, there was a period of adjustment. Most of the Russian Jews who did venture to a B'rith Kodesh service no doubt were as confused as the congregation's future rabbi, Philip Bernstein. Rochester-born, and from a traditional background, Bernstein first attended a Sunday morning service in 1915. He found little that was familiar in the English language service at B'rith Kodesh, and told his mother afterwards, "That is no shule. That is a church."

One of the most important changes that Wolf and others wished to institute was the opening of its religious school to the children of non-members. Interested in the new field of the psychology of childhood and adolescence, Wolf wanted a child-centered religious education that emphasized moral values and the lessons imparted by Bible stories as the foundations for a Jewish life. Wolf's ideal Sunday school building would have

Table 3

1913 Plebiscite on Sunday Services at B'rith Kodesh

Type of Services	Number Voting
Friday and Saturday	81
Saturday and Sunday	98
Friday and Sunday	46

Horace Wolf,

"Anti-Semitism,"

sermon preached at

Temple B'rith Kodesh,

December 10, 1917

What shall be our reaction to anti-Semitic outbursts to-day? There are some among us who are spiritual descendants of Marranos, of course, who seek to disavow all affiliations with Jews. They may belong to a synagogue, but they never attend it; they associate chiefly with non-Jews and aim to pass as non-Jews whenever possible. Their reaction to anti-Semitism is simple; it consists of meek silence. However they may resent it inwardly, they never betray their displeasure; perhaps they feel none because they do not look on themselves as Jews.

A word has been coined in connection

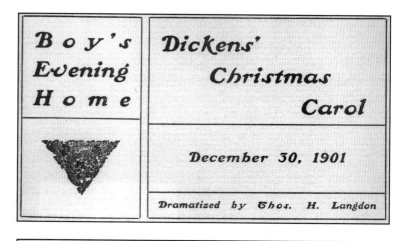

Though the Boy's Evening Home was non-sectarian, some of its programs provided an impetus for the Jewish community of Rochester to develop its own after-school programs. In this unusual production of Charles Dickens' A Christmas Carol, the Ghost of Christmas Present is played by Benjamin Goldstein, later the longtime executive secretary of B'rith Kodesh. (Courtesy Department of Rare Books and Special Collections, Rush Rhees Library, University of Rochester)

a pool, gymnasium, auditorium, and well-stocked library, all open to Reform and Orthodox children alike. At the same time, Hebrew instruction apparently lost its tenuous place in the B'rith Kodesh Sunday School. In 1921 the school committee tried to introduce Hebrew classes, though this suggestion was turned down by the Board of Trustees. Indeed, Wolf seems not to have been as interested as Landsberg in maintaining Hebrew in the Sunday school curriculum.

Starting in 1906 the religious school took measures to allow the children of non-member Russian Jews to attend at little or no cost. These efforts expanded in 1913, when the temple hired Benjamin Goldstein as a teacher of the religious school. A recent graduate of the University of Rochester, Goldstein would have a life-long involvement with the congregation. In 1914 the congregation noted that the Sunday school's current enrollment of 77, which included almost all the school-age children of members, left plenty of room for expansion. The temple decided to double the school's size, with the non-paying children of non-members to comprise as many as half of the pupils.

The religious school made a special effort to attract girls, given the inadequate provision for female religious instruction in traditional *cheders*. A young girl of Orthodox background, Elizabeth Schwartz was first brought to the temple's religious school by a friend around 1913. Her parents, wanting their daughter to have some religious education, and aware of the limited options, let her attend. The first lesson, on Moses in the bullrushes, convinced her parents and pious grandmother that, appearances aside, B'rith Kodesh was genuinely Jewish. Young Elizabeth always felt welcome in the temple, despite her background, in her words, "from the wrong side of the tracks," and from a family that was not a member of the temple.

Wolf related especially well to children and teenagers. Elizabeth Schwartz remembers that prior to her Confirmation in 1920, she had a meeting with Rabbi Wolf that made a lasting impression:

> He said to me, you're in high school, what are you going to do when you finish? I said, I don't know, I think I want to be a teacher. His response to me immediately was, anytime you want to come back and teach in our religious school, you're invited. I never forgot that. I graduated from high school, and attended City Normal School, a teacher training college. At the end of my first year there, when I was eighteen years old, I was asked if I wanted to start teaching at B'rith Kodesh.

Of the twenty members in Elizabeth Schwartz's Confirmation class, five others came, as did she herself, from Russian families that did not belong to the temple.

Wolf saw the growing presence of Eastern European Jews in B'rith Kodesh as more than a much-needed demographic infusion. It demonstrated for him the failure of the Reform movement's commitment to radical assimilation. He argued in 1915 that the belief that only "religious conceptions bind Jews to Jews" flew in the face of common sense. "The wish that Jews are not a race," Wolf stated, "is parent to the thought." Pride in being American should not become an excuse to hide from one's Jewishness. Reform Judaism too often, Wolf cautioned in an article in the *American Hebrew*, resulted in Jews adopting "protective mimicry," with the goal of fitting into American society at all costs. Had Reform Jews sold their heritage for a "mess of pottage," and become "amateur Gentiles" for the sake of harmony with non-Jews? To the extent that Reform Judaism had

with the Great War that describes the second group—camouflage. Camouflage is the science of concealing identity. In this class are many Jews who are professing members of the synagogue at home but practice the art of camouflage away from home. They are Jews at home and cosmopolitans abroad. If neither the names nor their features betray their Jewish origin they will not register as Jews at any anti-Semitic hotel. They will sit silently under any anti-Semitic tirade. They will enter any fraternity or sorority or club that ordinarily bars Jews provided they are not discovered in advance.

The next group is best described as unconscious anti-Semites. They flee to the defense of non-Jews whenever anti-Semitism is discussed. Yes, the Jews are vulgar; the Jews are loud; the Jews are clannish. They do exactly what the anti-Semite does—generalize from individual experience. They know some Jews who show little evidence of culture, who push themselves forward, who are vociferous—but they fail to see that the anti-Semite classes all Jews under the same heading—and there lies the injustice. These unconscious anti-Semites wail from the housetops if they are dubbed loud, vulgar, stingy—-but under their breaths agree with the GENERAL indictment.

Thirdly, there are the Christian Jews. I call them Christian because they seem to have absorbed the Christian philosophy of turning the other cheek when one has been smitten. I call

IN MEMORY OF

IDA BRAYMAN

17 YEARS OLD

who was shot & killed by an Employer Feb. 5th 1913 during the great struggle of the Garment Workers of Rochester.

Copyrigted 1913 by U. G. W. Local 14 Rochester N. Y.

The death of Ida Brayman, a recent immigrant to the United States, shot during a strike rally, sobered both sides in the labor struggle. (Courtesy Rare Books and Special Collections, Rush Rhees Library, University of Rochester)

made itself a religion that placed few demands on its adherents, Wolf argued, it had devalued itself, and made Jews unwilling to assume their obligations as Jews.

The United Garment Workers' Strike in early 1913 for recognition of the union, an eight-hour day, and a fifteen percent pay raise, marked by two months of rallies, marches and meetings in the city's garment district, was a turning point for the city's labor history. For many Russian Jews in Rochester it was a political coming-of-age, and ushered in an era of socialist activism. In the strike's aftermath, Rabbi Horace Wolf pushed B'rith Kodesh to become an advocate for the city's Jews as a whole, rather than for one particular faction. (Courtesy Rare Books and Special Collections, Rush Rhees Library, University of Rochester, and Stone Negative Collection, Rochester Museum and Science Center, Rochester, New York)

The presence of Eastern European Jews in America challenged Reform Judaism to advance beyond the old standard of assimilation at all costs. For Wolf, Reform Judaism had to become as diverse as American Judaism, and indeed American society itself. In 1916 Wolf hailed the waning of German-Jewish control of American Jewish institutions as "the passing of benevolent feudalism." German Jews could no longer control all the major Jewish organizations and philanthropies, or assume the right to speak for the latest immigrants. The new generation demanded a say in the future of American

them Christian because they are ready to return good for evil, to kiss the hand that smites them. I call them Christian because of their readiness to forgive every insult. To love those that hate can never be justified in Jewish ethics. Is the Jew insulted? Very well, let us not pay any attention to it. Let us ignore the insult. Let us act as though it had not happened. What will the Christians say if we resent it?

Do you know the trouble of Jews of this type? They are not used to liberty. They are not accustomed to freedom, the equal rights and the equal privileges which are theirs are so new and strange that they do not know how to use them. They do not understand that the Ghetto walls are fallen, that we live in a land where Jews and non-Jews are on the same plane before the law—and that they have the right to protest against undemocratic treatment.

Judaism. To Wolf, this was more than the usual changing of the generational guard. The older generation of Jewish leaders, with their lack of sympathy for the nationalist aspirations of the recent immigrants, was unrepresentative of the vast majority of American Jews. The transition to genuine democracy, Wolf argued, will not be without its tensions, but only with the change could Reform Judaism remain strong and vital. Reform Jews had to find common ground with Orthodox Jews. Despite the many differences between Reform and Orthodox Judaism, Wolf argued, both movements had a common enemy and a shared task, that of fighting religious indifference and assimilation.

Wolf and the Rights of Labor

One of the many tributes to Rabbi Wolf after his death noted he had devoted the last decade of his life to the amelioration of "the lot of the laborer and employee." Remarkably, he emerged as the Reform movement's leading advocate for the rights of labor while serving as rabbi of a congregation long identified with the interests of garment manufacturers. That he did so without engendering much ill-will on the part of his congregants is a testimony to his powers of persuasion and leadership. Wolf applauded the liberal Christian denominations that worked for social change, for the disadvantaged, for the working poor and new immigrants. But for Wolf, the "Social Gospel" merely showed that Judaism had been right all along. By abandoning its emphasis on other-worldly salvation, and adopting a belief in changing things for the better in the here and now, Christianity was "forsaking her historical position and enlisting under the banner of prophetic Judaism." Reform Jews had a

By 1911 over 1200 garment workers were employed in the Adler-Rochester factory on Hart Street (near St. Paul Street) of the L. Adler Brothers & Co. The company was organized in 1869 by the brothers Abram, Levi, and Solomon Adler. All were active members of B'rith Kodesh.

special obligation to lead in efforts to ameliorate the evils of society.

In early 1913 Wolf had a chance to test his political convictions. Since the crushing of the Knights of Labor by the Clothier's Exchange in 1890, union organizing of Rochester's garment workers had made a slow if unspectacular comeback. In February 1913, the revitalized United Garment Workers went on strike, demanding an eight-hour day, a 10 percent pay increase, and overtime and holiday pay. The Clothier's Exchange responded by locking out of all of the garment workers. The bitter strike, which pitted Eastern European factory workers directly against German Jewish entrepreneurs, reached its tragic crescendo when Ida Brayman, a seventeen-year-old Russian immigrant who had been in the United States for only nine months, was killed on a picket line by a fearful subcontractor. At the funeral at Congregation Va'ad Hakolel, Ida's father remarked that his daughter's murder brought back memories of the Zhitomir pogroms.

On February 25, a five man-committee from the Minister's Association of Rochester, including Horace Wolf, offered its services to help mediate the strike. Some of his colleagues on the committee, including Unitarian minister E. A. Rumball and Dr. Algernon Crapsey were Christian Socialists who spoke at strike rallies; Wolf was more circumspect. Nevertheless, the Clothiers Exchange rejected the offer of mediation, perhaps because of the somewhat partisan makeup of the panel. The strike eventually ground to its conclusion on March 20, with an abolition of subcontracting (the existence of which the Clothier's Exchange had regularly denied), a 52-hour week, and overtime pay.

The strike became a turning point in Wolf's attitude toward labor questions. He became a national leader within the Reform movement on questions of social justice. In 1916, Wolf became the first chairman of the CCAR Committee on Synagog [sic] and Industrial Relations. Its report addressed the two linked social issues most important to Wolf—the increased participation of Russian Jews within Reform life, and the role of the synagogue in settling industrial disputes. When such a dispute arose, the report argued, rabbis needed to investigate the matters carefully, especially when faced with a confrontation between Jewish management and Jewish labor. If possible, rabbis should try to mediate the conflict without partisanship. But when clear moral issues were involved, such as child labor, the establishment of a living wage, or the right of collective bargaining, "the rabbi must speak out from his pulpit boldly and unambiguously." In subsequent years Wolf's committee, renamed the Committee on Social Justice, called for a more equitable distribution of the profits of industry, a minimum wage, an eight-hour day, and workman's compensation.

Horace J. Wolf, The Alternative to Bolshevism, sermon preached at Temple B'rith Kodesh, April 27, 1919

[The] social question is nothing more nor less than an organized demand that every willing workman shall be permitted to obtain for himself and his family the things of life that are worth having. At the bottom of the social unrest of our day is the elementary statement that there are certain things in life, running all the way from physical health on the one hand to love and consecration on the other, which alone make life worth living, and which every man born into this world must have at least a fair opportunity to secure... Is Bolshevism

117

coming to America? It depends upon whether the reasonable or the unreasonable group prevails, not so much in labor as in capitalist circles. The day has arrived when labor demands that industry be humanized, that conditions, wages and hours conform to the best standards that will insure happiness. If reactionaries in the employing class have their way, industrial unrest will grow like a weed…

During the last few months many an observer of social conditions, whether he was a mild reformer, a sympathetic observer or an ardent patriot found himself labeled "Bolshevist": it was a convenient peg on which to hang any critic of the present order of things no

World War I

Over the weekend of June 28, 1914, the Federation of American Zionists held its annual convention in Rochester. The highlight of the convention was a mass meeting, where a crowd estimated at around 5,000, heard the noted Zionist orator Shmaryahu Levin give an address on the renaissance of the Hebrew language in Palestine. For many the conference produced long and lasting memories. Philip Bernstein, who was thirteen years old at the time of the gathering, remembered the conference as the beginning of his life-long commitment to Zionism. The conference also marked the beginning of a rapprochement between B'rith Kodesh and Zionism. The congregation's president, Max Lowenthal, opened the conference and welcomed the delegates to Rochester. For the first time, Zionism was preached from the B'rith Kodesh pulpit when a Reform Zionist, Rabbi Max Raisin, addressed the congregation. Wolf, who jocularly introduced Raisin as "my enemy," remained noncommittal on the question of Zionism.

The conference was full of optimism, both for the future of Palestine and for cooperation among Russian, German, and American Zionists. But the mood would soon change. The assassination that same weekend of Austrian Archduke Ferdinand in far-away Sarajevo led to a series of ultimatums that within a month would plunge Europe into World War I. America stayed on the sidelines until 1917, but the outbreak of the war marked the end of the era of massive immigration to the United States. For Jews worldwide, the war brought the Balfour Declaration, the November 1917 promise of the British government to help establish a Jewish homeland in Palestine. But it also brought unparalleled suffering, especially in Eastern Europe, where Jews were caught between hostile armies. In light of subsequent events, it is easy to overlook the magnitude of Jewish tribulation during and after World War I. The plight of the Jews was summarized by Horace Wolf in what was probably the last sermon he ever preached at B'rith Kodesh, in October 1926:

> It is not easy to tell the story of the atrocities of Eastern Europe. It is too ghastly. There were wholesale deportations of women and old men and children. Cattle trucks were filled with the sick and helpless and were abandoned on railroad sidings in the forests, carts and sleighs were loaded with starving women and children and sent off into oblivion in the dead of night. Everywhere there was terror and flame and carnage.

The horrors of the war forced the American Jewish community to coordinate its relief efforts for Jews overseas, and to assert Jewish interests

During World War I all the major Jewish organizations in Rochester coordinated their activities to support the war effort and Jewish men in the service. Horace Wolf was president of the Jewish Military Welfare Society, an organization that embraced all the major synagogues, Jewish fraternal societies, and Zionist organizations in the city. The Jewish community participated in many civic functions during the war, including this 1918 bond rally. (Courtesy Stone Negative Collection, Rochester Museum and Science Center, Rochester, New York)

more actively. In November 1914, the Joint Distribution Committee was organized in New York City to assist Jews caught in the conflict. Though horrified by the war, Wolf saw it as an opportunity for American Jews to overcome their complacency. The war effort provided them with the means to transcend the petty barriers between German and Russian Jews. Wolf wrote of a Reform Jew, "Mr. Deutsch," and an Orthodox Jewish Zionist, "Mr. Posen." The two men, who had spent a lifetime despising one another, discovered their common Jewish bonds when they joined together in an American Jewish Relief Campaign.

Before the American declaration of war in April 1917, Wolf actively supported the preparedness campaigns, which aimed at making the United States ready for combat. He attended a preparedness camp in Plattsburg, New York in the summer of 1916, reporting enthusiastically on his experiences in the *American Hebrew*. The members of B'rith Kodesh strongly supported the war effort. With the American declaration of war against Germany in April 1917, they subscribed $30,000 to one of the major Liberty Loan campaigns. By the fall of that year, twenty-one sons of the congregation were in the service.

The war provided an opportunity for Wolf to put his egalitarian spiritual ideals into practice. In January 1918 he went on leave for a month to serve

matter how temperate or sane his point of view might be. You can't silence dissatisfaction by calling it names; you can't calm righteous dissatisfaction by stopping the ordinary channels of expression with force... [Employers] have looked on men as so many isolated units, each utterly responsible for his own conditions and have shouted the shopworn sociological truth that all men have the same opportunity. They have answered the cry of poverty with charity—which is ameliorative but not remedial. Now the time has come for the reconstruction of society along such lines as shall insure to every man, woman, and child the things that make life different from mere existence.

The situation of the Jews in Eastern Europe at the end of World War I was more tenuous than ever. In this 1919 demonstration, Rochester Jews held placards denouncing Ignzcy Paderewski, the prime minister of a newly independent Poland, for backtracking on promises made to Jewish leaders in the United States during the war. (Courtesy Stone Negative Collection, Rochester Museum and Science Center, Rochester, New York)

as a chaplain at Fort Dix, New Jersey, where troops trained prior to their service overseas. Wolf lauded the army as a place where social status, privilege, and wealth were immaterial. The army was a "true democracy," which swept away all artificial distinctions, and fostered the rapid integration of Eastern European Jews into the mainstream of American life. Wolf was sure that Judaism would emerge from the war stronger than before. The new Judaism could not be contained "within synagogue walls, within the bounds of theology, within the mechanism of ritual or ceremony." Its responsibility for social involvement was essentially religious in character. "Every effort to eliminate the forces which drag men downwards helps to raise them Godwards," Wolf claimed.

But Wolf's version of Judaism balanced a commitment to universalism with a strong sense of ethnicity. In time Wolf recognized the legitimacy of the Zionist quest for a Jewish homeland. In his early years he was a non-Zionist, but unlike Landsberg, was never a die-hard anti-Zionist. The Balfour Declaration in 1917 made the Zionist enterprise far more tangible. Wolf was one of the signers of the Reform movement's official response. The response welcomed the Declaration as a sign of good-will to the Jews, but made clear that the Reform movement believed that Jews were at home in every land where they lived, and that Palestine was not the national homeland of the Jews.

In the remaining years of his life, Wolf became increasingly friendly toward Zionism, and he slowly brought the congregation along with him. By 1924 B'rith Kodesh was sending delegates to meetings of the Jewish National Fund, using the transparent subterfuge that they were not "official" representatives of the temple. In his final sermon at B'rith Kodesh in October 1926, Wolf gave his most passionate defense of Zionism. "After 1800 years of Goluth the wandering people are on their way back!…Only a few thousand thus far—brave souls—pioneers, halutzim, who are literally recreating the land with their bare fingers, a few thousand." In 1936, almost a decade after Wolf's death, Horace Wolf, Jr., made *aliyah* to Palestine. "Is it really such an amazing development," wrote Wolf's successor, Philip Bernstein, "seeing that in the last years of his life the father had become such a good Zionist?"

Jewish Rochester in the Early 1920s

In 1922, the approximately 15,000 Jews in Rochester attended twelve synagogues, one Reform, one Conservative, and ten Orthodox. With approximately 500 members, B'rith Kodesh remained the largest Jewish congregation in the city. It was closely trailed in size by the new conservative synagogue in the city, Temple Beth El. Founded only in 1917, Beth El already had 360 members. But its Sisterhood had 400 members, in comparison to B'rith Kodesh's 390; and Beth El had a considerably larger religious school, with 270 students to the 175 at B'rith Kodesh. The ten Orthodox shules had a combined membership of 1260.

The Jewish Young Men's Association had 500 members in somewhat cramped quarters at 3 Franklin Square, with activities that included a well-attended monthly dance, a dramatic club, a radio club, a basketball league, and several clubs for women. The director of the JY after 1921 was Tobias Roth, an active member of B'rith Kodesh. In his previous work in New York City as the director of Temple Emanu-el outreach and settlement work on the Lower East Side, he had already demonstrated an ability to straddle the German-Russian divide. The clientele of the Baden Street Settlement, with almost 400 participants, remained overwhelmingly Jewish—99% according to the 1922 report—but most of its staff was non-Jewish, and none of its activities had a specifically Jewish character. The settlement's former music program, now an independent institution, the David Hochstein Memorial Music School, named after a young Russian-Jewish violinist from Rochester who died in World War I, was located on Joseph Avenue, in the heart of the Jewish neighborhood. It had 360 pupils, 90 percent of them Jewish.

In 1922 there were over thirty Jewish organizations, including several sizable Zionist groups. The largest Jewish fraternal organization in Rochester was the Workman's Circle, with four branches and a combined membership of 750. The local section of the National Council of Jewish Women had 530 members, and held its meetings alternatively at B'rith Kodesh and the Leopold Street Shule, the oldest Russian Jewish shule in Rochester. Two fraternal organizations held their meeting at B'rith Kodesh, the Zerubabel Lodge of the B'nai B'rith, and the Rochester Lodge of the Independent Order of the Free Sons of Israel, with 160 and 125 members, respectively.

By the early 1920s, B'rith Kodesh was, under Wolf's direction, reintegrating itself into the broader Rochester Jewish community. This was a

The Jewish Orphan Asylum of Western New York on St. Paul Street opened in 1884. The institution also served Jewish orphans from the Buffalo and Syracuse areas. These quarters served needy orphans from central and western New York until 1915, when a new orphanage opened on Genesee Street.

The Orthodox and Conservative alternative to the Jewish Orphan Asylum was the Jewish Sheltering Home, which opened on Gorham Street in 1914. (Courtesy Stone Negative Collection, Rochester Museum and Science Center, Rochester, New York)

long-standing interest of Wolf. Between 1910 and 1925 B'rith Kodesh membership doubled, from 220 to over 500 members. Most of the increase came from Eastern European Jews and their children. Over the same period enrollment in the Sunday school almost quadrupled, from 65 to over 200 children. With the expansion of its numbers, the religious school became seriously overcrowded. The School Committee complained in 1923 that the classes of the religious school were "scattered everywhere in every possible corner" of the Assembly Hall, and the temple had been forced to convert the antechamber to the Ladies' Rest Room into a classroom. The next year an annex to the Assembly Hall was built to relieve the overcrowding.

Wolf's effort to democratize the congregation contributed to its growth. In January 1919 he called for the congregation to eliminate fixed pews, which he saw as one of the most glaring manifestations of class bias remaining in B'rith Kodesh. The congregation waited over a year, until April 1920, to approve an experiment in unassigned seating. At that point, it voted that all seats would be "lent" back to the congregation starting in February 1921, and people would be free to sit wherever they wished. This arrangement was soon made permanent, though some were reluctant to relinquish the old ways. Sophy Bernstein remembers that when she and her husband arrived at B'rith Kodesh in 1926 some members continued to feel they owned their pews by right, and few challenged their prerogatives. This did change over time. In 1936, a poll taken on the subject showed sixty-one respondents favored the unassigned pew system, with only four dissenters. In January 1919, Wolf also called for a sliding scale for membership fees, ranging from $25 to $500 annually, so no one wanting membership would be denied. This system was adopted in May 1926.

A further sign of Wolf's leadership was the 1921 election of Sol Applebaum as president of B'rith Kodesh. Applebaum was the first Eastern European Jew to serve in that office. A physician, he was also the first president of the temple in half a century not to be associated with the garment industry. Increasingly, the new members of B'rith Kodesh would be, like Applebaum, upwardly mobile Eastern European families with professional careers—doctors, lawyers, teachers—rather than entrepreneurs. Applebaum was committed to Wolf's vision of the re-integration of B'rith Kodesh into the Rochester Jewish community. In his address on the 75th anniversary of B'rith Kodesh in 1923, Applebaum reminded the members that the temple had been founded to serve the entire Jewish population of Rochester, and that "as a religious institution we can continue to exercise our influence as a vital force in the community, only as we are ready to serve the community, and make our facilities available to all who are in need of them."

It was one of Wolf's fondest hopes that the Reform and Orthodox communities of Rochester could combine their relief efforts. As early as 1914, he played a significant role in trying to form a council of all the Jewish organizations in Rochester. In May 1917, the Military Welfare Society was organized, with Wolf as its president. The society, which looked after the interests of Jewish men joining the military, was a joint effort of all the major synagogues and organizations in Rochester. It later associated with the Jewish Welfare Board. In early 1918, Wolf was elected its local field representative of the Jewish Welfare Board.

After the war Wolf continued to press for heightened levels of cooperation between B'rith Kodesh and the broader Jewish community. Combining the (Reform) United Jewish Charities and the (Orthodox and Conservative) Associated Hebrew Charities had been a goal of Wolf's since 1915, though he was initially rebuffed by both sides. By the early 1920s, the Associated Hebrew Charities was the larger of the two, with 1922 expenditures of $37,000, compared to $20,000 for the United Jewish Charities. The Community Chest, established in 1918 as an outgrowth of war-relief efforts, provided much of the funding for both organizations, and balked at the needless duplication of their relief efforts. In 1924, the two organizations merged to form the Jewish Welfare Council, one of the culminating moments of Wolf's career in Rochester. Wolf also hoped that the two Jewish orphanages in the city, the Reform-sponsored Jewish Orphan's Home and the Orthodox-run Jewish Sheltering Home, would combine their services. He did not live to see this happen, but in 1928 the Jewish Orphan Home closed, its functions subsumed by the much larger Jewish Sheltering Home.

By the end of the war the long domination of B'rith Kodesh by

In the 1920s B'rith Kodesh sponsored many youth programs and activities, including this Girl Scout troop.

assimilated German-Jewish culture was slowly waning. Visiting speakers at the temple, such as writers Mary Antin and Anzia Yezierska, spoke of the concerns of the new immigrants. Though most members of the temple personally remained at some distance from the culture of Eastern European Jews, in their public outreach to the rest of the Jewish community there was a new openness. In a book representing the tastes of B'rith Kodesh members, the Sisterhood's *Flower City Cookbook*, first published in 1911, and subsequently reprinted in many editions, there were more recipes for pork and seafood than for latkes and kreplach. But in their public programming, there was a new consideration of the sensibilities of the new immigrants. A turning point occurred in 1920, when the renowned Orthodox Cantor Yossele Rosenblatt appeared at the temple in a benefit concert sponsored by the temple Sisterhood, singing in a style long absent from B'rith Kodesh.

An Untimely Death

Horace Wolf was a person of unbounded confidence and enthusiasm in the early 1920s, occupied with thoughts of integrating the disparate strands of American Judaism in Rochester, and with broader ambitions for political, economic, and social reconstruction in postwar America. Towards the end of 1923 he became seriously ill, probably with tuberculosis. In November of that year, he requested a six-month leave of absence. During this time, Rabbi Benjamin Friedman of Syracuse came to Rochester every other Sunday to conduct services, while Tobias Roth, president of the JY, conducted the Torah service on Saturday mornings. Benjamin Goldstein also led occasional services. Wolf left Rochester for the warmer Mediterranean climate. On May 27, 1924, he wrote to the congregation from Royat-Les-Baines, France, where he had gone to take the "cure," that his health had totally broken down while in Algiers, and that his physicians insisted that in order to return to full health, he had to refrain from work for a year. The congregation extended Wolf's leave of absence for another six months, until the spring of 1925. In the fall of 1924, Samuel S. Cohon, a leading theologian at HUC, conducted the High Holy Day services.

Wolf returned to Rochester in the spring of 1925, but his health remained precarious, and Friedman continued to lead every other Sunday service. In the fall of 1925, the Board of Trustees decided to hire an assistant rabbi. They interviewed several unsatisfactory candidates. The Board wrote to Rabbi Stephen S. Wise at the Jewish Institute of Religion in February 1926, asking if he could recommend any suitable candidates. Wise's response is unknown. It hard to imagine that he would not have recommended his protégé, the Rochester native and one-time B'rith Kodesh Sunday School teacher, Philip Bernstein, for the opening. But there is no evidence that Wise contacted Bernstein about the position, and Bernstein always insisted that he heard of the opening by chance while he was spending the year in Palestine. Bernstein applied for the position in April 1926, came to Rochester the next month, and was hired as Wolf's assistant.

Wolf's health did not improve. At the end of 1926, he took a turn for the worse, and he died on February 17, 1927, at the age of forty-one. At Wolf's funeral service, Sol Applebaum observed that though Wolf died a young man, "the promise and vision of his earlier years met with an unusually large measure of fulfillment."

Though Wolf's rabbinate lasted more than a decade, it seems short in comparison with the tenures of the two rabbis who came before and after him. Nevertheless, his fifteen years at the temple may have been the most significant in the development of the congregation. Wolf engineered a decisive reorientation of the congregation away from an identification with its German Jewish founders and their social and economic interests. Wolf was searching for a Judaism that would go beyond the rationalist platitudes of classical Reform, and one that

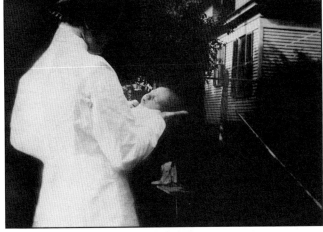

Wolf Family Photos. Top (l. to r.): Back: Rabbi Wolf and Ruth Levi Wolf. Front: Paul Louis Wolf and Horace Louis Wolf. Bottom: Ruth Levi Wolf with son, Horace.

was committed to the quest for social justice. His successors would build on his legacy. Let one of them, Philip Bernstein, have the last word. "Wolf had a warm, sunny temperament. What was lacking in religiosity among his congregants, he compensated by the charisma of his person. He built a whole new generation of B'rith Kodesh members around his own charm."

Chapter IV

Rabbi Philip Bernstein in Peace and War, 1927–1948

Introduction

Philip Bernstein's apprenticeship at Temple B'rith Kodesh lasted all of eight months, from May 1926 until the death of Horace Wolf in February 1927. Taking over from his predecessor, Bernstein would remain the senior rabbi of B'rith Kodesh until 1973. If he became a much beloved figure at the temple, rabbi to several generations of B'rith Kodesh members, his influence extended far beyond the boundaries of Rochester. By the 1930s he was a leader of American Jewry, and in the 1940s he played a vitally important role in the Jewish response to World War II and its aftermath. Any account of the first two decades of Philip Bernstein's tenure at B'rith Kodesh has two connected dimensions; the growth of a Reform congregation in a moderate-size city in upstate New York, and the struggle of the Jewish people to survive the cataclysms of the mid-century.

Young Philip Bernstein

Feivel Shimmel Bernstein was born at 9 North Cumberland Street on June 29, 1901, the son of Sara Steinberg Bernstein and Abraham Bernstein, both immigrants from Lithuania. By the time he attended

The teenage Philip Bernstein with a group of his friends, around 1915, standing in front of the Leopold Street Shule. l. to r. back row: Arnold and Harold Goldstein, front row, Philip Bernstein, William and Bob Berman. (Courtesy Division of Rare Books and Special Collections, Rush Rhees Library, University of Rochester)

126

school, he was given the name Philip Sydney Bernstein. Bernstein always credited his mother, a woman with little formal education, with instilling in him and his brothers a reverence for education and "an appreciation for the life of reason, for the educated heart, and for the disciplined mind." He often said that until B'rith Kodesh moved from Gibbs Street to Elmwood Avenue in 1962, most of the important events of his life had taken place in a one-square-mile area of central Rochester. He was born in the heart of the Jewish section of the city, attended No.10 School, East High School, and then, after a few years away, returned as rabbi of B'rith Kodesh. His parents arrived in the United States when they were quite young. Bernstein's family moved to New York City when he was two. They lived on the Upper West Side and in Brooklyn. In 1912 his family returned to Rochester; the reasons for the moves remained somewhat obscure to Bernstein. Back in Rochester his father opened a moderately successful men's trousers shop, one of the many independent contractors in Rochester's thriving men's ready-made clothing industry.

Bernstein received the conventional Orthodox upbringing common to most children of Eastern European immigrants. His mother, who kept a kosher home all her life, was more observant than his father. When Bernstein's parents returned to Rochester they became members of The Leopold Street Shule. Its rabbi was Paul Chertoff, a young American-born graduate of the Jewish Theological Seminary (JTS). Bernstein remembered him as a person of "sensitivity and a deep Jewishness," who played a decisive role in orienting young Philip toward a life dedicated to Judaism and Jewish affairs. Like many JTS graduates, Chertoff was comfortable with American culture and the English language, and organized a number of youth organizations within the congregation. Bernstein served as the first president of the synagogue's Young Judea Club. He was also president of the JY's Teen Council, a position that would have placed him in contact with the children of B'rith Kodesh members.

Bernstein became active in Beth Israel at a time when the congregation, like many traditional Jewish synagogues, was separating into Orthodox and Conservative factions. In 1916 internal wrangling led to the resignation of Rabbi Chertoff, who was identified with the Conservative tendency. The same year, dissatisfied members of Beth Israel left the congregation to found Temple Beth El, Rochester's Conservative congregation. Late in his career, Bernstein speculated that if a Conservative synagogue had been active in Rochester during his childhood, he might well have become a Conservative rabbi. This did not happen, but, especially in his later years, he was convinced that the division between Reform and Conservative Judaism had no theological or ceremonial basis. For years he worked to move the Reform movement to a more traditional understanding of the role of ritual.

The early lessons Bernstein learned from Chertoff in Beth Israel were some of the longest lasting.

Bernstein graduated from East High School at age sixteen, and entered Syracuse University in 1917. There he joined a Jewish fraternity, and began his connection to the Reform movement by teaching in the religious school of the Temple Society of Concord, supposedly because it was the only congregation in the city that paid its Sunday School instructors. While in college he later served as part-time secretary to the temple's new rabbi, Benjamin Friedman; in 1925 Bernstein married Friedman's niece, Sophy Rubin. While at Syracuse University he served as president of the local chapter of the Menorah Society, an organization of Jewish university students and teachers. When B'rith Kodesh Rabbi Horace J. Wolf came to Syracuse in 1920, he was impressed by the chapter's president, writing Henry Hurwitz, national director of the Menorah Society, that "Bernstein is a fine fellow and a capable worker."

Bright, verbally adept, and passionately concerned with politics, Bernstein seriously considered a career as a lawyer, and was admitted to Harvard Law School in his senior year at Syracuse. But his father took ill, and Bernstein was forced to return to Rochester to help out in the family business. Back in Rochester, Bernstein involved himself in a variety of Jewish activities. He led Young Judea clubs for Beth El, was active in the JY, and taught in the B'rith Kodesh Sunday School. Bernstein also came to consider Rabbi Wolf as a mentor. Bernstein's previous connection to B'rith Kodesh had largely been limited to playing pool with his cousin Milton Steinberg (later a distinguished rabbi) in Sunday afternoon settlement recreation programs sponsored by the temple Sisterhood. The one time Bernstein worshiped at B'rith Kodesh the lack of Hebrew in the service left him uncertain about the congregation's Jewishness. But the year of involvement in Rochester's Jewish life convinced Bernstein to enter the Reform rabbinate.

Bernstein had two choices. Wolf expected him to attend the Hebrew Union College (HUC) in Cincinnati, as had almost all American-trained Reform rabbis since 1875. But Bernstein was wary of the HUC. He disliked its opposition to Zionism, and feared that it would prove a narrow and somewhat insular place to study. Instead, he was drawn to the Jewish Institute of Religion (JIR), the new seminary in New York City,

Rabbi Stephen S. Wise, Philip Bernstein's mentor and close friend, founder of the Jewish Institute of Religion and the American Jewish Congress, and one of the dominant figures within Judaism in the first half of the twentieth century. (Courtesy American Jewish Archives)

founded and headed by the charismatic **Rabbi Stephen S. Wise.**

Wise viewed the JIR as a major tool for realizing his goal of a new liberal Judaism that was supportive of Zionism, fully open to the diversity of American Jewish life, and committed to social and political involvement. During its twenty-five years of operation, the JIR would have a remarkable history. In its early years, before losing many of its most distinguished teachers to better-paying institutions, its faculty included philosopher Harry A. Wolfson, historian Salo W. Baron, and theologian Mordecai M. Kaplan. Wise's institution was pro-Zionist, celebrated Jewish ethnicity, and found the label of "Reform Judaism" to be limiting. Nevertheless, it shared with classic Reform a highly rationalistic understanding of Jewish ritual, theology, and law.

By the time Bernstein entered the JIR, he had long since lost his Orthodox faith. Though his calling to the rabbinate came from a desire "to be of spiritual and moral service to Jews and my fellow man," he later recalled, it was "not specifically a religious commitment." Bernstein found the instruction at the JIR, which deemphasized "God-talk, " sympathetic to his outlook on religion. But he was also deeply troubled, wondering whether an agnostic like himself should pursue the rabbinate.

Bernstein found some answers to his queries in conversations with John Haynes Holmes, a leading Unitarian minister and close friend of Wise. Holmes convinced Bernstein that his values and attitudes toward life were more important than his religious beliefs, which would grow over time. Holmes, a religious humanist, did not consider himself a theist. He was also a passionate pacifist, seeing this as the major moral challenge of his time. Bernstein came to share in much of Holmes' religious and ethical thinking; no single individual shaped Bernstein's thinking in his early years as a rabbi more than John Haynes Holmes. It was Holmes, "this non-Jewish clergyman," wrote Bernstein, "who more than any other helped me to stay in the rabbinate."

Bernstein was awarded a Guggenheim Fellowship for 1925–26 that permitted him to spend half a year studying at Cambridge University, where he met Chaim Weizmann, later the first president of Israel. He and Sophy then traveled to Paris, Amsterdam, Berlin, Poland (where he investigated local conditions for the American Jewish Congress), Vienna, Rome, Naples, and Egypt, before arriving in Palestine, where he studied for six months at the newly opened Hebrew University. It was still quite unusual for American rabbinical candidates to study in Palestine, and Bernstein spent his time there improving his Hebrew, and getting acquainted with the land and the kibbutz movement. While at Hebrew University he met Judah Magnes, the former rabbi at Temple Emanu-el in New York City. Magnes was an important figure in the emerging Jewish pacifist movement, and another

PHILIP S. BERNSTEIN

Born at Rochester, N. Y., June 29, 1901. He attended East High School, Rochester, N. Y., Syracuse University (A.B.), Columbia University, Cambridge University, England; Hebrew University, Jerusalem. He served as acting rabbi at Temple Israel, Amsterdam, N. Y. The title of his Thesis is "A Study of the Personality of Jeremiah."

Philip Bernstein in his 1926 graduation photograph from the Jewish Institute of Religion. B'rith Kodesh hired Bernstein as assistant rabbi the same year. (Courtesy Sophy Bernstein)

example to Bernstein of how to combine a rabbinic career with a commitment to social change and an opposition to war. While in Jerusalem, Bernstein finished his rabbinic thesis on Jeremiah, arguing that Jeremiah's most important contribution to Judaism was his realization that true religion lay not in laws or institutions, or even in acts of righteousness, but in the moral and rational faculties of the human heart.

Bernstein was unsure of what to do after graduation. Two synagogue openings seemed particularly interesting. His friend James Wise, son of Stephen S. Wise, encouraged him to apply for a rabbinical position at a congregation in White Plains, New York. Bernstein later acknowledged that this was the position he was most interested in taking, but the congregation's Board of Trustees was slow to make a decision. The other position was at B'rith Kodesh, and due to the illness of Rabbi Wolf, a suitable candidate had to be hired promptly. In March 1926, Bernstein heard of the opening for an assistant rabbi at B'rith Kodesh from two Rochester couples, Mr. and Mrs. Simon Steefel, and Mr. and Mrs. Samuel Wile, passing through Jerusalem on a tour of the Middle East. Bernstein applied for the position in April, and was in Rochester by May.

A Young Rabbi's Religion

To the end of his life, Bernstein remained surprised that he had been hired by B'rith Kodesh in 1926. He was all of twenty-five, untested as a rabbi, uncertain of his faith, and uncompromisingly pacifist in his politics. His previous experience as a rabbi was limited to two years as a weekend rabbi in Amsterdam, New York, a congregation he had found "provincial, parochial, dull, and unchallenging." Though Rabbi Wolf had changed B'rith Kodesh somewhat, it was still widely perceived as a congregation radical in its liturgy, conservative in its politics, and German-Jewish in its membership. If Bernstein's youth wasn't enough, his trial sermon all but challenged its hearers to find a political or theological objection to the candidate rabbi.

Though Bernstein often wrote about his trial sermon, the first of several thousand that he preached at B'rith Kodesh, it was always with a slight sense of embarrassment, especially for its consistent use of the term "minister" rather than "rabbi" throughout. The sermon was based on his article, "The Minister," published in the *Jewish Institute of Religion Annual* for 1926. Bernstein later said of his trial sermon that it "contains remarkably clear statements about my own remarkably unclear attitudes about religion." Nonetheless, "The Minister" is interesting for what it discloses about Bernstein's understanding of Judaism in 1926, and for its anticipation of his characteristic homiletic style. In "The Minister," he speaks to the congregation not from a position of clerical privilege, but as a fellow sojourner, full of his own doubts and uncertainties about God and Judaism. And for all his agnosticism, he speaks with passion and certainty of the connection between spiritual values and political commitments.

Philip S. Bernstein, *"The Minister,"* Jewish Institute of Religion Annual, *1926*

It is possible to look upon the ministry as a job. He who does, will perform his duties; he will preach and teach; he will marry and bury, and will be satisfied. But he who has been called, like Jeremiah, has a fire burning in his soul. He will bring to his ministry the first fruits of his heart and the tallest flowers of his mind…

What should be the equipment of a man who looks upon the ministry as a calling? In the first place he must have a spiritual attitude toward life. I use this term advisedly and do not say that he must have a definite belief in God, for if I did, I would have to quit the ministry. There is a popular belief that because a man is a minister, his is a firm and unshakable faith, that he is not touched by the same questions and doubts as others. That is wrong, for he is not blind. Life can serve him quite as cruelly as the next man. He ministers to others in their hours of grief. He sees the shadow that accompanies the sunshine of life.…

Questioning God is inevitable. I believe it is healthy. But a man must have a spiritual outlook on life. If he sees life in purely mechanistic or materialistic terms, he has no place in the ministry. For the ministry deals with souls. The ministry is predicated on the assumption that there is something different and higher than his body. I do not know how to define this word, spiritual, but it seems to me that there is potentially a spirit that makes for the high and good, a something that will not let ourselves be content with ourselves as we are, or with conditions in the world as they are, a spirit that forever reaches out and on and beyond to heights we descry in vision, a power that struggles within us and with our lower selves and constantly aspires toward a nobler, purer and more unselfish life. Call this your higher self or God or Christ or Buddha or Abdul Baha—call it what you will—that is not important. The recognition of its reality is important, and he who responds to its call lives a spiritual life.

Nor is this enough. A man to be spiritual must see life whole and not as a disconnected series of causes and effects. It is possible to see the world as a vast multiplicity of things, to see ripples of sunlight, the floating clouds, the fleeting colors and think of them as the world. But he who sees life steadily and sees it whole knows that these are not the world, knows that these things come and go. He goes down underneath. He sees how these things all hold together and belong to one another, how all things in the universe seem to interpenetrate...

Thus, though a minister's God be uncertain, he must have a spiritual attitude toward life. But an attitude is only an attitude and he must have more. He must have a mind that is open and honest. I believe that today there is not enough ringing sincerity in the pulpits of America. There is too much of a tendency to mouth phrases and, I fear, too much willingness to compromise. But a man who is ready to sacrifice principle to expediency does not belong in the ministry. For if he is a minister, his service in the last analysis is not to his congregation nor his sect, but to the total of all perfection, to the source of all ideals, to God as he conceives Him.

What are the implications of this? First, that a minister with an honest mind must call a spade a spade. Is there oppression, does he see injustice anywhere? Then it is not for him to explain or excuse or apologize or palliate. Rather it is for him to point out the ideal, and as a minister to declare unequivocally, "Thus saith the Lord." Is it the question of war? Shall the ministers join the diplomats and warriors in praising war as sometimes good, or excusing it as sometimes necessary? War may be sublime or inevitable, as you please. It may be glorious to defend our country or invade another's as the poets have told us. Every proposed method of abolishing war may have proved a failure. But these do not affect the question.

For it is my conviction and it amounts to a sort of faith with me, that the destruction of human life is the worst sin of which a human being is capable. That is why I hate war. I hate it with every fiber of my being. And I believe it is the duty of the minister to proclaim the Brotherhood of Man and the laws of Love and Justice. These know no qualifications, they are as shining as the stars, as unalterable as the laws which hold the planets in their course. With them war is always inconsistent. The message may be impracticable, it may be unpatriotic. But it is the only position that a minister of religion has the right to preach.

Any man who preaches less, any man who calls upon his God to bless an army that goes out to kill, though he do it in the integrity of heart, that man is faithless to his God. The minister must stand for the uncompromised ideal. The way for such a man may be hard, the rocks along the way may be sharp, but where he goes with bleeding feet mankind shall march to a peace undreamt of by us, the children of a happier era.

Bernstein's early religious views, expressed in a typically straightforward and uncompromising fashion, challenged conventional ideas of God and Judaism. In the late 1920s and 1930s he denounced petitionary prayer (prayer to influence God) as "contrary to our experience and knowledge," and argued that it should have no place in the Reform ritual. He argued for a faith based on experience and reason, going so far as to state unequivocally that he did not "believe in a revealed religion." Divine transcendence, omnipotence, and omniscience were some of the traditional theological notions that Bernstein felt modern Judaism must discard.

In "Changing Gods," a sermon from around 1930, Bernstein argued that the three most important contributions to modern theology had been made by three Jews, Benedict Spinoza, Henri Bergson, and Felix Adler. They were an odd trio to praise from a synagogue pulpit. One (Spinoza) had left the faith; one (Felix Adler, the founder of Ethical Culture) had actively renounced Judaism; and the third (Henri Bergson, a French philosopher) was a non-practicing Jew who sympathized more with Roman Catholicism than with his birth religion. What they all had in common, and shared with Bernstein, was a rejection of the transcendent God of traditional Judaism.

Bernstein had a lifelong admiration for Spinoza, the seventeenth-century philosopher, who had been raised as a Jew in Amsterdam before being expelled from the Jewish community for his outspoken rejection of Jewish Orthodoxy. At the 1932 B'rith Kodesh Confirmation service, Bernstein described Spinoza as the noblest and most honorable Jew who had ever lived, and held him up as a model for all the confirmands to emulate. Bernstein admired Spinoza's stoic realism, his refusal to anthropomorphize God, his determination to see both God and humanity exactly as they are, and especially his refusal to be intimidated by the disapproval of those around him. As late as 1956 Bernstein staged a debate in the temple on the subject "Should the Jews Take Spinoza Back?" He himself argued the affirmative side.

Before World War II, Bernstein identified with Spinoza's theology as much as with his moral philosophy. For Bernstein, Spinoza knew that science and religion were compatible, and he understood that "God was not outside the universe miraculously imposing his will on it." He admired Spinoza's identification of God with the works of nature. Like Spinoza, Bernstein at times verged on pantheism. "To me, God is in the whole process, and not apart from it," he preached around 1930. "With Spinoza and Einstein, I find God in the laws which hold the planets in their courses." (Einstein was another non-practicing Jew whom Bernstein frequently cited as a religious model.) This view of divinity left little room for God as an independent moral arbiter, and at times Bernstein seemed to agree with Spinoza that God is neither moral nor immoral, but just *is*.

Henri Bergson was one of the most influential religious thinkers of the early twentieth century, particularly for his notion that God was incomplete and evolving, a view that came to be known as "process theology." In a 1929 sermon, which is perhaps the clearest statement of Bernstein's prewar theology, the rabbi praised Bergson's notion of a limited God perpetually trying to overcome matter. There is no final resolution. There is only, said Bernstein, "an incomplete victory on the part of a struggling and imperfect

God." Bergson's God was neither omniscient nor omnipotent. "God is the life urge," Bernstein argued. "He is not all-powerful nor all-wise, he is obstructed by the dead weight of matter, struggles against it sometimes victoriously, sometimes not." A limited God provided a solution to the problem of evil. People would no longer be obliged to accept the world's imperfections as manifestations of God's incomprehensible plan.

Bernstein acknowledged that Bergson's God seemed at first glance to be incompatible with the traditional teachings of Judaism. But he maintained that further study revealed a deep affinity between the idea of covenant and Bergson's limited and imperfect God. Both brought God down from the mountaintops, and renewed, in a profoundly intimate fashion, the connection between God and humanity:

> It seems to me that Bergson has brought God very close to us. There was an aloofness about God in the old conception. He was a king, to be obeyed, a majesty to be adored. He was sufficient unto himself. He did not need us. Our deeds did not affect his life. But in this God, who struggles as we do, who suffers and aspires, who falls and rises again, we have a fellow-laborer. He not only means something to us, we mean something to him.

Spinoza, Bergson, Felix Adler, as well as Albert Einstein and Louis Brandeis, provided Bernstein with different models of how one could accept the cosmology of modern science, reject the traditional view of God, and still be authentically and spiritually Jewish.

A Political Pulpit

In the 1920s and 1930s, the main purpose of theology for Bernstein was to eliminate the notion of a transcendental God. A truer notion of God would enable Jews to utilize Judaism to explore the essential questions—politics, pacifism, and the future of the Jewish people. Though Bernstein preached on a wide variety of topics, the most common focus of his sermons was politics. As early as his time in seminary, his homiletics professor, Joel Blau, who was briefly the first rabbi of Temple Beth El in Rochester, criticized his sermons as sounding like editorials from *The Nation* (a journal of political commentary). Bernstein, who became a frequent contributor to periodicals, including *The Nation*, took this as a compliment. He once called himself the "writingest rabbi in the country."

To Bernstein, there was no single aspect of his rabbinate as important as his preaching, and he went to extraordinary lengths to ensure that his sermons were successful, regularly working more than twenty hours a week in preparation. His major sermons commonly lasted three-quarters of an

Rabbi Bernstein in his study during the 1930s. During the decade, Philip Bernstein emerged as a prolific commentator in the national press on Jewish affairs and the crises of the era. (Courtesy Division of Rare Books and Special Collections, Rush Rhees Library, University of Rochester)

hour, and many non-members (including many non-Jews) came to the temple to hear him preach on the issues of the day. Bernstein also circulated copies of important sermons to leading figures within American Judaism and, depending on the subject, to local and national political figures. Whatever the national impact of a sermon, however, its primary function was to inform and instruct the congregation. Bernstein believed that rabbis were essentially teachers. "A rabbi doesn't try to have people get religion," he once said. "He doesn't try to save their souls. He tries to teach them about Torah and help them to live by its doctrines." For Bernstein, the best way to do this was through sermons.

Most of Bernstein's sermons had little in common with traditional rabbinical preaching, and were rarely based on a set biblical or talmudic text. (Unlike, for example, Rabbis Landsberg and Wolf, who generally built their sermons around prooftexts). Many of Bernstein's sermons reported on current affairs, and required extensive and careful research. At the same time, his style was personal. He often drew illustrations from his own life, with its various successes and failures, and tried to connect himself to the struggles of his listeners to be better citizens, better persons, and better Jews. Humor, much of it self-deprecating, was another key element in Bernstein's sermons. Beyond its role in holding the attention of the audience, humor helped to minimize the distance between the pulpit and the pew.

A modern preacher, Bernstein avoided flowery language and emotional flourishes. Though his sermons always displayed his wit and cleverness, his arguments were sober, carefully constructed, and well documented. According to one account of Bernstein's sermons in the early 1930s, "there was not oratory, just facts and logic. Bernstein was never an orator but always a great persuader." Rather than shouting or gesticulating fervidly, Bernstein favored a calm and cool presentation, as one might find among 1930s film stars. Indeed, in 1930, writing to Stephen S. Wise, he envisioned a time when film would become an integral part of the Reform service. "The time may come when Reform congregations will install talking picture apparatus, and once or twice a month, sermons will be delivered through the medium of the talking picture by the outstanding Jewish preachers of all time."

Bernstein generally preached twice a week, giving a short commentary on the Torah portion on Saturday mornings, and a longer sermon, generally on the issues of the day, on Sunday mornings. (After Sunday services were abandoned in 1941, he delivered his main weekly sermon on Friday evenings.) The Saturday morning service was something of a stepchild. As Garson Meyer, who joined B'rith Kodesh in the 1920s, remembered some years later, the Saturday morning service was "very limited, more pro forma than anything else. The real service attended by most of the congregation was on Sunday morning."

In a 1936 analysis, Bernstein divided his sermons into four main categories: book and film reviews, sermons on personal religious topics, discussions of Jewish questions, and discussions of general religious topics. Throughout his career, generally once or twice a year, he offered extended book or theater reviews, generally on a work of Jewish interest, such as *The Deputy, Marjorie Morningstar,* or *Fiddler on the Roof.* (After the war, he sent annual letters to the congregation that provided capsule reviews of his summer reading.) Though he preached frequently on personal religious topics, Bernstein acknowledged in 1936 that he had neglected the private spiritual dimensions of Judaism in his overwhelming interest in the political issues of the mid 1930s. Bernstein felt most comfortable in delivering— and according to a prewar poll, the congregation was

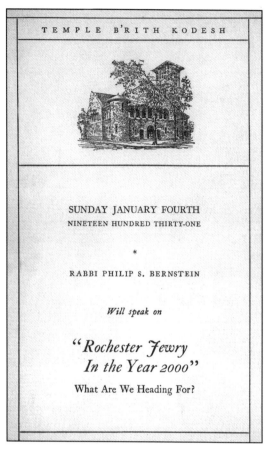

TEMPLE B'RITH KODESH

SUNDAY JANUARY FOURTH
NINETEEN HUNDRED THIRTY-ONE

*

RABBI PHILIP S. BERNSTEIN

Will speak on

"*Rochester Jewry In the Year 2000*"

What Are We Heading For?

(Courtesy Division of Rare Books and Special Collections, Rush Rhees Library, University of Rochester)

most interested in hearing—those sermons having to do either with general issues of the day or Jewish politics. A fifth class of sermon, Bernstein's annual Purim lectures on "Jewish Wit and Wisdom," was always a congregational favorite.

In his 1936 sermon, Bernstein tried to explain his emphasis on political topics. He acknowledged that the pulpit was neither a classroom nor a soapbox, but he felt that "religion is meaningless unless it flows out into life" and that Judaism had to try to make the world a better place. In both religion and politics, he hated abstractions and obscurity, and felt that true religion and good politics had the same goal: to puncture illusions and help people to see the world exactly as it is. He never apologized for filling his sermons with facts, dates, and figures. If rabbis were going to speak on politics they had to be informed on their subject.

The most important early statement by Bernstein of his views on preaching appear in a sharply negative review of a 1929 sermon collection of the prominent Brooklyn Conservative Rabbi Israel Levinthal, which he

1936 Religious School Graduation: From left, front row: unidentified, Janet Gates Goldberg, unidentified. Back row: two unidentified, Jane Sanger Edelstein, Rabbi Bernstein, Goodman Sarachan, Janice Hurwitz Birnbaum, unidentified.

found to be "dull, shallow and totally inadequate." In the review, Bernstein argued that "in both Reform and Conservative Judaism preaching has become the most important activity of the rabbi. Through preaching the rabbi attracts people to the synagogue, and wins them, if he can, to his views on Judaism." Good preaching, he argued, had two elements, a core of Jewish teaching, and a message that could "satisfy the intellectual and emotional needs of the congregants." Levinthal tried to discuss contemporary political issues through the elaboration of a few biblical or talmudic maxims. This wasn't sufficient:

> Rabbi Levinthal's preaching suffers, as does much of our Jewish preaching, from a failure to respect sufficiently the intelligence of the modern congregation. A publicist who was to engage in a public debate, a journalist who planned to write an article for a good magazine, would take good care to develop a reasonable and orderly argument. He would not dare to come before his congregation, as apparently Rabbi Levinthal does, bringing only one or two simple and often thin ideas, embellished with quotations, myths, trite phrases, and commonplaces.

The mainstays of Bernstein's politics in his early years at B'rith Kodesh were pacifism, socialism, and Zionism. Of the three, probably the most deeply held was pacifism. This was a major theme in the very first sermon he preached at the temple, and until the outbreak of World War II he held no conviction with more fervor. Like many young men and women of his generation, Bernstein arrived at pacifism through a sense of revulsion at the carnage in World War I. When America entered the war, Bernstein had been as eager as many other young boys to join the fray. He had lied about his age in the summer of 1918 to get into the training camp at Plattsburgh (the same base where Rabbi Wolf had trained two years earlier.) On hearing of the armistice in November 1918, he "regarded it as something of a personal tragedy that the war did not go on a little longer to permit me to destroy my share of these horrible Huns."

But Bernstein's enthusiasm for combat soon soured. Like so many in his generation, his pacifism came out of the realization that World War I had been a massive exercise in both death and futility. Benrstein's beliefs were also shaped by the knowledge that the war had been especially traumatic for Jews. Religious pacifism had never been especially popular among Jews, and Bernstein was one of its pioneers. His closest colleagues in the pacifist crusades of the 1920s and 1930s were not his fellow rabbis, but liberal Protestant clergy such as John Haynes Holmes, Norman Thomas, and Reinhold Niebuhr. Even as a pacifist, Bernstein never rejected violence as such, but he was convinced that in the post-war setting, violence could only beget more violence. He devoted his first Yom Kippur sermon in 1926 to an explanation of his pacifism. If he or his family were personally attacked, he told the congregation, he would not hesitate to defend himself. But wars do not resemble street-corner fisticuffs. "Nations," he argued, "do not suddenly decide without reason to attack the helpless of another nation. Wars grow out of the blunders and alliances of statesmen, out of blind prejudices and hatreds, out of unreasoning ambitions and prides, out of a combination of circumstances. Usually, as we learned in the last war, out of nothing worth dying for."

Bernstein was probably the best known American Jewish pacifist of his time. In 1931, as chairman of the CCAR's Committee on International Peace, he introduced a resolution that came close to committing the Reform rabbinate to the renunciation of war. He also worked actively with the National Council of Jews and Christians. In 1934, with Roman Catholic Priest T. Lawrason Riggs and Protestant Minister Everett Ross Clinchy, he toured a number of southern cities as a member of "The Good-Will Trio," spreading a message of ecumenism and pacifism.

Bernstein believed that serious discussion of pacifism and other contemporary problems had to begin with a recognition of their economic and sociological roots. He was scornful of any appeal to pacifism simply on moral grounds. Like those of many progressives of his time, Bernstein's politics were broadly socialist. Socialism began to attract Bernstein while he was an undergraduate at Syracuse University, where he presided over the Socialist Study Club. When the college newspaper refused to print notices of club meetings, he tossed off a characteristically feisty letter to the editor. "Honorable editor, are you a parrot? Do you repeat, after other newspapers, the flag-waving patriotism, without a thought? Is your loyalty measured by the depth of the hole you can burrow with your head in the sand?...Rational social advancement can only come about through a synthesis of all the forces toward the better society."

Bernstein's socialism was moderate and non-Marxist. If Marx had any influence on Bernstein, it was in the conviction of both men that moralizing without careful economic and social analysis was of little use. Even if Marx's analysis of the problems of capitalism was basically correct, Bernstein felt his prescriptions for violent revolution and the suppression of democratic rights were always counterproductive. In the early 1930s, Bernstein described himself as a "Norman Thomas socialist." When Thomas ran for president in 1932 as the candidate of the Socialist Party, Bernstein actively campaigned for him. This was one of the two times in Bernstein's career— the other coming during Lyndon Johnson's bid in 1964—that he advocated the election of a political candidate from the B'rith Kodesh pulpit.

Socialism never seemed more necessary to Bernstein than in the early years of the Depression. "The capitalist system has broken down," he wrote in 1934. "Apparently, like Humpty-Dumpty, it can't be put back together again, even by progressive presidents with recovery programs. Mild palliatives won't work; that seems to be the lesson of the Roosevelt failure. Only some sort of collective society with production not for profit but for use holds out a reasonable hope for life, liberty, and the possibility of happiness for the masses of the world." Only through the rational control of industrial output could the poverty and demoralization that Bernstein associated with the Great Depression be ended.

But if Bernstein was a socialist, he always kept his distance from Communism. Extremely interested in the Soviet experiment with socialism, Bernstein visited the Soviet Union in 1928 and 1933. In 1928, accompanied by a Soviet agronomist, he visited several experimental farms in the Crimea where former yeshiva students were being retrained as farmers and remolded into exemplars of the "New Soviet Man." Bernstein was unimpressed, but only the pleas of his wife, Sophy, prevented him from taking the two-week trip on the Trans-Siberian Railway to visit the "Jewish Autonomous Region" of Birobidzhan.

In retrospect, like most progressives of the interwar period, Bernstein gave the Soviet Union more credit than it deserved for trying to build a better and more equitable society. He admired the Soviet Union's attempt to realize the principles of social and economic justice, and he also accepted the Soviet contention that in the new Russia, anti-Semitism and discrimination against Jews was a thing of the past. But from his earliest writings on the subject, Bernstein felt that progress in the Soviet Union was being gained at a terrible cost—the systematic suppression of Judaism, and the forced assimilation of Jews. In a 1928 sermon, "On Jews in Soviet Russia,"

Bernstein was forthright. "Judaism, the religion, is dying in Russia. This is owing largely to the efforts of the communists, who have set out to destroy all of Russia's religious faiths." In his 1933 Rosh Hashanah sermon, after his second trip to the Soviet Union, during which he saw the bloated victims of the Ukrainian famine dying in the streets, he was even blunter. Soviet Communism "has meant the destruction of Judaism and probably the assimilation and annihilation of the Jewish community."

Love for the Jewish people and a commitment to Zionism constituted the third pillar of Bernstein's political faith. His attendance at the 1914 American Zionist Conference in Rochester, where he worked as an usher, along with other members of Young Judea, was a turning point in his life. It imbued within him a "mystic feeling of the Jewish people [which] became one of the strongest elements in my whole life, and ultimately on my religious outlook on life. It led me into the rabbinate." The next year, at another Zionist conference, Bernstein had his first encounter with Louis Brandeis, who became another of the non-practicing Jews who profoundly influenced Bernstein's conception of Judaism.

Bernstein's Zionism complemented his socialism, and he was convinced that there was no better model for socialism than in the flourishing kibbutz movement, a point he emphasized in a 1928 article in *The Nation*, "Where Communism Is Real." Like many Zionists of the era, Bernstein was fond of sweeping and rather invidious comparisons between the weak-willed and sickly Judaism of the Diaspora with the newly proud and assertive Jewish culture that was being forged in Palestine. As events deteriorated in Europe in the 1930s, the importance of the Jewish National Home and the need to ensure the access of Palestine to all Jews were increasingly important themes in Bernstein's preaching. Still, his commentary on the events in the Yishuv was not as prominent as it would become during and after World War II. Through 1939, the two dominant themes of Bernstein's sermons were the economic crisis at home and the political crisis in Europe.

B'rith Kodesh in the 1930s

In February 1929, Stephen S. Wise wrote to Philip S. Bernstein concerning the latter's progress in the B'rith Kodesh pulpit. On a recent trip to Rochester, Wise had noticed "a rather different attitude towards you from that which I found a year ago. You were still looked upon experimentally, but I think the congregation now feels that the experimental period is over and that you have won your way and finely met the test of leadership."

Some long-time members of the congregation had indeed resisted Bernstein initially, rejecting Bernstein both for his youth and for his radical politics. In 1928, Henry Stern, president of B'rith Kodesh, had to remind the

DEBATE OF THE CENTURY

CLARENCE DARROW

VERSUS

RABBI STEPHEN S. WISE

Congressman Meyer Jacobstein will preside

Saturday Evening, February Eighteenth

AT

Temple B'rith Kodesh

Subject: "THE PROBLEM OF THE JEW—Will a homeland in Palestine solve it?"

Rabbi Wise says—YES   *Clarence Darrow says*—NO

The Temple Club, founded as the Men's Club in 1911 on a suggestion from Rabbi Horace J. Wolf, presented provocative and intellectually stimulating forums such as this 1928 debate between Clarence Darrow and Stephen S. Wise on the future of the Jews. (According to Philip S. Bernstein, perhaps a somewhat biased source, Wise was the clear winner.) Wise spoke before the Temple Club as early as 1915. Another leading American Zionist spoke there the following year, with other speakers following over the years including Walter Lippman, Lincoln Steffens, Judah Magnes, Gershon Scholem, and Sen. John Fitzgerald Kennedy.

congregation that the days of Landsberg and Wolf were not going to return. Too many older members of the congregation, Stern charged, were using the changing of the guard, and their lack of familiarity with Bernstein, to absent themselves from the temple. They had never heard the new rabbi preach. "Men die, times and conditions change. We give young doctors, lawyers, and teachers an opportunity. Why not rabbis?"

If most members of B'rith Kodesh came to accept Bernstein, many congregants continued to object to his radical social views. In 1936, Bernstein wanted to sponsor a meeting at the temple of the Socialist-affiliated League for Industrial Democracy with Socialist Party leader Norman Thomas. The Board of Trustees took a dim view of this, and one member that argued the organization was "subversive of American traditions and institutions." The majority of the trustees were inclined to agree, and turned down Bernstein's request. After much importuning, however, the board relented and allowed Thomas to appear so as not to seem to be repudiating Bernstein's leadership. Opposition also came from Henry Kirstein, a retired optics executive, who, in Bernstein's somewhat jaundiced memory, "had nothing to do but harass the rabbi." Kirstein

Into the middle decades of the twentieth century, wealthy German-Jewish families such as the Kirsteins formed the backbone of B'rith Kodesh membership and set the social tone of the congregation. Edward Kirstein (l.) came to Rochester in 1859, and soon became a nationally recognized leader in the wholesale optical business, manufacturers of "Shur-on" glasses, a well-known brand name in the early twentieth century. Edward and Jeannette Kirstein's four children included Louis E. Kirstein, later a prominent department store magnate and father of the Rochester-born Lincoln Kirstein, founder of the New York City Ballet. Henry Kirstein (r.), born in 1865, took over the family optical business, and remained active in B'rith Kodesh long enough to become very annoyed by Philip Bernstein's radical sermons in the 1930s.

regularly complained about the leftist political slant of Bernstein's Sunday morning sermons, and wrote a letter to the leading men of the congregation, urging them to attend only on Saturday mornings, when Bernstein gave but a brief Torah commentary. In one case, Bernstein's politics had so offended a member of the board that his family asked the rabbi not to officiate at the man's funeral.

If the Depression spurred Bernstein's social thinking, it

```
        SCHEDULE OF DUES FOR 1936

Regular and Annual Members..........$150.00 plus tax
Married Men under thirty................ 125.00   "      "
Intermediate Jr. Members............... 100.00   "      "
Junior Members............................... 75.00   "      "
Non-Resident Members....................  75.00   "      "
Non-Resident and Wife.................... 100.00   "      "
Associate Playing Member...............  75.00   "      "
Associate Non-Playing Member........  60.00   "      "

One Child of Member........................  15.00   "      "
More than one child..........................  25.00   "      "

The tax in each case is the Federal Tax of 10%.
```

Schedule of B'rith Kodesh dues in 1936.

obviously presented a challenge to the financial health of B'rith Kodesh. The Rochester area was as hard hit as any area of the country. Members of the Sisterhood remember that their fundraising activities took on a new seriousness during the Depression. The annual revenue of the congregation plummeted from $37,000 in 1928 to $23,000 in 1937. Many wealthy members were unable to contribute their accustomed share to support the temple and Jewish activities in Rochester. Largely as a consequence of financial problems, the number of family members declined from about 500 to 350 over a ten-year period. In the fall of 1929 Bernstein offered to forgo a recent salary increase of $2,000. He later wrote, "I nobly volunteered to cut back my salary from eight to six thousand dollars. I must say slightly to my amazement and with great alacrity the board accepted my offer."

The Great Depression contributed to a sense of flux within B'rith Kodesh. By the eve of World War II, Reform Judaism in America was almost a century old. But in many ways it was almost starting out again, with a new core population. As the second- and third-generation descendants of the German Jewish immigrants of the nineteenth century lost their economic clout and social coherence, the upwardly mobile, American-born children of Russian Jews increasingly came to dominate and define the Reform movement, and to remake B'rith Kodesh. After a decline in membership in the early 1930s, there was a rapid increase in the years before World War II. According to Manuel Goldman, president of the congregation during the war, the number of family members "went from 300 to 500 very quickly, practically all of whom were the descendants of Eastern European Jews."

The newcomers rejected traditional observance, but they generally did so without the hostility that had previously characterized Reform Judaism. As the popularity of Reform Judaism grew among the children of the Russian Jews, families often ended up divided among the branches of Judaism. Various members of the family of Florence Sturman, for example, affiliated with the Leopold Street Shule (Orthodox), Temple Beth El (Conservative), and B'rith Kodesh. Rather than cause tension, this mixing, Sturman suggested, built good will and

Having outgrown their old headquarters on Franklin Street, a new home for the JY opened on Andrews Street in 1931. (Courtesy Stone Negative Collection, Rochester Museum and Science Center, Rochester, New York)

erased boundaries among the three branches. Indeed, there seems to have been a remarkable lack of rancor within Rochester Judaism in the 1930s. Jews ranging from militantly secular Zionists to pious Orthodox were able to overcome their differences and work together for a common purpose.

The reintegration of B'rith Kodesh with the other Jewish institutions of Rochester was one of the fondest wishes of Horace Wolf, and by the 1920s it was coming to pass. Participation in B'rith Kodesh did not preclude membership in other Rochester synagogues. Maurice Forman, born in Rochester in 1904, and the son of clothier B. Forman, remembered that his father "was very active in the Jewish community, and I think that there wasn't a temple or synagogue that he wasn't a member of in those days. I myself was confirmed by Horace Wolf at Temple B'rith Kodesh and I was also bar mitzvahed at Temple Beth El."

Bernstein built on this legacy, and his reputation as a speaker with insight into the issues of the day brought to the synagogue many people who lacked sympathy with the Reform movement. Nathan Goldberg was a long-time member of Temple Beth El and treasurer of Congregation Beth Sholom (Orthodox). He also contributed annually to B'rith Kodesh because of his fondness for Philip Bernstein. In the 1930s and 1940s, he later recounted, he and his father, an Orthodox cantor, would often come to services at B'rith Kodesh. "My father liked to go on Friday nights to B'rith Kodesh. People would criticize my father for going to a Reform temple but he enjoyed listening to speakers and rabbis. So on Friday night after dinner, if there were no guests, we would walk together from Hanover Street to Gibbs Street." The temple also attracted members from the other end of the spectrum. As Bernstein noted, many members of B'rith Kodesh were not religious, but "affiliated with the Temple because of the contribution it [made] to Jewish life."

Within B'rith Kodesh, Bernstein tried to bring his peers, college educated American-raised Jews, into positions of leadership. Around 1930, Bernstein started a Sunday Night College Group at the temple, at which he or some other speaker would deliver an address, followed by dancing to the accompaniment of jazz records on the temple's victrola. If some of the older members looked askance at this, the members of Bernstein's Sunday Night Group became his staunch admirers. In the troubled times of the Depression, when many young college graduates were bitter and unemployed, Bernstein encouraged optimism and social action, together with a new, less formal, approach to Judaism.

The Sunday Night College Group became Bernstein's first triumph at B'rith Kodesh, according to one of its members, Chester Leopold. "The sons and daughters of his detractors now became his constituency; they were his friends, he was their rabbi. The older members were impressed with the

A new breed of leader emerged at B'rith Kodesh in the 1930s: young professionals of Eastern European background. One of the most prominent was Manuel D. Goldman, temple president from 1937–1948.

children's devotion to the temple, and soon the anti-Bernstein syndrome disappeared." Bernstein reached out to the younger generation in other ways as well. In 1938, he surprised Manuel Goldman by asking him to become president of B'rith Kodesh. Until then, Goldman had not been closely involved in running the temple. "When I was first approached to be president of the temple, men of great wealth had been president…I was unmarried to start with. I was a young practicing lawyer. I'd gone through the depression. I didn't know the members who ran the temple, all in their seventies, and I was in my late thirties." Goldman was a good choice, and would go on to have one of the longest tenures of any B'rith Kodesh president, serving until 1948.

Both Rabbi Landsberg and Rabbi Wolf had fought for the freedom of the B'rith Kodesh pulpit, including the right of the rabbi and guest speakers to choose any topic they wished. Despite occasional grumbles from the Board of Trustees, this tradition was proudly upheld during Bernstein's early years. He noted that B'rith Kodesh differed from some other old-line Reform temples, which prevented their rabbis from making Zionist appeals during their sermons.

One of Bernstein's most controversial guest speakers in the 1930s was Margaret Sanger, the leading figure in the birth control movement. Sanger came to B'rith Kodesh only after being turned away from several other Rochester institutions. The invitation resulted in the resignation of one of the leading families of the temple. Sanger spoke at B'rith Kodesh on January 17, 1932, and her defense of contraception was strongly supported by Bernstein: "Why shouldn't human life be as intelligent and as happy as possible? Why should any religion set up its dogmas as an obstacle to human welfare?" His comments did not deter Roman Catholic opponents of birth control from attempting to disrupt Sanger's appearance at B'rith Kodesh. A "plant" in the audience asked Sanger where to obtain birth control devices. When she answered, a sympathetic police officer arrested her for violating New York State's birth control laws, which made the public dissemination of specific information about contraception illegal. Sanger and her defenders maintained that she had not violated the state's laws, and the resultant case brought much publicity to Sanger's cause and the temple.

Bernstein's involvement in city affairs and stature as a Rochester civic leader also grew during the 1930s. According to the distinguished church historian Winthrop Hudson, Bernstein was one of the three most influential opinion leaders in the city, along with University of Rochester history professor Dexter Perkins, and Baptist minister Justin Wroe Nixon. Bernstein's participation was sought by every municipal organization, and his opinions were frequently quoted in local newspapers.

In 1935 Bernstein served as president of the Rochester City Club, at the time of its greatest importance as a local institution. At the same time, he was chairman of the City Planning and Housing Council, and was, as he wrote a friend that year, "on practically all the boards in town, including the Council for Social Agencies, Family Welfare Society, and the Civic Music Association." In 1932, in an effort to cut costs, the local administration proposed to close the Rochester Museum of Arts and Science (now the Rochester Museum and Science Center), all of the branch libraries of the Rochester Public Library system, and all evening classes in the schools. Bernstein led a successful fight against the budget cuts.

Public housing was another of Bernstein's primary concerns. In a 1935 sermon he reminded the congregation that "those who have had occasion to visit the homes of the very poor in Rochester know that in our city are to be found slums that have no place in any decent American community. In Rochester thousands of people live in shacks and hovels." As chairman of the Housing Council, he played a significant role in building some of the first low- and moderate-income housing projects in Rochester. In 1934, Bernstein was appointed chairman of the Rochester Labor Board, established under the National Industrial Recovery Act (NRA) to arbitrate labor/management disputes.

Bernstein was also a leader in interfaith activities in Rochester. In the 1930s, B'rith Kodesh established the Clergy Institute, an annual meeting of prominent figures to discuss matters of general religious interest. Perhaps the most significant inter-religious activity in Rochester in the 1930s was the Inter-Faith Good Will Committee, an organization of Jewish, Protestant, and Roman Catholic leaders, created specifically out of concern with the problems in Germany. Bernstein had a number of close friends among the non-Jewish clergy, including Justin Wroe Nixon and the Unitarian Minister David Rhys Williams. Nixon was the author of a pioneering history of Christian anti-Semitism, much admired and promoted by Bernstein.

Bernstein's interest in racial equality grew steadily in the 1930s and 1940s. His first extensive exposure to the South came as part of his ecumenical-pacifist "Good Will Tour" of 1934-35. What he saw horrified him. American anti-Semitism, he argued in a 1935 sermon, though a serious problem, paled in comparison to the systematic discrimination practiced against Southern blacks. Bernstein actively supported the Rochester chapter of the defense committee for the Scottsboro Boys, the nine black Alabama teenagers falsely accused of rape. In early 1942, at a joint service with the Mt. Olivet Baptist Church, the leading black Baptist congregation in

Rochester, Bernstein pointed to the lessons of Hitler, arguing that the persecution of any group could only undermine all democratic institutions. In 1946, with the depression and war over, Bernstein argued that no domestic issue was of greater importance to Americans and American Jews than the Negro struggle for full equality.

If Bernstein's range of civic and political interests was far reaching, his concern with Jewish affairs, and above all, with Zionism, lay at the core of all of his public involvements. Bernstein opened the temple to Zionist organizations of all kinds, ranging from the Orthodox Religious Mizrachi Zionists to Hashomer Hatzair, a radical Marxist movement. Rochester had been a stronghold of Zionism since early in the century, and Bernstein now became the leader of the local movement. In 1938 he hosted several meetings with Golda Meir, who thanked him for his splendid cooperation in arranging fundraising meetings for her. The next year Bernstein, with publisher Frank Gannett, staged a large rally for Palestine.

Most Rochester Jews admired Bernsten's Zionism, but some still opposed it, especially those members of B'rith Kodesh who has been raised on Landsberg's inveterate anti-Zionism. In 1932, after a pro-Zionist radio address by Stephen S. Wise, Bernstein wrote him (jocularly, one hopes) that "even some of the anti-Semites in my congregation" admired his speech. Bernstein's efforts to bring the Reform movement into the Zionist fold culminated in his support in 1936 on behalf of the Columbus Platform, which repudiated the anti-nationalist Pittsburgh Platform of 1885. (At the CCAR convention that ratified the Columbus Platform, Bernstein was a close ally of CCAR President Felix Levy, the former B'rith Kodesh assistant rabbi.) While Bernstein used his powers of persuasion to mollify and neutralize the anti-Zionist elements within the congregation, resistance still remained. As late as 1946, Hazzan Samuel Rosenbaum of Temple Beth El was asked not to sing Hatikvah at the opening rally of the Jewish Welfare Fund Campaign, so as not to offend anti-Zionist members of B'rith Kodesh.

Bernstein's greatest achievement in Rochester in the 1930s was his central role in the formation of the Jewish Community Council (JCC) in 1937. Bernstein felt there was a need for an organization that would embrace the interests of all the Jewish groups in the city, rather than having "some six or seven groups going out on their own, each approaching community relations from their own particular point of view." The umbrella organization combined the efforts of, among others, the local chapters of B'nai B'rith, American Jewish Congress, American Jewish Committee, Jewish Labor Committee, Jewish War Veterans, the major synagogues, and fraternal groups such as the Workmen's Circle.

One of the major tasks of the JCC was to expose and confront local incidents of anti-Semitism. Jewish groups, including B'rith Kodesh, waged a successful campaign in 1932 to have Shakespeare's *The Merchant of Venice* removed from the reading lists in Rochester's high schools. The JCC also tried to address a number of other instances of genteel (and not so genteel) anti-Semitism. Nearly all Rochester Jews believed that the University of Rochester had a quota that restricted the enrollment of Jewish students. A number of Rochester suburbs, notably Brighton, utilized restrictive covenants on real estate contracts to prevent Jews (and African-Americans) from purchasing property in certain housing tracts. Many local firms hired very few Jews. Garson Meyer, a chemist, remembers that when he was hired at Kodak around 1920, he was one of the first Jews employed there. Philip Bernstein frequently wrote about the prevalence of informal anti-Jewish discrimination during these years, complaining in a 1939 article in *Harper's* that "there is not a single Jewish officer in any Rochester bank."

In one of its first successful actions, the JCC persuaded a local Rochester radio station to end the weekly broadcasts of the Roman Catholic priest, Charles Coughlin. A Detroit-area priest whose weekly broadcasts had a national following, by the late 1930s Coughlin increasingly colored his commentaries on world events with anti-Semitism. Bernstein, as president of the JCC, met with local Roman Catholic priests, and a group of Jewish and Christian clergy went to the radio station and demanded that it discontinue Coughlin's broadcasts. Bernstein remained president of the JCC until 1942, when he invited Elmer Louis to come to Rochester and become its first full-time professional executive director. Louis served as the president of the JCC for over thirty years, overseeing a vast increase in its size and influence.

There was no greater test for Bernstein's talent for making friends and placating potential antagonists than his effort to remake the B'rith Kodesh liturgy. From the time of his appointment as rabbi to the congregation, he found the ritual "thin and attenuated." But he was aware that most in the congregation were satisfied with the liturgical status quo. A 1936 survey of the congregation's attitudes toward the service reveals no consensus for sweeping reform. Twenty-nine of the respondents wanted more Hebrew in the service, and twenty-six wanted less Hebrew. Thirty-three voted for more congregational participation in the liturgy; twenty-one members wanted less. Most opposed the institution of an all-Jewish volunteer choir to replace or supplement the professional singers. Few members expressed interest in hiring a cantor.

The B'rith Kodesh choir was often augmented by vocal students from the University of Rochester's Eastman School of Music, which was across the street from the Gibbs Street Temple. A Rochester resident from early boyhood, William Warfield sang at the temple in the early 1940s. In a 1998 letter, he spoke of "his fond memories of B'rith Kodesh. I sang there, and I'm very proud to be a part of your history." (Courtesy Sibley Music Library, Eastman School of Music)

Irma Frankenstein,

"Memories of Sisterhood
Presidency, 1932–1934,"
Fiftieth Anniversary
Celebration of
the Sisterhood,
May 1942

All was not well with
the nation. We had a
stock market failure and
we were in the midst of a
frightful depression.

We organized a
motor corps under the
Red Cross. We served
lunches to school
children who were sent
to school without food.
The jam and the peanut
butter were donated. This
was a real job for about
one hundred women.

We decorated the
Assembly Hall, the Dining
Room, and the Kitchen—
a rather hopeless job. It
didn't improve them
much.

We were so disturbed
about the rise of anti-
Semitism and a man

Given this situation, Bernstein proceeded warily on matters of liturgical reform. He tried at various times in the 1930s to introduce experimental services, but the Landsberg ritual remained the primary prayerbook. Throughout the 1930s, Bernstein appeared in the pulpit in formal attire, striped pants and a waistcoat. (Through the 1920s ushers wore frock coats and white gloves.) He eventually replaced morning clothes with a black robe, much like that worn by a judge. Until the end of his career he never officiated at services with his head covered.

By 1930 he was trying, in his words, to "Judaize" the music in the service. The visit for several months that year of the distinguished German synagogue composer and choir director Heinrich Schalit provided a taste of modern trends in synagogue music.

Save for this visit, the music in the temple remained typical for a "classical Reform" congregation. There was no cantor, and music was provided by a double quartet of professional singers, accompanied by an organ. The service conveyed a general feeling of order rather than religious ardor, and the lack of emotional intensity was reinforced by the invisibility of the choir in the high lofts of the Gibbs Street sanctuary. (This also permitted the choir to sneak out of the loft sometimes during some of Bernstein's longer sermons and play a few hands of cards.) Neither the choir leader, Mrs. Mollie Howland, who sang at B'rith Kodesh for over thirty years, from 1911 through the mid 1940s, nor most of the other singers were Jewish. Students from the Eastman School of Music often joined the choir, and in 1941–42 one of the choir members was William Warfield, at the beginning of his career as one of America's most distinguished American baritones. In November 1942, Warfield, the first African-American to sing at B'rith Kodesh, performed at the temple's annual meeting.

In the early 1940s, Bernstein's patient efforts at changing the service led to a number of significant transformations. Friday night services resumed at B'rith Kodesh in the fall of 1928 after a hiatus of almost twenty years. But this short service, generally held from 5:30 to 6:10, did not have a sermon, and was not intended as a replacement for Sunday. In the early 1930s, about 75 persons regularly attended Sunday services, and forty on Friday night. In late 1939, Bernstein pressed for an end to Sunday services and for the expansion of Friday night services into the major service of the week. By this time, Bernstein had persuaded a majority of the influential members to abandon Sunday services, but the congregation remained divided on this issue. In January 1941, for example, the Board of Trustees of the Sisterhood split fifteen to ten to end Sunday services. On April 22, 1941, the shift was finally made, and Sunday services were abandoned. The congregation adopted the *Union Prayerbook* and the *Union Hymnal* for Friday night services. Around this time B'rith Kodesh also reinstituted Bar Mitzvah and regular Hebrew instruction in its religious school.

Those conversant with the history of B'rith Kodesh in the 1930s have suggested that Bernstein and the German-Jewish pillars of the congregation arrived at a tacit understanding at the time; if Bernstein would leave the service intact, they would refrain from overt criticism of his politics. But whatever compromises he made at the time, Bernstein's deepest impulse was to fashion a worship service at B'rith Kodesh that was emotionally richer and more authentically Jewish.

From the beginning of his career, Bernstein's rational theology included to some extent an appreciation of and sympathy for the rites and ritual of traditional Judaism, and the power of deeply felt faith. In this regard a touchstone in his religious life was his visit to the hasidim of Ger, Poland in 1925. In later years he often spoke about how moved he was to observe the hasidim in prayer, and share in their religious passion. When he met the Gerer Rebbe, it was "not as a Reform rabbi to quarrel with him, but to learn from him." These two sides of Bernstein's religious personality—the rationalist and the pietist—were perhaps never fully reconciled.

By the late 1930s, Bernstein was fully at home in B'rith Kodesh. If he did not quite have the authority of the Gerer Rebbe, he certainly had earned the complete devotion and respect of the congregation. Some of the usual duties of the senior rabbi of a large congregation did not come easily to him. In his early years he was an uncomfortable fundraiser. He wrote to Stephen S. Wise in 1932, "I find discussions about money very embarrassing and very difficult, and therefore, I do it very poorly." In time he overcame his diffidence in this regard, though until the building of the new temple in the late 1950s he spent little time in directly soliciting large donors. By the end of the 1930s, however, there was no lack of individuals willing to support Bernstein's pet projects. Though he carefully consulted with the congregation about important decisions, he was a man who knew what he wanted, and he generally got his way. "Whatever Bernstein wants, Bernstein gets," soon became bywords in the congregation.

B'rith Kodesh in the 1930s was a vigorous, thriving, and rapidly expanding congregation. By 1940 the temple, in addition to weekly services, was hosting regular Friday Evening Suppers, and meetings of the Sisterhood, the Temple Club, the Sunday Niters, the College Group, the Post Graduate Class, and various Boy and Girl Scout troops. The largest temple organization remained the Sisterhood, which continued its social service activities, as well as fundraising both for the temple and for general good works. Members of the Sisterhood still worked at the Baden Street Settlement, teaching classes for new immigrants. They often ran fundraising campaigns, like the one that raised $3,000 for the HUC Dormitory Fund. They sponsored many entertainments. Mrs. Julian Wiley, president of the

named Hitler.

We had plenty of money in our Treasury in these lean years. I was told to see that the Treasury remained that way.

We spoke a great deal about something called Peace—an almost forgotten word.

We gave a delightful Mothers and Daughters meeting based on A. A. Milne's When We Were Very Young, *and we had some tableaux.*

President Franklin D. Roosevelt had been inaugurated and Dr. Meyer Jacobstein [a Jewish congressman from Rochester] came from Washington to tell us about something bewildering called the New Deal.

These were serious times, but in comparison with today, these were only depression years.

Sisterhood in the early 1920s, remembered that the Sisterhood had its "plays, operettas, fashion shows, coffee clatches, and garden parties." Some of the garden parties were quite elaborate. Mrs. Henry Stern, president of the Sisterhood in 1918, regularly entertained the group on her large estate at 1501 East Avenue, in a garden with a stream, trees, and beautiful flowers.

If the women of the Sisterhood enjoyed themselves, they also worked very hard. Sewing clothes for the poor and for refugees was one of the Sisterhood's main activities. Sewing sessions often took place on Sunday afternoons, and Esther Lowenthal remembers sitting in the sewing room on Gibbs Street one December afternoon, and hearing the news of the Japanese raid on Pearl Harbor. The serious events of the Depression and World War II colored the work of the Sisterhood. During the war and its aftermath the fund raising and sewing took on a new urgency.

Through the middle of the century, the Sisterhood was dedicated to upholding a domestic ideal of Jewish womanhood. The women of the Sisterhood were good wives and mothers, taking care of their households and their children. Few members of the Sisterhood worked outside the home, and the afternoon meetings discouraged the participation of working women. Irma Frankenstein, president of the Sisterhood from 1932 to 1934, who worked in her family's dress shop, was remembered as the exception to this rule. In 1942, at the fiftieth anniversary of the Sisterhood, Terese Cohn, spoke of the purpose of sisterhood. "We as mothers dare not shift the responsibility, for the home should be the strongest influence in forming the character of our children." She was worried that these values were in danger of being lost—overcome by the new movies about drinking, gambling, and sex outside of marriage—but she was sure that Jewish women could "make the home an influence fine enough and strong enough to arm our daughters with the right sort of ideals and the right values in life."

Benjamin Goldstein

No one in B'rith Kodesh in the twentieth century has occupied the unique role of Benjamin Goldstein. In the middle decades of the century he acted as the general factotum of the congregation, the assistant rabbi in all but name, a teacher and director of the religious school, the executive secretary of the temple, and Philip Bernstein's right-hand man.

The child of immigrants from Russia, Goldstein was born on Staten Island on December 25, 1883. His family soon moved to Rochester, where he spent the rest of his life. After graduating from East High, he attended the University of

Benjamin Goldstein in 1907. A prize-winning athlete and debater as an undergraduate at the University of Rochester.

Rochester, where he was captain of both the track team and the debating team. Philip Bernstein first became aware of Benjamin Goldstein through the latter's impressive skills as a debater, which he continued to hone after his graduation in 1907. In February 1909, Goldstein captained a team from the JY that debated the YMHA of Syracuse on the pertinent question of whether "the open shop promotes the interest of the working men better than the closed shop." Rabbi Nathan Krass of B'rith Kodesh was one of the judges.

Benjamin Goldstein was just the sort of person that Horace Wolf wished to recruit into B'rith Kodesh. He was of Eastern European background, well educated, and interested in Judaism but alienated from Orthodoxy. Goldstein began to teach in the religious school, and eventually became principal of the school. During Horace Wolf's fatal illness in the 1920s, he increasingly assumed responsibility for running the business of the congregation. Philip Bernstein sought Goldstein's counsel when trying to decide whether to return to Rochester as assistant rabbi at B'rith Kodesh, and eventually took his old friend's advice. In turn, Bernstein persuaded Goldstein to quit his day job as a manager of a ketchup manufactory to work full time for B'rith Kodesh.

Benjamin Goldstein was the longtime executive director of the congregation, and for many years served as assistant rabbi in all but name.

To compensate for Philip Bernstein's extreme case of wanderlust, B'rith Kodesh needed an assistant who could fill in during the rabbi's many absences.

A typical example of Goldstein's indispensability occured in the summer of 1937, when, before a fact-finding mission to Germany, Philip and Sophy Bernstein contracted nearly fatal cases of influenza. Seeing to it that the Bernsteins were well cared for at such a great distance was no easy task. When the crisi was over, Philip's brother, Irving, wrote Goldstein, "you have been wonderful and terribly efficient in all of this—as usual."

In the years before and during World War II, Benjamin Goldstein generally played that role. Bernstein and others urged Goldstein to acquire rabbinical ordination, but he refused to do so. Temple president Manuel Goldman remembered Goldstein as a "devoted, religious man. And he quit his job and became an assistant rabbi without any rabbinical training whatsoever. He was a better rabbi than 90 percent of those who had all the degrees in Cincinnati." During World War II, the temple successfully petitioned New York State to permit Goldstein to officiate at marriages, a move made necessary by Bernstein's absence from the congregation. Goldstein's gruff exterior belied his heart of gold. He remained indispensable at B'rith Kodesh until his death in 1958. In the temple on Elmwood Avenue, the chapel is named in his honor.

Elizabeth Schwartz, 1976 Interview

My experience as a teacher in the TBK school started in the kindergarten classes, and I had the opportunity through the years of covering all the elementary classes. In those days children attended school on Sunday, and we never thought in terms of anything but a Sunday School. Classes were for about an hour and a half, and an assembly period, a junior service, for about half an hour. At the service there would be a hymn book and singing, responsive readings, and we always had a kind of story or sermonette. It was an opportunity for children to learn responses and important hymns. In the classroom originally we had no textbooks, but

154

The principal of the B'rith Kodesh Sunday School from 1944 to 1958, Elizabeth Schwartz, significantly improved the quality of religious education at the temple. (Courtesy Nancy Kraus)

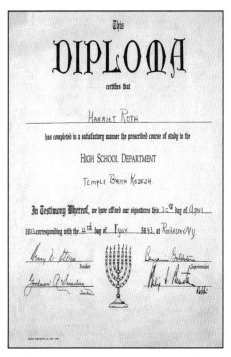

Diploma of Harriet Roth, long-time member of Temple B'rith Kodesh. (Courtesy Harriet Roth)

Education in the 1930s

In the 1930s the educational programs of the temple were growing in both scope and substance. If the school offered religious instruction to the students, it often provided an education for the teachers as well. For many instructors, notably Benjamin Goldstein and Philip Bernstein, teaching in the B'rith Kodesh Sunday School was a decisive step toward a full-time professional involvement with Judaism. For others, it was a crucial part of their understanding of what it meant to be a committed Jew. The teachers at the Sunday School had diverse backgrounds. Some of the instructors also taught in the public school system, as did Elizabeth Schwartz, who later became the principal of Rochester's largest elementary school. Others were businessmen, government employees, store clerks, and housewives. All were united by the desire to teach Judaism to the next generation.

The Sunday School at B'rith Kodesh also brought together teachers from a diversity of religious orientations. While most were members of the Reform movement, a surprisingly large number had been raised in

LESSON XVII

KINDNESS IN THE FAMILY

Aim of Lesson—To teach the child that in being helpful he is also kind. This lesson illustrates kindness in the family.

Greeting.

Quiet Music—"Little Drops of Water" (1st and 3d verses).

Hymn.

Prayer.

Songs—"God is always near me." Teach "God Sends His Bright Spring Sun" with the coming of Spring.

Nature Talk—Guide yourself in accordance with the season of the year and the condition of the weather.

Conversation—Who learned the verse on the cover of the book you took home last week? Let different children recite the verse. Who showed the pictures to the parents? Who told them the stories about the pictures? Who did a helpful thing during the past week? Let the children relate their personal experiences, the teacher bringing out clearly the fact that through the children's acts of helpfulness they were also kind. Review the story of Pharaoh's dream. I know another story about Joseph.

Physical Activity.

Sunday School lessons, from Eva Landman, A Kindergarten Manual: *Union Graded Series, 1918.*

Orthodoxy. Herman Sarachan had been born in Vilna in 1894, and remained an active member of the Leopold Street Schule (Congregation Beth Israel) for almost his entire life. In the 1920s and 1930s he regularly taught at the B'rith Kodesh Sunday School. During the Depression, he later recalled, the few extra dollars a week was helpful, but the attraction was more than financial. "I enjoyed the work and when the high school department was organized my brother taught the highest class in comparative religions and I taught the next class, the eleventh grade, on the history of the Jewish country and the Bible." William Greenberg, later director of the Jewish Home of Rochester, started teaching at the B'rith Kodesh religious school after World War II, when he needed some extra money. Raised Orthodox, he recalls that "when I first walked into the sanctuary without a yarmulke, I was sure that those bricks were going to fall." In time he became a member of the congregation.

The fortunes of Hebrew instruction at B'rith Kodesh are somewhat difficult to trace. It appears that under Rabbi Wolf the Sunday School ceased to offer classes in the language. Herman Sarachan remembered that early in his career at the B'rith Kodesh Sunday School, he taught his fifth-grade class "a few Hebrew words. The next thing I know the principal calls me in. The phone has been ringing, the parents are all excited. What's the idea of

rather leaflets. The youngsters would get a leaflet each week and compile a notebook. In the lower grades we did a great deal with Bible stories and told an ethical lesson from the story. We would do a great deal with the holidays when they came.

Over the years I have been able to see an enrichment in the classes. Many of the children today attend a mid week or twice-a-week classes as well as on the weekend. Therefore we no longer call it Sunday School, but religious school. And we saw the introduction of Hebrew. In the early days none of the youngsters read Hebrew. They used transliteration instead. We now introduce Hebrew and a majority of the youngsters know how to read Hebrew and many of them are bar and bat mitzvah. There is also a concentration on the holidays in a much deeper way than the superficial study of the past. We stress observance of the holidays, Shabbat in the home. And I think it's a much richer experience.

starting to teach Hebrew. You've got to cut it out. And that was the first and the last time." By the late 1930s this attitude had changed again, and in 1940 a Hebrew department, offering twice-a-week instruction, was organized under the direction of Jerome Gordon. Born in Rochester, Gordon trained for the rabbinate at Yeshiva University but never received ordination. Nevertheless, he spent his career in synagogues, including many years as executive director of Temple B'rith Kodesh.

The person who had the longest and closest involvement with religious education at B'rith Kodesh was undoubtedly Elizabeth Schwartz, who taught at the school for almost forty years, serving for many years as principal. Along with Benjamin Goldstein, and later, Aaron Braveman, she played a crucial role in the growing professionalism of the religious school. Over the years she saw a vast improvement in the rigor, seriousness, and accomplishments of the educational programs at B'rith Kodesh.

But if the 1930s saw much growth at B'rith Kodesh, they were not a happy time, framed by the start of the depression on one end, and the beginning of World War II on the other. In February 1939, the temple and the Sisterhood performed a pageant celebrating B'rith Kodesh's first ninety years. Such events are typically celebrations of triumph and progress. In early 1939 the B'rith Kodesh pageant struck a more somber note. The opening scene portrayed a family Passover seder in Germany 1840, just prior to the journey to America that would end in Rochester. Filled with sadness at departure, the participants expressed hope for the future. The final scene depicted some of their descendants celebrating a Passover seder in Germany in 1938, trapped, without the means to escape, and praying for a miracle.

Watchman, What of the Night?

Philip Bernstein experienced his first extensive exposure to European anti-Semitism in the summer of 1930. At the behest of the American Jewish Congress, he toured Romania, where in July there had been a fearsome pogrom in Balaceano. The thirty Jewish families in the town received no police protection as a mob of three hundred gathered in the town square. Most of the Jews escaped to a nearby field, where they were unharmed. Meanwhile the mob rampaged through the town.

Bernstein described the destruction in an article in the *Menorah Journal*. "The attackers entered every Jewish house, smashed every window, every dish, every piece of furniture, and then broke or tore or burned or stole every article of merchandise in the Jewish shops…The Jews were left homeless, without a livelihood, and without compensation for their losses, while their attackers remained free." Bernstein's article explored the complicity of the Romanian government in the pogroms, the rise of parliamentary anti-Semitic parties, and the efforts of the government to curtail Jewish communal life in an effort to "Romanize" the populace. Bernstein called for strong, decisive measures by American Jewish groups to bring the anti-Semitic excesses in Romania to the attention of the world, and to combat them in a forceful and decisive manner.

Subsequent events have reduced 1930s Romanian anti-semitism to a mere sideshow to larger tragedies, but this was not how it appeared at the time. Bernstein wrote to Stephen S. Wise shortly after his return to the United States: "I very much wanted to talk to you about the Jewish situation in Roumania. It is simply terrible. I have never been as heartsick or as indignant in my life as when I came upon the desolation." In September 1930, Bernstein devoted much of his Rosh Hashanah sermon to a discussion of the Balaceano pogrom. In the opening of the sermon he placed the Romanian incident in a broader European perspective, in which he mentioned the rise of radical anti-Semitism in Germany. Bernstein recalled this initial mention of Nazism from the B'rith Kodesh pulpit in his Rosh Hashanah sermon of 1944. "In these fourteen years, we have lived through an experience so horrible, so frightful, as to have been utterly inconceivable." If the catastrophe facing European Jewry in 1944 was indeed inconceivable in 1930, Bernstein's sense of the resolute response required by American Jews changed little in the intervening years.

Philip S. Bernstein, "Rosh Hashanah 1930," sermon preached at B'rith Kodesh

Would that a mood of optimism did rest to-night upon him who has been sent to stand upon the watchtowers of Israel. Would that circumstances justified your asking him, "Watchman, what of the Day?" Is the sun rising, bringing with it promise of light and hope and cheer and warmth for the children of Israel, bringing with it the assurance that the dark night of our suffering is coming to an end?

But no, the question that must be asked is "Watchman, what of the Night?" For the answer to these questions lies not in what we desire, lies not in the sweetness and peace of our life here in America, but in the inescapable realities of life in Europe. The answer lies in the economic persecution, squeezing the very life-blood out of our people in Poland, in the religious persecution in Russia, in the rise to power in Germany of the viciously

"Hitler—Is He
Germany's Messiah or
Greatest Menace?,"
Philip S. Bernstein,
sermon preached at
B'rith Kodesh,
January 10, 1932

I did not really
understand the
significance of Hitlerism
until I saw [in 1930] on
a large bulletin board at
a prominent street
corner in Munich this
sign in flaming red
letters. "Vote for Adolph
Stricker. He is the enemy
of the Jews. The Jews
started the war. The Jews
profiteered from the war.
The Jews are the
betrayers of Germany. If
Adolph Stricker is
elected, he will drive
them out of the
country." I could not
believe my eyes. I could
not believe it possible
that in this modern
enlightened Germany,
such open appeals to

anti-Semitic party, whose public appeal has been, "We are
the enemies of the Jews"…

For better or worse, the mantle of leadership has
fallen on us, the American Jews. We must use our voice,
which is now the most authoritative in the entire world, to
cry out again, in the words of this torn Book, "It is enough.
Now stay thy hand." And we must fight with every ounce of
energy against the recrudescence of such medieval
barbarity. Every Jewish faction, every Jewish leader, must
set aside their individual enmities in order to meet this
enemy with a united front. Every individual Jew must be
informed, must feel a sense of historic obligation to his
people, must use whatever voice, whatever influence he
has, [to see] that these things shall cease.

For the next seven years, Bernstein would begin each Erev Rosh Hashanah eve sermon by quoting the same imploring, unanswered question from Isaiah 22:11, "Watchman, What of the Night? " And he would then deliver a sermon on the year's events in Europe and Germany. By the end of 1931 it was clear to him that Hitler and the Nazi Party presented the greatest threat to European Jews and international stability. With a growing sense of urgency, Bernstein tried to alert his congregation, and through numerous articles and public appearances, the larger Jewish community and the American people, to the dangers posed by Adolf Hitler. In a January 1932 sermon that asked the very rhetorical question, "Hitler—Is He Germany's Messiah or Greatest Menace?," Bernstein recalled his trip through Munich in 1930, and his incredulity at the blatant anti-Semitic appeal of Nazism. Very sympathetic to post-war Germany's economic plight, he argued that the triumph of political anti-Semitism in Germany could only be averted by rethinking the onerous financial obligations imposed on Germany by the victors of World War I in the Treaty of Versailles. But he feared that the time for such remedies was already too late.

Bernstein's fears about the triumph of Nazism in 1932 were off by only a few weeks. On January 30, 1933, Hitler became chancellor of Germany, and the reign of terror against Germany's Jews began almost immediately. In a sermon, "Hitler: Chancellor of Germany," preached less than a week later, Bernstein said that "Hitler is a menace to the Jews, to Germany, and to the peace of the world." In the spring, on behalf of the American Jewish Congress, Bernstein undertook a speaking tour of American cities, denouncing Hitler. Bernstein had no illusions that Hitler's reign in Germany would be short, or that there would be any easy way to drive him from office. In his Purim sermon that year, he compared Hitler and Haman:

> The situation in Germany to-day is almost as bad as in ancient Persia when Premier Haman announced that on the fifteenth of Adar, the Jews were to be destroyed. In my judgment, Hitler will be the dictator of Germany now for an indefinite period. The Jews in that country are destined to suffer as is hardly conceivable in this so-called enlightened, western nation.

What would happen next, Bernstein wondered. "How far will the analogy between Haman and Hitler go? Will the German ruler, like the Persian, intoxicated with power, demand even crueler persecution of the Jews? And will his end be the same as Haman's? The lessons of Jewish history suggest that ultimately it will."

In the summer of 1933, Bernstein embarked on a dangerous trip to Germany to evaluate the situation there for himself and the American Jewish Congress. Some thought the trip foolhardy, especially Stephen S. Wise, who used all of his powers of persuasion to try to convince Bernstein not to go. "What in the hell is the use of your going?" Wise somewhat pointedly asked. "What Jews tell you, you cannot repeat lest they be inculpated; what Goyim tell you, you cannot repeat unless you want to exculpate Hitler. I ask you, as my younger friend and disciple, as a matter of sheer respect, to stay out of Germany."

Though Bernstein was taken aback by Wise's criticism, and spent some time pondering the wisdom of his plan, he decided to go ahead with it. Needless to say, he was horrified by what he saw, and as he viewed the situation in its larger dimensions, he saw little reason for optimism. He found systematic discrimination and exclusion of Jews from society, and abject fear on the part of many of the Jews he met. Some were even afraid to meet him, and many were bewildered about what step to take next. Bernstein returned to America with no illusions about the Nazis, or about the efficacy of any standard form of protest to dissuade Hitler from pursuing his anti-Semitic policies. In his major sermon on the trip, "Hitler's Germany: An Eyewitness Report" (see page 162), preached at B'rith Kodesh on October 29, 1933, he frankly told the congregation that the mass murder of German Jews was a distinct possibility.

Bernstein saw it as one of his primary obligations to publicize the horror of Nazi Germany. Throughout the 1930s, he continued to preach on the dangers of Hitler, and his articles appeared regularly in both Jewish and general magazines. He regularly reminded his audiences and readers of the

hatred could be made...

That this sort of silly and vicious prejudice should have affected a small group of wild, irresponsible people in Germany might have been perhaps expected in a country so heavily burdened. But the terrifying thing is that Herr Stricker was elected. The Hitler National-Socialist Party has gone from strength to strength, and reliable observers have come to the conclusion that the year 1932 will witness the Hitlerite triumph in Germany. What does this mean for our people? If we accept the threats of the Nazi Party at face value, it means the disenfranchisement of the entire community of German Jews, and the expulsion from Germany of those Jews who entered the country since 1914. It means further, according to Herr Hitler's own words, the expulsion from Germany of all Zionists. The wildest of these irresponsible fanatics have even gone so far as to threaten the sterilization of all Jews in Germany. It is simply impossible to believe that such things could happen. It is impossible to believe that in an enlightened, modern country in the twentieth century, such things could be done. I would rather hope that if and when Hitler achieves power he will become more moderate, and yet, there is the danger that without a really practical program for rehabilitating Germany, and facing the possibility of unfulfilled promises and internal chaos, and continued, if not greater oppression from France, Hitler may proceed as

growing dimensions of the unfolding catastrophe. Bernstein went on another, even more dangerous fact-finding trip to Germany in September 1937, and in an article in *The Nation* the following month, his prognosis was stark. "The Nazi assault upon the German Jews moves on from segregation, to pauperization, to emigration, to annihilation…For the Jews of Germany the choice is between emigration and death."

Bernstein's pacifism greatly complicated his response to Hitler. This was far too deep a moral commitment for him to relinquish it lightly. Indeed, in the mid 1930s, as rearmament became a leading political issue, his public support of the pacifist cause increased. In 1936 Bernstein, as a co-leader, with author Dorothy Canfield Fisher, of the People's Mandate to End War, interviewed the presidential candidates on their attitudes toward military preparedness. When he met with Franklin Roosevelt at Hyde Park on August 23, the president said little to alleviate Bernstein's suspicions that Roosevelt was basically a militarist, committed to steady increases in American armament expenditures, and fanning the flames of another world war. In later accounts, Bernstein related a different version of the meeting. Roosevelt had already decided that a war with Germany was unavoidable, but had, because of the prevalence of isolationist sentiment, refrained from making a public statement. Though Roosevelt was respectful to the members of the ecumenical pacifist group that met with him, he found them naive. Bernstein remembered that Roosevelt kept saying to him, "Rabbi, you don't know what Hitler's up to."

But Bernstein's quandary was that he knew all too well what Hitler was up to. In a 1934 article, "Pacifism in Hitler's World," in *The World Tomorrow*, the leading pacifist journal in the United States, he acknowledged that his pacifism had been "tried by fire since Hitler has come to power." But a second world war, with all of the technological advances in airplanes, poison gas, and other weapons of mass destruction, and against a foe far worse than the Kaiser, would lead to unimaginable carnage. "No matter how great the dangers of Hitlerism, war is worse." For the Jews, a war against Hitler would be catastrophic. The victory over Nazism would not be easy. Hitler would have plenty of time to have his way with Germany's Jews, and a Europe-wide war could only place more Jews in harm's way. Bernstein wrote in Rochester's *Jewish Ledger* in March 1935, "Let the Jew take no comfort from a war against Hitler. German Jews will be slaughtered, and evil forces let loose that will hurt every Jewish community in the world."

Bernstein's warnings were prescient, but they were also, as he came to realize, increasingly irrelevant to the European situation. By 1938, it was clear that the main issue was not whether to wage war against Hitler. Hitler had no interest in confining his regime to the area within Germany's boundaries, and a new conflict, for all this implied for the Jews, was increasingly likely, whether the anti-Hitler nations wanted one or not. Facing the inevitability of war, Bernstein's views changed. In a speech he delivered at the 1937 CCAR convention in Charlevoix, Michigan, Bernstein spoke of his growing doubts about pacifism. But his renunciation of pacifism was not yet complete. As he later recalled, "My last pacifist speech was delivered at Willamstown [Massachusetts] on September 1, 1939, the day after Hitler invaded Poland. I had prepared my address weeks before *der Tag* and I delivered it as written. But the ensuing days and months blasted the ground from under me."

Bernstein's decision to abandon pacifism was prolonged and agonizing. As a result of the pressure to forswear the single most important political and moral commitment of his career, he related in his unpublished autobiography, he very "nearly cracked up." He wrote to a pacifist friend that the events in Europe shook "my entire outlook on life and created the most difficult insoluble spiritual problems for me." Leaving his family behind, he spent most of the summer of 1939 by himself, searching his soul while climbing the Rocky Mountains in Colorado. Bernstein's conversion from pacifism was greeted by skepticism in some Jewish circles, who viewed him as an isolationist. Writing in November 1940, though he strongly defended his support for the war against Hitler, he did not apologize for his earlier pacifism:

> It seems to me that at least up to the outbreak of the war it was possible and legitimate for Jews and all Americans to be divided about America's relationship to the European situation. In fact it was probably beneficial to the Jews at that time for some rabbis publicly to urge the United States not to become involved. Until the time that labors for peace became fruitless it was I believe, entirely right that each of us should work along the lines of his own convictions. However that time is past and now there is not much room for differences among us about the international situation.

Rochester as a City of Refuge

Rabbi Bernstein and Temple B'rith Kodesh did more than make speeches against the Nazis. The best way to help German Jews, Bernstein argued, was to get them out of Germany, and the Jews of Rochester did what they could. The stringent immigration laws adopted by the United States in the 1920s made this process far more complex and difficult than it should have been. The Depression spurred xenophobia and anti-Semitism among large segments of the American public, which were frightened by the

impotent rulers in the past have often done to divert the attention of the people from their real problem, to some scapegoat, that scapegoat being readily available in the presence of the Jews. I shudder to think of what may happen to the Jews of Germany this year, if Adolf Hitler is lifted to control of the country.

"Hitler's Germany: An Eyewitness Report,"
Philip Bernstein, sermon preached at B'rith Kodesh, October 29, 1933

I was shocked not only as a Jew but as a human being, when I read these things in Germany this summer. Hitler in Mein Kampf: "If, at the beginning of the war, twelve or fifteen thousand of these Hebrew corrupters of the people had been held under poison gas, then the sacrifices of millions at the front would not have been in vain." Goering: "The Third Empire will treat Jews like plant lice." Alfred Rosenberg [a leading Nazi ideologist] "On every telephone pole from Munich to Berlin, the head of a prominent Jew must be stuck."...
There is an

CONCERT
Of Compositions by
HEINRICH SCHALIT

Temple B'rith Kodesh

NOVEMBER SEVENTEENTH, NINETEEN HUNDRED AND THIRTY

PROGRAM

I   ORGAN SELECTIONS — Heinrich Schalit
   (A) D Major—*Choral Prelude*
   (B) F Minor—"*Longing for God*"

II   HEBREW CHORUSES — Mixed Choir
   (A) Mah Tovu
"How goodly are thy tents, O Jacob, thy dwellings, O Israel! Through Thy great mercy, O God, I come to Thy house and bow down in Thy holy temple in devotion to Thee."
   (B) V'shomru
"The children of Israel shall keep the Sabbath, to observe the Sabbath throughout their generations, for a perpetual covenant. It is a sign between Me and the children of Israel forever."

III   RELIGIOUS SONGS — Nicholas Konraty
   (A) "Our Father, Our King"
   (B) *Loud through the World resounds the Name of the Eternal.*

IV   VIOLIN SOLO — Gustave Tinlot
"*Jacobs Song*" (After a Lithuanian Jewish Folk Melody)

V   HEINE SONGS — Nicholas Konraty
   (A) "*Break forth in loud lamentation.
O mournful song of martyrdom!*"
   (B) "*Away with the lyre of Greece.
I shall praise the Lord of Creation—Hallelujah!*"

VI   HYMN—"*In Eternity*" — Mixed Choir, Organ, Harp, Violin Solo and Violin Chorus

"*Sun, Moon, true servants of God, for ever keep their watch;
Day, night, in ordered way they hold the appointed course.
They were as symbols given unto Jacob's seed,
God's people they, eternal, ne'er to be destroyed.
When God's left cast them off, His right hand drew them nigh.
Not e'en in dark distress have they despaired of life.
Yea, firm is their belief that ever they shall be, that
Ne'er their end shall come ere endeth day and night.*"

(From the Hebrew of Yehuda Halevi)

CHORUS: Mesdames Bootes, Brightman, De Visser, Howland, Lewis, Seibold, Messrs Emanuel, Frank, Kaufman, Lowenthal.

VIOLIN SOLO—Mr. Tinlot.   VIOLIN CHORUS, Messrs Friedman and Donato, HARPIST, Mr. Marthage.

A reception will be tendered to Mr. Schalit in the Assembly Hall.

Steinway piano used through the courtesy of Levis Music Store

Heinrich Schalit at age forty-five in 1931. One of his era's foremost composers of Jewish liturgical music, Schalit first visited B'rith Kodesh for several months in 1930. During his time in Rochester he led a concert of his sacred compositions at the temple. A decade later, through the concerted efforts of Rabbi Bernstein and Benjamin Goldstein, Schalit was able to emigrate from Europe, and for the next three years served as the temple's music director.

prospects of large numbers of destitute refugees arriving on American shores at a time of massive unemployment. Though about 150,000 German Jews entered the United States between 1933 and 1941, far more would have immigrated if they had been allowed.

B'rith Kodesh experienced the difficulty of bringing German Jews to this country first hand. It took a full decade for the temple to gain entry of Heinrich Schalit as its music director. In 1930, Bernstein attended services at Munich's main Reform synagogue. There he met Schalit, the congregation's music director, and one of the most distinguished Jewish liturgical composers of his generation. Schalit was eager to visit the United States, and Bernstein was eager to have someone of Schalit's stature at B'rith Kodesh. The temple's minutes for 1930 note that Bernstein "was not satisfied with the music in the Temple and saw little prospect for its improvement so long as one, not a Jew, was responsible for it… He was convinced that Mr. Schalit was the man we were looking for, and Schalit was interested in coming."

Schalit came in 1930, stayed for several months, and led a concert of his liturgical compositions. During the Depression, however, the congregation failed to raise the necessary funds for a permanent position, and Schalit returned to Munich in the spring. In the spring of 1933, Schalit, understandably eager to leave Munich and come to Rochester under any workable financial arrangement, contacted Bernstein again. B'rith Kodesh responded by offering him a two-year position at $125 a month, his duties to consist of playing the organ and directing the choir. When Schalit went to the American consulate in Munich in August, however, his visa application was denied on the grounds that his eyesight was poor, and if the arrangement with B'rith Kodesh failed, he was unlikely to be able to support himself. The consular official in Munich, though presumably without much expertise in the field of Jewish liturgical composition, decided that Schalit was not sufficiently distinguished as a musician to warrant an exception to the immigration laws.

Despite protest from B'rith Kodesh, no visa was granted. Schalit and his family managed to get out of Germany and he found a position at a synagogue in Rome. But Fascist Italy was only a slight improvement over Nazi Germany. In 1937, Schalit renewed his plea to come to Rochester, but once again he was unable to obtain a visa. Only in October 1940 did Schalit and his family finally arrive in Rochester. During the three years that Schalit served as music director of B'rith Kodesh, he contributed greatly to improving the quality of the temple's music. After leaving Rochester, he maintained a connection with B'rith Kodesh. In 1954 a newly composed Saturday morning liturgy, composed by Schalit, had its world premiere at B'rith Kodesh.

instrument of protest available to us which we have the right and duty to use, viz., the economic boycott. But nothing will change the basic attitude and program of the Nazis toward the Jews, not even the economic boycott. I will add this further statement: the boycott, however successful, will not dislodge Hitler. He is there to stay. Any foreign movement against him, especially one that is inspired by the Jews, will only strengthen the German people's devotion to him…

Hitler is preparing for war. That war will not come tomorrow or the day after. He is much too clever to involve his country before he is ready. But the time is coming—and German efficiency will bring it soon—when Hitler will be prepared to insist on Germany's "rights" either through threat of war or war itself...

I cannot forget what Nazi Reichstag Deputy Boerger said in Cologne the other day, "If a Frenchman steps over the German frontier, then on the next day, all the Jews of Germany will die." I know enough about Nazi ruthlessness to know that this was no idle threat but was seriously spoken and would be carried out. An invasion of Germany would mean the instantaneous destruction of the German Jews...

There is only one thing that we can do for the Jews of Germany that will really help them, and that is to get them out of that country. We must rebuild Palestine as a haven of refuge for them, we must use

TEMPLE HONOR ROLL

☆ ☆ ☆

Robert M. Adler	Sanford M. Epstein	Arthur F. Horwitz
M. S. Apperman		George Horwitz
Mark Attie	David A. Falk	Sydney M. Hyman
Charles August	Albert O. Fenyvessy	Elliot L. Hose
	Stanley J. Fenyvessy	
Monroe Blumenstiel	Maurice R. Forman	
William J. Bakrow	Richard C. Frank	Dr. George B. Joel
Leonard L. Babin	Irwin F. Fredman	Jerome Jacobs
Morton J. Baum, Jr.	Stanley Z. Fredman	Myron V. Jacobs
Joseph Beckler	Dr. Harold A. Friedman	Marvin Jacobstein
Harry Benewick, Jr.	Myrtle M. Fox	Milton Joffe
Donald L. Berlove		
Irving Bernstein	Alfred W. Gans	Jerome Kahn
Roger D. Blank	Reuben Garner	Jack A. Kaman
Lee Bloch	Emil Gersten	Robert A. Kaman
Richard M. Bloch	Lee J. Goldman	Hyman J. Kaplan
Ralston Bloom	Dr. Jacob D. Goldstein	Philip Kates
Marvin Brudno	Harriet S. Goldstein	Harold W. Katz
Paul Bloch	Robert K. Goldstein	Herman Z. Katz
	Burton Gordon	Dr. Benjamin Keyfetz
Harold H. Caplin	Gay Given	Stanley Kleeberg
Harold Caplan	Albert Goldberg	Lawrence D. Kushner
Isadore Caplan	Charles H. Green	Dr. Lawrence A. Klein
Daniel C. Cohen	Edward Dale Green	Norman M. Kline
Donald Cohen	Burton J. Greene	Allan S. Klonick
Martin S. Cohen	Elmer Guggenheim	David E. Klonick
Robert Cohen	Alwyn L. Gumberts	Richard S. Knopf
*Eugene R. Cohen	Irving Guttenberg	Edward Kochenthal
Peter Cohen	Nelson Greenberg	Robert Kochenthal
Howard Cohn	Louis L. Gup	Dr. Bernard S. Kristal
Jerome B. Cohn		Earl J. Komesar
Stanley B. Corris	Frederick L. Harrison	
	John Alan Hart	B. M. Lauer
Alan W. David	James H. Heilbrunn	Dr. George R. Lavine
Robert L. David	David M. Heller	*Marvin Lee
Dr. Bernard Drexler	Arthur H. Herz	Isidor Leventhal

☆

Honor Roll of B'rith Kodesh congregants who served in World War II.

Not all German refugees experienced Schalit's difficulties in getting to the United States and Rochester. The city had one of the most active refugee committees in the country. Under the guidance of Rabbi Bernstein, B'rith Kodesh President Manuel Goldman, Mortimer Adler, and others, the Jewish Community Council saw to it that Rochester was one of the first cities in the nation to make out a community affidavit to support German Jewish refugees and have it approved by the government. Without such an affidavit, a pledge to support immigrants so that they would not become wards of the state, it was very hard to arrange for the generally penniless immigrants to enter

TEMPLE HONOR ROLL (Cont.)

☆ ☆ ☆

Austin R. Leve	*Wesley J. Robenstein	Leonard D. Shavlan
Chester M. Leopold	Gerald L. Robenstein	Marvin A. Shulman
Charles J. Levine	Henry Rautenberg	Milton J. Shurr
Sherwin E. Levine	Herbert Rehbock	Miller Simon
Charles S. Levinson	Barton James Raz	Willard J. Simon
Dr. Murray D. Lewis	Samuel Rolick	Milton Smith
Edward List	Norman Rose	Dr. Ellis B. Soble
David M. Levy	B. Robert Rosenberg	Dr. Samuel J. Stabins
Ruth Loewenstein	Edward Rosenberg, Jr.	Dr. Edward A. Stern
Arthur E. Lowenthal	George L. Rosenberg	John H. Stern
Eugene M. Lowenthal, Jr.	Gerald Rosenberg	Charles D. Snyder
William S. Magill	S. William Rosenberg	Dr. E. G. Sternberg
John O. Moser	Edward Rosenstein	Betty Jane Lubliner Stone
James A. Marine	Stewart H. Rosenthal	Dudley A. Striker
Bernard Masling	Paul L. Ross	
Joseph M. Masling	Mark R. Rosenzweig	Elmer Teklin
Arthur H. Messinger	Herbert N. Roth	Harold Temkin
Samuel A. Meyer	George G. Roth	Dr. Joseph Thaler
John H. Mitchell	Norman R. Roth	Elizabeth H. Turk
Ralph Mitchell, Jr.	Howard J. Samuels	Oscar Turk
Dr. Morris E. Missal	Hans M. Schiff	Alwyn N. Tyser
Herbert Fred Mock	Bert Sanger, Jr.	Dr. Alvin L. Ureles
Paul M. Mock	L. E. Schaffer	
Walter L. Mock	Robert E. Schoenberg	Edwin Wyner
Richard C. Nast	Howard J. Schonfeld	Sherman B. Weiner
Nelson K. Neiman	Seymour Schonfeld	Elmer Weiss
Robert H. Neiman	Jack H. Schooler	Julian Wiley, Jr.
Melvin B. Neisner	Kermit K. Schooler	Louis Wiley
Dr. Hans Neuberg	Lawrence Schooler	Richard F. Wolin
	Donald M. Schwartz	Sanford F. Wolin
Jack Oppenheimer	Louis R. Schwartz	*Paul L. Wolf
	Peter D. Schwarz	Dr. Horace L. Wolf
William Packer	Ralph C. Schwarz, Jr.	David F. Wolfe
Arthur R. Posner	Bernard R. Schweid	
Henry L. Posner	Paul M. Schweid	Dr. Howard Yalowich
Dr. Arthur J. Present	*Marvin J. Shavlan	Doris A. Yanowitch
David H. Present		Robert E. Yanowitch
		Harold M. Yanowitch

☆

whatever influence we can to open the bars of immigration in this country. Of course, until that time we must continue to feed, clothe, and shelter those who can no longer provide these things for themselves, but we must recognize that this is purely palliative and that we must get the Jews out of Germany.

America. With this strong community backing, a number of German Jews came to Rochester, where they found jobs in various branches of the clothing industry. A bakery staffed by German-Jewish refugees opened on Monroe Avenue. The Jewish Social Service Bureau and the Baden Street Settlement helped the newcomers acculturate by offering English classes and preparation for Regents' examinations. Many German Jews who came to Rochester in this period joined B'rith Kodesh and remained lifelong members.

Arthur Herz, born in Berlin in 1921, in some ways typified the younger

Over two hundred men and women of B'rith Kodesh served in World War II. Six young men-Eugene R. Cohen, Marvin Lee, Wesley Robenstein, Sanford Schubiner, Marvin Shavlan, and Paul Wolf, the son of Rabbi Wolf— died in battle. Among the B'rith Kodesh combatants was Arthur Herz, a young refugee from Berlin who arrived in Rochester in the late 1930s. He has been an active member of the temple ever since. (Courtesy Arthur Herz)

generation of German refugees that came to Rochester. His family went to Cuba in the late 1930s, seeking refuge in Latin America due to the restrictive immigration policies of the United States. Herz arrived in Rochester in 1939 to study photography at the forerunner of Rochester Institute of Technology; the rest of the family came to Rochester the following year. The Herz family joined B'rith Kodesh, though the service struck Arthur as rather Episcopalian in character. His real connection to B'rith Kodesh began during World War II, when he was stationed in an army base in the Carolinas. One day a message came over the loudspeakers, asking Herz to report to the main headquarters. Philip Bernstein, making a tour of military installations, had learned that Herz was present at this particular base, and spent several hours talking with him. Herz remembers that he was grateful for the opportunity to get out of KP duty. When he returned to Rochester after the war, he became an active member of B'rith Kodesh, and remains one today. He has taken a special interest in social action, and particularly the right of free immigration to the United States.

A Rabbi At War

After 1939, Bernstein supported America's war-readiness programs with all the fervor of a convert. But in 1940 and 1941, with the United States on the sidelines, there was little to cheer as Hitler's armies ripped their way through Europe. "Every important Jewish center on the European continent has been ruined," Bernstein wrote in 1941. "All important religious and cultural institutions have been destroyed. The scholars and rabbis have been imprisoned, scattered to the four winds." A new responsibility had been thrust upon the Jews of America, and an obligation to do more than indulge in lamentations.

In this situation, Palestine was one of the few available antidotes to despair. Though Bernstein had always been a Zionist, Palestine now began to occupy an ever increasing share of his attention. He demanded an end to the White Paper restrictions on Jewish immigration to Palestine, and called for the right of Palestinian Jews to form their own military units in the campaign against Hitler. In 1942 he celebrated the 25th anniversary of the Balfour Declaration with a sermon, "The Greatest Day in Jewish History." When Chaim Weizmann came to Rochester in March 1941, Bernstein welcomed him with an address that argued for the crucial spiritual importance of Palestine in the midst of the European carnage:

From 1943 through 1946, Philip Bernstein was the executive director of Committee on Army and Navy Religious Activities (CANRA) of the Jewish Welfare Board, and the supervisor of the over three hundred Jewish chaplains in the armed forces. During the war years, Bernstein wrote with passion and eloquence on the desperate plight of European Jewry, and on the need for a Jewish state in Palestine. His wartime prominence further strengthened his friendship with Stephen S. Wise, president of the American Jewish Congress. Bernstein and Wise, shown in a meeting with military chaplains, are third and fourth from left.

It is my profound conviction that what the Jews have done in Palestine to create a new life out of desolation, to substitute courage for degradation, to give hope to the hopeless, is not only the most important development in Jewish history for nineteen hundred years, but is one of the bright and hopeful signs for mankind in this dark and tragic time. When in their despair men ask themselves why should we hope, why should we struggle to preserve spiritual values, why should we suffer for the unknown future, they may turn to what the Jews have done in Palestine.

Religious faith offered Jews one more source of hope. Though Bernstein's sermons and writings were never more concerned with political matters than during World War II, he also began to place more stress on the spiritual dimensions of Judaism. It was not enough for Jews to survive the war. Judaism had to survive as well. He wrote in 1941:

For Jews to survive simply as part of a frenzied, meaningless struggle for existence is pathetic and pitiful. But for Jews to live on because they have a great faith to live by, because they have a message of healing and hope for unhappy mankind—that is not to merely make a virtue of our necessity, but to give our people dignity, courage, and self-respect.

Under the pressure of war, Bernstein slowly discarded his religious radicalism of the 1920s and 1930s and reevaluated the core teachings of Judaism. His earlier hyper-rational, optimistic Judaism slowly disappeared. If there was no single moment of conversion, as with his transformation from pacifist to advocate of rearmament, the change was equally profound. Though he continued to admire Spinoza as a person, he had less and less sympathy with the efforts of Spinoza and others to purge all elements of mystery from God. In the 1920s and 1930s, Bernstein often claimed that modern theology had solved the problem of evil. What religious Jew during the years of World War II could make such a claim?

A Friday night sermon delivered on December 5, 1941 illustrates Bernstein's move away from his earlier positions. In "What Do Jews Believe—Messiah, Mission, Mankind?" Bernstein noted that, like most liberal Jews, he had once rejected the idea of a personal messiah. But the war caused him to rethink many of his older beliefs. Over the past decade, the world learned "how much evil one man with an idea can do in a short time." If evil could do this, why not goodness? Perhaps, he speculated, the time was not too distant when one "great historic man with a good idea" would capture the loyalty and support of all mankind. And this person was long overdue. Two days later the Japanese bombed Pearl Harbor. Within the week the United States was at war with Japan and Germany.

After the United States entered World War II, the Jewish community set out to organize chaplaincy programs for the Army and Navy. Jewish men and women would be serving in the armed forces in unprecedented numbers. The director of the chaplaincy program would have to be an energetic advocate for Jewish interests, as well as a rabbi on good terms with all three branches of Judaism.

Many thought Philip Bernstein would be an ideal choice, and in December 1942 the National Jewish Welfare Board appointed him executive director of the Committee on Army and Navy Religious Practices (CANRA). He was given the ultimate responsibility for selecting and supervising the over three hundred Jewish chaplains who served with the United States military during the war. Bernstein received a leave of absence from B'rith Kodesh. Though he returned annually to Rochester to conduct High Holy Day services, he moved with his family to New York City for the duration of the conflict. It would be over five years before Bernstein returned to Rochester on a full-time basis.

Bernstein spent much of the war traveling to meet with Jewish personnel and chaplains stateside and in every theatre of combat. He often spoke of spending Chanukah on Saipan Island, in the South Pacific, where it was so hot the candles in the menorah melted before they were lit. In the Aleutians, north of the Arctic Circle, Bernstein faced the problem of determining when to begin Sabbath services at latitudes where the sun either never rose or never set. Everywhere he went, he encountered lonely GIs who needed an encouraging word or the consolation of religion.

CANRA was a successful experiment in cooperation among the three main movements within Judaism, with a level of coordination that probably could not be duplicated today. One of CANRA's first tasks was to fashion a prayerbook for the soldiers, combining (in separate sections) the rituals of Reform, Conservative, and Orthodox Judaism. Over a

As executive director of CANRA, Rabbi Bernstein visited American armed forces throughout the European, Pacific, and Alaskan theaters. Over the graves of fallen Jewish soldiers in a New Guinea cemetery, Chaplain Albert G. Gordon, Rabbi Philip S. Bernstein, and Chaplains Aryeh Lev and Samuel W. Chomsky intone the El Malei Rachamin (memorial prayer).

million copies were printed. Bernstein's experience with the chaplaincy program confirmed his growing sense of the limitations of the Reform movement. One of Bernstein's duties was to interview prospective Reform chaplains to make sure that they were willing to work with Conservative and Orthodox GIs. As Bernstein noted in his little volume on CANRA, *Rabbis at War*, serving GI congregations from diverse Jewish backgrounds forced many Reform rabbis to go beyond the *Union Prayer Book* and use the Conservative or Orthodox rituals in the military siddur.

During his years in New York, Bernstein continued to agitate and organize for Palestine. In September 1943, he helped found the American Zionist Emergency Council (AZEC), which proved to be extraordinarily effective in gaining recognition for the idea of Jewish statehood. At the same time, with his cousin, Milton Steinberg, the distinguished rabbi of the Park Avenue Synagogue, and Protestant theologian Reinhold Niebuhr, he helped organize the Christian Council for Palestine, which was closely associated with the AZEC. Bernstein also hosted dinner parties at his New York home, helping to make a number of important converts to the Zionist cause, including journalists Max Lerner and Norman Cousins, and Freda Kirchway, editor of *The Nation*.

On November 24, 1942, Stephen S. Wise, president of the American Jewish Congress, held a press conference in Washington, in which he declared that reliable reports, confirmed by the U.S. State Department, described a systematic campaign by the Nazis for the extermination of the Jewish population of Europe. This was the first widely publicized acknowledgment of the final solution in Eastern Europe. Barely a month after Wise's press conference, Philip Bernstein began a four-part series in *The Nation*. This, along with another article by Bernstein in the *New Republic* in April 1943, "What Hope for the Jews?" was among the earliest and most important efforts by American Jewish leadership to deal with the implications of Wise's revelations. In *The Nation*, Bernstein began by reviewing the harrowing news of 1942. Piecing together fragmentary accounts from Berlin, Lodz, Warsaw, and other locations in Eastern Europe, Bernstein concluded that the reports "reveal the most horrible suffering of this war and most frightful desolation in all of Jewish history."

The Jewish question, Bernstein insisted, was not a question for Jews alone. It had been a major cause of the war. The fate of Europe was inextricably tied to the fate of the Jews. Tolerance of European anti-Semitism and the failure of Christians to condemn it in unequivocal terms were among the weak links in European society that permitted the rise of Hitler:

> It is imperative to recognize that what is happening to the Jews is but the foreshadowing of the fate of other peoples under Nazi rule. It has been the strange role of this unhappy people to mirror in its life the destiny of mankind. The oppression of the Jew has been the symbol of decay, it has led inexorably to tyranny, war, and collapse. In their early attacks upon the Jews, the Nazis revealed the pattern of their treacherous and ruthless assault upon the whole western world. And now in the mass slaughter of Jews they demonstrate what is in store for other people as further frustration embitters their mean spirits in the fourth year of war. What we can do to prevent this is still unclear.

What could be done to save European Jewry in January 1943 was indeed unclear. In the long run, Bernstein argued, the only way to bring an end to Jewish suffering was to win the war as quickly as possible. "The destruction of Hitler is the sine qua non of Jewish survival," he argued. Nevertheless, Bernstein suggested, in his articles in early 1943, a number of possible methods of assisting European Jewry: allowing Jews to have official representation to the allied powers; to allow Palestinian Jews to form an army under their own flag; permitting new Jewish settlement in Palestine; opening the borders of the United States and other nations for Jewish refugees; encouraging wavering Axis allies, especially Hungary and Romania, to keep their Jews out of the clutches of Hitler; and getting food to

Jewish children behind enemy lines.

Most of these proposals, Bernstein knew, were either unlikely to be implemented or to result in an immediate improvement in the condition of European Jews. In January 1943, with the borders of Europe almost hermetically sealed, and the forthcoming D-Day invasion over a year away, there was little practical military assistance to be offered to the trapped Jews of Europe. Bernstein recognized this tragic truth, even if some later critics of the American Jewish wartime leadership have not. Bernstein hoped most of all that Jews would have a place at the table at the inevitable discussions of a postwar settlement. There would be no lasting peace in Europe, he argued, without addressing the status of the Jews. The right of Jews to live in peace in all European countries must be protected, but many survivors would have little interest in returning to their former homes. The United States and other nations would have to accept more refugees after the war, but the only way to avert another Jewish tragedy would be to establish a Jewish homeland in Palestine.

In his writings during the war, Bernstein was among the first to use the term "Holocaust" in something close to its current meaning. "A clearer perception ten years ago of the meaning and intent of Hitlerism," he wrote in *The Nation* in January 1943, "might have spared the world this holocaust." Elsewhere in *The Nation* series he wrote of Western European countries such as France, where "such of their Jews as survive the holocaust may hope, however scarred, to regain their former status." Later that year in his Rosh Hashanah sermon at B'rith Kodesh, he called on American Jewry to not be "diverted from our ultimate objectives of seeing to it that this holocaust shall not be again."

During his visits to B'rith Kodesh during the

Arthur Herz in battle fatigues, in the aftermath of the Battle of the Bulge in the Ardennes Forest in Belgium, December 1944–January 1945. For Herz and many other B'rith Kodesh members in the service, the liberation of Germany had a personal meaning, an occasion for both sorrow and heartfelt rejoicing. (Courtesy Arthur Herz)

1942 Confirmation Class. The growing sense that American Jews now had a special responsibility for maintaining Judaism led many at B'rith Kodesh to a new sense of religious conviction. (Courtesy Department of Rare Books and Special Collections, Rush Rhees Library, University of Rochester)

war, Bernstein found his congregation doing its utmost for the war effort. The minutes noted in early 1943 that "the temple has become a beehive of defense activity. There are first aid and nutrition courses given here, sewing groups in our rooms and in the homes of members. We operate a seven day a week center of spiritual and social service." Over 220 young members of the congregation served in the armed forces during the war. There were six fatalities, including one of the sons of Rabbi Horace Wolf.

At the same time, something about the home front troubled Bernstein. Despite their concern about the fate of European Jewry, Rochester was still too calm, too normal. Berstein searched for ways to translate the depth of his feelings about the war into language that wouldn't seem to be mere ranting. In a 1964 interview, he discussed the ambivalence he felt on his frequent returns to Rochester during the war:

> I found that American Jews, even the most sympathetic, couldn't always comprehend the depth and the awfulness of the tragedy if they hadn't seen it or experienced it personally. But it was always difficult for me, returning to Rochester… to bridge what I had left and what I had come to. People here were living normally, activities at the country club were going on as usual… At the same there had befallen our people the most awful catastrophe in their history… I say this with understanding rather than blame. Because that's the way it is… I found when I came back to talk, that I had to adjust what I had to say to the capacity of the people to take it in.

Aftermath and Exodus

Most American Jews became aware of the dimensions of the Holocaust only after the war ended. Even such clear-sighted observers as Bernstein had been unable to imagine its full magnitude. During the war, like most American Jewish leaders, he regularly spoke of the urgent postwar needs of the millions of Jewish refugees and survivors displaced by Hitler. By the summer of 1945, no more than half a million Jews remained alive in what had been German-occupied Europe. The fate of the displaced persons (DPs) was high on the agenda of both the allied nations and international Jewish organizations, and would provide the background for the single most dramatic episode of Bernstein's career. After spending all of 1945 tying up loose ends at CANRA as the U.S. military demobilized, Bernstein returned to Rochester in February 1946. His return was short lived. That March, all of the major Jewish organizations concerned with the DPs—the Joint Distribution Committee, the American Jewish Congress, the American Jewish Committee, the Jewish Agency for Palestine, and the World Jewish

Congress—unanimously asked Bernstein to serve three months as Special Advisor on Jewish Affairs to General Joseph McNarney, Commander of U.S. Forces in Europe.

Bernstein was an excellent choice as advisor for Jewish affairs for several reasons. CANRA personnel had been the first representatives of organized Judaism to enter the concentration camps. They played an important role in convincing the occupation armies to establish separate DP camps for Jews. Moreover, Bernstein's familiarity with the U.S. Army, his extensive contacts in all branches of American Judaism, and his

Philip Bernstein, Special Advisor to the U.S. Army on Jewish Affairs, in Germany in 1946, with General Joseph McNarney, Commander of U.S. Forces in Europe, and General Dwight D. Eisenhower, Supreme Allied Commander in Europe. (Courtesy Department of Rare Books and Special Collections, Rush Rhees Library, University of Rochester)

commitment to Zionism made him a natural candidate for the position. After careful consideration, he decided to accept the position. In May of 1946 Bernstein and his family arrived in Frankfurt.

In Germany, Bernstein served as a civilian on the staff of General McNarney (and afterwards on that of his successor, General Lucius Clay). At the same time, he acted as an official representative of the major American Jewish organizations in Europe. He told McNarney upon his arrival that he intended to perform both jobs, and would try to work out any conflicts between the positions, but he would consider resigning if the conflict appeared to be irreconcilable. McNarney, himself, was sympathetic to the plight of the Jews, but Bernstein had to educate other army officials about Jewish concerns. Bernstein remembered that one of Gen. McNarney's chief assistants, who had little previous contact with Jews, thought "a Zionist was a Communist." Bernstein tried to enlighten him about the situation of the Jews, and brought him along on visits to the DP camps. The officer eventually became an active supporter of their cause.

In the summer of 1946, there were approximately 100,000 Jews in Germany, most of them living in DP camps. Conditions were spartan and often difficult. There was often tension between the DPs and the local German police and American GIs. Though black market activities were rampant everywhere in postwar Germany, the DP camps often became a

להציע הראשי בעיני היהודים באיזור אמריקאי
הרב גנרל ברנשטין נ"י
מתנת לדי בית-הילדים של הפועל-המזרחי בלינדנפלס
[7 XII 1946. כ"ד כסלו תש"ז

TO RABBI P. BERNSTEIN WiTH THANKS FON ALL.
HE HAS DANC FOR THE JEWiS iN EVROPE
A GIFT FROM THE CHILDERN OF MiSRACHi
LINDENFELS 17/XII 1946.

LINDENFELS
JULY 4, 1947

Dear Rabbi Bernstein.
        Enclosed are the
pictures which were taken on
the evening of your very
welcome visit to our camp.
        Not only were we delighted
to have the bananas but your
very own person.
        I do hope that you will
find it possible to make a
return visit.
        In the event you want
duplicates, please let me know.

                Sincerely yours
                James J. Markus.

Philip Bernstein's main responsibility in Germany was to be an advocate for the Displaced Persons (DPs), Holocaust survivors in central and eastern Europe to the U.S. Army. Bernstein worked to improve the conditions in the refugee camps, and to assist refugees in leaving Europe for Palestine. Bernstein's admiration and affection for the DPs were returned by individuals and groups covering the entire spectrum of Jewish belief and practice. The young boy in the Chanukah dreidl was participating in a presentation staged for Bernstein at the Lindenfels DP Camp. In the same camp, a Mizrachi group, an Orthodox Jewish Zionist organization, paid tribute to Bernstein's efforts on their behalf. (Courtesy Sophy Bernstein and Department of Rare Books and Special Collections, Rush Rhees Library, University of Rochester)

special focus of attention by authorities. A raid against black market operations in the Landsberg DP camp left one dead and many wounded. Bernstein often had to intervene with Army authorities in instances such as this, and to see to it that the DPs had adequate food and shelter. Working closely with Major Emanuel Rackman—later a leader of modern Orthodoxy and president of Bar Ilan University in Israel—Bernstein tried to ensure that observant Jews could resume their religious practices as fully as possible. He sometimes had to mediate factional disputes within the camps. More than one camp was bitterly divided between Hasidim and secular Zionists.

Both in and outside of the camps, Bernstein worked to reestablish Jewish life in Germany. He fought for and received recognition by the U.S. Army of the Central Committee of Liberated Jews as the official representatives of the DPs; he helped initiate a Jewish property restitution program; and he publicized the work within the DP camps in the American and Jewish press, working closely with noted Zionist author Marie Syrkin. In addition, he secured

A B'rith Kodesh committee working for the betterment of the DPs in January, 1948. (Courtesy Rochester Democrat & Chronicle*)*

funding and permission for the publication of a new edition of the Talmud, issued by the Central Committee of Liberated Jews. Dedicated to Bernstein, it was one of the most striking indications of the determination to return Judaism to Germany. Bernstein participated actively in numerous efforts in German cities, including Frankfurt and Wiesbaden, to rededicate synagogues after their defilement by the Nazis. One large part of this task was locating Torah scrolls; many were found. Through Bernstein's efforts, B'rith Kodesh acquired one of the rescued Torah scrolls.

Bernstein did not know what to expect from the DPs. He feared that many of them would be so battered by their wartime experiences that he would meet with "neurotic, psychotic groups of Jews." He did not find this. For the most part, the determination of the inmates of the DP camps to build new lives inspired Bernstein. Despite a decided lack of privacy in the barracks, many saw marriage and parenthood as a top priority. Equally heartening to Bernstein were the efforts by the residents of the camps to assert their Judaism. Bernstein found the deep faith of many Orthodox Jews and Hasidism, unshaken by the Holocaust, to be profoundly moving. In 1946 he found himself celebrating Simchat Torah in a DP camp with a group of Lubavitcher Hasidim, who had fled into Russia in 1940, been sent into Siberia, and had been unable to practice their faith for the duration of the war. Somehow they had made their way to Germany, and their wild rejoicing struck Bernstein as "in that atmosphere, almost miraculous."

Sophy Bernstein
Interview, April 1997

The wonder of the Jewish people is their hope. A man who had lost his wife and children in the war, and a woman who lost all of her family meet in a camp, get married, and have a baby. The dormitories were one great big bunker, and the couples had a bed, curtained off one from another. It was the coldest winter I could ever remember. They had big wood-burning stoves in the middle of the bunker. And they had lines where the women hanged their baby clothes. I had the idea of getting them new baby outfits, because they had nothing to speak of. I wrote to my husband's mother in Rochester, who was a member of a sewing group in temple. I asked the sewing groups to make layettes, simple layettes, nothing fancy, just a nightgown and a shirt, along with lots of diapers, booties and sweaters. And they proceeded to do it. And I would be in the office in Frankfurt, gathering up the layettes made by the women of B'rith Kodesh, the layettes for the boys were tied with a blue ribbon, the ones for the girls were tied with a pink ribbon.

176

For his father, Stephen Bernstein's 1947 Bar Mitzvah in Frankfurt, the first in the city in over a decade, was an assertion of the power of the God of the Jews. The service was attended by military personnel of all faiths. (Courtesy Department of Rare Books and Special Collections, Rush Rhees Library, University of Rochester)

The personal highlight of Bernstein's efforts to reestablish Judaism on German soil took place on January 25, 1947 when his son Stephen became the first Bar Mitzvah in Frankfurt since 1940. The Bernsteins experienced some special difficulties in arranging the service. Few buildings or auditoriums of any size were standing in Frankfurt in 1947, and of course there were no functioning synagogues. The service was held on the top floor of a former Jewish community center that had been turned into a German army hospital and was still filled with convalescing soldiers. A fresh coat of black paint covered over swastikas and other Nazi insignia that had only recently been emblazoned on the walls and windows. About three hundred people attended the service, including several U.S. army generals, and representatives of the DPs.

Bernstein's sermon that day was later reprinted as the final chapter of his 1950 introduction to Judaism, *What the Jews Believe*. He had never doubted, throughout the 1930s and 1940s, that the Jewish people would survive Hitler. The Bar Mitzvah of his son in Germany was proof he had been right:

Rabbi Bernstein in center of a group of DPs, probably in Poland. Bernstein was one of the first Amercans to observe the aftermath of the Kielce pogrom in Poland in the summer of 1946. (Courtesy Sophy Bernstein)

The oppressor may triumph for a moment. He may enjoy for a short time the rewards of his gangsterism, but his house is built on sand. It cannot stand against the wrath of the Lord. It cannot withstand the irresistible moral laws of history. But Israel survives. This very Bar Mitzvah in these very extraordinary circumstances demonstrates the indestructibility of our people and our faith. "Am Yisrael Chai."

Bernstein's time in Germany formed a unique period of his life. He kept up a hectic pace, shuttling among DP camps, attending appointments with prominent politicians, religious officials, and generals. Bernstein wrote to Stephen in August 1946 that in the previous two weeks he had been to Warsaw, Berlin, Vienna, and Paris. His work in Europe, he later felt, was in some ways the culmination of his entire career, the perfect marriage of his passion for the Jewish people with his administrative and diplomatic skills. He did his job well, advancing what he saw as the best interest of the DPs, while winning the trust of the generals. In a humorous letter to Orthodox Rabbi David de Sola Pool of Shearith Israel in October 1946, he wrote about some of the satisfactions of his work in Germany:

1) I don't have to deal with rabbis.
2) The generals let me finish every sentence I begin.
3) I don't have to administer anything, just give gratuitous advice.
4) I have a large house in Bad Homburg, but have reduced my retinue to four servants. (I *just* don't know how I get along.)

That was such a terrible, terrible time, because these people saw no hope. Every time Phil would go to a camp, they would ask him, "Rabbi, when are you getting us out of here?" Where were they to go? Our immigration laws were closed except to a select few. What other country would take them? The only hope was Palestine, but the British wouldn't permit it. But while we were in Germany, Haganah men would secretly go into the camps and get a group of young people and escort them over the mountains into Italy. The Haganah men were not supposed to come into Germany, you know. Phil and I put them up in our house in Bad Homburg.

5)   Emanuel Rackman takes care of the Orthodox Jews for me.

6)   There are no Conservative or Reform Jews...

10) I don't have to choose between Wise and Silver, nor even between Wise and foolish.

But moments of levity in Germany were few and far between, and became fewer after July 4, 1946. On that date, in the small Polish town of Kielce, a traditional blood libel led to a violent pogrom that killed 41 persons. Bernstein, one of the first observers on the scene, went to Kielce a few days later to survey the damage and interview survivors for a report to the army. The Kielce pogrom greatly heightened the desire of Jews to leave Poland. The U.S. Army worried, understandably, that a massive influx of Polish refugees would further tax the already badly overcrowded DP camps. Having gone to Poland to investigate the situation and make recommendations to the army, Bernstein played a central role in convincing the military authorities to keep the Polish border open, and to permit 100,000 Jews in Poland to enter Germany. Within six months, the number of Jewish DPs in Germany almost doubled. Because of this heightened activity, Bernstein felt compelled to remain at his post for another year. His remarkable 1946 Rosh Hashanah sermon at B'rith Kodesh was one of the very first accounts by an American Jew of the situation in postwar Poland.

Philip S. Bernstein, *"Rosh Hashanah 1946," sermon preached at B'rith Kodesh*

My friends, it is not in my heart this year to preach to you in accordance with the established patterns of High Holy Day sermons. I have had neither the time nor the books nor the mood to prepare them. Fate has lifted me up and placed me in the center of the greatest catastrophe of all Jewish history, and the same fate has given me an opportunity for service unparalleled in my lifetime. It would be unworthy of this, our history, unworthy of the needs of the Jewish people, unworthy of the sacrifice this congregation has made if I did not share my experience with you.

I am conscious as I do it of the unbridgeable chasm between this world and that. Rochester seems so pleasant, so serene, so normal that it is almost impossible to realize that a twenty-four-hour flight across the sea brings you into the very heart of the most ineffable tragedy of history.

This very night as we sit comfortably in our own Temple and take for granted our return thereafter to our own pleasant homes, there are undoubtedly hundreds of Jews—men, women, and children, the old, the sick, the infirm, the babies, scurrying across borders from lands where they are can no longer live to lands that do not want them. This very evening, the second Rosh Hashanah after liberation, two hundred thousand Jews still find themselves in camps living in the graveyard of memories confronting a desperate and uncertain future.

I shall try to depict the "shearit haplaytah," the surviving, scattered remnants of Israel as I saw them. Let us begin with the fourth of July. Early that morning a maddened mob of Poles gathered outside the Jewish Community House in Kielce. A little Christian boy had returned from a three-day's unexplained absence from home and told his family the Jews had detained him in a house in the woods. The blood accusation spread like wildfire, fanned of course by those who were deliberately exploiting it either through sheer elemental anti-Semitism or in order to embarrass the government of which three Jews were members. The Jews showed signs of resistance. Then a second hoax was perpetuated. Some of the officers of the local militia knocked on the door and promised safe conduct for the Jews if they would come out and entrust themselves to the military for transfer to promised safe headquarters. Some of the Jews put down their arms as requested. The officers thereupon turned them over to the crowd and they were beaten to death on that very spot before the eyes of their families and friends who were watching out of the Community House Windows. The mob broke into the house to the others and clubbed them or stoned them to death—women and children joining with the men in a sheer orgy of bestiality. They seized Jews on trains, took them off and pounded them into pulp on the very platform of the stations...

One day, hundreds of people gathered around us in a repatriation center near where the Ghetto had stood in Lodz. They pleaded with me, "Save us! Take us to safety out of Poland!" In the hospital in Lodz I called upon those who lived through the Kielce pogrom. For some it was only a temporary respite from death. One woman, whose body had been almost pounded out of human shape, told me how miraculously she and her husband had survived the war and the Nazi concentration camps. They had been separated by a thousand miles but managed as if drawn by a magnet of love to find each other when the holocaust gas passed and now with a newborn child had settled in Kielce when the pogrom struck and her husband was slain. Yes, I could understand why the Kielce pogrom deprived the Jews of whatever sense of security they had formerly possessed....

I was drawn to the Warsaw Ghetto as with a dark fascination. It was the last word in desolation and sorrow. Except for an empty, unused church on the very edge of it, an apt symbol of the ineffectuality of Christianity in preventing or mitigating the most un-Christian barbarism of all time. The Ghetto was a vast sea of rubble. Every house, every building had been systematically destroyed. There was a strange, weird deathly silence about the area. Nothing living stirs in it. No traffic passes through it. The only people seen were the human vultures, the poor Poles who dug in the ruins searching for money and valuables which Jews buried, hoping vainly to return from the camps where they were exterminated. I stood at the quiet, unused railroad siding at which Jews were loaded into the loaded box cars, and carried to the extermination chambers at Auschwitz and Treblinka.

There is a public memorial to the Ghetto resistance. But much more poignant were the un-meant memorials, the little heaps of bone fragments, the belt buckles, the utensils which the victims wore or used before they were killed. The stench of death was still in the air.

I could easily see why the Jews would want to leave Poland. Every stone cried aloud of the blood of their loved ones. The very people with whom they were now being asked to help rebuild their families were those who had helped to destroy their families. A Rabbi in the Polish army told me, "I loathe this uniform. These Poles killed my wife and two children. I will stay here only long enough to help the survivors to escape."

My heart is heavy when I report that not a single government in Europe has been prepared to offer more than temporary shelter to these people. In spite of all that these Jews and the others have suffered together at the hands of the Nazis, these Jews are still unwanted, still stigmatized, still excluded from the normalities of life.

When my predecessor laid down his responsibilities he said that there were one hundred thousand displaced Jews in the occupied countries. Today, there are two hundred thousand. In these few months, we have saved more Jews from death and despair than perhaps has ever been accomplished in so short a time in all of our tragic history. For the privilege which has been my share in this vast undertaking of rescue and for the generous ever-cooperative congregation that has made this possible, I express my profoundest gratitude.

Praised art Thou, O Lord our God, King of the universe, who has sustained us and kept us alive and brought us to this day of gratification.

Bernstein's two missions were to get the Jews from Poland into Germany, and then, since very few Jews saw Germany as their final destination, to get them out again. As he regularly said at the time, as many as ninety percent of the DPs wished to go to Palestine. As a representative of both the United States government and the American Jewish community, Bernstein sought to help the DPs attain this goal by meeting with numerous high European officials, including the prime ministers of Great Britain, Poland, Czechoslovakia, and Italy. He had a frosty meeting with the firmly anti-Zionist British Foreign Minister Ernest Bevin. In the United States he had interviews with Gen. Dwight D. Eisenhower, Secretary of State Dean Acheson and Secretary of War Robert Patterson.

On September 11, 1946, Bernstein traveled to Castel Gandolfo, the summer residence of the Pope, to ask Pius XII to use his influence to encourage the Italian government to permit the temporary settlement in Italy of 25,000 Polish-Jewish refugees. When Bernstein arrived he found two "kibbutzim" of DPs in the town, awaiting transit to Palestine. When Bernstein spoke of the positive role the Church had played in saving Jews from the Nazis, especially in France, Belgium, and Italy, the Pope was deeply moved. "At this point he said the persecution of the Jews 'was dreadful.' He used that word 'dreadful' again and again in the conversation, as he referred to the martyrdom of the Jews. The word seemed to have special significance to him, as if connoting something vile and unholy."

The Pope expressed outrage at the Kielce pogrom, and on the matter

"Strength, Not Idealism,"
Philip Bernstein,
Christian Century 66
July 20, 1949

What has become clear to me is that in a world which permitted the slaughter of six million Jews and denied asylum to their survivors, Jews were only saved by the force of their own determination and by their own strength. Christendom did not save them; it was unwilling or unable to do so. Appeals to humanitarian considerations and to law or justice were futile. It was Jewish strength, moral and military, which alone salvaged hope from the wreckage.

There is a connection between the two basic ideas which

of the Polish refugees, he agreed to speak to the Italian government. Bernstein urged Pius XII to offer a forthright condemnation of Polish anti-Semitism. The Pope said he would ask the Church to do so, but also said that communication with the Church had become difficult, and the Church's position in Poland, under attack from the Soviet authorities, was far from secure. At the end of the audience, the Pope offered a benediction, and Bernstein asked Pius XII to bless some rosaries he had brought for Catholic friends.

During his return to the United States for the High Holy Days in 1946, Bernstein also had a chance to report directly to President Harry Truman, and to urge the president to work to liberalize America's immigration policy. Bernstein discussed the plight of the DPs, focusing on the difficulties they were having in getting to Palestine and in gaining permanent status in any European country. Truman—Bernstein's favorite among the seven presidents he met—was impressed by the presentation:

> **President Truman:** I can't understand it. The Jews have been good citizens in the United States. I intend to ask Congress to liberalize our immigration laws so as to admit more of these people. These people would be assets to any country. I can't understand the attitudes that the others take.
> **Rabbi Bernstein:** The world is sick, Mr. President. This is a symptom of it.
> **President Truman:** I believe you are right, Rabbi. The world is sick.

After returning to Europe in the fall of 1946, Bernstein continued to work on behalf of the DPs. To the extent permitted by his official status, he worked with the *Bricha*, the quasi-secret effort by the DPs to leave Europe and enter Palestine, often supported by representatives of the Haganah. The final act of Bernstein's tenure in Germany was his presentation, on August 8, 1947, to the United Nations Special Committee on Palestine (UNSCOP). The committee, in Europe to investigate first hand the conditions in the DP camps, invited Bernstein to make a presentation. Bernstein later regarded this as the most important address of his life. He told the committee that 90 percent of the DPs wished to go to Palestine, though if the United States allowed them in about 30 percent would go there. If the United States opened its doors while Palestine remained closed, half of the DPs would come to the United States; the other half would fight their way into Palestine. Bernstein spent much of his time with UNSCOP trying to allay the suspicions of the delegates from countries with large Islamic populations—India, Iran, and Yugoslavia—that the demands for immigration to Palestine were

Bernstein family photo at about the time of Rabbi Bernstein's return from Europe. left to right: Philip Bernstein, Jeremy, Alice, Sophy, Stephen. (Courtesy Sophy Bernstein)

genuine and not the product of Zionist propaganda. Bernstein always felt that he had played a part in shaping UNSCOP's recommendations to the full United Nations that an independent Jewish state be created in a part of a partitioned Palestine, and that the displaced Jews of Europe be given the right of emigration to the new entity.

Bernstein returned to Rochester in the fall of 1947, this time to stay. More cautious and subdued, he had discarded both his religious radicalism and commitments to pacifism and socialism. Israel stood at the center of his changed view of the world, together with the obligation of American Jews to support and defend the new state. In May 1948 Israel was born. For Bernstein, the establishment of Israel was "the most revolutionary event that has occurred in Jewish history in untold centuries."

Bernstein's rethinking of Judaism culminated in his well-known 1950 volume, *What the Jews Believe.* This was probably the first significant synthesis of American Judaism to be decisively shaped by the experiences of the Jews in World War II. The Holocaust figures into almost every chapter of *What the Jews Believe,* and the volume concludes with the sermon Bernstein delivered at his son's 1947 Bar Mitzvah in Frankfurt. Bernstein viewed the Holocaust not as a challenge to faith, but as a spur to more genuine belief. He quotes an Orthodox rabbi to the effect that the most important lesson the rabbi learned from the concentration camps was the need to keep the Sabbath. Elsewhere, Bernstein writes that although at first he found this a surprising and perhaps inadequate lesson to draw from the Holocaust, on further reflection, he found it entirely appropriate.

Bernstein returned to Rochester with a new attitude to politics. He now

the past decade has forced upon me. It is that strength is indispensable to survival and to progress. Christian principles, ethical idealism, humane internationalism resting on weakness are destined to futility in the face of the cynicism, the indifference, the brutality of which human beings have proved capable.

God's Kingdom will be achieved not through a general soft humanitarianism, pacifism, social idealism, but by organizing men's basic interests into the pattern of a just and workable society. The American colonies gave the world a great example. Facing profound conflicts of interests, they established a government based on mutual respect for the right of the states and resting ultimately on police power. In this kind of society, stable and strong, there is a place for the kindlier virtues. But the point is that strength establishes and maintains the framework in which love is possible, not the other way around.

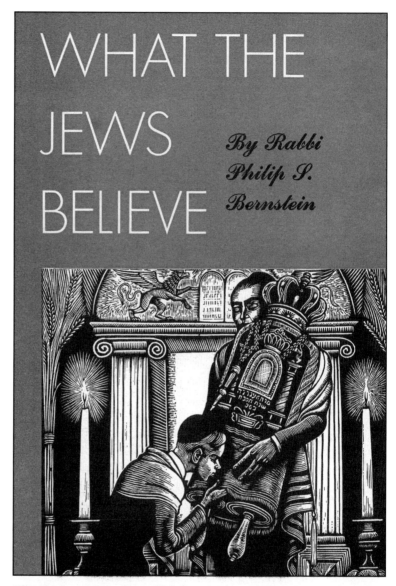

What The Jews Believe, *first published in 1950, was Philip Bernstein's best-selling account of the meaning of Judaism, and a personal distillation of the lessons he had learned over the past decade.*

believed that among the strengths of traditional religion was its ability to withstand passing theological and political fads, and its recognition of the human potential for sin. Bernstein and many others saw the Cold War as the first test of the lesson of World War II that evil had to be resisted by force. In one of his first sermons after his return to Rochester, "Can We Make Peace With the Russians," delivered on October 24, 1947, Bernstein cautioned against anti-Soviet hysteria, but argued that Americans shouldn't shirk from the ultimate implications of the confrontation between the United

States and the Soviet Union. "There was a time when I thought that nothing was worse than war. Now I know that Hitler was worse than war and the gas chambers were worse than war, and Jewish homelessness is worse than war."

Bernstein was hardly alone among religious thinkers who in the postwar world repented of their earlier enthusiasm for religious and political radicalism. There are striking parallels between Bernstein's spiritual evolution and that of his good friend Reinhold Niebuhr, probably the most widely respected American theologian of the midcentury. Bernstein's major statement of his new views on politics and religion appeared in the non-denominational Protestant *Christian Century*, a journal heavily influenced by Niebuhr. Bernstein was asked to contribute to a series of articles the journal ran every ten years, "How My Mind Has Changed in the Last Decade." There was no lack of lessons to be found in the 1940s, the most terrible (and in some ways also the most miraculous) decade in all of Jewish history. In his 1949 article, "Strength, Not Idealism," Bernstein argued that pacifism had proved ineffective against Hitler, and that idealistic professions of goodwill toward the Jews had neither prevented the Holocaust nor assisted Jews in the creation of their own state after the war. Jews had to deal with their problems from a position of strength, and not as supplicants. The world was better off dominated by strong governments that used their power to shape international relations for the common good. This would remain Bernstein's political credo for the rest of his life.

Sanctuary of Gibbs Street Temple.

Chapter V

Post-War Growth and Contemporary Challenges, 1948–Present

Introduction: Berstein's Return to Rochester

Rabbi Philip Bernstein's return to Rochester after his postwar service in Germany was not a foregone conclusion. He had long entertained the possibility of going elsewhere. As early as 1929, Stephen S. Wise told Bernstein of openings in other congregations, and urged him to spend no more than a few more years in Rochester. Wise felt that Rochester was too small a city for a rabbi of Bernstein's abilities. During the 1930s and 1940s, Wise regularly tempted his disciple with offers from larger and more prestigious pulpits, including KAM Isaiah Anshe Mayriv in Chicago, and Boston's Temple Israel, which was twice a serious suitor for Bernstein's services. Temple Emanu-el in New York City also made discreet inquiries as to Bernstein's availability. He was not interested. When Bernstein extended his leave of absence in 1946, some B'rith Kodesh trustees were not pleased, and wondered when the congregation would again have a full-time rabbi. But the majority of the board

Demolition of the Gibbs Street Temple in 1965 by the Atlas Wrecking Company.

From Old to New: The spanking new Elmwood Avenue Temple viewed from the portico side at its opening in 1962. The new temple marked the movement of most B'rith Kodesh members from the city to the suburb. (Photo by Molitor)

refused Bernstein's offer to resign, and extended his leave of absence for another year.

The serious illness of Bernstein's mother prompted his return to Rochester in the fall of 1947. Except for this, Bernstein would likely have remained as Advisor on Jewish Affairs until the creation of the state of Israel. How the B'rith Kodesh trustees might have reacted to a proposal for an additional leave of absence is unclear. Even after Bernstein came back to Rochester, Wise tried to lure him away, and in 1948 offered him the position of secretary of political affairs for the World Jewish Congress. For the last time, Bernstein turned down his mentor's offer, and opted to stay in Rochester.

Philip Bernstein dearly loved B'rith Kodesh, but his postwar return was not based simply on sentiment. The situation was comfortable. He wished to

Consecration, 1953. New children are welcomed to the Religious School by Rabbis Philip Bernstein and Joel Dobin.

remain a pastoral rabbi, and at the same time wanted to continue his efforts on behalf of Jews and Judaism in the national and international arena. At B'rith Kodesh, Bernstein made his own schedule, and played an undiminished role in American Jewish affairs as what he called the "oldest established permanent floating rabbi in the world." In 1949, the CCAR elected Bernstein president, at age forty-eight he was the youngest ever. In 1954 he was a co-founder of AIPAC (American-Israel Public Affairs Committee), a powerful lobbying organization. During the fifteen years he was president of the organization, he traveled to Washington, D.C. almost weekly. Along with this activity, Bernstein was rabbi at B'rith Kodesh for another quarter century after his return from Germany.

B'rith Kodesh and the Baby Boom

In the fall of 1948, B'rith Kodesh celebrated its centennial. It was commemorated by an elaborate costumed pageant, in a series of mounted tableaux representing the various stages of B'rith Kodesh history. Rabbi Abba Hillel Silver spoke at the centennial celebration in the fall, and in March 1949, only a month before his death, Stephen S. Wise gave the last of his many sermons at B'rith Kodesh. In commenting on the centennial in his 1948 Rosh Hashanah sermon, Philip Bernstein honored the founders of B'rith Kodesh as being "neither sinners nor saints but typical Jews who were deeply attached to the religion of their fathers." In dedicating the new congregation to the holy covenant, Bernstein argued, the founders were both affirming the covenant established at Sinai, and pledging to be good citizens in their new country, the United States. Over its first century, nurtured by countless acts of affirming Judaism and devotion to the temple, B'rith Kodesh had grown and prospered.

Despite the horrors of the recent past, the mood of the centennial was generally optimistic. As Bernstein pointed out in 1948, as Jews celebrated the High Holy Days, for the first time in two thousand years there was a sovereign Jewish state in the Holy Land. There was much to be optimistic about in the

A scene from the B'rith Kodesh Centennial Pageant, January, 1949, l. to r., Mort Adler, Michael Miller, Bertram Hershberg, Joan Miller, Mrs. David Francis. (Photo by Len Rosenberg)

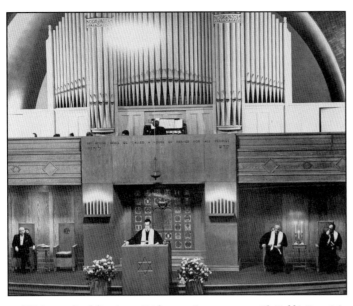

Mrs. Harold Feldman (l.) and Julia Berlove (r.) at the tercentenary celebration. Julia Berlove was one of the leaders of TBK for many decades, a national leader in Hadassah, and a close associate of Rabbi Bernstein.

Rabbi Bronstein delivering a Friday evening sermon, with Rabbi Bernstein seated on the bimah. The organist is at the massive pipe organ in the Gibbs Street sanctuary with choir members to his left.

United States as well. The prosperity of B'rith Kodesh in the 1950s made the depression a distant memory. The congregation included among its ranks many doctors, dentists, and lawyers. Increasing numbers of members worked for Xerox and Kodak and other large corporations in the Rochester area. Jews had never been more secure in America; incidents of anti-Semitism were in a steep decline, and the full acceptance of Jews in American life was an unremarkable, everyday reality.

The period of greatest growth for B'rith Kodesh and for organized Judaism in America waas the fifteen years after World War II. There were 550 members of the congregation in 1942, and over 1,200 members by 1960. The religious school increased fourfold in a decade, from 273 children in 1950, to over a thousand by 1960. The Hebrew school had over 200 students. In 1966, B'rith Kodesh was the largest congregation in Rochester, with 1,311 member families. Almost thirty percent of all those affiliated with synagogues in the Rochester area were B'rith Kodesh members. The facilities on Gibbs Street were never intended for a congregation of this size. In 1962 a new temple building opened on Elmwood Avenue in Brighton, just outside the Rochester city limits.

Some wondered whether post-war American Judaism was not in some ways the victim of its own success. Were the newly improved temples soulless, and the larger congregations impersonal? Philip Bernstein lamented the limitations imposed by growth in a 1958 article:

As on many other festive occasions B'rith Kodesh commemorated the 1954 tercentenary of Jewish settlement in North America— the arrival of twenty-three Jewish refugees from Brazil in New Amsterdam in 1654—with a pageant. The fashion of amateur theatricals in the temple lasted from the late nineteenth century into the 1970s. The practice was at its height in the post-war years, when the source of the evening's entertainment was usually a popular Broadway musical, refitted with a Judaized and lightly Yiddished text; "Finian's Rainbow," for example, was reborn as "Finklestein's Rainbow." The highlight of the social season at B'rith Kodesh in 1954–55 was the "Tercentenary Revue," presented on March 5, 1955. The six-episode musical drama was followed by an elaborate buffet, and the evening concluded with dancing to the music of Len Hawley and his orchestra. "All this," the flyer for the event promised, "for three dollars a person." A typical scene of the revue underlined Jewish support for American independence. Tercentenary Revue Staff l. to r. James Feldman, Mrs. Harold Feldman, Miriam Morris, Peggy Savlov, Pinny Cooke, Sara Elizabeth Goldblatt, Sylvia Nadritch (Photos by Louelen)

Tercentenary Revue scene of Revolutionary War period set in 1775 Philadelphia with Mr. and Mrs. Julius H. Michaels as Mr. and Mrs. Haym Solomon.

(Many Jews, both officers and enlisted men, helped the colonies struggle for freedom. Haym Solomon, Philadelphia broker, helped the new government during a period of economic struggle and distress.)

1775. YOU ARE THERE.

I'm a Yankee Doodle Dandy
—I'm a Yankee Doodle Doo
A regular native of the U.S.A.
And happy that I am a Jew
I've got a dandy Uncle Sammy
And I'm his Yankee pride and joy-
I've even got a Yankee dolly
—I am Hymie, She is Mollie
I am a Yankee Doodle Boy
I'm his Yankee Doodle Dolly-
I'm a Yankee Doodle girl
A friend to all of the community
They tell me that I am a pearl.
I'm just a Yankee Doodle Sweetheart
So gay and full of fol-de-rol
I'm simply great at Yankee dishes
—oh my knishes are delicious
I am a Yankee Doodle Doll!

> I find this year, for the first time, that I do not know the sixty-
> one members of our Confirmation class by name. When I blessed
> them personally at the ceremony I really didn't know what to say,
> apart from innocuous generalities. Gone are the days, probably
> forever, when each youngster had a personal meaning for me and I
> could reach out to his innermost being at the most sacred moment
> of his life. When I recall what a certain rabbi meant to me in a
> similar crucial state of my development, I question the value of our
> "success." No efficiency of administration, no adequacy of facilities
> can compensate for the loss of the personal touch.

Though B'rith Kodesh's growth in the post-war years was impressive, there was a general sense that there was a declining level of piety and Jewish education and knowledge among the Reform laity. In 1961 the percentage of Rochester Jews who either never attended services or attended only on the High Holy Days was thirty percent. This percentage more than doubled over the next two decades. By the late 1940s, Bernstein felt there was a need to return to the basics, to Hebrew instruction and study of the Torah. The attempts to address this perceived decline were central to the history of B'rith Kodesh after World War II.

In the fall of 1948 Bernstein complained that "our educational program is basically unsatisfactory," that it was mere "Melba toast education," very thin and without much substance; most students attended religious school for only two hours a week. The level of Jewish knowledge among the children of the congregation left him disheartened:

> As teacher of the Confirmation class, I find it very discouraging
> to test the children on the knowledge they have acquired throughout
> the years of Sunday School. Most of them cannot even read a single
> Hebrew word. Maintaining our Hebrew school on a voluntary basis,
> only some 10 to 15% of our children get any kind of Hebrew
> education.

After World War II Bar Mitzvah (and later, Bat Mitzvah) became a near-universal rite of passage at B'rith Kodesh. Bar Mitzvah, reintroduced at B'rith Kodesh around 1940, took a while to assume its current level of acceptance and prestige. In the mid-1950s, fewer than half of the young boys in the congregation became Bar Mitzvah. Over the next fifteen years, the growing demand for Bar Mitzvah ceremonies (and of course, for the obligatory catered affair afterward) led to an increased enrollment in the religious and Hebrew schools, but not necessarily in the seriousness of the students.

In the late 1950s, due to the lax requirements at B'rith Kodesh, Rabbi Herbert Bronstein noted in a 1970 sermon, "there were a good number of people who were trying to make this congregation into a Bar Mitzvah factory. They would join it four years before the Bar Mitzvah, get through the Bar Mitzvah and leave." The clamor for Bar Mitzvah was an opportunity for the temple to tighten its standards. In 1959, the religious school instituted a policy that required Bar Mitzvah candidates to start Hebrew School by the fourth grade and complete four years of Hebrew education, attend religious

Rabbis Philip Bernstein and Herbert Bronstein in front of open ark in the Gibbs Street sanctuary with young congregants.

Due to overcrowding, from 1956 through 1962, High Holy Day services and Confirmation ceremonies were held in the 3,100-seat Eastman Theatre. The post-war baby boom swelled up religious school enrollments, and the 1962 Confirmation Class, with 83 confirmands, was the largest in the history of the temple.

Temple B'rith Kodesh
ROCHESTER · NEW YORK

SHAVUOT
CONFIRMATION SERVICE

Saturday, June 9th, Nineteen Hundred Sixty-Two

SIVAN 5722

CONFIRMANDS

Nancy Joy Ackoff	Marcia Lynn Goldstein	David Eli Ness
Susan Lee Allen	Suzanne Nancy Golfe	Nancy Ellen Rabin
Maybelle Joy Altman	Jane Susan Gordon	Susan Wynn Relin
Lois Atkin	Stanley James Haber	Carol Diane Rosenberg
Rose Ann Atkin	Suzanne Naomi Haber	Barbara Ann Rosenbloom
Elaine Roberta Baker	James G. Hart	David Lee Rosenbloom
Robert Becker	Karen Sue Horn	Joan Margaret Rothstein
Robert S. Berger	Frederic A. Itkin	Sharon Leslie Rothstein
Barbara Ann Berman	Dodye A. Kahn	Vicki Lee Salin
Suzanne Carol Bernhardt	Owen James Kaplan	Dianne Sattinger
Jeffrey B. Blanchard	Robert E. Kates	Dale R. Schaffer
Sima Sharon Bogorad	Robert Lewis King	Kathryn Schwartz
Sanders Harold Borisoff	Patricia Bennett Koren	James A. Singer
Naomi Ruth Carson	Richard Alan Kroll	James Harvey Sloan
Lynne Carol Cramer	Carol Leslie Lang	Lawrence Bloom Slotnick
Tamar Diesendruck	Linda Ann Levin	Wendy Lee Smith
Richard A. Feinberg	Barbara Levine	Randa Jean Sokol
David G. Flaum	Kathryn Ellen Lewis	Barbara Jane Solomon
Gail Ann Friedman	Joel Raymond Lipshutz	Susan Jane Strassberg
Nancy Friedman	Stanley M. Litwin	Robert Joseph Tishler
Arthur James Gallancy	Carol Anne Louis	Gary William Ware
Sharyn Bette Gelb	Janet Beth Lovenheim	Amy Lynne Weg
Lawrence Richard Gersh	Robert David Luss	Susan Ellen Weinberg
Kenneth David Gilman	Della Huette Metzger	Ellen Weiss
Nancy Goldberg	Carol B. Michaels	Sue Ann Winkler
Robert Ira Goldberg	Lawrence L. Miller	David Myron Wolk
Sandra Jane Goldberg	Nanci Miller	Laurie Gail Zeitz
Malcolm Anthony Goldstein	Marlene Toby Morris	

school three times a week, and agree to stay in religious school through Confirmation. Over the 1960s and 1970s, Bat Mitzvah became a standard ceremony for Jewish girls at B'rith Kodesh; as common, in fact, as the Bar Mitzvah. Within Rochester's Jewish community as a whole, the percentage of girls celebrating Bat Mitzvah increased fivefold from 1966 to 1980.

If Bar and Bat Mitzvah were increasingly important at B'rith Kodesh, for many, the main ceremony for young people in the congregation was Confirmation. From the 1850s, this had been a ceremony celebrated at B'rith Kodesh with considerable pomp; for many experiencing the rite, it remained one of the highlights of their life. There were many changes over the years. In the earliest days, each confirmand read a prayer, and the Confirmation class conducted a short service. Rabbi Horace Wolf believed that individual participation in the service by the Confirmation class emphasized the individual over the group, weakening the unity of the service. The highlight of the service, he thought, should be the sermon by the rabbi and the rabbinic blessing afterward. Despite this limited participation by the students, Confirmation was an important life passage. Elizabeth Schwartz has retained vivid memories of her 1920 Confirmation for over seventy years:

> We wore white dresses and carried little nosegays of sweetpeas. The whole Sunday school marched into Assembly Hall at Gibbs Street, singing a hymn, with the Confirmation class coming in last and sitting in front. Rabbi Wolf delivered a sermon, and then called each of us to the altar, a boy and a girl at the same time, standing on either side of him. I don't really remember the message Rabbi Wolf gave to me after the blessing, but I remember what he said to the boy I was paired with, Louis Black. He told Louis that he was the oldest boy in the family, and he had a special obligation to be a role model and role setter for his siblings.

The Confirmation service at B'rith Kodesh reached its apex in the 1950s and 1960s both in the numbers of participants—peaking at 83 in 1962—and in the intricacy of the ceremony. During the 1960s the highlight of the Confirmation ceremony was a cantata, created and arranged by Tamar Bronstein, Herbert Bronstein's wife, who carefully rehearsed the students for months. Carol Yunker remembers her Confirmation in 1962 as one of the special days of her life:

> We marched solemnly into the Eastman Theatre in our robes, each girl carrying an elegant bouquet of roses, a gift from Sisterhood. We were carefully instructed on how to hold it, at a

Pastoral Visits

In the 1950s, the greater size of the congregation made it more difficult for B'rith Kodesh rabbis to perform their pastoral functions. The Board of Trustees at one point suggested that Rabbi Bernstein forgo pastoral visits, with all of the duties to fall on rabbinic associates. Bernstein rejected this idea, but acknowledged that visiting the needy members of the congregation was a necessary but difficult obligation. In the late 1950s, Rabbis Philip Bernstein and Herbert Bronstein often paid between ten and twenty pastoral calls a week. The counsel of both B'rith Kodesh rabbis was greatly respected, both in and out of the temple. Hazzan Samuel Rosenbaum of Temple

specific angle and cradled in the crook of our elbow. The theater was filled to capacity with our family, friends, and relatives. We each had a special role; mine, along with two girlfriends, was to present the floral offering.

The Confirmation service has changed since the 1970s. Through 1975 confirmands classes wore robes—white for girls, dark for the boys. Many saw adoption of the robes as an egalitarian decision. During the depression, the use of robes was a way to spare people the embarrassment of not being able to afford new clothes. In 1975 the Confirmation class voted to abolish "conformity," and the wearing of robes was abolished. Confirmation ceremonies have become less elaborate, and the size of the Confirmation class has dropped considerably, reaching a nadir of ten in 1996. In 1998 there were fifteen in the Confirmation class. Despite the changes, Confirmation is one of the most important ceremonies in the B'rith Kodesh annual cycle.

There were two main architects of the B'rith Kodesh religious curriculum in the 1960s and 1970s: Rabbi Herbert Bronstein and Director of Education Aaron Braveman. Braveman became director of education in 1959, remaining in the position until 1983. A Rochester native who spent most of his formative years in Palestine, Braveman had no specifically Reform Jewish background before he became involved in teaching Hebrew

Confirmation service, in Eastman Theatre in the late 1950s.

Aaron Braveman, Education Director, 1960–1983, and current leader of senior adult activities at Temple.

Harold Movsky surrounded by Lovenheim cousins whom he had prepared to become B'nei Mitzvah. l. to r.: Barbara, David, Bob, Martha, Harold Movsky, Janet, John, Peter, Lisa, Jennifer, Helene, on the occasion of Helene's Bat Mitzvah. (Courtesy Roberta Lovenheim)

in Rochester-area synagogues. In 1954 he started teaching Hebrew at B'rith Kodesh, and in 1957 he became principal of the Hebrew department. Encouraged by Rabbi Bronstein to obtain professional training in education, Braveman became the first full-time professional educational director of B'rith Kodesh in 1960. Braveman and Bronstein introduced many innovations into the religious school, including a new curriculum for social issues, and a more comprehensive Hebrew program. The Cohn and Dworkin institutes, developed by Herbert Bronstein, gave teenagers in the post-Confirmation years an opportunity for extended periods of retreat, study, and spiritual reflection. The institutes attained national recognition as programs that developed Jewish commitment and leadership.

Harold Movsky was a significant figure at the B'rith Kodesh religious school during the postwar years. In the 1940s he began to teach Hebrew and instruct Bar and Bat Mitzvah candidates at B'rith Kodesh. A much beloved figure in the congregation, he knew every nook and cranny of the Gibbs Street sanctuary, and later, the Elmwood Avenue building. After his retirement, Movsky's involvement with the temple increased. Through the 1980s he was an indispensable figure at the congregation, helping to coordinate the planning for wedding ceremonies and other major temple events.

Herbert Bronstein and the Revival of Tradition

Assistant rabbis assumed a new importance at B'rith Kodesh during and after World War II. During Bernstein's war-related absence, Horace Manacher assisted Benjamin Goldstein in conducting services. Rabbi

Beth-El remarked in an interview in 1976, "In times of personal problems of my own I've frequently gone to Rabbi Bernstein, whom I consider a friend and a very wise person, and felt no compunction about it. And I know others who feel the same way."

Installation of Rabbi Herbert Bronstein in 1958. l. to r. Rabbi Samuel Blumenfield (Mrs. Bronstein's father), Tamar Bronstein, Rabbi Bronstein, Rabbi Bernstein. (Courtesy Herbert Bronstein)

Martin Zion's rabbinic career began at B'rith Kodesh in 1946. Rabbi Zion remembers B'rith Kodesh as a wonderful place to launch a career. The congregation was supportive, and when Rabbi Bernstein returned from Europe, he was an excellent model for a young rabbi, charismatic and caring, witty and wise. Rabbi Zion, who for many years was rabbi at Temple Israel in New York City, remembers the three years he spent in Rochester with great fondness. (Courtesy Martin Zion)

Benjamin Friedman of Syracuse came to Rochester about once a month to lead services, much as he had during the illness of Horace Wolf during the 1920s. In 1945, with the continued absence of Rabbi Bernstein, Herbert Weiner became the interim rabbi, succeeded the following year by Martin Zion. In 1949, Myron Weingarten became assistant rabbi at B'rith Kodesh. Weingarten devoted several sermons to the implications for Judaism of such post-war intellectual movements as psychiatry and existentialism. In 1954 Weingarten was appointed rabbi at a congregation in Wilkes-Barre, Pennsylvania. He died the following year, at the shockingly young age of thirty-four. He was followed at B'rith Kodesh by Joel Dobin. After several years, Dobin left Rochester in 1957 for a congregation in Alexandria, Louisiana.

In the fall of 1957, Herbert Bronstein joined B'rith Kodesh as the new assistant rabbi. He served as rabbi for fifteen years in Rochester, where he had a profound influence in shaping the direction of the congregation. Born in 1930, Bronstein was a native Cincinnatian, and, like Rabbi Wolf, also a graduate of the University of Cincinnati and Hebrew Union College (HUC). Bronstein, who had grown up in an observant household, and attended Conservative and Reform synagogues, was also active in Habonim, a Labor Zionist organization that, if ostensibly secular, deepened his experience of Judaism as both a religious and cultural phenomenon. After deciding to become a rabbi, he was uncertain whether to attend HUC or the main Conservative rabbinical school, the Jewish Theological Seminary in New York. Though he did attend HUC starting in 1952, he was uncomfortable with the elements of classic Reform that persisted there, and formed a student group that petitioned—unsuccessfully—to permit student rabbis to wear kipot while conducting services.

When he graduated from HUC in 1957, Herbert Bronstein received several offers for assistant rabbi positions. He chose B'rith Kodesh, he recounted in an interview, because "I sensed in Phil Bernstein someone who would be open to a young rabbi who would bring more tradition into the congregation. I felt in the congregation a warmth, a sense of possibilities, a willingness to try new things." Reform of the liturgy would be one of Rabbi Bronstein's major roles at B'rith Kodesh, acting as, in his words, Philip

Bernstein's "cat's paw," the person who took charge of the efforts to inject elements of the traditional liturgy into the religious life of the congregation.

Since returning to Rochester in 1947, Bernstein himself had tried to include more elements of the traditional liturgy in B'rith Kodesh. In 1948, he complained in a sermon that "Reform Judaism made the fundamental mistake of assuming that men can live by ideas alone. We need institutions, customs, ceremonies, laws." He called for a codification of Reform practices, and spoke particularly of restoring the Jewish holidays to an older, richer sense of Jewish meaning. Conservative Judaism, he argued, "has wisely avoided the extremes to which Reform Judaism went. It has more Judaism to build on than we do." One way to return to this tradition was to re-emphasize the importance of the Jewish holidays and the annual ritual cycle, as he articulated in his 1950 volume *What The Jews Believe.*

From our contemporary perspective, the B'rith Kodesh service in the early 1950s had not moved far beyond the strictures of classic Reform. In 1950, the only Hebrew in the Friday evening service was the first line of the Sh'ma. In 1954, following some discussion, Bernstein persuaded the Board of Trustees to agree to use a shofar—rather than a French horn—during High Holy Day services.

Even small changes in the liturgy provoked a not unjustified fear among the upholders of classical Reform that the addition of traditional worship elements was a harbinger of more comprehensive revisions. There had been enough changes in the service to prompt Bernstein to preach a 1953 sermon, "Is B'rith Kodesh Getting too Orthodox?," a question he answered in the negative. But Bernstein was moving toward a more ritual-based and God-centered view of Judaism. In many ways, the change was quite dramatic. In the early 1930s Bernstein argued that Jewish prayer did not require a direct address to God. In 1958 he preached that "services without religion are meaningless; religion without God is a mockery. At the center of the Sabbath service must be prayer, worship, an 'I to Thou' relationship. Otherwise it is a sham." Though Bernstein remained true to the liberal, rationalistic Judaism he had espoused since the beginning of his career, he linked it to a new emphasis on ritual. In a late sermon, from 1971, Bernstein stated that in many ways he had become Reconstructionist in his principles, "liberal in theology and traditional in practice."

There was a considerable element in the congregation that viewed with alarm any evidence of "creeping Orthodoxy." In 1972 members were still criticizing "wearing the yarmulke and other Orthodox customs that have crept into the Congregation." One former president of the congregation complained in the mid 1970s that "we still have members at B'rith Kodesh who think we have too much Hebrew. They can't understand why you need Hebrew in a Reform synagogue."

Herbert Bronstein,
"The Continuum of Reform and Tradition in Judaism," c. 1958

The founding fathers of Reform Judaism, the heroes of our movement, those who lived and breathed during the age to which we now refer as the period of classical Reform, never made any innovation in a willful or irresponsible way. As Solomon Freehof, one of the greatest living experts on Reform Judaism puts it, "in all cases the principle which all the Reform rabbis consciously followed, was that no changes should be made that were not justifiably on the basis of the spirit of the Jewish tradition." The early reformers justified innovation itself only on the basis that dynamism and

Milton Sandell, shofar blower, with Rabbis Bronstein and Bernstein, 1970 High Holy Days.

The most visible indication of the tension over liturgical changes in the temple was the split in 1959 that led to the formation of Temple Sinai. The main issue at contention, as one observer noted, was that the founders of the new congregation "wanted Sunday services and the austerity of the old Reform service and its church-like quality." There was also a desire to return to a smaller, more intimate worship space, and there was ample evidence in the late 1950s, notably the expensive campaign to build a new sanctuary complex, that the older ways of doing things were not likely to return. Like the Greentree Schule that broke away from B'rith Kodesh in 1869, however, the new congregation soon found itself in retreat from its founding ideological presuppositions. Within several years, worship at Temple Sinai was probably more "traditional" than at B'rith Kodesh.

Given the strong divisions in the congregation over the questions of liturgy, the rabbis carefully introduced changes in the service. As in the 1870s, the question of head coverings became one of the most visible battlegrounds between classic Reform advocates and neo-traditionalists. Though Rabbi Bronstein does not remember wearing a kipah on the bimah during his years at B'rith Kodesh, members of the congregation were free to cover their heads during services, and in increasing numbers did so. Some viewed this with alarm. A former temple president sat in the balcony on the High Holy Days, taking an annual census on the number of covered heads, then reporting to the Board on the extent of their proliferation. Bronstein tried to persuade Bernstein to drop —at least for the High Holy Days and festivals—the standard black robes, which had little sanction in Jewish tradition, for more customary white robes. One of Bronstein's most controversial innovations, and one having little to do with the Classic Reform/Neo-Traditional debate, was his decision to offer an aliyah to a woman on the High Holy Days.

These changes affected relatively external matters. The heart of the dispute over the nature of the direction of the Reform movement was the worship service. In Herbert Bronstein, B'rith Kodesh had as rabbi one of the most gifted liturgists in Reform Judaism, someone who had definite ideas about how to transform the worship service. When he arrived at B'rith Kodesh, he found the standard service to be exceedingly formal and devoid of spiritual spontaneity. Given a free hand by Bernstein, Bronstein added additional elements of Hebrew and congregational chanting to the service, and successfully lobbied for the hiring of a cantor. Bronstein eliminated the choir from Saturday morning services to foster spiritual intimacy; he shaped the festival services, which, even more than the regular Shabbat service, emphasized older liturgical customs. In addition, he introduced weekend study sessions that exposed teenagers to an intense period of religious reflection. "The real genius of Reform Judaism," he commented in a 1966 sermon at B'rith Kodesh, "was to examine the overall pattern of Jewish observance, not to destroy it, but to revitalize it: to eliminate what was inauthentic or what actually inhibits the preservation of our Jewish values in order to strengthen the rest and develop new patterns of observance."

Herbert Bronstein has been in the forefront of the dramatic transformation of Reform worship over the past four decades, and considers himself today one of the most traditionally minded rabbis within Reform Judaism. He was a member of the CCAR liturgy committee that in 1975 produced *Gates of Prayer,* the successor to the *Union Prayer Book,* and remains active on the committee. Rabbi Bronstein edited *A Passover Haggadah,* produced under the auspices of the CCAR, which since its initial appearance in 1974 has sold over a million copies, making it the best-selling work of Jewish liturgy of our time.

In his view of Jewish liturgy, Bronstein emphasizes the importance of the symbolic component of the worship service. One steady influence has been the renowned historian of religion Mircea Eliade. In 1968–69, Bronstein took a sabbatical from B'rith Kodesh to study with Eliade at the University of Chicago. Like Eliade, Bronstein sees didactic rationalism as the

creativity were themselves the hallmarks of really traditional Judaism, and that Orthodoxy was the betrayal of this spirit. True, the primary reason for early reforms was to adjust Jewish life to the needs of modern times. But only those changes that were justified as a development of a historical Jewish tradition have remained permanent in Judaism.

Reform Judaism represents continuity in our tradition, because the entire elaborate edifice of Reform Judaism was based from its very beginning on the foundation of massive and solid scholarship and Jewish learning. The respect felt by the founders and developers of Reform Judaism for the authority of Jewish learning, their respect for the knowledge of Jewish tradition, as the authority for changes in Jewish practices, is in dramatic contrast to the cavalier and philistine disregard for learning and knowledge as the authority for change in practice which is manifested in many quarters today.

enemy of authentic religious belief. By taking the symbolic function of religion seriously, one can participate in what Bronstein called the "recovery of transcendence," the discovery of the irreducible spiritual element that makes for genuine religious worship.

From Gibbs Street to Elmwood Avenue

By the early 1950s the sanctuary on Gibbs Street was over 50 years old and in the minds of many, had not aged particularly well. With its dark interior, it often presented a gloomy place for worship, especially at late Friday evening services during Rochester's long winters. Some considered the sanctuary to be an exemplar of the "best penitentiary architecture." A 1950s repaneling of the interior and the bimah in lighter woods somewhat alleviated its dimness.

The problems with the Gibbs Street temple were more basic than its aesthetic appeal. Built for a congregation of 250 families, and with a seating capacity of around 850, its size was simply not adequate for a congregation of over 1,000 families. For several years, B'rith Kodesh held double services on the High Holy Days. From 1956 until the opening of the new temple, the congregation held Rosh Hashanah and Yom Kippur services at the nearby Eastman Theatre. The Assembly Hall on Gibbs Street was now too small for larger temple functions. Parking was a serious problem, and bathroom facilities were inadequate. There was similar pressure on the religious school, straining under the enlarged enrollments of the Baby Boom decades. By the early 1960s, classrooms that were originally intended to accommodate at most three hundred children now were filled with almost a thousand students. Every room that could possibly be turned into classroom space was utilized; much of the space, in the basement and elsewhere, was hardly conducive to an atmosphere of learning. Of necessity, the religious school held high school classes in alternative locations, such as Cutler Union on the University of Rochester campus on University Avenue, now part of the Memorial

Groundbreaking ceremony at Elmwood Avenue site, May 7, 1961. l. to r. Hy Freeman, past president, Rabbi Bernstein, Garson Meyer, building committee chairman, Rabbi Bronstein, Jack Rubens, Clifford Lovenheim, president.

Art Gallery.

Dissatisfaction with the Gibbs Street Temple was not new. As early as 1923, the Board of Trustees seriously considered selling the temple to the Order of the Moose and building a bigger sanctuary complex elsewhere. Over the next two decades, the trustees deferred the question of a new temple building, as more pressing matters—the illness of Rabbi Wolf, the depression, and the war—intervened. Many raised the question of change after 1945. In his 1948 Rosh Hashanah sermon, Bernstein called the existing physical facilities "not worthy of our history nor equal to the needs of our children." It was a theme he would return to repeatedly. By the early 1950s, the efforts to rebuild the congregation grew increasingly serious, and, spearheaded by Bernstein, fundraising efforts for a new temple complex began in earnest.

Like most older synagogues, the Gibbs Street sanctuary was downtown. There had long been pockets of poverty in the area, and these increased after the war, as the move to the suburbs gathered strength. Bernstein spoke to the congregation on the problems of slums around the temple as early as 1948. By 1956 the Board of Trustees acknowledged that the temple, "in a deteriorating neighborhood situation," required serious thought about relocating the temple elsewhere.

In the post-war years there was a movement of Rochester Jews to adjacent suburbs. For many Jewish families in Rochester, the suburb of choice was Brighton, to the immediate southeast of the city. The memories of the restrictive covenants that had kept Jewish families from moving to

Table 4

Jewish Population of Rochester (in percentages).

Area	1961	1980
Rochester Neighborhoods		
West Side	5.4	0.5
St. Paul	13.3	4.0
North Central	6.3	2.5
Downtown	0.6	0.7
Northeast	1.6	0.7
Monroe-Park	33.8	13.6
Winton-Browncroft	2.6	2.0
Rochester Totals	**63.6**%	**24.0**%
Rochester Suburbs		
Irondequoit	9.7	11.7
Brighton	22.4	44.3
Pittsford	0.3	5.5
Henrietta	2.8	2.7
Other towns (1961)	1.1	—
Penfield	—	4.2
Fairport	—	3.5
Webster	—	2.0
Other towns (1980)	—	2.1
Suburban Totals	**36.3**%	**76.0**%

Sources: Jewish Community Council of Rochester, *Leisure Time Study,* 1966; Jewish Community Federation, *The Jewish Population of Rochester, New York* (Monroe County), 1980.

Rabbis Bronstein and Bernstein welcome new students at consecration ceremony. During his fifteen years at B'rith Kodesh, 1958 to 1973, Rabbi Bronstein's commitment to a more traditional version of Reform Judaism exerted a profound influence upon the many young people he taught.

Abe Feinbloom, General Chairman of the Building Fund, prominent clothier and co-founder of Champion Knitwear.

Stephen Weingarten hands Rabbi Bernstein a stone of Jerusalem at Consecration Ceremonies for the new temple site on October 20, 1958. Mrs. Samuel Wile, granddaughter of Henry Michaels, leader of drive to erect Gibbs Street Temple, looks on. (Courtesy Rochester Public Library)

Isaac "Ike" Gordon, a successful real estate developer. Before his passing in 1965, Ike Gordon was a major contributor to many temple projects. The most important of his many benefactions was donating the plot on Elmwood Avenue that became the new home of B'rith Kodesh.

Brighton in the interwar years were largely forgotten.

By the beginning of the 1960s, only an insignificant fraction of the Jewish population of Rochester—0.2%—lived in the immediate vicinity of the temple. Almost a quarter of the area's Jews lived in Brighton (see Table 4). The movement toward Brighton, and away from Rochester, continued over the following decades. By 1980, over forty-four percent of all Jews in the metropolitan area were living in Brighton, while only half as many Jews remained in Rochester proper. Temple B'rith Kodesh also relocated to Brighton.

In May 1958, Mr. and Mrs. Isaac Gordon, Brighton real estate developers, donated fifteen acres along Elmwood Avenue to the temple. (One reason the site was available was the stream in the back of the lot that made it unsuitable for residential development.) The building committee interviewed a dozen architects for the project, before commissioning Pietro Belluschi of Cambridge, Massachusetts, to design the temple. Belluschi was an accomplished religious architect, who had designed a number of churches and

A guard of honor brings the Sifrei Torah from Gibbs Street to the new Temple on Elmwood Avenue, Simchat Torah, 5723/October 19, 1962.

Aerial View of the new Elmwood Avenue Temple, before the parking lot was finished and the surrounding area landscaped. (Photo by Molitor)

one previous synagogue, Temple Israel in Swamscott, Massachusetts.

A Consecration service for the land was held on October 20, 1958. Several years of preparation and vigorous fundraising transpired before the groundbreaking ceremony on May 7, 1961; the cornerstone was laid June 11, 1962. On Friday, October 19, 1962, the congregation transferred the Torah Scrolls and Ner Tamid to the Elmwood Avenue sanctuary. The formal dedication of the new sanctuary complex took place over the weekend of April 19–21, 1963.

Jerome "Jerry" Gordon (1915–1995), executive director of B'rith Kodesh from 1958 to 1984, supervised the growth of the temple during the period of its greatest expansion.

The new ark in the Benjamin Goldstein chapel with a close-up of the shredded metal ark doors, designed by Richard E. Filipowski, faculty member at M.I.T. (Photo by Molitor)

Luise Kaish supervising the assembly of the sanctuary ark she designed and built.

The new sanctuary was set back a good distance from Elmwood Avenue, to keep the congregation separated from the bustle of traffic. The main sanctuary, named for Rabbi Bernstein after his death, was 65 feet high and 62 feet in diameter, with a seating capacity of 850. The twelve sides of the sanctuary correspond to the twelve tribes of Israel; the dome on the roof of the sanctuary represents the Ohel-Moed, the tent of meeting of the tribes of Israel in the wilderness. The auditorium has a seating capacity of 2,000, making possible a High Holy Day seating of almost 3,000 persons.

The new temple building was filled with distinguished art. The ark in the main sanctuary, designed by Luise Kaish, was unusual for its use of figurative representations of biblical characters. The ark in the Goldstein chapel, designed by Richard E. Filipowski in welded and meshed metal, was strikingly abstract. It presented an image which the designer described as a randomness that reveals after careful scrutiny a subtle symmetry. Herbert Bronstein described the ark as depicting "order arising out of disorder, concord out of discord, harmony out of disharmony, structure out of randomness."

The Elmwood Avenue building cost over $2 million to build, in pre-1970s dollars. This called for creative fundraising, and the driving force behind this effort was Philip Bernstein. This would be, as he knew, his last great contribution to Temple B'rith Kodesh. He had long since overcome whatever diffidence he had about asking for contributions for good causes, and as one admirer put it, "he could raise water from a rock." His success came about less from any high-powered style than the immense respect he carried with his congregants.

Elmwood Avenue Temple under construction, 1961. (Courtesy Rochester Public Library)

Working closely with Philip Bernstein in this endeavor was Jerome Gordon. He first came to B'rith Kodesh in 1940 as head of Hebrew instruction, in which capacity he directed the first Bar Mitzvah candidates at the temple in almost sixty years. Gordon left B'rith Kodesh in 1944, and later spent a number a years as educational director of a Conservative synagogue in Miami. Gordon returned to Rochester at the express request of Philip Bernstein in the late 1950s after the death of Benjamin Goldstein to take the position of executive director. Gordon headed the administration of the temple during the hectic years of the building campaign for the Elmwood Avenue complex. He brought a new level of professionalism to the management of B'rith Kodesh finances. Gordon remained executive director until his retirement in 1984. He was followed by Marvin Walts, who stayed through 1992. Rona Wyner was executive director from 1992 to 1997.

Garson Meyer was chairman of the Building Committee, and the individual most responsible for supervising the construction of the new temple. He brought to the task a wealth of experience as a practical chemist, and the perspective of a long-time officer of B'rith Kodesh. Meyer was born in Rochester in 1896, the son of one of the first Hasidic families in Rochester. After getting a degree in chemical engineering from the University of Rochester in 1919, Meyer was one of the first Jews hired at Kodak. (His regular tasks included waterproofing the hiking boots of George Eastman.)

Meyer joined B'rith Kodesh in the early 1920s because he felt his children, especially his daughters, would have a better Jewish education at B'rith Kodesh than in an Orthodox shule. He soon became active in temple affairs. Elected to the Board of Trustees in 1930, Meyer stayed on the board for over forty-five years, serving as president of the temple from 1954 to

The "clerk of the works," Chairman of the Building Committee, Garson Meyer personally supervised every aspect of the building of the Elmwood Avenue Temple.

Garson Meyer,
Interview, 1976

I was originally scheduled to retire in 1963, which was beyond my 65th birthday, but Kodak wanted me to

1960 2nd Annual Board of Trustees Institute held at Letchworth State Park, September 25, 1960. (l. to r.) 1st row: Lester Berlove, Rabbi Bernstein, Theodore Applebaum, Herbert Elins, Jerome Gordon, Emanuel Goldberg, Milton Berger, Louis Rappaport, Louis Perlman, Max Farash, Philip Liebschutz, Meyer Katz, Rabbi Bronstein. 2nd row: Sophy Bernstein, Julia Berlove, Betty Elins, Sylvia Applebaum, Florence Gordon, Nathalie Goldberg, Helen Berger, Edith Perlman, Rose Rappaport, Marion Farash, Betty King, Betty Katz, Elizabeth Schwartz, Tamar Bronstein.

stay on for a couple of years. And meantime we started to construct the temple. And I felt that we needed somebody to watch every brick that went into the building, being the kind of guy I am. So I retired. I set up a clerk's station at the Works Office, right on the field. And I became the official clerk of the Works, with no pay. I really watched every nail and screw that went into the place. The land had quite a slope; there was I think a six or eight foot difference between the front and

1956. Thereafter, he was on the Executive Committee for fundraising for the new temple, chairman of the Building Committee from 1958 to 1962, and on the Dedication Committee in 1962–1963. The construction of the temple became his personal project.

From the Sisterhood to Women of Reform Judaism

The temple Sisterhood, the oldest and largest temple organization, also expanded in the post-war years. By 1950 it had almost 800 members. For many, participation in Sisterhood was a tradition, passed on from generation to generation. Joan Hart, president of the Sisterhood in the early 1950s, had been initiated into the Sisterhood by Sadie Steefel, a friend of her mother, who had been president of the Sisterhood before the turn of the century. Margie Sabath, president of the Sisterhood from 1988–1990, was the daughter of a former president, Hannah Guggenheim, and from the time she became active in the Sisterhood felt her presidency was preordained.

For other women, the Sisterhood helped to alleviate the sense of being strangers in a new city. Lelia Keyfetz, who was president of the Sisterhood from 1953 to 1956, remembered that she was "a brand new bride, intensely lonely in a new community. I was from Chicago, and I needed an extended family, so we joined Temple, and I joined Sisterhood." Linda Fuhrman, president of the Sisterhood from 1972 to 1974, originally became active because she was new to town, and eager to make friends.

In the 1940s and 1950s, the highlight of the fund-raising year was the rummage sale. Often, Rochester-area notables, such as Senator Kenneth Keating, attended the opening session of the sale, and it received extensive publicity in the local press. Mrs. Horace Hart remembers the excitement:

At the annual B'rith Kodesh Sisterhood Rummage Sale, November 1–3, 1948, sorting and marking accumulated rummage in the temple basement, l. to r.: Mmes. Robert Hart, Milton Nusbaum, Horace Hart, Mark Goodman, Morris Missal, Sam Appelbaum.

Rabbi Bernstein congratulates the weary co-chairs Mrs. Horace Hart (center) and Mrs. Morris Missal on the successful outcome of rummage sale. A rack of unsold menswear is to their right. November 3, 1948. (Photos by Ed Potter)

My big project was the Rummage Sale. The most exciting one was the year we made an arrangement for *Life* magazine to cover it. We decided that *Life* should "go to a Rummage Sale" because they were *the* thing throughout the country at that time. We had a spectacular sale, but something really important happened in the country at the last minute, and *Life* had to devote their whole magazine to that. A year later, *Life* "went to a rummage sale" somewhere in California, and we were all furious.

Once the craze of rummage sales peaked, there were other ways the Sisterhood raised funds: antique shows, auctions, and bulb sales. The Temple Judaica Shop, staffed by the Sisterhood, opened in the late 1940s, in part, as Lillian Hershberg remembered, to give temple members an alternative to cheap tin menorahs.

the rear of the site. There were thousands, several thousands of loads of landfill that had to be brought in. We were charged for each load. And I had orders that no fill should start until I got there at eight o'clock in the morning. And I counted every load that went in there, and signed for every load that went in, so we wouldn't pay for any truck that didn't have a full load. …The temple is a very, very fine building. And I feel very proud that I had a great deal to do with its construction. I'd get there in the morning, come back in the evening with my shoes all full of mud and catch hell from Mrs. Meyer.

At the 100th anniversary of the B'rith Kodesh Sisterhood in 1992, members could look back at a century of dedication to the temple, American Judaism, and the Rochester community. Past leaders at the centennial celebration. l. to r. top row: Judy Schwartz, TBK Sisterhood president, Esther Lowenthal, Mrs. Horace Hart (Joan), Harriet Croog, Sophy Bernstein. Front row: Belle S. Gitelman, Johanna Gitlin DePuyt, Mildred Feinbloom, Florence Rubens.

Judy Schwartz, President of TBK Sisterhood with Judith Hertz, president of Women of Reform Judaism, Federation of Temple Sisterhoods.

In the 1950s, the Sisterhood, spurred by Philip and Sophy Bernstein's hobby of collecting Judaica, opened a small in-house museum. The collection, in addition to memorabilia from the temple's history, includes an impressive collection of artifacts, including some items from pre-exile times. The B'rith Kodesh museum stages regular exhibitions, including a comprehensive retrospective of the temple's history for the sesquicentennial in 1998.

In the 1960s and 1970s there was a new emphasis on religion and social action in the Sisterhood. The Sisterhood started a Bat Mitzvah class and a Torah study group. There was also a greater involvement with politics. In the mid-1970s, a current affairs program, "Keeping Posted," was started because, as Betsy Bobry, president of the Sisterhood at the time stated, "I felt it was important that we shouldn't just discuss temple business. We should also be conscious of what was going on in the world." The Sisterhood in the late 1980s and early 1990s took numerous stances on controversial issues, including support of reproductive rights and civil rights for gays and lesbians. In 1996 the B'rith Kodesh Sisterhood adopted a new name, the Women of Reform Judaism, to denote their broader role within the Reform movement.

One of the greatest monuments of the Temple B'rith Kodesh Sisterhood, the Baden Street Settlement, will celebrate its centennial in 2001. It has been many decades since it served a Jewish clientele. For 35 years the Baden Street area, formerly the heart of the Jewish neighborhood of Rochester, has been largely African-American. The Baden Street Settlement continues to be active in serving its community. In 1997–98, a group from the settlement and the B'rith Kodesh Confirmation class worked together on a social service project at St. John's Nursing Home, renewing the historic links between the temple and the settlement.

Much has changed since the Sisterhood was founded in 1892, but not its commitment to developing among its members a "warmer and more active interest in the prosperity of the temple . . .the higher purposes of life, and mutual improvement among its members, and to further works of charity, philanthropy and education."

Troubles Foreign and Domestic

Philip Bernstein returned to Rochester in the late 1940s with a deep sense of the importance of America's role in the world as a protector of democracy, and of the need to support Israel. These were his primary political principles for the rest of his rabbinate. One of his first sermons after his return in October 1947, "Can We Make Peace with the Russians?," argued that World War II taught that "peace at any price" was a slogan for defeatists, and that America had to stand up to the Soviet challenge. In all of Bernstein's sermons on the subject of Communism, however, he always cautioned against hysteria, and that an overreaction might lead to a general curtailment of civil liberties. His feelings on the most prominent anti-Communist of the era are clear from the title of a 1953 sermon, "Haman, Hitler, and McCarthy."

Israel was the other keystone of Bernstein's foreign policy concerns. His long-standing Zionism, involvement with the Exodus, and friendship with most of the leading Zionists and Israeli politicians of the era confirmed in him the sense of the necessity for Israel's statehood and the essential justness of its cause. Bernstein supported Zionism without becoming entangled in the thickets of Israeli politics. In March 1948, Stephen Wise wrote Bernstein, asking him to join a Committee for Progressive Zionism within the Zionist Organization of America. Bernstein declined, telling Wise that he had long refrained from involvement in internal Zionist politics, and planned to continue to do so.

The proper role for American Jews, Bernstein believed, was to provide Israel with moral, political, and financial support, and to be an advocate for Israel's interests with the American government. Bernstein's efforts on behalf of Israel culminated in 1954, when he became the first president of the American Zionist Public Affairs Committee, renamed American-Israel Public Affairs Committee (AIPAC) in 1959. AIPAC was an outgrowth of the American Zionist Emergency Conference lobbying efforts in Washington, which began during the war. Bernstein, as president of AIPAC, made frequent trips to Washington on its behalf, while I.L. "Si" Kenen, whom Bernstein had met in Germany, was executive director and in charge of day-to-day

Rabbi Bernstein with his long-time friend David Ben Gurion (1886–1973), then retired as Prime Minister of Israel, at Ben-Gurion's home at Kibbutz Sde Boker, during a Temple trip to Israel in the late 1960s. (Courtesy Sophy Bernstein)

operations of AIPAC from its Washington office.

AIPAC strongly supported Israel during the Suez Crisis in 1956, and opposed United States efforts to sell arms to Iran and Iraq in the mid 1950s, on the plausible ground that "the pro-western regimes there might be overthrown." AIPAC and Bernstein urged before the U.S. Congress that Israel and the United States form a formal defensive alliance. (This has never happened.) AIPAC played a significant role in securing U.S. Hawk missiles for Israel in 1962, the first significant example of the transfer of military technology between the two nations. In the mid-1960s, AIPAC was one of the first organizations to widely publicize the Arab boycott against Israel. Bernstein left the presidency of AIPAC in 1969, when it was on the verge of becoming, in the words of *The New York Times*, "the most powerful, best-run, and most effective foreign policy interest group in Washington," the key player in the "Israel lobby."

If Bernstein was a passionate supporter of Israel, he was never an uncritical apologist. As early as 1950, Bernstein was criticizing the lack of legal status afforded the Reform and Conservative movements in Israel, and demanded that all the branches of Judaism be granted equal status. (The issue remains unresolved, and has been one of the major concerns of Rabbi Laurence Kotok, who became senior rabbi of B'rith Kodesh in 1996.) Bernstein, writing in the late 1950s, felt that for too many American Jews, Israel had become an object of sentimental affection, conveniently distant, rather than a real sovereign state, with its own internal dynamics:

> We have pat answers about our relationship to the Jewish State, a sort of dichotomous pattern—a sentimental, spiritual attachment to Israel which is for the Jews over there, and loyal citizenship here. But is it really so simple? What if Israel should make some grave moral blunders as most states do, at some time or another? Will we not be altogether free of the responsibility or the consequences?. . . Would American Jews not be caught in the middle?

By the mid 1960s, Philip Bernstein had been the senior rabbi of B'rith Kodesh for forty years. He watched the rise of student activism in that decade with interest and concern. He saw the rebirth of anti-war sentiments among the new generation of student radicals, and wondered whether the new generation was repeating what he considered to be his old errors. Bernstein now believed that it was sometimes necessary to use force in support of a good cause. With Israel's three major wars in two decades as a reminder, Bernstein argued that sometimes "terrible things have to be done for survival." Rather than antiwar idealism, Bernstein advocated, like Noah in Rashi's characterization, a righteousness appropriate "to the requirements of the age."

Bernstein's discomfort with the anti-war movement of the 1960s was most obvious in his attitude toward the Vietnam War. He was an ardent supporter of President Lyndon Johnson, and in 1964, along with Herbert Bronstein, for the first time since advocating the presidential candidacy of socialist Norman Thomas in 1932, he endorsed a candidate from the B'rith Kodesh pulpit. As the American involvement in Vietnam intensified after 1965, Bronstein soon regretted that endorsement from the pulpit, and criticized the escalation of the war. Bernstein was uncharacteristically tight-lipped. Finally, in a sermon in December 1967, "Vietnam: Where I Stand," he made known his views. He rejected the withdrawal of American forces or a halt to the bombing of North Vietnam. He feared there would be slaughter of the Vietnamese if U.S. forces left, a disastrous loss of American prestige, and a triumph of Communism throughout Southeast Asia. The United States, he said, had no choice but to stay the course until the North Vietnamese could be persuaded to adopt a comprehensive peace treaty.

Rabbi Bernstein addresses congregation in front of newly installed ark. (Photo by Len Rosenberg)

Philip Bernstein often circulated copies of his important sermons and articles to persons of influence. He did so with his December 1967 sermon on Vietnam; a number of high-ranking officials in the Johnson administration responded. Secretary of State Dean Rusk, by this time fairly desperate for any support for the war policy, praised Bernstein's sermon, and invited Bernstein to meet with him and other cabinet officers in Washington. Bernstein's next sermon on the topic, "Washington-Vietnam-Israel," delivered in March 1968, was even more outspoken in its support of President Johnson's Vietnam policy.

Bernstein's sermons on the Vietnam war were among the most controversial he ever delivered at B'rith Kodesh. Much of the congregational response was hostile. His stance outraged many long-time members of the congregation, admirers of Bernstein for decades. "The first letter I composed after your sermon of March 22 was too vituperative. I have torn it up," read one typical letter. "This one perhaps you will be willing to read and answer." Bernstein responded that he was just expressing his own opinions, and was comfortable with criticism of his views, either on the pulpit or from the congregation. The week after Bernstein's first pro-Vietnam war sermon, Bronstein came to the congregation with a strong criticism of American involvement. Bernstein had always been committed to Stephen Wise's notion of open and untrammeled debate within a "free synagogue." This principle could have no greater illustration than at B'rith Kodesh in the late 1960s, when its two clerical leaders took strongly contrasting views on the major issue of the day.

If any political issue rivaled the Vietnam War in the 1960s, it was the crisis of the cities. This was not a crisis in a faraway land, but one, in Rochester and many other urban areas, uncomfortably close to home. By 1960, Rochester faced kindred problems with many cities in the North, especially the declining and overcrowded housing stock in downtown areas. Those city residents with the means often moved to the suburbs; those without had little choice but to remain where they were. The stark reality was clear to Bernstein as early as 1948. "The slum areas in our own city have both have increased and deteriorated. There are neighborhoods within a stone's throw of this Temple where most of us would not put animals and which I would be ashamed to show even to DPs. The areas in which we still outrageously compel Negroes to live are a disgrace to Rochester." Bernstein strongly opposed efforts to build public housing that would reinforce existing residential segregation patterns, and championed the right of African-Americans to live wherever they wished. He saw public housing, properly implemented, as a critical tool in reviving urban communities. Bernstein and B'rith Kodesh were deeply involved in such undertakings throughout the 1950s. Members of the temple were active in the Civil Rights Movement; Rabbi Bronstein led a contingent to the March on Washington in 1963. Nonetheless, urban decline in Rochester continued.

After 1960, there were rising tensions between the growing African-American population of Rochester and the city authorities, especially the police force. Rochester was one of the first cities in the United States in the 1960s to undergo the travail of a "long, hot summer." In July 1964, simmering resentments between blacks and the police sparked a weekend of violent rioting. Almost 1,000 persons were arrested, and 300 persons were injured. There was extensive damage to local businesses from burning and looting. The center of the riot was in the area of Joseph Avenue and Hanover Street, formerly the center of the Jewish population of Rochester. In 1964 it still housed a number of Jewish businesses. The leading historian of Rochester, Blake McKelvey, has written that "Never before had Rochester experienced such a shocking ordeal as that of the riots of 1964." Herbert Bronstein remembers spending a sleepless weekend visiting the site of the riots, trying to calm distraught congregants whose livelihoods were in ruins.

The July 1964 riots were a traumatic event for the Jewish population of Rochester. If Jews disagreed over whether the rioters were anti-Semitic or simply anti-white, it disturbed most Rochester Jews that so many Jewish-owned stores were the targets of violence. In the aftermath of the riots, the Jewish business presence in the Joseph Avenue area dwindled away to insubstantial levels.

If there was anger, there was much soul searching as well. How could this have happened? What were the roots of black rage? Rabbi Bronstein, speaking at the temple in February 1965, argued that too many had simply averted their eyes from the poverty and anger of the black population of Rochester. Many in the city "had not been aware of the enormity of the problems caused by the sudden growth of a Negro ghetto of over 30,000 living in two wards of the city. When riots occurred, there was the childish search for outside groups or agitators, an unwillingness to face the cruel facts of human suffering, despair, hostility, hopelessness, in the core of our city." Bronstein warned that Jews of Rochester had to be prepared for black anger and militancy, and not to let that deter them from the needed tasks of social reconstruction.

B'rith Kodesh played an important role in the efforts to address the urban problems of Rochester. In January 1965 the Rochester Board of Urban Ministry, a Christian inner-city mission, invited the Chicago-based professional organizer and neighborhood activist Saul Alinsky to come to Rochester. Alinsky had achieved a national reputation as an advocate of "empowerment" (a term he popularized) encouraging poor and laboring people to acknowledge their grievances, confront persons of power, and organize themselves into effective organizations that could be articulate advocates for their cause. One of the first consequences of Alinsky's stay in Rochester was the organization of a black community organization, Freedom, Integration, God, Honor, and Today, commonly known as FIGHT. Alinsky and FIGHT demanded black community participation in urban planning decisions, and hiring and job training programs for African-Americans from major Rochester employers. If the program in retrospect seems fairly moderate, there was heated rhetoric on both sides. B'rith Kodesh members disagreed over the merits of FIGHT. Some joined the white support organization, Friends of FIGHT. (Whites were not allowed to join FIGHT directly.) Others felt threatened by FIGHT, often because of a fear of black militancy. In some cases the dislike was personal. One of FIGHT's early demands was the dismissal of the Jewish director of the Baden Street Settlement, and some felt that Jews, especially social workers and educators, were special targets of FIGHT.

A central event in Alinsky's campaign in Rochester took place in the spring of 1965, when Rabbi Bronstein invited Alinsky—a non-practicing Jew—to speak about FIGHT and its campaign at the temple. This would be his only public address in Rochester during the height of his campaign. Many in the temple were uncertain about the wisdom of the invitation.

Tempro Development Co. Inc.

(Courtesy Richard Rosen)

1. *Emergency House for Monroe County Department of Social Services (DDS), one of three built in Rochester in 1970.*

2. *One of three two-family houses built for Monroe County DSS Emergency Housing Program in 1991.*

3. Adopt-a-Cop *Rehab House, 39 Scio Street.*

4. *Adopt-a-Cop, 64 Ontario Street.*

5 Adopt-a-Cop, *105 Woodward Street.*

6. *New two-family house,* Adopt-a-Cop *, 6 Wait Street.*

7. *New two-family* Adopt-a-Cop, *182 Second Street.*

8. *Second Street Recreation Center, rebuilt for Genesee Settlement House.*

Under Rabbis Bernstein and Miller, Social Action became one of the most important of temple activities. Spurred by the urban crisis of the 1960s and early 1970s, the Tempro program has provided temporary housing for Rochester families in emergency situations.

Adopt-a-Cop *was a Tempro program that helped pay for the housing of a police officer in a poor inner-city neighborhood.*

Since 1995, B'rith Kodesh has sponsored an annual Mitzvah Day, a time for the collective undertaking of works of tzedekah. Hundreds of temple members have participated in this annual event. Temple B'rith Kodesh Annual Mitzvah Day, First year, 1995 (Photos by Arthur Lind)

1. *Coordinating committee: standing: Ellen Solomon, Arthur Herz, Nettie Sheiman, Tom Fink, seated: Irwin Solomon, Sid Rayburn.*

2. *B'rith Kodesh teenagers polishing Temple windows.*

3. *Religious School volunteers raking leaves in front of Temple.*

Bronstein persuaded the Sisterhood to invite Alinsky to speak at the temple, in part because Mrs. Harper Sibley, "Mrs. Rochester," long the doyenne of social activism in Rochester, agreed to chair the meeting. Alinsky agreed to speak, in large part because of the critical role played by Jews in local affairs.

The B'rith Kodesh sanctuary and auditorium were filled to capacity, and television cables and reporters crowded the corridors of the temple. Alinsky received a police escort to and from the temple. When someone asked what to do to help FIGHT, Alinsky advised them to stay away and let FIGHT develop its own strategies. Herbert Bronstein wrote to a friend at the time, that Alinsky "could have won the congregation very easily that day, instead he managed (perhaps deliberately) to offend people."

Despite the equivocal response to Alinsky, the controversy energized many in the congregation to continue the struggle for racial equality. FIGHT and kindred organizations such as Rochester Jobs Inc. (RJI) had considerable success in the late 1960s in employment and job training programs. B'rith Kodesh and the Jewish Community Council were active in the effort to establish a Police Advisory Board, the Interfaith Council, and other civil rights initiatives. In the late 1960s B'rith Kodesh held the largest convention of religious groups on race relations in the Rochester area, with over 1,000 people in attendance.

One of the most important social action projects of B'rith Kodesh in the 1970s developed out of the urban problems of the time, the Tempro Program, which provided emergency housing for families in need. The Tempro program purchased and refurbished the houses; the Monroe County Department of Social Services maintained the properties. The program started with three units on Lewis Street, and six additional units were added in 1990. In 1991, the Social Action Committee of the congregation participated in the refurbishing of the First Street Recreational Facility as a community center. Tempro remains one of the most important social action projects of the congregation.

Social action is one of the firmest commitments of the temple. The social action program has involved many members of the congregation in work in local homeless shelters, in senior residences, and hospices. It also is active in a number of campaigns for social change. In 1985 the congregation declared itself a sanctuary for refugees from Central America, and helped to shelter several families in the Rochester area. In 1995 B'rith Kodesh inaugurated Mitzvah Day, a congregation-wide program of general involvement in a variety of tzedekah or charitable projects.

Temple Visitors

Bernstein's stature within American Judaism ensured that many prominent visitors would come to Rochester and B'rith Kodesh. During the 1950s and 1960s many prominent Israeli politicians visited, old friends like Golda Meir, and such acquaintances as Abba Eban and Moshe Dayan. Governors Herbert Lehman and Nelson Rockefeller spoke at B'rith Kodesh on more than one occasion. In 1959, early during his bid for the presidency, Massachusetts Senator John F. Kennedy spoke at the temple. When the Roman Catholic Bishop of Rochester, Fulton J. Sheen, spoke at B'rith Kodesh in the early 1960s, he was, thanks to his extremely successful radio and television programs, probably the best-known Roman Catholic cleric in the United States. His appearance at B'rith Kodesh was his first address to a Jewish congregation. Speaking

Rochester Bishop Fulton J. Sheen and Rabbi Herbert Bronstein on the bimah. The national press covered Bishop Sheen's address to the B'rith Kodesh congregation in the mid 1960s. (Courtesy Rabbi Herbert Bronstein)

shortly after Vatican II, Sheen's exposition of the new Roman Catholic position—that the covenant between God and Israel was eternal and of everlasting validity—received national attention.

In recent years there has been a number of interesting speakers at B'rith Kodesh. On occasion they have been able to fill the entire sanctuary and auditorium. In November 1991, as a part of Jewish Book Month, 2,500 came to hear lawyer Alan Dershowitz offer his prescriptions for Jewish

Massachusetts Senator John F. Kennedy on his visit to B'rith Kodesh on October 1, 1959, with Abe Feinbloom, Philip Bernstein, and Arthur Lowenthal. At the time of his appearance at the temple, Kennedy was already considered a front-runner to be the Democratic presidential candidate in 1960; he would go on to win the nomination and the general election in November.

survival in America. In the spring of 1997 an equal number came to the annual lecture sponsored by the Philips S. Bernstein Society, at which Daniel Goldhagen lectured on his controversial thesis of the responsibility of ordinary Germans for the Holocaust.

Music at B'rith Kodesh

The first visit of German liturgical composer Heinrich Schalit to Rochester in 1930, highlighted by a concert of his music, and later his three-year stint as music director in the early 1940s, marked a turning point in the role of music at B'rith Kodesh. The congregation slowly abandoned the quasi-Mendelssohnian hymnody that characterized much of its liturgical music in the late nineteenth and early twentieth centuries in favor of music using authentically Jewish themes and compositions by contemporary Jewish composers. An important indication of this was a well publicized 1938 performance at the temple of Ernest Bloch's *Sacred Service* with Bernstein as the narrator.

An interest in contemporary Jewish music continued after the war. In 1948 Philip Bernstein tried to persuade Leonard Bernstein to compose a service setting for B'rith Kodesh, though the rising young composer and conductor was too busy to accept the commission. Another important American-Jewish composer, the Rochester-born and raised David Diamond, composed a Sabbath eve service, which premiered in Rochester at B'rith Kodesh in 1953. (In the spring of 1997, with the eighty-year-old composer in attendance, and B'rith Kodesh Cantor Martha Rock Birnbaum as soloist, this rarely heard work was performed again in the temple sanctuary in a

Virginia McConnell first joined the B'rith Kodesh choir in 1947, and remains a member in 1998.

Virginia McConnell, Interview 1998

My official association with Temple B'rith Kodesh began in 1947. But before I started singing at the temple, my mother, my

brother, and my aunt all sang at B'rith Kodesh. At that time, a double quartet provided the primary music for the temple. I used to come on Friday nights to listen to the singing. I first sang at B'rith Kodesh in 1943 at a High Holy Day morning children's service led by Ben Goldstein. Four years later I joined the quartet on a permanent basis. After Music Director Heinrich Schalit left the congregation in 1943, my aunt, Mrs. Lucille Brightman, became the substitute music director. She remained the director of music at B'rith Kodesh for almost twenty years. She was a professional singer and expected all the singers to be prepared, and looked dimly upon the occasional high jinks by choir members. My aunt

Cantor Martha Rock Birnbaum teaching songs for Tu B'Shvat at pre-school event organized by Yoran Hackmon, 1995. (Photo by Arthur Lind)

special concert.) In the early 1950s, the Rochester Philharmonic Orchestra and its conductor, the Austrian émigré Erich Leinsdorf, held annual Jewish music concerts at the temple. Newly composed services were often performed, such as new Sabbath services by Heinrich Schalit in 1954, and Lazare Saminsky in 1958. Since 1995, the Rochester Philharmonic Orchestra has played an annual summer concert at the temple.

For many years, the B'rith Kodesh trustees were reluctant to hire a cantor. Like many Reform congregations, B'rith Kodesh had traditionally used a music director and a vocal quartet or double quartet. As the move toward a more traditional liturgy gathered strength in the 1960s, so did the call for hiring a cantor. In May 1967 Temple B'rith Kodesh hired David Unterman, its first cantor since the early days of the Civil War, who also served as youth director. Stephen Richards followed him in the fall of 1969. Hired in 1971, Hazzan Joseph Gutherz served primarily on a part-time basis. In the fall of 1973, the temple hired Rochester-born Richard Allen as cantor and music director; Allen stayed for three years. In 1976 Steven Pearlston came to B'rith Kodesh for a one-year term as cantor.

In 1977, due primarily to financial considerations, the temple did not hire a cantor and made do with cantorial soloists, primarily hired from the Eastman School of Music. This would be the congregation's policy for a number of years. It would not be until 1988 that the temple again hired a cantor on a full-time basis, Barbara Ostfeld Horowitz, the first woman to be invested by the Hebrew Union College's School of Sacred Music. After her two-year tenure at the congregation, B'rith Kodesh returned to the practice of hiring cantorial soloists. In the fall of 1993, native Rochesterian Martha

Rock Birnbaum was hired as cantor. After her retirement in the summer of 1997, the congregation hired Cantor Joel Colman.

A New Era

In January 1960, B'rith Kodesh appointed Herbert Bronstein associate rabbi. In March of 1963, he was named co-rabbi of the congregation. He remained at B'rith Kodesh until June 1972, when North Shore Congregation in Glencoe, Illinois, one of the largest synagogues in the Midwest, appointed him senior rabbi. In his farewell, he thanked the congregation for allowing him "to teach Torah in the widest and fullest sense" in Rochester, "to be a part of the *kehila kedosha*, [the holy community] of B'rith Kodesh." Bronstein was senior rabbi at the North Shore Congregation until 1997, when he assumed emeritus status.

In the summer of 1972, Philip Bernstein announced his retirement, to become effective in May 1973. He had been the senior rabbi for forty-six years. The congregation, the Jewish people, and the world had changed in unimaginable ways since his first sermon at B'rith Kodesh in May 1926. In December, 1974, the University of Rochester inaugurated the Philip S. Bernstein Chair in Judaic Studies. Bernstein's old friend, Golda Meir, the former Prime Minister of Israel, spoke at the ceremonies. The first holder of the chair, fittingly, was Abraham Karp, long-time rabbi at Rochester's largest Conservative congregation, Temple Beth-El. He had been Bernstein's rabbinic colleague in Rochester for almost two decades, and a leading scholar of American Jewish history. Philip Bernstein gave his last public speech in 1978, a commencement address at Nazareth College in Rochester. Thereafter, slowed by Parkinson's and Alzheimer's disease, he lived a quiet life in Rochester, devotedly attended by his wife, Sophy. Philip Bernstein died on December 3, 1985.

In the mid-1970s there were other changes in the congregation. The baby boom was receding, and the rapid expansion of B'rith Kodesh was a thing of the past. It was a time of consolidation. The religious school of B'rith Kodesh declined from around 1000 students in 1970 to about 600 by 1977. If the total number of family members did not undergo a similarly dramatic decline, there was also a falling off from the peak membership numbers of the mid-1960s. By 1973 the exuberance of post-war expansion gave way to a tenser mood in the congregation. America seemed less secure and morally rudderless, while the place of the Jews in the world appeared more problematic. To remedy this problem, many in B'rith Kodesh felt the need for a rabbi who could inspire spiritual renewal and social transformation.

In the fall of 1973, Judea B. Miller became the senior rabbi of B'rith Kodesh. Miller was born in the Bronx in 1930 and raised in an Orthodox

had learned much from Schalit, and she maintained many of his innovations in the temple's liturgical music. We were very carefully rehearsed, and the music was very expressive and quite powerful.

Over the years there have been many changes. The main service for the quartet was Friday night, though in recent years we almost never sing on Fridays, and primarily sing on Saturday morning. The double quartet was gradually replaced by a single quartet for most Shabbat services, though the double quartet was retained for the High Holy Days. The regular quartet was often supplemented by voice students from the Eastman School. In the late 1960s, at the suggestion of the cantor, David Unterman, I also started singing with the volunteer women's choir on Saturday morning. Over time the quartet was slowly phased out, and the choir was enlarged. When I joined we were professional singers. Now the singers are mostly volunteers. The music has changed over the years as well. We have performed in a number of different musical styles. In recent years there has been more congregational singing, and some of the arrangements have become simpler. We have sung the liturgical works of all the important Jewish liturgical composers of the century, from Heinrich Schalit, Isadore Freed, and Max Janowski, to contemporary composers, such as

Temple B'rith Kodesh
117 GIBBS STREET
Rochester, N.Y.

THE RABBI'S STUDY

March 22, 1938

Dear Friend,

Mrs. Goldie Myerson, who is an outstanding leader of the labor movement in Palestine, will be in Rochester next week. I am inviting a small number of influential people to have lunch with her at the J. Y. M. A. on Monday noon, March 28, at 12:15.

Mrs. Myerson was a school teacher in Milwaukee until 1923 when she settled in one of the collective colonies in Palestine. She has recently played an effective part in the building of the Tel Aviv port.

Consistent with the policy of our United Jewish Welfare Fund there will be no appeal for funds. But I am inclined to believe that Mrs. Myerson will attempt to interest people in modest investments in the Tel Aviv port which thus far has been a remarkable success and a significant venture. In any event, I am sure you will find it interesting to meet and listen to the story of one of the most remarkable Jewesses of our time,

Will you indicate on the enclosed card whether you plan to attend?

Cordially,

From the mid-1950s. From left, Stuart Rosenberg, Rabbi of Temple Beth-El, Golda Meir, Philip Bernstein, and Samuel Byron Dicker, Mayor of Rochester, 1939–1955, and a member of B'rith Kodesh. (Courtesy Sophy Bernstein)

Like-minded contemporaries, Philip Bernstein and Golda Meir (1898–1978; Prime Minister of Israel, 1968–1974), shared much in common, especially an unshakable commitment to Zionism, and to the creation and defense of the state of Israel. Both before and after World War II, Golda Meir often spoke in Rochester, frequently staying with the Bernsteins. Their final public appearance together, at the Eastman Theatre, December 16, 1974, for the dedication of the Philip S.

Bernstein Chair for Judaic Studies at the University of Rochester, spoke to the strength of their life-long friendship. (Courtesy Sophy Bernstein)

220

Philip S. and Sophy Bernstein at around the time of Philip Bernstein's retirement as rabbi of B'rith Kodesh in 1973.

household. After attending New York University and obtaining a degree in psychology, he studied at HUC-JIR in New York City and Cincinnati, graduating in 1957. He served as an army chaplain and then a congregational rabbi at Temple Emanu-el in Wichita, Kansas; in 1965 he became rabbi at Temple Tifereth Israel, in Malden, Massachusetts, a suburb of Boston.

One of the formative influences on Judea Miller was the Civil Rights Movement. He campaigned for fair housing legislation in Kansas in the late 1950s, and participated in voter registration campaigns in the Mississippi Delta in 1962 and 1963. He was arrested at least three times, doing time in Mississippi jails in Hattiesburg, McComb, and Jackson. As he wrote a friend in 1965, "I remember the saliva on my cheek after I was spat upon, the black-and-blue marks on my buttock where I was kicked, the fear and frustration I experienced in Mississippi." In Boston, he was chairman of the Social Action Committee of the Massachusetts Board of Rabbis, where he played an important role in exposing urban poverty and housing discrimination in the Boston area. He was active in the grape boycotts of the United Farm Workers in the late 1960s and early 1970s, and became a friend of United Farm Workers President Cesar Chavez. His synagogue in

Samuel Adler, Michael Isaacson and Bonia Shur. Many composers have conducted their music at the temple, including Herbert Fromm and Lazar Weiner. It's always a balancing act. Some people like new music; some people want us to stick to familiar melodies.

I always have found singing at B'rith Kodesh to be a religious experience. Singing at a temple or church should never be a mere performance. The choir should participate in the worship service, and not just concentrate on the music. The temple is a very special place. For my 25th anniversary in the choir, Rabbi Bernstein made me an honorary Jew, and gave me a menorah from his personal collection. For my 50th anniversary in the choir, Rabbi Gruber called me and my husband, David, up to the bimah and blessed us. All my family was there, and it was a very special occasion. The fall of 1998 marks my 52nd consecutive year singing at B'rith Kodesh for the High Holy Days. I always feel surrounded by warmth when I come to the temple. When I sing at B'rith Kodesh I feel very cared for and protected. I feel that I am a part of B'rith Kodesh, and B'rith Kodesh is a part of me.

Engagement portrait of Anita and Judea Miller, 1951. (Courtesy Anita Miller)

Malden was available for "sanctuary" for draft resisters, and he was a leader of an anti-war sit-in by Boston area rabbis in the Kennedy Federal Office Building in Boston.

Judea Miller brought his passionate concern for social justice to B'rith Kodesh. He was a leader in Rochester of efforts to support the imposition of sanctions against the white minority government of South Africa, and to put pressure on local banks and colleges to divest from their portfolios the stock of corporations doing business with South Africa. In the summer of 1983 he was an active supporter of the Women's Peace Encampment for Nuclear Disarmament in Seneca Falls. In 1985, through his efforts, B'rith Kodesh declared itself a sanctuary for refugees of oppression from Central America and Southeast Asia. Miller vehemently opposed the death penalty, and testified before the U.S. Congress on this issue. Its restoration in the 1980s angered him intensely. He wrote in 1985, "The death penalty is a spiritual link between primitive savagery, medieval fanaticism and modern

Rabbi Judea Miller in Washington D.C., to offer the opening invocation for the U.S. House of Representatives. With Anita Miller, Rochester Congressman Frank Horton, and Speaker of the House, "Tip" O'Neill. (Courtesy Anita Miller)

Judea B. Miller, senior rabbi of B'rith Kodesh 1973–1995, in March 25, 1974. This picture accompanied one of the first of his many guest editorials and articles in the Rochester Democrat & Chronicle. *(Courtesy* Rochester Democrat & Chronicle*)*

totalitarianism. It stands for everything that humanity must reject if it is to be worthy of survival."

Miller's passionate engagement with social justice connected to his deep involvement with the spiritual dimensions of Judaism. He rejected the notion that there was a division between "religion as piety and religion as social activism." For Miller, influenced by the work of Jewish philosopher Abraham Joshua Heschel, Judaism required a "leap of action" as much as a "leap of faith." This involved "a willingness to learn by doing, by participating actively in fulfilling God's will." By so doing, "we go beyond ourselves, we surpass ourselves, and become co-workers in the task of redemption." Miller believed that in contemporary life, "The supreme issue is whether we are dead or alive to the challenge and the expectation of the living God. The crisis engulfs us all."

Miller's understanding of the prophetic responsibility of Judaism was also intensely personal. Miller agreed with Heschel that the true prophetic gift was the ability to empathize with the "pathos of God," to identify with human suffering, and to provide solace to the sick of heart. Miller's passion for social change flowed from a deep and compassionate understanding of the shared pain and misery of all humankind.

Judea B. Miller, Sermon Delivered at Temple B'rith Kodesh, August 10, 1974

The Haftarah portions for this time of year are particularly lovely. Just before the solemn fast of Tisha B'Av, there were three very somber, almost threatening Haftorot. These three prophetical portions castigate the people of Israel for faithlessness and threaten all sorts of retribution and punishment if they do not repent. But immediately after Tisha B'av, the mood changes, and there follow seven very lovely, comforting Haftorah, all with the theme of nechama, "comfort"; as in "comfort ye, comfort ye, my people." Here the prophet promises that his people will be restored, Jerusalem will be rebuilt; and there will be peace and abundance for all...

This past Thursday night President Nixon was forced to announce his resignation under ignominious circumstances. It was for all of us a sad spectacle. I had a feeling of the U'nesane tokef prayer, which we say on High Holy Days, that reminds us never to be self-satisfied, because we never know who, in the coming year, will be raised high and who will be brought low. President Nixon was brought low, very low indeed. From the highest political office in the nation—indeed in the world! And it was a sad spectacle to behold. ...

Few would want to see the man further prosecuted. His public humiliation and shame many of us believe were punishment enough. The high office of President of the United States was one that most of us respect. He disgraced it just as he disgraced himself, and this was shame and humiliation and punishment enough, that to continue prosecution now may tear the nation even further apart.

The pity that many of us felt Thursday night may invoke the sort of public compassion that may now allow us at long last to grant amnesty to draft resisters and also to resist the mad drive, the stampede to reinstate the public barbarism of the death penalty. This would be the sort of moral enlightenment that should come from tragic drama that Aristotle called catharsis. Otherwise we would have learned nothing from the tragedy of the President, and the agony of the nation would have been in vain. If a result of this, all of us, of all political suasions, would now be less self-righteous, less arrogantly positive about our own rectitude and rightness, and more and more tolerant and forgiving of others who differ, then we would have grown from this tragedy...

This is what we have learned from the Haftarah portions, the prophetical readings, from this time of year. We usually think of a prophet as someone with great courage who gets up before people in high places and tells them off when they deserve it, who pokes a finger of judgment at them and at a corrupt society, who dares to say when it is justified, "shame, shame." But that is only half of the story of prophecy. There is another aspect.

First, there are what we call in Hebrew the Divre Tochachot, "words of condemnation," when people are corrupt and arrogant. But then there is also the other half of prophecy. There must also be what are called Divre Tachunim, "words of comfort," when the tragedy and punishment that has been foretold has finally come about. A true prophet has to be able to do both: to castigate and to comfort, and to know when to do which.

Up until Thursday, Divre Tochachot, "words of condemnation," and castigation and criticism were necessary. These were vital if we were ever to retain our free institutions and our respect for law and decency. The President in his arrogant disregard for the rights and liberties of other Americans, his hypocritical belief in his own absolute rectitude and rightness to the end that almost everything could be justified, any means no matter how foul and illegal, if it were to achieve his ends and political goals; his perversion of the electoral process and the legal processes of our nation—all this required an alert citizen opposition.

But now his fall has come. His public humiliation has taken place. So now other words are required. Divre Tachumim, "words of comfort," words of solace, and yes, of forgiveness. Now words of comfort are needed so that we may bind up the wounds that were tearing us apart so that now we can unite our nation and ultimately the world for peace. This is our hope. This is our prayer.

Judea Miller, Eulogy for Rima Braave, B'rith Kodesh, June 24, 1984

Our sages compare a life to a book. For just as a book cannot be judged only by its length, so, too, a life. There are long endless tomes that are boring and trivial. There are other books that are brief, but interesting and exciting, and, like a lovely sonnet, have significance. So, too, with the life of Rima Braave. Her years were brief as we consider a life. But those years were rich in quality and in decency. She could not have accomplished this alone. It required the love and support of all of you who loved her and stayed with her to the end. Now when we come to the conclusion of a good life, as we do when we conclude a

If Judea Miller upheld the longstanding commitment of Reform Judaism to prophetic universalism, many of the issues that touched him most deeply had to do with the fate of the Jews. The future of Israel was always of paramount concern. In 1974 Miller was a delegate to the World Zionist Congress, and he was the only rabbi in attendance to travel to Arab countries, including Lebanon, Syria, and Jordan, visiting several PLO camps on his journey. Miller's views on Israeli politics were sometimes critical of official government actions, but he did this within a framework of basic respect for Israel, and its right to make its own choices about its future. Despite Miller's liberal politics, he did not hesitate to challenge potential allies on the left who engaged in what he considered to be uninformed or irresponsible criticism of Israel.

Anti-Semitism in any guise and from any quarter always earned Miller's sternest condemnation. When Jesse Jackson, during his 1984 presidential campaign sought the endorsement of the openly anti-Jewish Nation of Islam leader Louis Farrakhan, Miller's response was scathing. Though Miller was sympathetic to Jackson's political goals, his campaign, he argued, "brought out the worst in American politics."

The promise of Zionism for Miller was the right of all Jews to live wherever they wished, and their ability to leave the countries of their oppression. Miller was one of the leaders of efforts by American Jewish leaders in the mid 1980s to assist in the emigration of Ethiopian Jews to Israel. In September 1986, he arranged for a "Rabbinic Call to Conscience" in Washington to lobby for Ethiopian Jews, and Miller later served as the director of the American Rabbinic Network for Ethiopian Jewry. Miller frequently spoke on the issue at B'rith Kodesh and elsewhere in Rochester, developing good ties with the local African-American clergy.

The question of the freedom of Russian Jews was a central concern for Miller, long before it became a major international issue. As early as 1964, he engaged in a two-day Passover Fast to bring attention to the plight of Jews in the Soviet Union, neither able to practice their faith freely nor emigrate. When freedom of Soviet Jews did attain political significance in the late 1970s, Miller saw it as a basic question of human rights, and he bitterly rejected the common accusation that the campaign was a right-wing effort to wage the Cold War through other means. Miller offered Soviet émigrés free memberships in B'rith Kodesh, and encouraged them to participate in congregational affairs.

In 1984, Larissa Shapiro, a Soviet émigré living in the Rochester area, brought the case of her sister, Rima Braave, a Soviet "refusenik" diagnosed with a serious form of cancer, to Miller's attention. He started a vigorous campaign to achieve her release, which succeeded in December 1986, and she lit the *shamas* candle in the B'rith Kodesh Chanukah celebration that year. Rima Braave succumbed to cancer in June 1987.

For Rabbi Miller, the child of Polish-Jewish immigrants, the Holocaust was at once a deeply personal loss, a theological conundrum, and a constant reminder of the need for persons of good will to forcefully oppose evil. In 1990, during a trip to Poland, with the aid of a local guide, he searched for the graves of his deceased relatives. (Courtesy Anita Miller)

good book, we Jews say, "Chazak, Chazak, Venitchazak, let us be strong and love one another."

Like many Jews of his generation, the Holocaust haunted Judea Miller. Miller's connection was more personal than most. Two half-brothers, living near Poland, died during the war, and in 1990, he told the congregation of his great sorrow in finding their name in the records of the Majdanek extermination camp. Miller's involvement with the spiritual and religious implications of the Holocaust came together in one of the last great campaigns of his life, his witness against ethnic slaughter in Bosnia in the early 1990s. He spoke and wrote of his concerns in numerous sermons and articles in both Jewish and national journals. One of the highlights of his effort to bring attention to the ethnic cleansing was a unique joint worship service of August 19, 1992. Jews, Muslims, and Christians participated in "A Service of Worship in Common Concern." The service, coordinated by Martha Rock Birnbaum, mingled surahs from the Koran, traditional Jewish prayers, and excerpts from the Roman Catholic Mass, in calling for "an end to the political and physical oppression of people because of their religious belief, ethnic origin, or racial background." Miller wrote in September 1992:

> What can the nations of the world do? Let us care enough so that any helplessness we claim is not used to trivialize the murder of innocent civilians. And let us admit that we all "have a dog in the fight." To lose is to lose in the struggle for justice and law and decency everywhere. Brand the perpetuators of genocide as war criminals who will be held accountable by the nations of the world. For these are indeed crimes against humanity. Let us not repeat that mistake again. Never again!

Rabbi Miller in the B'rith Kodesh sanctuary. (Photo by Martin Adwin, Alwyn Studio)

Rabbi Miller's love for young children is apparent as he interacts with these pre-school congregants and their parents. (Photo by Arthur Lind)

Members of B'rith Kodesh were not indifferent to Judea Miller's vigorous rabbinic manner. Many loved the intensity, spontaneity, and passion he brought to the congregation. A few found his style uncomfortable and disturbing. One former B'rith Kodesh president said in 1977 that "Rabbi Miller is a sort of Hasid at heart. I think much about him reminds me of Orthodox Hasidic life." If the B'rith Kodesh service previously was characterized by an excess of formalism, some now found the services too loosely structured. Rabbi Miller sometimes surprised cantors and cantorial soloists by asking them to repeat parts of the service he found especially moving. Some loved his penchant for peppering his sermons with Yiddish expressions; others found it off-putting. One of Rabbi Miller's most controversial innovations was his decision to wear sneakers on Yom Kippur (following the injunction against putting on any leather products on that day.) This incurred the anger of the opponents of "creeping Orthodoxy."

One of Rabbi's Miller's great strengths as a rabbi was his unpredictability, his conviction that only by transgressing and breaking down barriers, by asking unanticipated and probing questions, by making unexpected pronouncements, and by challenging the congregation, could Jewish worship get beyond externals. Cantor Birnbaum found working with Rabbi Miller to be

Rabbi Miller carrying the Torah at a pre-school Sukkot celebration in the Temple's courtyard. (Photo by Arthur Lind)

228

THE 'REAL' RABBI

Rabbi Rosalind Gold

I n her early months at Temple B'rith Kodesh, a Reform congregation in Brighton, Associate Rabbi Rosalind Gold was frequently asked, "Where is the real rabbi?" Not a surprising question, perhaps, when you consider she's one of only a handful of women rabbis in the world — there were only seven when she joined the congregation in 1978 at the age of 28.

Yet for a faith with a strong tradition of male leadership, the 1,400 families who belong to the Temple at 2131 Elmwood Ave. seem to have made a smooth transition. "Many congregants especially invite me to officiate at their important religious occasions," Ms. Gold says now. "I'll never forget the first wedding I officiated at. It was my birthday, and I was so nervous, it was hard to keep from crying."

In recent years, Reform Judaism has moved toward equalizing the place of women by encouraging them to study at rabbinical school. Traditionally, though, most women graduates have worked with Hillel Founda-tions located on college campuses which provide religious and social support to Jewish students.

Ms. Gold's decision to become a congregational rabbi was influenced by service as an intern rabbi at Sherith Israel Congregation in San Francisco. She set up programs to teach Jewish culture, song and dance, conducted worship services and got a feel for a rabbi's daily routine.

"I enjoyed all the different parts of the life process that I dealt with at Sherith Israel," she says. "It was more appealing and challenging to me than limiting myself to working only on the university level."

She says she enjoys researching and writing sermons ("I wish I had more time for study"), visiting the sick ("it's an intimate kind of sharing that I really look forward to"), and working with converts ("we get into some good, heated discussions").

She enjoys, in short, being a rabbi, one who happens to be a woman. Her goal? "To be the best Rosalind Gold, the best rabbi, I can." — **Grace Kraut**

The first female rabbi at B'rith Kodesh, Rosalind Gold, assistant rabbi 1978–1980.

exhilarating. His spontaneity and commitment to improvisation and keeping things fresh were challenging, but when everything came together the service could be quite remarkable. When Rabbi Miller's preaching was "on," and he was speaking on a topic of great concern to him, his remarkable intensity was often quite electric. If Rabbi Miller's refusal to play it safe was in the eyes of his supporters his greatest strength, for those troubled by his style, it was his greatest weakness.

In his almost quarter century as senior rabbi of B'rith Kodesh, Judea Miller was helped by a number of assistant and associate rabbis. Robert Baruch was assistant rabbi from 1973 to 1976. Ron Shapiro followed, fondly remembered for his warm personality and guitar playing during services. In 1978 Rabbi Rosalind Gold became the first woman rabbi in Rochester, and one of the first female congregational rabbis in the nation. Though her coming to B'rith Kodesh produced a mild controversy, she was warmly accepted by the congregation after her arrival, both by the members of B'rith Kodesh, and by most other rabbis in Rochester. Rabbi Gold, who became the first female rabbi to be accepted as a member of any regional Board of Rabbis, was especially active in leading youth activities.

In 1980 Robert Eisen became assistant

Co-Directors of Education Eleanor Lewin (with puppet) and Carol Leichtner, 1996.

229

Present president of Temple B'rith Kodesh, Carol Louis Yunker.

Librarian and former temple president Nettie Sheiman, reading to group of young congregants, supervised the expansion of the temple library. (Photo by Arthur Lind)

rabbi, eventually becoming an associate rabbi, remaining at B'rith Kodesh until 1985. Rabbi Judy Cohen-Rosenberg, active in defending the rights of women, gays, and lesbians, succeeded him. She was succeeded by Rabbi Brian Daniels in 1990. In 1992, the congregation, wanting an assistant for Judea Miller with more experience, hired Marc Gruber as an associate rabbi.

Over the 1980s and 1990s, there were many new social issues that confronted the congregation. After a century of effort, women finally achieved full equality in the governance of the congregation. In 1988, Nettie Sheiman became the first woman president of the congregation. In 1997, Carol Yunker, the daughter of Elmer Louis, the longtime director of the Rochester Jewish Federation, became the second woman president.

Like many other congregations, in the 1980s B'rith Kodesh confronted the question of gay and lesbian rights. Judea Miller was among the first American rabbis to write extensively on this subject, notably in "The Closet: Another Religious View of Gay Liberation," in 1979. Miller argued that gay liberation and feminism freed all people, by enabling everyone to become more tolerant of others and of ourselves. A temple should be open for all Jews, Miller argued. The choice of partners was a private issue. It was not the place of a rabbi or a synagogue Board of Trustees to delve into the private lives of its members. But even in a congregation as liberal as B'rith Kodesh, the full acceptance of gays and lesbians took time. In 1989, after a stormy debate at the annual meeting, a same-sex couple, Trudy Baran and Beth

Bloom, were at first were denied the right to join the congregation as family members. With much discussion and soul searching, in December 1989, the congregation reversed this decision in a special meeting several months later. Since then, B'rith Kodesh has actively welcomed gays and lesbians as family members.

New Directions

Judea Miller remained active and maintained a vigorous travel schedule into the 1990s, and his comprehensive enthusiasm for religious and social change remained undiminished. By 1994 he developed a heart ailment, and during the High Holy Day services that year he was visibly weakened, and he found standing for long periods of time difficult. His Kol Nidre sermon that year reflects Miller's reflections on the meanings of life and death, and his deep commitment to the possibility of true spiritual renewal. Over the course of the year his physical deterioration was evident. Judea Miller passed away on July 9, 1995. The congregation, the religious community of Rochester, and the Reform movement hailed Miller as one dedicated to the ideals of justice, and as one who had devoted much time to improving relations among the different religions and ethnicities of Rochester. The Rev. Dwight Cook of the Mt. Olivet Baptist Church praised Miller as one who had done much to build bridges between the black and Jewish populations of Rochester. Miller's abundant compassion for all who needed help led to tributes from some unexpected places. The official publication of the Monroe County chapter of the American Legion praised Miller as a proud veteran who spent much time in pastoral work for disabled veterans in local hospitals. Rabbi Miller would have been pleased by an editorial in the *Rochester Times-Union,* which eulogized him as one who embodied the spirit of *Tikkun Olam,* and "had taught us all how to repair the world."

Rabbi and Anita Miller with their children, Rabbi Jonathan Miller and Rebecca (Betsy) Gottesman and spouses and their grandchildren. (Courtesy Anita Miller)

Two recent temple presidents, Gerald Zakalik (1993–1995) on left, with David Feinstein (1995–1997). (Photo by Arthur Lind)

Judea Miller, Kol Nidre Sermon, 1994

I recently came across this obscure passage in the Talmud: "People coming to pray at the Temple would enter through the right hand gate, bring their offerings, and depart through the gate on the left (that is, they would travel counter-clockwise). But mourners, people suffering from a serious illness and people searching for a lost object would enter through the gate on the left (moving in a clockwise direction) and leave through the gate on the right."

Did you have the same reaction to that passage that I did? What is the lost object doing there? I can understand having a different category for people who are in mourning or are desperately ill. I can understand that they would feel out of sync with the normal worshippers who were going to the Temple to celebrate the birth or marriage of a child, or to express gratitude for a good harvest or a successful business deal. But why put people who have lost something in the same category?

I can think of two possible answers. One answer is the feeling we have all had when looking for something and cannot locate it. You put your car keys right there a moment ago, and now you are running late and cannot find it. You know how that can drive you crazy.

The second possibility is that the lost object the passage speaks of is not just any lost object, your glasses or your car keys, but refers to something specific, to a person who lost his faith and comes to the Temple hoping to find it. I sense that every year when we gather here for Yom Kippur, we come to temple, most of us, in a festive mood. We are wearing our nicest clothes, we have our friends and family around us, we look forward to the familiar melodies, to the sermon, to the shofar. There is an air of celebration as we begin the New Year together.

But every year there are some people among us who are coming from a totally different direction. Some are coming to temple from the doctor's office, and when the rest of the congregation joins in chanting B'rosh Ha Shanah Yikatevun uv' Yom tzom Kippur Yehatemun, "It is decided on Rosh Hashanah and sealed on Yom Kippur who shall live and who shall die," they hear the words differently from the way the rest of us do. They sit here wondering if they are going to be inscribed one more time in the Book of Life, wondering if they are hearing these words for the last time.

I suspect there are a lot of us here in the third category as well, men and women coming to the temple in search of a lost object, in search of the faith they had as a child but lost somewhere along the way. They see their neighbors familiar with the traditional prayers, joining in the chants, and they ask themselves, "what are they feeling that I can't feel?"

They think of the devoutly religious people they know, Jewish and gentile, and wish they had a little of their certainty, their serenity.

In ancient Jerusalem, people like that had their own special entrance to the Temple. They were asked to go the wrong way on a one-way street, to enter by the door through which everybody else was coming out.

I suspect this was done, not to embarrass them or to isolate them, not to keep them away from normal people. I suspect it was done in some way to heal them, that somehow the other worshippers coming out of the Temple would comfort the mourners, give hope to the suffering, and restore faith to those who had lost their faith. Tomorrow afternoon toward the conclusion of Yom Kippur, we will read the story of Jonah, the reluctant prophet. God commanded Jonah to go to the wicked city of Nineveh in Assyria, and to call on the people there to repent. Jonah does not want to. He does not want to save the Ninevites. He does not think they deserve it. So he gets on a ship going in the opposite direction. A storm comes up and the ship is about to founder. Jonah is thrown overboard and swallowed by a huge fish and the story goes on from there.

A rabbinic comment on the passage remarks, "There are three places in the Bible where we read of a wind so strong that it threatens to destroy the world: in the story of Jonah, in the story of Job—where a massive wind storm destroys his house with his family in it, and in the story of Elijah, who runs away from Israel because it is so filled with idol worship. Elijah runs back to Mount Sinai where God appears to him in a great wind." — A wind so great it could destroy the world.

I take that as a symbol of a despair so deep, so stifling that if everybody got sucked into it, all life would end. It would be an emotional black hole. Nobody would have the energy to go on living.

That is what happened to Job when his family died. He could no longer believe in God. Life had lost all meaning. That is what happened to Jonah when God asked him to preach to the wicked people of Nineveh. He gave up on humanity. He could not convince himself that they were worth saving, that they were capable of becoming better. And that is what happened to Elijah. He gave up on the Jewish people. According to the Talmud, the cure for all of them was to go in the door that everybody else was coming out of.

The answer to Job, who lost his faith in God when he saw people around him suffer and die, was not theology but people, not explanation but consolation. As a wise Hassidic rabbi put it, "human beings are God's language." When we cry out to God, "how can you let things like this happen?" God answers by sending people, people to work

233

day and night to try to make us whole, people to sit with us to assure us that we are not alone, we are not rejected, people to bear witness that they once stood where you are standing and they have survived and you will survive too—because that is what you do with tragedy. You do not explain it, you do not justify it, you survive it.

Most of the prayers in the Jewish prayerbook may be said at home by yourself. You do not need a minyan (a quorum of ten people). But the Mourner's Kaddish can only be said with a minyan because when you are depressed and hurt and confused, it is hard to find God by yourself. It is easier to find God in the people around you because they want to help. People reach out to you, people show that they care (if you let them) and wash away that sense of rejection, and there is holiness in that.

When the tornado demolished Job's home and family and blew away his faith in the world as a livable place, his prescription was to go to the Temple and enter through the left hand door so that people coming the other way could stop for a moment and offer him a word of condolence, could perhaps hug him and comfort him and witness to him that they too had suffered and survived, and so would he.

God's promise is not that everything will be all right. God's promise is that when things are not all right, you will be all right because God will be with you. God will be with you in friends and good people who will help.

Jonah did not lose his faith in God. He lost faith in humanity. Jonah had no problems about God. It was in people he could not believe in. They were not worth saving because they had fallen so far short of what God demanded of them. God calls upon us to be honest, and we hide behind evasions and rationalizations. God calls on us to be generous, and we choose to be selfish, blinded by our own needs to where we cannot see anyone else's. God calls on us to be strong and we reply, "Hey, I'm only human."

Jonah did not want to urge the people of Nineveh to repent, not because they were far off but because they were Assyrians. They were Israel's enemies, they had done terrible things to his people, and he did not believe they were capable of changing. In effect, he says to God, "I know these people are not going to change for the better because I know myself. I'm a much nicer person than they are, and I know how hard it is for me to shed bad habits and form good ones."

If Jonah were around today, he would see more evidence to reinforce that feeling. You look at what is going on in Bosnia where people have had 600 years of practice nurturing grudges and polishing hatred. You look at the mind-boggling horror of genocide in Rwanda—

where hundreds of thousands, even millions of people have been slaughtered because they were Hutus or Tutsis.

Then there are the random killings almost daily in our urban centers. Husbands who kill their wives, and boy friends who kill their girl friends, and strangers who kill other strangers because they are angry or bored.

Jonah saw things like that in his lifetime, and it robbed him of his ability to believe in human goodness. That is why, when God told him to go to Nineveh, he answered, "What's the point? What difference will it possibly make?" Human nature is human nature.

But God says to him, "Look, I know human nature at least as well as you do. But you only see the headlines; I see the hearts behind the headlines. You read of the crimes; I see the hundreds of people who grieve, who protest, who reach out. You read about the child who disappears and the police suspect foul play, and all your worst suspicions about people are confirmed. I see the hundreds of people who give of their time to search for her. You see selfishness and fraud, and I see the people who open their hearts and their pocketbooks for so many deserving causes."

"More than that," God goes on to say, "you only see people in one dimension of time, where they are now. I see them in three dimensions. I see where they started, and I see where they are capable of ending up. I see the potential for growth and change."

That is why people like Jonah, people who have lost their faith in humanity, are told to go to the Temple and go in a different door than everyone else. Do not see people on the way into the service, when they are a lot like you, burdened by doubts and overwhelmed by a sense of their own shortcomings. Meet them on the way out, after the encounter with God has worked its magic on them.

One of the offerings that people would bring to the Temple in Jerusalem, and especially on Yom Kippur was the Korban Hattat, the sin offering brought by the person who was ashamed of something he or she had done. Fasting on Yom Kippur is the modern equivalent of the sin offering. People brought it, not to bribe God to forgive them or to balance the books by doing something good to make up for whatever bad they had done. They brought it to acquaint themselves with their better nature, their nobler, more generous side. They brought it in the same spirit that people give to charity or come to services today, so that they should say to themselves, "sometimes I am petty and narrow-minded and unresponsive, but you know, sometimes I am capable of being good and kind and generous."

The Talmud tells us "there was no happier person in all of

235

Jerusalem, than the person who brought his sin offering and left feeling forgiven." That is why the Talmud wants the person who doubts whether human beings can grow and change, to go through the left hand door, to meet people on the way out, people who feel cleansed, people who feel forgiven, and let them testify to him to what people are capable of.

The case of Elijah and his loss of faith in some ways may be the most relevant for us today. Elijah lost faith in the Jewish people. He saw them becoming ordinary, like everybody else. He saw them put idols in their living rooms like their Canaanite neighbors. According to the narrative in the book of Kings, he ran away in despair. He ran all the way back to Mount Sinai where the Jewish enterprise began. There he called out to God, who had revealed Himself at Sinai and given Moses the Torah.

Elijah said to God, "You entered into a covenant with Israel at this place, but they have forsaken your covenant. They refuse to be a special people. They worship the gods of nature, of impulse, as the pagans do. They chase after material success, and trample Your values in the process."

God replies to Elijah, "not in thunder, not in a whirlwind, but in a still small voice." But we're not told exactly what God says to him. So Jewish tradition fills in the blanks.

There are two occasions when the prophet Elijah is welcomed into our homes, when we set a place for him as an honored guest. Do you remember what they are? One is the Passover Seder; we pour a cup for Elijah and open the door to welcome him.

The second is at the Bris of a baby. The chair on which the sandek sits to hold the baby is called "the throne of Elijah" and the opening words of the bris ceremony invoke his presence.

Why Elijah and why on those occasions? God is offended on our behalf when Elijah says, look at those people; they have forsaken Your covenant. So God orders Elijah to attend every bris, every Passover Seder, as a way of saying to him, "these are My people." They may not do everything I tell them to; they may not do very much of what I tell them to. But at crucial moments of their lives, they remember that they are Jews.

It is easy to lament about the future of the Jewish community in America. But if we let ourselves lose faith in the Jewish people as Elijah did, that despair can be a wind that threatens to destroy the world. We have to do what God told Elijah to do—stop looking at our people's flaws, and look instead at what continues to remind them that they are Jewish.

There is an old joke about the man crawling on his hands and knees around a lamp post at night, looking for something. A friend comes by and asks him what he is doing, and he answers, "I dropped my keys and I cannot find them." The friend says, "did you drop them here under the lamp post?" And the man replies, "No, I dropped them down the block, but I'm looking here because the light is better."

If you are looking for a lost physical object, keys or glasses—you will not find it unless you look where you lost it. But if you are looking for something spiritual, not physical, if you are looking for your lost faith—in God, in people, in Judaism—maybe it does make sense to search for it where the light is better.

Even as in ancient Jerusalem, people whose ability to believe had been blown away by a great wind went looking for it in the Temple. And there they met other people who had suffered but endured, and who found God in their ability to survive the worst that fate could deal them. There they met people who had been mean and petty and jealous and disliked themselves for it—but had grown and changed, and had found God in their own ability to grow and to change. There they met Jews who did not think often about their Jewishness, but when they did, they found it cleansing and calming, full of light and full of hope.

Walking into the Temple, they met these people walking out, saying, "You know we really ought to do this more often." And when they met them, and when they saw and heard what the life-giving contact with the Temple had done for them, that which had been lost was found. So may it be with each of us. Shana Tova—Have a good year.

Amen.

Following the passing of Rabbi Miller, Associate Rabbi Marc Gruber served as the spiritual leader of the congregation. He remained at B'rith Kodesh until the summer of 1997, when he assumed the position of senior rabbi of Temple Israel in Dayton, Ohio. Assistant Rabbi S. Robert Morais joined the congregation in the fall of 1997.

In 1995 and 1996 the B'rith Kodesh Board of Trustees conducted an extensive rabbinic search. In the spring of 1996 Laurence Kotok was hired as the fifth Senior Rabbi of Temple B'rith Kodesh; his tenure began in the summer of 1996. Kotok brought to B'rith Kodesh a wealth of experience both as a congregational rabbi and as a leader of the Reform movement. He was born in Bayonne, New Jersey in 1946. Kotok's family was Orthodox in their religious practice, but when he was nine years old, they moved to West Orange, New Jersey, where his family became members of a traditionally inclined Reform congregation. While an undergraduate at Rutgers University at New Brunswick, New Jersey, Kotok made the decision to enter the rabbinate. If this decision was cumulative, the result, in part, of positive Jewish experiences during his childhood and adolescent years, it was the turbulence and uncertainty of the years of the Vietnam War that finally convinced him to follow a religious calling.

After graduating from Hebrew Union College in 1972, Kotok became an assistant rabbi at Temple Sinai in Roslyn, New York, on the North Shore of Long Island in Nassau County. Two years later he became rabbi of Temple Ner Tamid in nearby Glen Cove, where he would remain for the next twenty-two years, building his congregation from 100 to over 300 families. During his years in Glen Cove, Kotok became a certified family therapist and drug and alcohol counselor. Deeply interested in international affairs, he served as an advisor on Jewish affairs to four members of the U.S. Congress. Kotok took many trips abroad on behalf of Jewish organizations: to Lebanon in 1982 in the aftermath of the Israeli invasion, to Poland in 1983 after the lifting of martial law, and twice to Amman in the early 1990s, prior to the signing of the formal peace treaty between Israel and Jordan.

One of Rabbi Kotok's chief concerns has been religious rights for non-Orthodox Jews in Israel. He formed the rabbinic cabinet of ARZA (Association of Reform Zionists of America), and serves as its national chair. In the winter of 1997 he served as an ARZA delegate to the World Zionist Congress in Jerusalem. In Rochester, he has been active on the Ministerial Council, an interfaith clerical forum, and has been a leader in dialogues with both the African-American and Islamic communities of Rochester.

Current Senior Rabbi Laurence A. Kotok.
(Photo by Martin Adwin, Alwyn Studio)

Reflections on the B'rith Kodesh Sesquicentennial:
Interview with Rabbi Laurence Kotok, Senior Rabbi, Temple B'rith Kodesh, September 1998

Q: In the oldest surviving sermon preached at B'rith Kodesh, Simon Tuska told those assembled on Rosh Hashanah in 1854 that in their determination to build a Jewish congregation in Rochester, they demonstrated that in "this glorious land, Israel does not deny its God and has not forgotten the saving hand that led it through great waters to a land of religious and civil freedom." In 1998, how are the members of B'rith Kodesh seeking to affirm God and affirm their identity as Jews and Americans?

Rabbi Kotok: *I think there's a real renaissance taking place at B'rith Kodesh, a real desire to find out about what it takes to be*

Jewish. Perhaps things have reversed since 1854. In the early days of the congregation, the members were pretty secure in their identity as Jews, but were still exploring what it meant to be American. Today, we all feel so very comfortable in America that our American identity doesn't trouble us. But many of us are uncertain about the meaning of Judaism, and how to make religious faith a part of our lives. People are coming forward, people of all ages, seeking to claim the Jewish tradition and make it meaningful for their own lives.

This new feeling can be felt throughout the temple. This starts with the children. The director of the religious school, Eleanor Lewin, is committed to the process of change and the development of new educational programs at the religious school, and to make the experience of religious school as rewarding as it can be, both intellectually and Jewishly. We have regular "Tot Shabbats" for very young children, and Junior Congregation services, an alternative to the regular Saturday morning service. Cantor Joel Colman has done an excellent job in bringing musical involvement to the young people of the congregation. For grades four and higher we have been organizing social events so that the students can feel a real connection to the temple, and make

Rabbi Kotok teaching young congregants in front of open ark in the sanctuary. (Photo by Arthur Lind)

it one of the centers of their lives. There are higher levels of parental involvement in the religious school. This is essential, if we want to fully eliminate the adversarial and inter-generational tensions that sometimes enter into Jewish education.

We are trying to enrich the experience of Confirmation. This year, for the first time, there will be a Confirmation class conclave, a weekend gathering where the class will meet with similar classes from other Reform congregations in Rochester, Buffalo, and Syracuse for study and prayer. We have other long-range plans as well. We are trying to achieve full accreditation for the religious school, and trying to restart the Cohn and Dworkin Institutes, programs that will

Associate Rabbi Marc A. Gruber with congregant Lynda Bowen, 1995. (Photo by Arthur Lind)

Images of Temple life. *(Photos by Arthur Lind)*

provide for annual retreats for high school-age students in the religious school. Assistant Rabbi Robert Morais, who joined us last year, has brought an enormous wealth of energy and experience to young people's programming at the temple.

People are very excited about the Kollel, the adult education program we are starting in the fall of 1998. B'rith Kodesh is once again taking the lead. We are the first congregation in the United States to start a Kollel, an institute of higher Jewish learning. The Kollel is an opportunity for our congregation, for members of other congregation, and for non-Jews to engage in the serious study of Jewish texts, concepts, history, and practice from a liberal perspective, to interact with the texts in a serious fashion, so that we can become a generation of participants within the community.

We also have a number of programs for older members of the congregation. The TBKers has a very vibrant director in Aaron Braveman, the former director of the religious school, and Aaron and the other leaders have done a superb job in creating educational and social opportunities for the many long-time members of the congregation. Throughout the lifecycle there are several havurot, and we are always trying to start more. We have become very busy and very active, and it is very exciting.

Q: *Let me quote another of your predecessors, Rabbi Horace J. Wolf. He wrote in 1915, "The motto I would like to offer to every Reform Temple, which I would urge it to chisel over its doors and the spirit which I would insist should animate its every purpose is: 'Here let no Jew feel himself strange.' B'rith Kodesh is a large congregation. It's easy to feel like a stranger or an outsider. As it approaches its sesquicentennial, there are over 1,250 member families; 200 families joined in just the past two years. What are some of the special problems faced by a congregation of this size?*

Rabbi Kotok: *We are a large congregation. We should be proud of this, and the size of B'rith Kodesh doesn't have to make it impersonal, or keep people at arm's length. Over the past two years we have tried to build a vibrant and inclusive program here at the congregation. I have stressed the importance* *of making B'rith Kodesh a "caring community." The goal is to break down barriers, and eliminate the potential for people to become alienated and feel like outsiders. B'rith Kodesh is large, energetic, and diverse, and we need to make it even more accessible, so that individuals will feel a part of it in any way they want to connect. We want the congregation to project a sense of warmth and welcome. I think our efforts to make B'rith Kodesh a "caring community" have been very successful.*

People are attending services in larger numbers. We have introduced a new prayer book, one that uses gender neutral language. I think that throughout the congregation there is a new sense that people care, and that we are acting on this sense of inclusion. We have dramatically increased the number of programs. Our program coordinator, Carol Leichtner, has done a sparkling job in planning programs for all ages. We've created the Etz Mishpacha, the tree of the family, for families that have just had their first child. Twenty-five to thirty families gather once a month for Shabbat. There are other programs for singles, for married couples without children, for interfaith couples. Lynne Goldberg has brought the spirit of "caring community" to the office and the administrative work of the temple. The new spirit is everywhere.

Q: *Reform Judaism has a long and special connection to the prophetic*

tradition. In their different ways, all of your predecessors, from Rabbi Max Landsberg to Rabbi Judea Miller, have invoked the prophets to descry injustice. What role does social action play in Temple B'rith Kodesh today?

Rabbi Kotok: *Social action is very, very powerful in this congregation. The ongoing work of the Social Action Committee demonstrates its importance for B'rith Kodesh. But in recent years there has been a new emphasis. We need to seek the importance of social action and change for us as Jews, and not just as liberal Americans. There is a greater understanding now of the Jewish values systems that have shaped the historic commitment for social change. We have to find the nexus between doing right and being Jewish. We have gone through a period of universalism in Jewish life— certainly we have done so in the Reform movement. Universalism is very important, but it is equally important for our aspirations for universal justice to be rooted in our specific identity as Jews. There's no point in trying to homogenize our religions and our value systems. Though we share much with people of other faiths, it is important for us to cherish our own faith, and to know who we are and what we are, in order to better interact with the world. We have to live our lives according to our value base as Jews.*

Every month I meet with the Social Action Committee and we study a biblical text before the meeting, to give the subsequent discussion a specifically Jewish context. The legacy of the prophets has been a powerful motivation for Jewish thought and behavior throughout our history. The goal for me is to help people understand their acts of social involvement specifically as mitzvot, as commandments from God, inherent in a sense of Jewish responsibility, as an integral part of the way they wish to live their lives as Jews. I think we are succeeding in this. The broader objective, for all of us, is to give our lives a fullness, to make the different parts of our existence cohere, and to set our diverse and often contradictory obligations in a specifically Jewish context.

Q: Historically, this congregation has maintained a special connection to Israel. How is B'rith Kodesh realizing this obligation today?

Rabbi Kotok: *Israel is very important to this congregation's past and future. We are proud of our positions of leadership in the local federation, of our role in raising funds for Israeli bonds, of our efforts to send our young people to Israel for the summer. We are starting a program called "Gift of Israel." Our young people will, from their earliest grades in the religious school, put some money away for their first trip to Israel, so that when they are old enough to go they can feel that they helped to pay their way over. One of my most important commitments to Israel, and I think for the congregation as well, is to see to it that Israel becomes a country where religious pluralism is a reality, where every branch of Judaism is treated equally, and none is given preferred legal status. As the national chair of ARZA (the Association of Reform Zionists of America) this has long been for me an issue of paramount concern. Though there is a long way to go, the issue is finally beginning to get the attention it deserves. As liberal Jews in the Diaspora, we care deeply about Israel, about keeping the Zionist ideal alive and promoting the values of religious pluralism. There are few issues as important as these.*

Q: You are only the fifth senior rabbi at B'rith Kodesh over the past 130 years. Given the long tenures in office customary here, after two years as senior rabbi you are still a relative newcomer. Philip Bernstein became senior rabbi here in 1927. By 1929, in the judgment of Rabbi Stephen S. Wise, Bernstein's "experimental period" was over, and he was fully accepted as the rabbi of the congregation. Now that your "experimental" period is over, what are some of your impressions of B'rith Kodesh?

Rabbi Kotok: *All of us start new experiences with excitement and anticipation, perhaps mixed with a little anxiety. I found this congregation warm and welcoming from the time I arrived. They were eager to listen to me and to work with me. I never felt that I was being tested. I was a little older than Philip Bernstein when I became senior rabbi at B'rith Kodesh. I saw my service at B'rith Kodesh as another step, a continuation of my quarter-century of work as a congregational rabbi.*

Let me tell you a story. My first job as rabbi, while I was still a student at Hebrew Union College, was as a rabbinic assistant to a congregation in Brunswick, Georgia, where the senior rabbi had recently passed away. I flew down from Cincinnati every other week. While I was there, I became friends with the widow of the former rabbi. He had maintained a large collection of books on Jewish topics, and she invited me to take some of the volumes. They have ever since been a cherished part of my personal library, and I have taken them with me wherever I have gone. In 1982, when my congregation in Glen Cove was firebombed by arsonists, there was fire and water damage to many of the books. I salvaged whatever I could, and of course I brought the books with me to Rochester.

Once I was here for a while, I was asked by a congregant who had experienced a tragedy in his life if I could suggest an appropriate reading for a memorial service for his son. I went to my bookshelves, and reached for one of my favorite volumes. I don't how many times I had read it before. This time, as I looked through it, a few pamphlets left in the pages of the book fluttered to my desk. They were printed sermons of Philip Bernstein! I had never seen them before. My entire career as a rabbi, I have been carrying around his words without knowing it. Call it providence or call it serendipity, there was something about the event that convinced me that my presence in Rochester, at B'rith Kodesh, had somehow been preordained.

But of course it's never easy becoming the rabbi of a congregation with the history of B'rith Kodesh. What makes this temple so unique is that it is much more than its 150 years. This is a congregation! This congregation is diverse, complex, and spiritually alive, and we are not just observing an anniversary for want of something better to do. The history of B'rith Kodesh lives within its walls, within the collective memory of its members. B'rith Kodesh sees its rabbis as part of its history, and not simply as part of its present. There is an awareness in this congregation of what B'rith Kodesh has been, and what it can be. Though all congregations require infusions of new members, what makes B'rith Kodesh unique is its historic stability, the large number of multi-generational families that constitute such an invaluable chain and source of information and experience. It's the combination of the old and the new that makes B'rith Kodesh so unique.

Q: How do you think the role of rabbi has changed at B'rith Kodesh over the years?

Rabbi Kotok: *This is a complex question, and the answer has less to do with the personalities of the individuals than the changing needs of Jewish congregations. There was a time, fifty, sixty years ago, when rabbis were looked to as sources of information, a time when the great orators of the Reform movement, a Stephen S. Wise, an Abba Hillel Silver, a Philip Bernstein, could regularly deliver hour-long sermons. People don't need this, or expect this, today. If they want news reports they can watch CNN, or access the internet. They want rabbis to teach, and interpret the tradition. They want rabbis to provide ethical and moral leadership.*

There are also new requirements for rabbinic leadership today, I think. B'rith Kodesh has a history of strong, decisive rabbis. Nothing is wrong with that, and I hope that I am

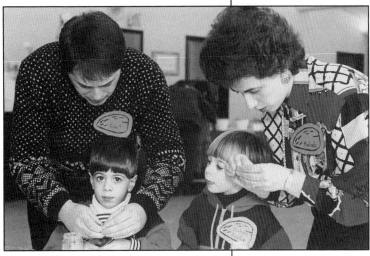

continuing the tradition. But there's a difference between being strong and being imperious. I believe deeply in shared leadership, and in the closest possible collaboration between the clerical and lay leaders in shaping the future of this congregation. The role of the rabbi is to break down barriers, to be inclusive, to encourage participation, to empower, and to build coalitions. Rabbis have to be available. This is the way to

Fifty year members, 1982. (Photo by Len Rosenberg)

Sanctuary bimah with new chuppah (wedding canopy) at marriage of Joanne Serling and Stephen Fisher, October 3, 1998. (Photo by Martin Adwin, Alwyn Studio)

build strong congregations. A rabbi today has to encourage participation, and to motivate and energize people into taking responsibility for their own lives, for their religious community, and for maintaining the Jewish tradition. That is our goal and vision.

Q: *B'rith Kodesh has been in the forefront of the Reform movement for almost all of its history. In your view, what do you see as the future for Reform Judaism in this country, and what does the future hold for B'rith Kodesh?*

Rabbi Kotok: *One of the great strengths of Reform Judaism, and of this congregation, is its tremendous diversity. This goes back to the origins of B'rith Kodesh as an Orthodox congregation. And the entrance of B'rith Kodesh into the Reform movement made it more, not less diverse. When Isaac Mayer Wise visited Rochester in 1860, he commented that it was a congregation that reflected a large number of*

Tallit presentation to Bat Mitzvah Sarah Lovenheim from her parents Peter and Marie Lovenheim, in Rabbi Kotok's study, June 7, 1997. (Photo by Martin Adwin, Alwyn Studio)

B'not Mitzvah JoEllen and Lindsay Erin Lustig at Saturday morning service, September 17, 1994. (Photo by Martin Adwin, Alwyn Studio)

variant perspectives on Judaism, various degrees of Orthodoxy and Reform. And he also noted that the different views on Judaism complemented and reinforced one another and strengthened the congregation. I think that's the way it's always been at B'rith Kodesh. Sure, there was a period of radical Reform, in which diversity was not trusted, and seen more as something to be rooted out than to be embraced. But diversity never died at B'rith Kodesh, and in this temple, and in the Reform movement as a whole, we have come to see the wide spectrum of beliefs within our movement as one of its greatest strengths.

This congregation is an amalgam of many different religious styles and attitudes toward Judaism. It reflects a

Portrait of Temple staff. l. to r. standing: Lynne Goldberg, Executive Director; Joel Colman, Cantor; Eleanor Lewin, Director of Education; Carol Leichtner, Program Coordinator. Seated: Rabbi S. Robert Morais, Assistant Rabbi; Laurence Kotok, Senior Rabbi. (Photo by Martin Adwin, Alwyn Studio)

Rabbi Kotok with wife Merrill and children David and Rachel.

new awareness in the Reform movement in terms of its liturgy and its place in Jewish life. We are not caught up in the model that says, "I'm sorry, you can't do that here; we're Reform." I think that Reform Judaism is evolving to a concept of personal choice by authentically engaging the tradition, allowing the individual to see the whole history of Jewish experience and make informed choices. No longer should it be said that Reform Jews don't keep kosher, or that Reform Jews don't know Hebrew, or that Reform Jews don't observe mitzvot, or don't wear talisim or kipot or anything that is authentically Jewish. We have talisim, we have yarmulkes. If you want to wear them that's perfectly okay; if you don't, that's okay too. We teach Talmud in this congregation. Nothing that is genuinely Jewish is outside the scope of this congregation. Our message is: Reform Judaism is valid, Reform Judaism is authentic. Reform Judaism is an exciting, vibrant way for Jews to access their tradition. This is an exciting time to be a Reform rabbi, and it is an especially exciting time to be rabbi of B'rith Kodesh.

Night-time view of Temple exterior. (Photo by Len Rosenberg)

Temple B'rith Kodesh Presidents

Joseph Wile 1869-1874

Moses Hays 1874-1877

Levi Adler 1874-1879

David Rosenberg 1879-1880

Leopold Garson 1880-1882

I. M. Sloman 1882-1884

Julius Wile 1884-1886

Henry Michaels 1886-1888

Leopold Garson 1888-1891

Joseph Caufman 1891-1892

Henry Michaels 1892-1894

William Miller 1894

Max Lowenthal 1894-1901

Sol Wile 1901-1912

Max Lowenthal 1912-1915

Mortimer Adler 1915-1921

Sol Applebaum 1921-1928

Henry M. Stern 1928-1937

Manuel D. Goldman 1937-1948

J. H. Rubens 1948-1954

Garson Meyer 1954-1957

Hyman B. Freeman 1957-1960

Clifford B. Lovenheim 1960-1963

Milton R. Berger 1963-1965

Louis E. Perlman 1965-1968

Emanuel Goldberg 1968-1970

Henry J. Rubens 1970-1973

Murray I. Blanchard 1973-1976

Herbert J. Schwartz 1976-1978

Warren H. Heilbronner 1978-1980

Charles S. Chadwick 1980-1982

Lawrence S. Scott 1982-1984

Thomas A. Fink 1984-1986

Morris H. Weinstein 1986-1989

Annette R. Sheiman 1989-1991

Donald J. Onimus 1991-1993

Gerald A. Zakalik 1993-1995

David Feinstein 1995-1997

Carol Louis Yunker 1997-present

There were a number of presidents of Temple B'rith Kodesh before 1869; their proper sequence and tenures in office are murky. Extant records are incomplete and in some ways inconsistent. Both Meyer Rothschild and Elias Wolf probably were early temple presidents, though the long-standing tradition which grants them long uninterrupted presidencies, 1848-1854, and 1854-1872, respectively, is not accurate. Indeed, I have been unable to confirm their presidencies from independent sources. A list of early B'rith Kodesh presidents includes the following names:

Meyer Rothschild 1848
Joseph Katz 1851
Nathan Newhafer 1854
Elias Wolf 1854
Elias Ettenheimer 1855
Gabriel Wile 1856
Moses Hays 1859-1862, 1863
I. Katz (Joseph Katz?) 1862
H. Haas 1862
Sigmund Stettheimer 1864-1865
E. M. Moerell 1867

Temple B'rith Kodesh Religious School Educational Directors

Benjamin Goldstein	*Director of Religious School*	.1927-1944
Jerome Gordon	*Dir. Hebrew Instruction*	.1940-1944
Elizabeth Schwartz	*Principal Sunday School*	.1944-1958
Samuel Bloom	*Principal High School*	.1957-1958
Anita Feldman	*Principal Elementary Grades*	.1958-1960
Lillian Hershberg	*Principal High School*	.1958-1960
Aaron D. Braveman	*Director of Education*	.1960-1983
Eleanor Lewin	*Director of Education*	.1983-1990
Chanah Michaelli	*Director of Education*	.1990-1992
Barbara Goldman	*Director of Education*	.1992-1995
Eleanor Lewin/Carol Leichtner	*Director of Education*	.1995-1996
Eleanor Lewin	*Director of Education*	.1996-present

Education was one of the main duties of the early B'rith Kodesh rabbis. Both Rabbis Mayer and Guinzberg directed the Hebrew day school, closely associated with the congregation, that operated from 1856 to 1867. The B'rith Kodesh Sunday School was organized in 1869; its founders, Sol and Isaac Wile, were its likely supervisors in its first years. After his arrival in 1871, Rabbi Max Landsberg was the director of the Sunday School. After Max Moll joined B'rith Kodesh as an assistant rabbi in 1886, he became the supervisor of the Sunday School. After Moll left B'rith Kodesh in 1905, his successor assistant rabbis took a major hand in the running of the Sunday school. In 1922 Benjamin Goldstein became chairman of the school committee; in 1927, he started working for B'rith Kodesh full-time. One of his duties was director of the religious school. He continued in this position through the mid 1940s. Thereafter, the congregation's assistant rabbis played a major role in the direction of the religious school, as did Elizabeth Schwartz, who also held a full-time position in the Rochester public school system. In 1960 Aaron Braveman became the first full-time director of education. He came to B'rith Kodesh in 1954 as a Hebrew teacher, and in 1957 was appointed principal of the Hebrew Department. In the late 1950s and 1960s, a series of youth institutes were initiated, the Paul Dworkin Memorial Camp Institute, the Cohn Institute for the Arts, and Confirmation class weekend. By the mid 1960s, there were over 1000 children attending religious school on weekends, and three hundred in the mid-week Hebrew program.

Temple B'rith Kodesh Rabbis

Mordecai Tuska	*Rabbi*	1849-1856
Isaac Mayer	*Rabbi*	1856-1859
Ferdinand Sarner	*Rabbi*	1859-1860
Aaron Guinzberg	*Rabbi*	1863-1868
Max Landsberg	*Rabbi/Senior Rabbi*	1871-1915
Max Moll	*Assistant Rabbi*	1886-1905
Felix Levy	*Assistant Rabbi*	1907-1908
Nathan Krass	*Assistant Rabbi*	1908-1910
Horace J. Wolf	*Assistant Rabbi*	1910-1915
	Senior Rabbi	1915-1927
Philip S. Bernstein	*Assistant Rabbi*	1926-1927
	Senior Rabbi	1927-1973
Horace Manacher	*Interim Rabbi*	1942-1945
Herbert Weiner	*Interim Rabbi*	1945-1946
Martin Zion	*Interim Rabbi*	1946-1949
Myron Weingarten	*Assistant Rabbi*	1949-1954
Joel Dobin	*Assistant Rabbi*	1954-1957
Herbert Bronstein	*Assistant Rabbi*	1957-1960
	Associate Rabbi	1960-1963
	Co-Rabbi	1963-1972
P. Selvin Goldberg *	*Visiting Rabbi*	1968-1969
Judea B. Miller	*Senior Rabbi*	1973-1995
Robert Baruch	*Assistant Rabbi*	1973-1976
Ronald Shapiro	*Assistant Rabbi*	1976-1978
Rosalind Gold	*Assistant Rabbi*	1978-1980
Robert Eisen	*Assistant & Associate Rabbi*	1980-1985
Judy Cohen-Rosenberg	*Assistant Rabbi*	1985-1990
Brian Daniels	*Assistant Rabbi*	1990-1992
Marc Gruber	*Associate Rabbi*	1992-1996
Laurence Kotok	*Senior Rabbi*	1995-present
S. Robert Morais	*Assistant Rabbi*	1996-present

* At B'rith Kodesh during sabbatical of Herbert Bronstein.

(continued on next page)

The distinction between rabbi and senior rabbi is fairly modern and of little significance in congregations with only one rabbi; whether Landsberg ever used the title is unclear, but he definitely functioned as a senior rabbi after 1886. It was only since the 1940s that a second rabbi has been employed at B'rith Kodesh on a regular basis. Before that time, in the absence of the rabbi, services were often led by hazzanim or readers. Some hazzanim were paid professionals, and were, in effect, assistant rabbis. Abraham Schmidt (or Smith) led services at B'rith Kodesh during the two prolonged rabbinic interregnums in the 1860s, from 1860-63 and from 1868-71. Other hazzanim, such as Gabriel Wile, were members of the laity with facility in the liturgy. Tobias Roth, a member of the congregation, conducted services during the extended illness of Rabbi Wolf in the mid 1920s. Also at the time, Rabbi Benjamin Friedman came from Syracuse every other Sunday to officiate at services; Rabbi Friedman regularly conducted services at B'rith Kodesh during World War II. Benjamin Goldstein, a gifted service leader, was the de facto assistant rabbi after 1927, and remained so even after 1942, when Philip Bernstein's war-related absence made the formal hiring of an assistant rabbi necessary. The following is a list of the more important hazzanim/service leaders at B'rith Kodesh.

Joseph Steifel 1848-1850s
Gabriel Wile 1850s-1860s
Abraham Schmidt 1860-1874
Sigmund Mannheimer 1877-1884
Tobias Roth 1920s
Benjamin Goldstein 1927-1958

Temple B'rith Kodesh Cantors and Music Directors

Heinrich Schalit . . . . *Music Director* 1940-1943
Lucille Brightman . . . . *Music Director* 1943-1962
Theodore Hollenbach . . . . *Music Director* 1962-1965
Herbert Brill . . . . *Music Director* 1966-1967
David Unterman . . . . *Cantor* 1967-1969
Stephen Richards . . . . *Cantor* 1969-1971
Joseph Gutherz . . . . *Hazzan* 1971-1973
Richard Allen . . . . *Cantor* 1973-1976
Moshe Hoffman . . . . *Music Director* 1976-1977
Steven Pearlston . . . . *Cantor* 1976-1977
Peter Halpern * . . . . *Cantorial Soloist* 1977-1980
Ed Schall . . . . *Music Director* 1978-1983
Gene Scher . . . . *Cantorial Soloist* 1980-1982
Steven Kane . . . . *Music Director* 1983-1985
Laura Croen * . . . . *Cantorial Soloist* 1983-1984
Jeremy Pic . . . . *Cantorial Soloist* 1985-1986
Ann Sheradsky . . . . *Cantorial Soloist* 1986-1987
Jim Cochran . . . . *Music Director* 1986-1989
Larry Stratemeyer . . . . *Music Director* 1990-1991
Barbara Ostfeld Horowitz . . . . . . *Cantor* 1988-1990
Rachael Gottlieb . . . . *Cantorial Soloist* 1991-1993
Michael Messina . . . . *Music Director* 1991-1995
Martha Rock Birnbaum . . . . *Cantor* 1993-1997
Paul Frolick . . . . *Music Director* 1995-present
Joel Colman . . . . *Cantor* 1997-1999

* Later invested as cantor.

(continued on next page)

Information on B'rith Kodesh music directors prior to 1940 is difficult to ascertain. The only cantor at B'rith Kodesh before 1967 was Elkan J. Herzman, who served for a few months in 1860. There were music directors before 1940, however. One of the chief demands of the radical Reform faction in B'rith Kodesh was the introduction of an organ and a choir into the services. One of the leaders of the faction, Nimrod Rosenfield, was the first music director of the congregation, from 1862 into the 1870s. After Rosenfield, we know little of the choral or music directors at the temple. By 1927 Herman Genhart, a professor of choral conducting at the Eastman School, was the B'rith Kodesh music director. Mollie Howland, a member of B'rith Kodesh's choir from 1911 through the early 1940s, also on occasion assumed a supervisory role. By the late 1930s the music director was Emanuel Balaban, who also taught at the Eastman School. He directed and conducted a performance of Ernest Bloch's *Sacred Service* at the temple in 1938. When Heinrich Schalit became music director in 1940, Emanuel Balaban remained organist. From the mid 1940s into the early 1960s, Laura Remington was the regular organist.

The tables of congregational leaders are derived from a number of sources. Every effort has been made to confirm names and tenures from contemporary records. Without Virginia McConnell's meticulous record keeping over the past half century, it would have been impossible to compile a list of music directors and cantors.

Several secondary sources provide additional context for understanding the history of Temple B'rith Kodesh. Isaac Wile, *History of the Jews of Rochester* (Rochester, N.Y., 1912), written by a member of one of Rochester's most influential German-Jewish families, is a valuable collection of historical information, anecdotes and biographical notes on the first sixty years of Jewish settlement in Rochester. Stuart Rosenberg, *The Jewish Community of Rochester, 1843-1925* (New York, 1954) is the only comprehensive scholarly study of the subject. Though the present volume takes issue with some of Rosenberg's conclusions, his work is an indispensable guide for the time period he covers. There is no history for the post-1925 period, though Abraham Karp, *Haven and Home: A History of the Jews in America* (New York, 1985), contains a great deal of material on the history of the Jewish community of Rochester. Jean Walrath's centennial history, *Temple B'rith Kodesh, 1848-1948*, was not based on primary research, but contains much of interest. The best history of Reform Judaism is Michael Meyer, *Response to Modernity: A History of the Reform Movement in Judaism* (New York, 1988). The five-volume collaborative history, *The Jewish People in America*, under the general editorship of Henry Feingold, is a valuable resource. The second volume in the series, Hasia R. Diner, *A Time For Gathering: The Second Migration, 1820-1880* (Baltimore, 1992), is especially recommended, and is the best introduction to American Jewish history during the early decades of B'rith Kodesh. For an overview of Jewish congregational life in the United States, the essays in *The American Synagogue: A Sanctuary Transformed* (Hanover, N.H., 1987), edited by Jack Wertheimer, are generally excellent. The standard history of Rochester is Blake McKelvey, *Rochester on the Genesee: The Growth of a City,* (2nd edition: Syracuse, 1992), an updated abridgment of the author's classic four-volume history of the city.

The modern orthography, "B'rith Kodesh," is used throughout. The original spelling, "Berith Kodesh," was standard through the early decades of the twentieth century. It is retained only in direct quotations from sources. Transliteration from Hebrew are retained in their original form in direct quotations; otherwise Hebrew transliterations follow modern Sephardic usage.

Unless specified, all photographs used in the volume are in the possession of Temple B'rith Kodesh.

The following citations are intended as an aid to interested researchers, and concentrate on primary sources, both printed and archival. The notes are arranged by topic, and within a given chapter, are clustered by their order of appearance. Within a specific group of citations, sources follow their order of appearance, but are arranged chronologically by specific publications; periodicals are given precedence to books; written sources precede oral interviews; primary sources precede secondary accounts. Because the archival processing of the Philip S. Bernstein Papers, Department of Rare Books and Special Collections, Rush Rhees Library, University of Rochester, is not complete, I have cited items in this collection by series rather than giving a specific box number. Unless otherwise specified, all temple minutes are in the possession of Temple B'rith Kodesh.

ABBREVIATIONS

AH . . . . *American Hebrew*
AI . . . . *American Israelite*
ADJA . . . . .Advisor on Jewish Affairs
AJA . . . . .American Jewish Archives, Cincinnati
BoTM . . . . .Board of Trustees Minutes
BSS . . . . .Baden Street Settlement
CCAR . . . . .Central Conference of American Rabbis
CCARJ . . . .*Central Conference of American Rabbis Journal*
CCARY . . . .*Central Conference of American Rabbis Yearbook*
CM . . . . .Congregational Minutes
ES . . . . .Elizabeth Schwartz
HB . . . . .Herbert Bronstein
HJW . . . . .Horace J. Wolf
HUC . . . . .Hebrew Union College
JDB . . . . *Jewish Daily Bulletin*
JL . . . . *Jewish Ledger* (Rochester)
JM . . . . .Judea Miller
JM . . . . *Jewish Messenger*
JMP . . . . .Judea Miller Papers, AJA
JT . . . . *Jewish Tidings*
ML . . . . .Max Landsberg
PSB . . . . .Philip S. Bernstein
PSBP . . . . .PSB Papers, UR
RDC . . . .*Rochester Democrat and Chronicle*
RJCOHP . . . . .Rochester Jewish Community Oral History Project
Rosenberg . . . . .Stuart Rosenberg, *The Jewish Community of Rochester,*
1843-1925 (New York, 1954)
RPL . . . . .Rochester Public Library
RUA . . . . *Rochester Union and Advertiser*
SB . . . . .Sophy Bernstein
SBA . . . . .Susan B. Anthony
SSW . . . . .Stephen S. Wise
TBK . . . . .Temple B'rith Kodesh
TBKM . . . . .Temple B'rith Kodesh Museum
TBKS . . . . .Temple B'rith Kodesh Sisterhood
TO . . . .*The Occident*
UR . . . . .Department of Rare Books and Special Collections, Rush Rhees Library,
University of Rochester
Wile . . .Isaac Wile, *The History of the Jews of Rochester* (Rochester, N.Y., 1912)

Chapter I

TBK 50th anniversary: *Jewish Advocate* 1 #3 (Oct. 14, 1898); Wile's opposition to the prayerbook: AI 30 #26 (Feb. 1, 1884).

First Jews in Rochester: AI 34 #51 (June 20, 1884); Wile, 7-10; Abraham J. Karp, "An Eastern European Congregation on American Soil: Beth Israel, Rochester, New York, 1874-1886," in Bertram Wallace Korn, ed., *A Bicentennial "Festschrift" for Jacob Rader Marcus* (Waltham, Mass., 1976), 263. The obituary of Joseph Katz, Joseph Katz Collection, AJA, gives his date of arrival in Rochester as 1834. The *Rochester Democrat's* quoted in AI 2 #12 (Sept. 8, 1855).

Early Polish Jews in Rochester: JM 5 #11 (Mar. 11, 1858); TO 13 #9 (December 1855); Salo W. Baron and Jeanette M. Baron, "Palestinian Messengers in America, 1849-1879: A Record of Four Journeys." *Jewish Social Studies* V (1943), 286. 234-245, 286; early Jewish marriages in Rochester: Wile, 26, 57.

Founding of TBK: AI 34 #51 (June 20, 1884). *Jewish Advocate* 1 #3 (Oct. 14, 1898); TO 5 #4 (July 1847), 275; Wile, 10-13. For cemetery records, see the burial, lot, and internment records, Mt. Hope Cemetery. I would like to thank Jack McKinney of the Friends of Mt. Hope Cemetery for making these records available.

Alternative names and spellings for TBK: JM 5 #1 (Jan. 7, 1859); Baron and Baron, "Palestinian Messengers in America, 1849-1979," 286; "The Congregation Bris Kaudesch to . . . Ferdinand Sarner," July 22, 1860, TBKM.

Worldly success of TBK: AI 2 (Oct. 31, 1856); JM 12 #4 (July 15, 1862).

Women at TBK: AI 3 #17 (Oct. 31, 1856), 3 #48 (June 5, 1857), 10 #24 (Dec. 11, 1863); TO 14 (January 1857), 503.

Conversion ceremonies: AI 3 #40 (Apr. 16, 1857), 6 #33 (Feb. 13, 1860).

Sarah Stettheimer: AI 3 # 40 (April 16, 1857).

Joseph Steifel and Mordecai Tuska: AI 34 #51 (June 20, 1888). Steifel was hired at the recommendation of Dr. Morris Raphall, the rabbi of B'nai Jeshrun in New York City; TO 12 #3 (June 1854).

Simon Tuska: Benjamin Tuska, "Biography of Simon Tuska," Simon Tuska Papers,

AJA; Abraham J. Karp, "Simon Tuska Becomes a Rabbi," *Publications of the American Jewish Historical Society* 50 (December 1960), 70-73; Abraham J. Karp, *Haven and Home: A History of Jews in America* (New York, 1985), 70-73; Simon Tuska, *The Stranger in the Synagogue, or the Rites and Ceremonies of Jewish Worship Described and Explained* (Rochester, N.Y., 1854); Simon Tuska, "Opfer und Reue: Eine Predigt, gehalten am Neujahrstage 5615 von der Gemeinde, 'Berith Kodesh' in Rochester, N.Y," Library of Congress. The sermon was orginally published in Berlin in the 1850s; the excellent English translation is the work of Hildegard Herz of Rochester, N.Y. Tuska's later career: AI 3 #7 (Aug. 22, 1856), 4 #52 (July 2, 1858), 5 #27 (Jan. 7, 1859), 10 #1 (July 3, 1863), 17 #33 (Feb. 10, 1871); Isaac Mayer Wise to Simon Tuska, Jan. 5, 1855, Isaac Mayer Wise Papers, AJA.

Isaac Mayer: AI 3 #17 (Oct. 31, 1856), 3 #48 (June 5, 1857), 5 #17 (Oct. 25, 1858), 7 #3 (July 20, 1860), 10 #24 (Dec. 11, 1863); TO 13 #8 (October 1855), 13 #9 (December 1855), 14 #6 (September 1856); Benjamin Tuska, "Biography of Simon Tuska," Tuska Papers, AJA.

Ferdinand Sarner: AI 6 #7 (Sept. 23, 1859), 6 #33 (Feb. 13, 1860), 6 #45 (May 12, 1860), 7 #3 (July 20, 1860); JM 7 #18 (May 4, 1860), 7 #22 (June 8, 1860), 11 #2 (Jan. 6, 1865); "The Congregation Bris Kaudesch to . . . Ferdinand Sarner." Sarner in the Civil War: Bertram Wallace Korn, *American Jewry and the Civil War* (Philadelphia, 1961), 83-87; New York State Monument Commission for the Battlefield of Gettysburg and Chattanooga, *Final Report on the Battle of Gettysburg* (Albany, N.Y., 1900), I, 208-209, 402-405.

Rochester's "unsynagogued": AI 2 #12 (Sept. 8, 1855); TO 12 #3 (June 1854), 167; TO 9 #8 (October 1851) names an otherwise unknown "Rev. Mr. Doski" as minister of the congregation.

Size of TBK c. 1860: AI 2 #12 (Sept. 8. 1885), 3 #17 (Oct. 24, 1856), 7 #3 (July 20, 1860); I. J. Benjamin, *Three Years in America*, 1859-1862, 2 vols., trans. by Charles Reznikoff (Philadelphia, 1956), II, 282-283.

St. Paul Street temple: AI 2 #12 (Sept. 8, 1855), 2 #23 (Dec. 14, 1855), 2 #40 (Apr. 4, 1856), 3 #7 (Aug. 22, 1856); TO 13 #8 (October 1855); Wile, 16.

The "pious five": AI 5 #15 (Oct. 1, 1855), 6 #45 (May 12, 1860); JM 5 #18 (Mar. 11, 1859), 7 #22 (June 8, 1860).

Introduction of *Minhag America*: AI 9 #41 (Apr. 17, 1862), 10 #10 (Sept. 4, 1863), 10 #17 (Oct. 23, 1863); TO 13 #9 (December 1855); Rosenberg, 37. TBK social and charitable activities: AI 3 #17 (Oct. 31, 1856); TO 9 #8 (October 1851); Rosenberg, 36-37; Wile, 21; Henry Seligman speech, TBKM.

TBK religious education: AI 2 #12 (Sept. 8, 1855), 2 #51 (June 27, 1856), 3 #17 (Oct. 31, 1856), 3 #48 (June 5, 1857), 7 #3 (July 20, 1860); TO 14 #6 (September 1856), 14 #10 (January 1857); Isaac Mayer, *"Mayon Hashonah": Source of Salvation: A Catechism of the Jewish Religion* (New York, 1874); Isaac Mayer, *Systematic and Practical Hebrew Grammar* (Cincinnati, Ohio, 1856); Rosenberg, 27; Wile, 13.

Jews in other lands: TO 16 #12 (March 1859); Baron and Baron, "Palestinian Messengers in America," 115-196, 22-292.

"Three visitors": AI 7 #3 (July 20, 1860); RUA, May 22, 1865; I. J. Benjamin, *Three Years in America*, , II, 282-283.

TBK in the Civil War: AI 10 #24 (Dec. 11, 1863); JM 5 #11 (Mar. 18, 1859), 10 (May 27, 1864); TO 11 #46 (May 12, 1865); RUA, Oct. 17, 1862.

Henry Rice: speech, May 15, 1864, Confirmation files, TBKM. Another speech of Rice also survives, either his Bar Mitzvah or Confirmation address, dated Feb. 17, 1861, Confirmation files, TBKM.

Chapter II

Hazzan controversy: AI 10 #17 (Oct. 23, 1863), 10 #24 (Dec. 11, 1863).

Aaron Guinzberg: AI 2 #2 (July 20, 1854), 10 #1 (July 3, 1863), 11 #46 (May 12, 1865), 11 #49 (June 2, 1865); JM, May 27, 1864; RUA, Jan. 30, Feb. 6, 1865. In different sources, Guinzberg is spelled Gunzberg, Gunsberg, Guinsberg, and Guenzberg. Guinzberg seems to be the preferred version.

Drunkenness: RUA, Sept. 5, 1867. In March 1891, Solomon Schindler spoke at TBK on "Why There Are No Drunkards Among the Jews," JT (March 20, 1891).

Family seating: AI 16 #12 (Sept. 24, 1870), 17 #50 (June 17, 1871); Wile, 11. The B'rith Kodesh board of trustees approved family seating in the spring of 1868, though it apparently did not go into effect until the following year.

Greentree Shule: TBK BoTM 1867-1873, Jan. 30, 1870, AJA; Rosenberg, 86-87; Wile, 103.

Hiring of Landsberg: AI 16 #28 (Jan. 14, 1870), 17 #36 (Mar. 13, 1871); JM, Dec. 17, 1869; TBK BoTM 1867-1873, Jan. 23, 1870, Apr. 2, 1871, AJA; TBK CM, Oct. 20, 1878, July 1, Sept. 2, 1883, TBK; ML, Notebook, "Collectanea," ML Papers, UR; ML, "The Religious Movement After Abraham Geiger," ML Papers, RPL; Rosenberg, 90; Wile, 12.

Landsberg's religious views: AI 30 #27 (Jan. 14, 1884); JT, Dec. 30, 1887; Samuel Goldensohn, "Max Landsberg," CCARY 38 (1928), 237-239; ML, *Outlines of the Jewish Religion* (Rochester, N.Y., 1899), 22; ML, letter to RDC, Jan. 17, 1902; ML, "Four Sentiments: A Passover Sermon," in CCAR, ed., *Sermons by American Rabbis* (Chicago, 1896), 166-175; ML, "The Position of Women Among the Jews," JT (Sept. 8, 1893); ML, "The Duties of the Rabbi at the Present Time," CCARY (1895), 121-130; [ML] *Ritual for Jewish Worship* (Rochester, 1884); ii; ML, "Discussion of Concerted Action in Sabbath-School Reform," in *Conference Papers of Essays and Addresses Delivered at the First Conference of the Jewish Minister's Association of New York and Adjacent States* (New York, 1885) 25-30; ML, "Leopold Zunz," in *Conference Papers of the Jewish Minister's Association of America* (New York, 1888), 17; ML, "Zionism Again" (1918), ML Papers, RPL; SB interview, April 1997.

Religious education: JT, June 24, Dec. 3, 1888, Aug. 29, 1890, June 24, 1892; Wile, 13; Confirmation file, TBKM.

Ritual for Jewish Worship: AI 30 #25 (Dec. 21, 1883), 30 #26 (Dec. 28, 1883), 30 #27 (Jan. 4, 1884), 30 #31 (Feb. 1, 1884), 30 #51 (June 20, 1884); JT, Oct. 5, 1888, Aug. 29, 1891; TBK CM, Apr. 27, May 7, Dec. 16, 1883, Jan. 13, 1884, Oct. 4, 1885; [ML and Solomon Wile], *Hymnbook for Jewish Worship* (Rochester, 1888); ML to Kaufmann Kohler, Dec. 22, 1922, ML Papers, UR; ML to Bernard Felsenthal, Dec. 26, 1883, ML Papers, AJA; ML to his children, Jan. 15, 1918, ML Papers, AJA; David Einhorn to ML, Oct. 15, 1875, ML Papers, AJA; Isaac Moses, *Tefillah Le-Moshe* (Milwaukee, 1884); Rosenberg, 95. The Landsberg ritual service was used at B'rith Kodesh for weekly services until the abandonment of Sunday services in 1941. PSB, "My Last Friday Night Sermon on Gibbs Street," May 11, 1962, Sermons, PSBP. The *Union Prayer Book* was introduced at High Holy Day services somewhat earlier, in 1927.

Sunday services controversy: JT, Oct. 5, 1888, Feb. 22, 1889, Apr. 11, Aug. 15, Oct. 24, 31, Nov. 7, 28, 1890, Jan. 2, Oct. 23, Nov. 21, 1891, Mar. 4, May 27, Oct. 17, Nov. 28, 1892; ML, "Friday or Sunday: Which?" JT (Nov. 21, 1890); Wile, 96-97.

German-Jewish social life: anti-Semitism: JT, May 17, 1889; Max Moll, "Sermon on Prejudice," JT (July 22, 1892). Baseball game: JT, Sept. 19, 1890. Eureka Club: JT, Feb. 20, 1890. Fraternal organizations: JT, Aug. 23, 1889; Wile, 19. Theater: JT, Oct. 3, 1890, Feb. 20, 1891.
Gibbs Street temple: AI 30 #51 (June 30, 1884); *Jewish Advocate*, 1 #3 (Oct. 14, 1898); JT, June 19, Sept. 27, 1889, May 27, Oct. 3, 1890, Oct. 21, 1892, Jan. 27, 1893; TBK CM, Jan. 30, 1876, Dec. 18, 1887, Sept. 30, 1888.

Chapter III

TBK and UAHC: TBK CM, Apr. 5, 1874, Apr. 13, 1879; CCARY 6 (1895); ML to Kaufmann Kohler, Dec. 22, 1922, ML Papers, UR.

Charities: "Minutes of the Hebrew Ladies Aid Society," Vol. 1, Jan. 1, 1871, and undated, Vol. 3, UR; Wile, 21-22.

Women in choir and school: AI 10 #1 (July 3, 1863); JM 6 #10 (Sept. 9, 1859); JT, June 28, 1888, Oct. 31, Nov. 6, 1890, Sept. 8, 1893; TBK CM, Oct. 7, 1888. Women as TBK members: JT, May 1, May 8, May 24, 1891; TBK CM, Apr. 26, 1891.

Susan B. Anthony and Women's Suffrage: JT, Dec. 4, 1891; SBA to ML, Nov. 27, 1901, SBA Papers, UR; ML, "The Position of Women Among the Jews," JT (Sept. 8, 1893).

Miriam Landsberg: Rosenberg, 112-113; SBA to Miriam Landsberg, Feb. 12, 1899, SBA Papers, UR; *Reform Advocate*, Dec. 20, 1897 I wish to thank Prof. Pamela Nadel of American University for making this document available; Miriam Landsberg obituary, c. Apr. 16, 1912, ML Papers, UR.

New immigration: JT, Feb. 5, 1887, Dec. 14, 1888, Aug. 22, Dec. 26, 1890, Jan. 2, Apr. 3, 1891; TBK CM, July 7, 1903; Oscar Craig, "The Prevention of Pauperism," *Scribner's Magazine* 12 (July 1893), 124; ML, "Review of N. S. Shaler, *The Natural History of Human Contacts*," September 1904 (unpub.), ML Papers, RPL; Rosenberg, 63, 147-49; Wile, 21-28.

Sisterhood: Founding of Sisterhood: JT, Jan. 27, 1892; Fannie Garson at 50th anniversary, in "TBK Sisterhood: Looking Back Fifty Years," May 2, 1942, TBKS files, TBK. Lack of men at services: JT, Oct. 30, Nov. 28, 1890. Baden Street Settlement: *BSS Bulletin* 2 #9 (February 1909); BSS, *Year Book of the Social Settlement of Rochester, 1901-1902* (Rochester, N.Y., 1902); BSS, *The Social Settlement of Rochester, 1915* (Rochester, N.Y., 1915); BSS, *The Baden Street Settlement, 1901-1949* (Rochester, N.Y., 1949); Ruth Lebovics interview, July 29, 1976, RJCOHP, 106-108.

Labor: Max I. Guttman, "Anarchism and Atheism," JT (Nov. 19, 1887); *Report of the Committee on Manufacturers, House of Representatives*, 52nd Congress, 2nd Session, Jan. 20, 1893, 59.

Leopold Garson: JT, Jan. 19, 1890; *Rochester Post-Express*, Sept. 27, 1899, for the identity of the author as Louis Lipsky, see Rosenberg, 261; Emma Goldman, *Living My Life* (New York, 1931), I 10-18; Wile, 108..

ML and Russian Jews: JT, October 1891; *Annual Report of the Executive Council of the Judean Club, 1898-1899* (Rochester, N.Y., 1899), HUC Library; Samuel Goldensohn, "Max Landsberg," CCARY 38 (1928), 237-239; Thomas A. Kolsky, *Jews Against Zionism: The American Council for Judaism, 1942-1948* (Philadelphia, 1990), 37-56; Rosenberg, 73-74; Wile, 47-48; SB interview, Mar. 30, 1997; ES interview, Apr. 8, 1997.

Last years of Max Landsberg: TBK and ML: TBK CM, Mar. 5, 1899, Mar. 4, Oct. 7, 1900; Jan. 29, June 23, 1901; Oct. 26, 1902; ML, "Collectanea," ML Papers, UR. Rev. Brown controversy: TBK CM, Mar. 4, 1900; TBK to ML, May 5, 1901, ML to TBK, May 9, 1901, TBK Collection, AJA; PSB, "Rabbi Wolf's Old Sermons," Nov. 12, 1971, Sermons, PSBP; Rosenberg, 115-116. TBK's assistant rabbis: TBK CM, June 3, June 24, Aug. 24, 1906 (evidently, the congregation tried to hire Samuel Goldensohn, Landsberg's protégé, at the time, but nothing came of it; Rosenberg, 189), May 5, 1907, Mar. 8, 1908, Nov. 9, Dec. 9, 1909; Nathan Krass, "Morals and Manners," AH 84 (Apr. 30, 1909); Nathan Krass, "Patriotism," *Common Good* 1 #9 (February 1909). Landsberg in retirement: TBK CM, Oct. 15, Dec. 5, 1915; PSB, "My Last Friday Night Sermon at Gibbs Street," May 11, 1962, Sermons, PSBP; HJW, "The Functions of Ceremonies," AH 89 (Mar. 29, 1909); ML to his children, Jan. 16, 1918, ML Papers, AJA; ML to Kaufmann Kohler, Dec. 22, 1922, ML Papers, UR.

Fire: TBK CM, Apr. 13, May 2, Nov. 5, 1909.

Sunday services and religious education: TBK CM, Oct. 7, 1906, Nov. 5, Dec. 28, 1911, Dec. 13, 1913, Apr. 5, 1914, Dec. 4, 1921; PSB, "My Last Friday Night Sermon at Gibbs Street"; HJW, "Abuses of Confirmation," AH 96#30 (May 14, 1915); HJW, "Character Building and Child Worship," CCARY 25 (1915), 318-326; HJW, "Pesach-Then and Now," AH 96 #22 (Mar. 26, 1915); ES interview, Apr. 8, 1997.

HJW's background, his eastern European origins, SB interview, Mar. 30, 1997. HJW's first years at TBK: AH 87 #15 (Aug. 13, 1909); TBK CM, Oct. 3, 1911, Jan. 15, Apr. 7, Sept. 12, 1912, May 3, 1913, Jan. 15, 1914; HJW, "A Congregational Report," AH 97 #19 (Sept. 10, 1915); HJW, "Democracy and the Reform Temple," AH 94 #16 (Feb. 12, 1915); HJW, "Is Religion Dying Out?," TBK sermon, n.d., HJW

Papers, AJA; HJW, "The Rabbi and the Community," AH 94 #24 (Apr. 10, 1914); HJW, "Synagogue and Community," *Survey* 30 #3 (Apr. 19, 1913); HJW, "Time to Cry 'Halt," AH 94 #26 (Apr. 23, 1915).

HSW's religious and political views: HJW, "Anti-Semitism," TBK sermon, Dec. 10, 1917, HJW Papers, AJA; HJW, "The Ghost of Assimilation," AH (n.d.), HJW Papers, AJA; HJW, "Inconsistencies," AH 97 #33 (Dec. 13, 1915); HJW, "The Miracle," AH 102 #21 (Mar. 29, 1918); HJW, "The Passing of Benevolent Feudalism," AH 98 (Mar. 3, 1916); HJW, "Rochester's Welcome to the Jewish Immigrants," *Common Good* 4 #8 (May 1911).

HJW and labor: RDC, Feb. 25, 1913, RUA, Feb. 7, 1913; Nathan Stern, "Horace J. Wolf," CCARY 31 (1927); HJW, "Alternative to Bolshevism," TBK sermon, April 27, 1919, HJW Papers, AJA; HJW, review of Graham Taylor's *Religion in Social Action*, CCARY 19 (1910), 367; "Report of the Committee on Synagog and Industrial Relations," CCARY 26 (1917), 101-103, CCARY 27 (1918), 101-104.

World War I: RDC, June 29, 1914; "The Zionist Convention at Rochester," AH 92 #10 (July 3, 1914); HJW, "Barriers to Brotherhood," TBK sermon, Jan. 19, 1919, HJW Papers, AJA; HJW, "The Challenge of the Hour," TBK sermon, Rosh Hashanah 1917, HJW Papers, AJA; HJW, "Hayim Cohn—Late of Kiev," AH 103 #23 (Oct. 23, 1918); HJW, "The Miracle"; HJW, "A Month at Camp Dix," HJW Papers, AJA; HJW, "A 'Rooky' at Plattsburgh," AH 99 #12, 15, 18, 20 (July-September 1916); HJW, "Stranger Than Fiction" TBK Sermon, 1926, HJW Papers, AJA; HJW, "The Synagog, the War, and the Days Ahead," CCARY 29 (1919).

HJW and Zionism: TBK CM, Jan. 2, 1924; HJW, "Stranger Than Fiction," TBK sermon, October 1926, HJW Papers, AJA; PSB to SSW, Jan. 14, 1936, PSB Papers, AJA; "Resolution Adopted by the CCAR July 4, 1918 Anent the Balfour Declaration," ML Papers, RPL.

Jewish Rochester in the 1920s: AH 98 #27 (Mar. 14, 1914); TBK CM, Feb. 22, 1918, Nov. 23, 1925, Apr. 23, May 14, 1926; Jewish Welfare Board, *Study of the Social and Recreational Facilities and Needs Relating to the Jewish Community of Rochester, N.Y.* (Rochester, 1922); Rosenberg, 200, 223; HJW, "A Free Synagog," TBK sermon, Jan. 14, 1919, HJW Papers, AJA; HJW, undated notes c. 1925, HJW Papers, AJA; SB interview, Mar. 30, 1997.

HJW's illness: TBK CM, Nov. 2, 1923, June 10, Sept. 12, 1924, Nov. 1, 1925, Feb. 21, Apr. 2, May 14, 1926; PSB, "I Never Regretted Being a Rabbi," Miscellanea, 19, 21.

Chapter IV

PSB's youth: JL (Mar. 22, 1935); PSB, "I Never Regretted Being a Rabbi,"
Miscellanea; PSBP; PSB, "A Rabbi's Thirty Years," Apr. 17, 1957, Sermons, PSBP;
PSB, "Stephen S. Wise-Some Personal Recollections," 6-11, CCARJ 11 (April
1963); PSB interview with Thomas Liebschutz, Aug. 14, 1964, 172-173, PSB
Papers, AJA ; ES interview, June 1976, RJCOHP, 42.

Beth Israel and Rabbi Chertoff: Rosenberg, 172-173.

PSB on Conservative Judaism: PSB, "Should Reform and Conservative Judaism
Merge?," Mar. 3, 1971, Sermons, PSBP; PSB, "What's Ahead for Reform Jews?,"
Nov. 26, 1948, Sermons, PSBP.

PSB at Syracuse University: "Letter to the *Syracuse Orange*," Addresses, PSBP;
PSB, "Stephen S. Wise-Some Personal Recollections"; HJW to Henry Hurwitz, Dec.
28, 1920, Henry Hurwitz Menorah Collection, Box 63, AJA.

PSB at JIR: PSB, "John Haynes Holmes," *American Jewish Congress Bi-Weekly*
(June 15, 1964); PSB, "I Never Regretted Being a Rabbi"; "I Was a Teenage
Atheist," Feb. 12, 1960, Sermons, PSBP; PSB, "Stephen S. Wise-Some Personal
Recollections"; PSB, "A Study of the Personality of Jeremiah the Prophet," Mar.
1926, JIR thesis, HUC Library.

PSB's prewar theology: PSB, "Bergson and Judaism," Jan. 20, 1929, Sermons,
PSBP; PSB, "Changing Gods," n.d. (c. 1930), Sermons, PSBP; PSB, Confirmation
speech, 1932, Confirmation files, TBKM; PSB, "I Was a Teenage Atheist"; PSB,
"The Minister," *Jewish Institute of Religion Annual* (1926), 38-40; PSB, "On
Prayer," n.d. (c. 1930), Sermons, PSBP; PSB, "Should the Jews Take Spinoza
Back?," Dec. 14, 1956, Sermons, PSBP; PSB, "What My Religion Can Do for You,"
n.d. (c. 1930), Sermons, PSBP. On Amsterdam, N.Y., PSB, "I Never Regretted
Being a Rabbi," 17.

PSB's prewar politics: PSB, "FDR Eulogy," 1945, Sermons, PSBP; PSB, "Hungry
Russia," RDC, Nov 6-8, 1933; PSB, "My Last Friday Night Sermon on Gibbs Street,"
May 11, 1962, Sermons, PSBP; PSB, "On Being a Rabbi," 1936, Sermons, PSBP;
PSB, "On Jews in Soviet Russia," 1928, Sermons, PSBP; PSB, "On Karl Marx," n.d.
(1930s), Sermons, PSBP; PSB, "On Racism and the Scottsboro Case," n.d.
(1935?), Sermons, PSBP; PSB, "On the Good-Will Pilgrimage," n.d. (c. 1935),
Sermons, PSBP; PSB, "On the History of His Thinking and Experiences in

Germany," October 1933, Addresses, PSBP; PSB, "A Pacifist Demurs," Opinion 5 (November 1934), 10-11; PSB, "Religion in Russia," Harper's (May 1930); PSB, "Rosh Hashanah,"1931, Sermons, PSBP; PSB, "Rosh Hashanah," 1933, Sermons, PSBP; PSB, "Stephen S. Wise-Some Personal Recollections"; PSB, review of Levinthal, Steering or Drifting—Which? *Menorah Journal* 16 (May 1929), 569-571; PSB, Yom Kippur sermon, 1926, Sermons, PSBP; PBS to Samuel Karff, 1976, CCAR, PSBP; PSB to SSW, May 28, 1930, Box 44, SSW Papers; Chester Leopold, "Impact of a Modern American Reform Rabbi"; SB interview, March 30, 1997; Garson Meyer interview, June 1976, RJCOHP, 72.

TBK in the 1930s: TBK CM, Feb. 16, 26, 1936; PSB to SSW, July 1, 1932, Box 44, SSW Papers; SSW to PSB, Feb. 25, 1929, PSB Papers, AJA; Chester Leopold, "Impact of a Modern American Reform Rabbi on a Young Modern Reform Jew," PSB Papers, AJA; "Program of Eightieth Birthday Party and Year Book, 1927-28," TBK, PSBP; SB interview in Carol Yunker, ed. "Do You Remember?: Reminiscences of Sisterhood," 1992, TBKS; Maurice Forman interview, September 1976, RJCOHP, 1; Nathan Goldberg interview, August 1976, RJCOHP, 9; Manuel Goldman interview, RJCOHP, 12; Mordecai Lurie interview, June-July 1976, RJCOHP, 74; Florence Sturman interview, June 1976, RJCOHP, 21.

PSB in Rochester: PSB, "The Future Leadership of American Jews," *Opinion* 16 (April 1946), 9; PSB to James Waterman, Jan. 9, 1936, Correspondence, PSBP; Justin Wroe Nixon, "The Interfaith Dinner: Celebrating One Hundred Years of Religious Progress in Rochester," *Rochester Historical Society* 13, 35-38; Winthrop Hudson interview, June 1976, RJCOHP.

PSB and Zionism: JDB, June 23, 1935; RDC, May 3, 1998; PSB to SSW, July 1, 1932, SSW Papers; Frank Gannett to SSW, May 23, 1939, SSW Papers; Samuel Rosenbaum interview, August 1976, RJCOHP, 31.

Formation of JCC: TBK CM, Feb. 5, 1932; Elmer Louis interview, July 8, 1977, RJCOHP, 37-38.

Jewish quota at the University of Rochester: The University of Rochester did not publicly acknowledge the operation of a Jewish quota, but its existence was assumed by many Rochester Jews in the interwar period. Emanuel Goldberg spoke of a 7% quota (Emanuel Goldberg interview, July, 1976, RJCOHP, 1) and Philip Bernstein of a 5% quota (PSB, "I Never Regretted Being a Rabbi," 13). Garson Meyer remembered anti-Semitic comments by U of R President Rush Rhees, and the confirmation of the existence of a quota by faculty members (Garson Meyer interview, July 1976, RJCOHP, 27); see also Abe Hollander interview, July-August 1976, RJCOHP, 3, and Julia Berlove interview, June 1976, RJCOHP, 27. Chester Leopold wrote of restrictive covenants in Brighton in "Impact of a Modern Reform Rabbi"; see as well PSB, "Some Facts About the Jews," *Harper's* (April 1939), 501-502.

Worship at TBK: TBK CM, June 2, 1941. PSB unsatisfied with: TBK CM, Nov. 30, 1930; PSB, "My Last Friday Night Sermon on Gibbs Street," 10; PSB, "On Being a Rabbi"; experimental services, TBK CM, Dec. 13, 1932, Mar. 22, 1934; HB interview, Jan. 13, 1998; Manuel Goldman interview, RJCOHP, 3; Yunker, "Do You Remember," 1.

Music during the 1930s: TBK CM, Nov. 12, 1942; Sunday to Friday, TBK CM, Sept. 14, 1928, Feb. 2, 1929, Jan. 10, 1930, Jan. 5, 1940, Apr. 22, 1941, June 2, 1941; Virginia McConnell interview, Apr. 27, 1997; Samuel Rosenbaum interview, RJCOHP, 26.

PSB and the Gerer Rebbe: JL, June 23, 1935; PSB, "I Never Regretted Being a Rabbi," "Miscellanea." 28-29; PSB, "The Tears of St. Anne and the Laughter of the Baal Shem," Apr. 22, 1949, Sermons, PSBP.

PSB and TBK in the late 1930s; PSB as a reluctant fundraiser: PSB, interview with Lauren Deutsch and Menachem Kaufman, c. 1977, 6, Miscellanea, PSBP; SSW to PSB, July 1, 1932, PSB Papers, AJA; "Temple Activities," 1940-41, TBK, PSBP.

Sisterhood: "TBK Sisterhood: Looking Back Fifty Years," May 2, 1942, TBK Files, TBK; Carol Yunker, ed., "Do You Remember?, 2.

Benjamin Goldstein: AH 84 #17 (Feb. 26, 1909); TBK CM June 1927; TBK CM, Dec. 17, 1942; PSB, "In Memoriam Benjamin Goldstein," Feb. 2, 1958, Memorial Sermons, PSBP; *In Memoriam Benjamin Goldstein, Executive Secretary Temple B'rith Kodesh* (Rochester, N.Y., 1958); Manuel Goldman interview, August 1976, RJCOHP, 13.

Education at TBK: TBK, 90th Anniversary Pageant, TBKM; William Greenberg interview, July 1976, RJCOHP; Herman Sarachan interview, June 1976, RJCOHP, 13-16; ES interview, July 1976, RJCOHP, 47.

PSB and the rise of Hitler: PSB, "The Fate of the Jews," *The Nation* (Oct. 23, 1937); PSB, "Haman and Hitler: Lessons from Jewish History," Mar. 12, 1933,

Sermons, PSBP; PSB, "Hitler: Chancellor of Germany," Feb. 5, 1933, Sermons, PSBP; PSB, "Hitler's Germany: An Eyewitness Report," Oct. 29, 1933, Sermons, PSBP (the excerpt published here also incorporates material from its expanded form, PSB, "Can Hitler Be Trusted Now?" *The Nation* [Dec. 27, 1933]); PSB, "Hitler—Is He Germany's Messiah or Greatest Menace?," Jan. 1, 1932, Sermons, PSBP; PSB, "Rosh Hashanah," Sept. 27, 1930, Sept. 14, 1944, Sermons, PSBP; PSB, "Roumania Backslides," *Menorah Journal* 19 (October 1930), 177-178; PSB to SSW, Sept. 11, 1930, SSW to PSB, June 15, 1933, PSB to SSW, June 20, 1933, PSB Papers, AJA; ES interview, July 1976, RJCOHP, 31.

PSB's retreat from pacifism: PSB, "I Never Regretted Being a Rabbi," 65, 66, PSBP; PSB, "Pacifism in Hitler's World," *The World Tomorrow 17* (June 1934), 304-307; PSB, "Presidential·Candidates and Peace," *Unity* (Oct. 19, 1936); PSB, "Strength, Not Idealism"; *Christian Century* 66 (July 20, 1949), 864-866. PSB to Oswald Garrison Villard, Nov. 28, 1940, Correspondence, PSBP; PSB to Jonah Wise, Nov. 22, 1940, Correspondence, PSBP; SB interview, Feb. 25, 1998.

German refugees in Rochester: Manuel Goldman interview, RJCOHP, 8-9; Arthur Herz interview, June 30, 1998.

Heinrich Schalit: TBK CM, Oct. 20, 1930, Feb. 16, Mar. 6, 1931, Jan. 8, 1937, Sept. 3, 1943, Apr. 9, 1954; Heinrich Schalit to PSB, March 20, 1933, Correspondence, PSBP; memorandum from A. Dana Hodgon, chief, Visa Division, U.S. Department of State, to Congressman Samuel Dickstein, Sept. 30, 1933 (in Schalit file, PSBP).

The coming of war and CANRA; PSB, ms. review of Solomon B. Freehof, *Modern Jewish Preaching*, and Abraham Cronback, *Our Social Outlook*, 1941, Publications, PSBP; PSB, "The Greatest Day in Jewish History," October 1942, Sermons, PSBP; PSB, *Rabbis at War: The CANRA Story* (Waltham, Mass., 1971); PSB, "Welcome Weizmann," Mar. 30, 1941, Sermons, PSBP; PSB, "What Do the Jews Believe—Messiah, Mission, Mankind?," Dec. 5, 1941, Sermons, PSBP; PSB interview with Thomas Liebschutz, 13.

Holocaust: TBK CM, Jan. 1, 1943; PSB, "The Jews of Europe—1) The Remnants of a People; (2) Seven Ways to Save Them Now; (3) Alternative to Zion; (4) The Case for Zionism," *The ation* (Jan. 2-Feb. 6, 1942); PSB, "What Hope for the Jews?," *New Republic* (Apr. 26, 1943); PSB, "Rosh Hashanah," Sept. 29, 1943, Sermons, PSBP; PSB interview with Thomas Liebschutz.

PSB as special advisor on Jewish affairs: PSB, "Can We Make Peace with the

Russians?," Oct. 24, 1947; PSB, "The New Israel and American Jewry," CCARY 58 (1948); PSB, "The Rabbi in Communal and National Activities," CCARJ 1 (October 1953), PSB, "Rosh Hashanah," 1946, Sermons, PSBP; PSB, "The Tears of St. Anne and the Laughter of the Baal Shem"; PSB, *What the Jews* Believe (New York, 1950), 22; PSB to David de la Sola Pool, Aug. 10, 1946, ADJA, PSBP; PSB, conference with President Truman, Oct. 11, 1946, ADJA, PSBP; PSB, interview with Thomas Liebschutz, 19, 20, 58-59; memorandum to General Joseph T. McNarney, Sept. 14, 1946 (on meeting with Pius XII), ADJA, PSBP; Yehuda Bauer, *Out of the Ashes: The Impact of American Jews on Post-Holocaust European Jewry* (Oxford, 1989), 37, 38, 193, 218; Thomas Liebschutz, "Rabbi Philip Bernstein and the Jewish Displaced Person," JIR thesis, HUC, 1965, 48; PSB, "Strength, Not Idealism."

Chapter V

PSB's return to Rochester: *Life*, 1955 (cited in introduction to the register of the PSBP); PSB, "The Rabbi in Communal and National Activities"; SSW to PSB, Apr. 24, 1929, June 14, 1939, PSB to SSW, Oct. 15, 1947, SSW to PSB, Jan. 30, 1948, PSB Papers, AJA; SB interview, March 30, 1997.

Postwar growth: PSB, "The First Fifty Years-What's Ahead for American Jews," Jan. 6, 1950, Sermons, PSBP; PSB, "Time and Estrangement;" PSB, "What's Ahead for Reform Jews," Nov. 26, 1946, Sermons, PSBP; HB, "A Case for the Abolition of the Bar Mitzvah," Feb. 6, 1970; HB Papers; Jewish Community Council of Rochester, *Leisure Time Study* (Rochester, N.Y., 1966); Jewish Community Federation, *The Jewish Population of Rochester, New York (Monroe County), 1980* (Rochester, N.Y., 1980); HJW, "Abuses of Confirmation," AH (Apr. 23, 1915); Carol Yunker, "Some Thoughts on Confirmation," *TBK Bulletin* (June 1988); Aaron Braveman interview, April 1997; HB interview, Jan. 13, 1998; ES interview, Apr. 7, 1997.

Pastoral visits: PSB, "My Last Friday Night Sermon at Gibbs Street," PSB, "Time and Estrangement," CCARJ 5 (1958), 5-7; Samuel Rosenbaum interview, RJCOHP, 29.

Temple Sinai: HB, "Fallacies About Reform Judaism," Oct. 21, 1966; Samuel Rosenbaum interview, RJCOHP, 26-27

Herbert Bronstein: *TBK Bulletin*, Feb. 16. 1951, Nov. 18, 1955, Apr. 19, 1957; TBK CM, Oct. 6, 1954; PSB, "Is B'rith Kodesh Getting Too Orthodox?," Jan. 2, 1953, Sermons, PSBP; PSB, "Should Reform and Conservative Judaism Merge?," Mar. 19, 1971, Sermons, PSBP; PSB, "What's Ahead for Reform Jews?," Nov. 26, 1948, Sermons, PSBP; PSB, "Where Did You Go? To Temple. What Did You Do? Nothing," Apr. 11, 1958, Sermons, PSBP; Letters toRabbinic Search Committee, 1972, TBK, PSBP; Murray and Frances Blanchard interviews, July 1976, RJCOHP, 55; HB interview, January 1998.

Elmwood Avenue move: TBK CM, July 5, Sept. 26, 1923, Feb. 24, 1956; PSB, "If I Were President," Nov. 5, 1948, Sermons, PSBP; PSB, "Time and Estrangement," CCARJ 5 (1958), 5-7; *138th Annual Meeting Celebrating Our 25th Birthday on Elmwood Avenue* [1987]; HB, "The Art and Architecture of Temple B'rith Kodesh: Its Religious Meanings," c. 1963, HB Papers; HB, "The Chapel Ark," c. 1963, HB Papers; *A New Beginning . . . Elmwood Avenue, c. 1963, TBKM;* HB interview, January 1998; Garson Meyer interview, June 1976, RJCOHP, 18, 73-75, 80.

Sisterhood: Carol Yunker, ed., "Do You Remember? Reminiscences of Sisterhood."

Postwar politics: PSB, "Apologia Pro Actate Mea," CCARJ (April 1969), 96; PSB, "Communists USA-USSR: What Shall We Do?," Nov. 25, 1949, Sermons, PSBP; PSB, "Haman, Hitler, and McCarthy," Mar. 19, 1954, Sermons, PSBP; PSB, "Religious Freedom in Israel," Dec. 1, 1950, Sermons, PSBP; PSB, "Time and Estrangement"; PSB, "Vietnam: Where I Stand," Dec. 15, 1967, Sermons, PSBP; PSB, "Washington-Vietnam-Israel," Mar. 22, 1968; Dean Rusk to I. L. Kenan, Dec. 27, 1968; Walter Litman to PSB, Mar. 24, 1968, Sermons, PSBP; PSB to SSW, March 5, 1948; PSB Papers, AJA; HB, "The Jewish Role in Race Relations," (February-March 1965), HB Papers; HB, "Priorities for the '70s-A Position," Jan. 14, 1972, HB Papers, AJA; HB to Stanley Chyet, Jan. 24, 1966, HB Papers, AJA.

Music at TBK: PBS to Leonard Bernstein, Correspondence, PSBP; TBK music services, TBK Files, PSBC; for cantors, see *TBK Bulletins*; Virginia McConnell interview, April 1997; Martha Rock Birnbaum interview, August 1998.

Judea Miller: *TBK Bulletin*, Jan. 29, 1960, Mar. 23, 1960; HB, "Farewell Sermon," May 21, 1972; HB interview, January 1998; Bernard Schuster interview, June 1976, RJCOHP, 32-33. Background on JM: RDC, Sept. 14, 1985; Rochester Times-Union, Sept. 13, 1985; JM, "Abraham Joshua Heschel Reconsidered," JL (Feb. 2, Mar. 6, 1987), JMP; JM, "The Closet: Another Religious View of Gay Liberation," *Reconstructionist* (February 1979); JM, letter to *Commentary* (June 1977); JM, "Eulogy for Rima Braave," June 24, 1984, JMP; JM, "Eulogy for Sadie Miller," June 22, 1990," JMP; JM, "Genocide Again," *America* (Sept. 12, 1992); JM, "A Man Visiting the Women's Peace Encampment," *RochesterWOMEN* (June 1984); JM, "Passover, Freedom, the Jews, and Jesse Jackson," Apr. 20, 1984, JMP; JM, "Poland Revisited," Feb. 23, 1990; JM, "Resurrecting the Death Penalty," JL (July 18, 1985); JM, "A Service of Worship in Common Concern," Apr. 19, 1992, JMP; JM, "Until Liberation Comes," Jan. 17, 1988, JMP; JM, press release, Mar. 23, 1964, JMP; JM to Carl Rowan, Aug. 3, 1978, JMP; JM to Stanley F. Chyet, Mar. 2, 1965, JMP; Jack Taylor to JM, Jan. 27, 1985, JMP; Martha Rock Birnbaum interview, August 1998; Samuel Rosenbaum interview, RJCOHP, 27-29; Bernard Schuster interview, RJCOHP, 42-43; Carol Yunker interview, August 1998; JM, Kol Nidre sermon, 1994, courtesy Anita Miller.

Laurence Kotok: Kotok interview, June 1998.

INDEX

279